D1592380

Read this book online today:

With SAP PRESS BooksOnline we offer you online access to knowledge from the leading SAP experts. Whether you use it as a beneficial supplement or as an alternative to the printed book, with SAP PRESS BooksOnline you can:

• Access your book anywhere, at any time. All you need is an Internet connection.
• Perform full text searches on your book and on the entire SAP PRESS library.
• Build your own personalized SAP library.

The SAP PRESS customer advantage:

Register this book today at *www.sap-press.com* and obtain exclusive free trial access to its online version. If you like it (and we think you will), you can choose to purchase permanent, unrestricted access to the online edition at a very special price!

Here's how to get started:

1. Visit *www.sap-press.com.*
2. Click on the link for SAP PRESS BooksOnline and login (or create an account).
3. Enter your free trial license key, shown below in the corner of the page.
4. Try out your online book with full, unrestricted access for a limited time!

Your personal free trial **license key**
for this online book is:

8py4-cstv-69gb-xrzu

Configuring and Customizing Employee and
Manager Self-Services in SAP® ERP HCM

 PRESS

Jeremy Masters, Christos Kotsakis
Implementing Employee and
Manager Self-Services in SAP ERP HCM
2009, 431 pp., hardcover
ISBN 978-1-59229-188-5

Masters, Kotsakis, Krishnamoorthy
E-Recruiting with SAP ERP HCM
2010, 358 pp., hardcover
978-1-59229-243-1

Martin Gillet
Integrating CATS
2nd edition 2009, 232 pp., hardcover
ISBN 978-1-59229-260-8

Jeremy Masters, Christos Kotsakis
Enterprise Compensation Management
with SAP ERP HCM
2009, 405 pp., hardcover
978-1-59229-207-3

Martin Gillet

Configuring and Customizing Employee and Manager Self-Services in SAP® ERP HCM

Galileo Press

Bonn • Boston

Galileo Press is named after the Italian physicist, mathematician and philosopher Galileo Galilei (1564–1642). He is known as one of the founders of modern science and an advocate of our contemporary, heliocentric worldview. His words *Eppur si muove* (And yet it moves) have become legendary. The Galileo Press logo depicts Jupiter orbited by the four Galilean moons, which were discovered by Galileo in 1610.

Editor Florian Zimniak
Copyeditor Julie McNamee
Cover Design Graham Geary
Photo Credit iStockphoto.com/artlinegraphics
Layout Design Vera Brauner
Production Graham Geary
Typesetting Publishers' Design and Production Services, Inc.
Printed and bound in Canada, on FSC-certified paper

ISBN 978-1-59229-356-8

© 2011 by Galileo Press Inc., Boston (MA)

1st edition 2011

Library of Congress Cataloging-in-Publication Data
Gillet, Martin.
  Configuring and customizing employee and manager self-services in SAP
ERP HCM / Martin Gillet. — 1st ed.
    p. cm.
  Includes index.
  ISBN-13: 978-1-59229-356-8
  ISBN-10: 1-59229-356-5
  1. SAP ERP. 2. Personnel management—Computer programs.
3. Management—Employee participation. I. Title.
  HF5549.5.D37G55 2011
  658.300285'53—dc22
  2011005027

Contents at a Glance

Dear Reader,

What happens if you combine the creative power and expert knowledge of an SAP Mentor with the restraints of an SAP PRESS book project?

Well, first, as an editor, you learn things. Mentors are busy people, for example: Their multiple obligations in the community and at customer sites sometimes compete with deadlines set in a side-project such as writing a book. Also, they are sensitive in regards of netiquette: CAPITAL LETTERS in emails make them cringe.

But, second and far more important, you get a book that truly delivers expert and real-world advice. In all my years at SAP PRESS I have never (never!) seen any of my authors drill down that deeply into the depths of the IMG as Martin did in the book you're just about to read. I am sure that it will be a companion in your self-services project that you will not want to miss a single day!

We appreciate your business, and welcome your feedback. Your comments and suggestions are the most useful tools to help us improve our books for you, the reader. We encourage you to visit our website at *www.sap-press.com* and share your feedback about this work.

Thank you for purchasing a book from SAP PRESS!

Florian Zimniak
Publishing Director, SAP PRESS

Galileo Press
Boston, MA

florian.zimniak@galileo-press.com
www.sap-press.com

Contents

Contents

Acknowledgments

Writing a configuration book takes a lot of time, will, energy, and determination. It also takes a lot of help as this is somewhat of a team effort.

This book is the fruit of many years of gathering information, practicing the functionalities, and teaching them at SAP education centers. I have spent a great deal of time trying to keep up with the SAP offering and the technology shifts, and trying to piece the different workarounds or alternatives to known issues or functionalities not provided in the standard SAP offering. One of the conclusions I've come to over the years is that even though we think we know the product, each implementation is a new challenge. This is mainly because each customer has its own requirements but also because the technologies change, not to mention the new functionalities or roles provided by SAP. Among the many colleagues and customers I've met in my SAP career, I would like to thank colleagues Dieter Flack and Harald Reiter for their expertise and knowledge sharing during common project assignments.

Although this configuration book is built on knowledge acquired and information gathered since my first acquaintance with Employee Self-Services back in 1998 (thanks to Udo Waibel among the many authors for showing us the way with the first Employee Self-Service book in SAP release 4.6C), it is also a product of indirect influences from the people and peers I've met throughout my assignments, the online exchanges, and the training held either at customer locations or SAP education centers. This list is long and distinguished, and a special thanks goes to all the delegates I've met while teaching self-services courses (HR290, HR250, HR260, HR255, etc.). They have provided additional perspectives, questions, issues, and ideas concerning how these functionalities could, should, or would work: I'd like to express my gratitude to all SAP education center teams, and namely to Anne-Catherine Rampelbergs from SAP Belgium for her professionalism and flexibility.

I'm a big fan and supporter of communities and sharing experiences, findings, and expertise, which in my humble opinion are enhancing the foundation of our knowledge. I would like to express my gratitude to all my community peers met throughout the different channels, especially the following individuals:

- Jarret Pazahanick for his support on the new self-services technologies, such as the Employee Interaction Center.

- Markus Klein for his HCM knowledge sharing and the great detailed wiki article, "Employee Self-Services: Personal Information UI Enhancement without Modification."

- Siddharth Rajora for his HCM and self-services community expertise and spirit.

- Marcio Leoni for his outstanding wiki article, "How to Get Rid of Support Packages Mismatch Issues (in the Field of HCM Self Services)."

- I'd also like to show my appreciation of Craig Cmehil, who is quite an inspiration to me with his charisma, and especially his activities in the field of the blogger influencers sphere and the SAP world of Innovation, Technology, and Mobility.

I am heartily thankful to my social media peers and followers, whose encouragement, guidance, and support enabled me to gather even more understanding of the subject. There are too many to be named, but I am sure that most of them will recognize themselves here.

I would also like to thank the extended community family, also known as the SAP Mentors (the list is long and distinguished), who are pushing our learning curve up by interacting with us, providing access to the latest information and rampup products, as well as leading us to beta testing, which helps us to better understand tomorrow's products. I must especially mention Mark Finnern and Aslan Noghre Kar for their faith, dedication, and leadership in the SAP Mentors program.

Also, as we are awaiting the Human Resources Self Services Certification, I would like to salute the team members of the Certification working group, also known as the "Certification 5," for taking certification into their own creative hands and spending countless hours to extensively improve SAP certification. Their expertise, broad experience, and talent combined with dedication and passion gave birth to white paper and exciting, challenging projects. Kudos to Leonardo De Araujo, Dennis Howlett, Michael Koch, and Jon Reed for "raising the bar," their camaraderie, and team spirit.

It sounds cliché, but I do believe that I would not complete any achievements if my family wasn't around to support me. I would like to thank my sweet wife, Bérengère, and my two sons, Collin and Julian, for their patience with late nights and sometimes decreased quality time over some weekends. I also would like to thank my brother Nicolas and my two sisters Hélène and Magali for their unconditional love and affection. I trust life, no matter how short it can be, is all about balance. Family plays a great part in that way. Since my first SAP book regarding the Cross-Application Time Sheet (CATS) with its 231 pages, I also realized that none of this would have happened without my mom's dedication and her ability to see through me. Don't we say that moms know best? While browsing through the myriad of Education offering after High School, she felt Human Resources management would suit me like a charm and she pointed it out back in 1994. I dedicate this book to the loving memory of Stéphane Rotsart de Hertaing (1947–2000). We dearly miss you everyday since life took you away from us. Quoting the band EELS: "P.S: You rock my world."

While writing this book, we unexpectedly lost our SAP HCM project business counterpart, Robert Grieder (1969–2011), who was a talented professional and meticulous SAP HCM analyst, philosopher, and artist. His professionalism and work dedication will be dearly missed. Godspeed, Robert.

I would like also to reiterate my loyalty to the best composer of all time, Hans Zimmer, who mastered the best original soundtracks ever in addition to the "usual suspects" also known as: Harry Gregson-Williams, James Horner, and the best band ever, Depeche Mode, which energized many of my sleepless nights while working on this book.

Last but not least, I would like to thank the SAP PRESS editorial team, not only for accepting this self-services book project but for their dedication, their professional commitment, their professionalism, and, most important, their patience. Writing a book takes a considerable amount of our time to build, as each chapter requires many revisions and inputs. This book was written often after normal working hours, so SAP PRESS's patience was quite challenged, but they always stood by me when many other editors would have dropped out. My gratitude goes namely to Florian Zimniak and Graham Geary, as well as to Julie McNamee, who did an outstanding job on copyediting this manuscript. I also would like to thank Jonathan Kent from SAP PRESS for his professionalism and dedication to promote my work.

Martin Gillet
SAP HCM Consultant, SAP Mentor, and SAP Trainer

This book unveils the SAP Self-Services functionalities, which employers and users use to view and maintain data for themselves or on behalf of their team members. This introduction lays out the structure of the book and explains some basic concepts and prerequisites.

1 Introduction

Throughout my 13 years in the field of SAP Human Resources, currently known as Human Capital Management (HCM), customers and users have wanted to access all relevant information through a simple but efficient web interface.

Most customers developed their own web interfaces when building intranets or basic web services available internally only.

When SAP products came into the market, it did not take long for SAP to develop a SAP Human Resources offering that would meet most common HR processes. After SAP successfully provided these tools to the customers, it became apparent that users needed more from the system. Indeed, the question was raised regarding the empowerment of users. The plan was simple: Provide users access to their personal master data, such as personnel administration, time management, payroll, and so on. This permanent access would be available when the user required it. This access would allow the HR department to handle basic requests, just by providing master data, which freed HR personnel to focus on more intensive HR tasks.

Since early 1998, Employee Self-Services (ESS) was provided by SAP to empower employees to maintain and access their personal data.

Employees could do the following:

▶ Maintain and access their personal data.

▶ Maintain their time entries.

▶ Request leave.

▶ Access their time statement.

▶ Access their payslip.

In my opinion, self-services are the next professional steps when dealing with Human Resources master data. It enables, through a dedicated user interface (which is most likely created from a web-based user-friendly interface) users to access and maintain their own data, triggers reports, or access forms.

Self-services is duly secured and checked with Business Rules, letting the employees master his own personal data. It provides great flexibility, as self-services can be used at any time by the employees. It also supports the HR department; HR personnel do not have to type employees' master data from paper-based forms into the system, not to mention the fact that this web enabling avoids other less productive administration tasks.

Self-services are provided as an access extension to the core system. This service has been around for quite a while, and is now shifting from the previous technology to the latest technology, as well as expanding the types of devices we can use. For example, employees or personnel working on the production plants can use self-services through kiosks, rather than computers.

Around 2004, the Manager Self-Services (MSS) provided employees' information to managers, including personal data, payroll information, and performance management, such as the following:

▶ General information

▶ Compensation

▶ Personal development

▶ Performance management

▶ Personnel change requests

▶ HCM Processes and Forms

▶ Travel

▶ Time

Later on (much later), came the portal administrator role to serve as the administrative role between employee and manager because although not everyone in the company is a manager, some have managerial responsibilities such as the Human Resources Business Partners (HRBP).

The user interface then only got better by extending the screens to Adobe® Portable Document Format (PDF), which can be either static (pulling out date for display) or interactive (encoding data and returning data to SAP).

The Employee Interaction Center (EIC) was also born and added to the proud family of HCM Self-Services to further enable the interaction with the employees through for example a Shared Services Center (SCC).

HCM also provides additional functionalities that may be identified as "satellites" because they come on top of standard functionalities. These well-known function-alities are the new generation of Training and Events Management (TEM), which is extended by the SAP Learning Solution (LSO), and the recruitment, which is extended by SAP E-Recruiting.

Although not directly part of HCM, users obviously need the proper inbox, such as the Universal Worklist (UWL), to follow up on notifications and workflows. They also need reporting capabilities to, for example, best comprehend the key perfor-mance indicators (KPIs), such as absenteeism, personnel turnover, identification of top performers, cost center and budget follow up, and so on. Those reporting capabilities can come in either the standard SAP ERP reports or the complementary reporting capabilities powered by Business Intelligence (BI), for example, SAP BusinessObjects or SAP NetWeaver Business Warehouse (BW).

Figure 1.1 illustrates the self-services functionalities, with a SAP NetWeaver Portal and its surrounding other functionalities.

I maintained and installed ESS as early as 1998, following up with close attention to the new releases and functionalities. I welcomed MSS with SAP R/3 Enterprise (4.70) and its extension sets, and I was thrilled with the introduction of the SAP NetWeaver Portal and the new user interface rendering, based in Web Dynpros.

Just like you, however, I have found myself in a difficult position, to fully com-prehend the self-services offering, including configuration, use, troubleshooting, and documentation.

I have led the early HR250 Employee Self-Services SAP course, as well the HR260 Manager Self-Services. This meant: many classes, many class delegates, many questions, and many confrontations concerning business requirements and SAP standard functionalities.

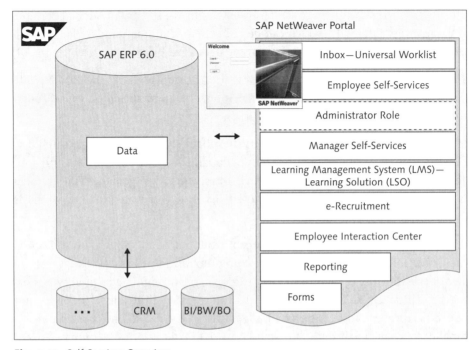

Figure 1.1 Self-Services Overview

Finally, the two self-services courses were merged into HR255 Human Capital Management Self-Services, but the business packages documentation and the screenshots samples were no longer available. We were left with the SAP Help Portal (*http://help.sap.com*). Fortunately, throughout 12 years of services in the field of consulting and training on behalf of SAP Education, I gathered a "war treasure" of nearly 200 MB of documentation.

I realized it was time to create a thorough reference book regarding the configuration of ESS and MSS as well as surrounding functionalities, questions, answers, known pitfalls, tips and tricks, lessons learned from the field, and workarounds.

You have in your hands the fruit of hard labor to compile all relevant information, with whenever possible, screenshots and configuration guidelines. We hope you will find this handbook useful and we look forward to your feedback.

1.1   What This Book Will Cover

SAP Self-Services is a challenging topic with plenty of configuration settings and information to cover. To set the expectations and the learning objectives for you, I have consolidated the topics and matters that this book will cover. Where relevant, I will also point out further documentation or useful information when dealing with topics that are out of scope for this book.

The primary learning objective of this book is to cover and provide in-depth descriptions of the customizing steps (also known as configuration) involved in self-services.

Some technical details are included to provide the most complete information:

▶ Implementation Guide (IMG) access paths

▶ Transactions to the Implementation configuration node, in place of the standard Transaction SPRO where applicable, based on table CUS_IMGACH and the IMG activity

▶ Table name

▶ Verification of customer naming convention, based on table TRESC, where applicable

▶ Additional tips and tricks and/or documentation where appropriate

Chapter 2, SAP NetWeaver Portal, introduces the SAP NetWeaver Portal and all relevant aspects for setting up and configuring ESS and MSS. The chapter also includes an overview of the different technologies and releases available. It provides a matrix with the service availability across each release, from Internet Transaction Server (ITS) versus Web Dynpro. Chapter 2 also gives you a glimpse of the ABAP Web Dynpro version, which will be released with enhancement package 5 (EhP 5) in June 2011.

Chapter 3, Backend Configuration, covers in-depth configuration settings available in the Implementation Guide (IMG) customizing, the Homepage Framework, the Internal Service Request (ISR), and the Object and Data Provider (OADP). It includes customizing of the different objects in the Overview menu on the SAP NetWeaver Portal, including the icon, description text, areas, subareas, and access to ESS. It also introduces the ISR used up to SAP ERP 6.0 in MSS, the personnel change request, and the relevant configuration tables. Detailed options, including the use of personnel development evaluation paths and function modules, are also introduced.

Chapter 4, Background Information on Self-Services Configuration, discusses some important considerations before venturing on an ESS or MSS configuration project. Topics covered here include the recent changes in technology and the available business packages. The existing release is also worth being considered.

Chapter 5, Employee Self-Services Configuration, covers the configuration of all settings available in the IMG for Employee Self Services (ESS), highlighting the key changes between SAP ERP 5.0 and SAP ERP 6.0. This includes customizing standard self-service configuration tables and highlighting useful SAP Notes for documentation. The chapter also introduces the workarounds and the known pitfalls in order to best answer the business requirements. The detailed options, including the latest functionalities provided through EhP 1 through 4, are also covered.

Chapter 6, Manager Self-Services Configuration, covers the configuration settings available in the IMG for the Manager Self-Services (MSS) offering for the personnel administration and the financial information provided to the manager. This includes customizing for compensation, personnel development, approval of working time, appraisals, display of the organizational structure, and management of competencies. The chapter also introduces the Human Capital Management (HCM) personnel change requests as well as the next generation of HCM Processes and Forms. This also includes the detailed options of the portal iView and page parameters.

Chapter 7, Reporting, briefly reviews the standard report offering in SAP ERP, from standard reports to ABAP and ad hoc queries. The chapter also covers the IMG customizing for HCM analytics and web enabling.

Chapter 8, Human Resources Administrator Role, introduces the administrator role as provided through the enhancement package, including a customizing overview for the different administrator role functionalities.

Chapter 9, Workflow, explains the integration of the Universal Worklist (UWL) as a common inbox for receiving workflow items and notifications. This includes the basic configuration, the setup of a substitution rule, a detailed example of a workflow setup, and a detailed troubleshooting guide.

Chapter 10, User Management, introduces the "need to know" configuration and setup regarding user management in SAP ERP and SAP NetWeaver Portal. This includes the Lightweight Directory Access Protocol (LDAP) and the Single Sign-On (SSO).

Chapter 11, Authorizations, discusses the configuration settings for authorization management through the profile configurator. This includes the setup of authorization object S_SERVICE for the self-services and the technical authorization objects. It also includes the management of SAP NetWeaver Portal permission for self-services. A useful troubleshooting guide and SAP UserID parameters are also provided.

The **Appendices** wrap things up by providing the following:

► List of tables name

► Cheat sheet of transaction codes

► SAP notes illustrated in this book

► Additional pointers to useful documentation

► List of acronyms and term of references

► Bibliography

As additional bonus material, you will find four overview chapters as PDF downloads on the book's web sites at *www.sap-press.com/H3154* and *www.sap-press.de/2430*:

► *Integrating Project Self-Services (PSS)* introduces the configuration settings available in the IMG customizing and the SAP NetWeaver Portal objects for the Project Self-Services (PSS) offering, provided through the enhancement package. The chapter also introduces detailed options regarding the integration with the Cross-Application Time Sheet (CATS).

► *Integrating the Employee Interaction Center* introduces the Employee Interaction Center (EIC) as provided through the enhancement package. This includes an overview of the customizing for the different EIC functionalities.

► *Integrating SAP Learning Solution* introduces the SAP Learning Solution, which is the next generation or extended functionalities of the standard Training and Event Management component. This includes an overview of the customizing for the different LSO functionalities. This chapter only covers an introduction because the functionality is vast enough that it has been covered in its own SAP PRESS book, *SAP Enterprise Learning* by Prashanth Padmanabhan et al. (SAP PRESS 2009).

▶ *Integrating SAP E-Recruiting* covers SAP E-Recruiting, including the next genera-tion of extended functionalities of the standard Recruitment component. This chapter includes an overview of the customizing for the different SAP E-Recruiting functionalities. This chapter also only introduces this topic because it has been covered in the SAP PRESS book, *E-Recruiting with SAP ERP HCM* by Jeremy Masters et al. (SAP PRESS 2010).

1.2   What This Book Does Not Cover

Although this book includes the best and most current information, it does not cover or provide code to fill in the multiple user exits and Business Add-Ins (BAdIs).

This book does not replace the standard SAP documentation made available through the SAP channels, and, of course, this book shouldn't replace appropriate hands-on training on a sandbox system.

1.3   Systems Used to Describe the Configuration

To provide the latest system screenshots and configuring options, unless specifically written, the following systems have been used:

▶ Latest release SAP ERP 6.0, also referred to as the backend

▶ Latest support package (SP) and enhancement package (EhP) 4

▶ SAP NetWeaver Portal, also referred to as the frontend, with SAP NetWeaver

▶ Employee Self-Services Business Package 1.0

▶ Manager Self-Services Business Package 1.0

▶ Business Package, where relevant for EhP 1 through 4

1.4   Assumptions, Prerequisites, and Disclaimer

Before delving into the configuration, we must underline a couple of assumptions and prerequisites. Carefully review the following non-exhaustive lists.

We assume the following are true:

▶ Although optional, you have read the standard product documentation.

▶ You are ideally running SAP ERP 6.0 (or at least SAP ERP 5.0).

▶ You checked whether or not enhancement packages have already been installed.

▶ You have assessed with the business stakeholders which functionalities to enable.

▶ You have assessed with other SAP component teammates what should be enabled.

▶ You have assessed the technical prerequisites such as support packages, and so on.

▶ You have access clearance to relevant technical transactions to install the enhancement packages.

▶ You are configuring all customizing activities in a sandbox system at first.

▶ You are duly testing all new configuration before transporting anything to a test or production system.

▶ You are doing your utmost to use SAP standard configuration at all times.

▶ You are abiding by SAP naming convention rules.

▶ You are only looking for SAP user exits, Business Add-Ins (BAdIs), or Business Application Program Interface (BAPI) as last remaining courses of action, if the SAP standard does not meet all your requirements.

▶ You are (daring) challenging the business requirements and the SAP configuration alternatives to best meet the business requirements and make the configuration as smooth as possible.

Following are the necessary prerequisites:

▶ You have SAP Human Capital Management (HCM) knowledge.

▶ You have some experience in the field of SAP configuration and customizing.

▶ Relevant configuration has already been done regarding functional areas such as personnel administration, personnel development, time management, payroll, reporting, and so on. (Self-services functionalities are being placed on top of functional areas.)

- ▸ (Sandbox) SAP ERP 6.0 (or SAP ERP 5.0) is up and running.

- ▸ (Sandbox) SAP NetWeaver Portal is up and running.

- ▸ Technical settings for connecting the SAP ERP system and the SAP NetWeaver Portal have been maintained (technical users, Remote Function Call [RFC] connections, system landscape directory, etc.).

- ▸ Relevant support packages have been installed.

- ▸ Relevant business packages have been installed.

- ▸ Relevant enhancement packages have been installed.

- ▸ Ideally, you have the International Education and Demonstration System (IDES) master data.

- ▸ You have the relevant authorizations on all systems (ideally, full authorizations, such as SAP_ALL and SAP_NEW because we are dealing with sandbox systems).

The information in this book is provided to the best of my knowledge, so there might be alternatives to the configurations introduced throughout these chapters. Feel free to challenge these configurations and chime in online through the SAP Community Network (SCN) and dedicated blog entries.

1.5   Standard Functionalities—Out of the Box Versus Alternatives

When deploying SAP, the primary approach is to deploy the standard functionalities—also known as the out of the box solution. However, we will also point out some useful alternatives to answer gap analysis or known pitfalls.

1.5.1   Standard Functionalities

As of SAP ERP 6.0, most services have been converted to Web Dynpro. You should therefore stick with the latest standard technology provided by SAP. However, for some reasons (e.g., time, budget, release, etc.), you might still want to use an ITS-based scenario.

Some ITS-based scenarios can still be used in SAP ERP releases. Serious limitations are effective. The best example is, under strict conditions, to use the ITS-based service PV7I—Training Center and PV8I—My bookings.

Unless you have deployed and are using EhP 4, the Performance Management (PM) process is still delivered through Business Server Pages (BSP) up to SAP ERP 6.0, EhP 3.

1.5.2 Employee Self-Services (ESS)

As of SAP ERP 6.0, the following countries are supported for the following services:

▶ **Address, bank information, family member/dependents and personal data**
Canada, Germany, Japan, South Africa, United States, France, Australia, Brazil, Great Britain, Malaysia, Mexico, Switzerland, South Korea, Denmark, Singapore, Netherlands, New Zealand, Belgium, Norway, Sweden, Spain, Portugal, Austria, and Italy.

▶ **Personal ID**
Singapore, Hong Kong, Indonesia, Malaysia, Taiwan, and Thailand.

1.5.3 Manager Self-Services (MSS)

Manager Self-Services provides the following functionalities through worksets:

▶ Team viewer

▶ Employee review

▶ Compensation review

▶ ESS in MSS

▶ Team calendar

▶ Personnel change request/forms

▶ Recruitment

▶ Reporting and headcounts

1.5.4 Alternatives

The SAP Self-Services configuration is achieved through the IMG, which provides access to customizing, and the SAP NetWeaver Portal Content Directory (PCD), which provides access to the portal objects configuration.

However, besides these standard configuration tools, there are some alternatives introduced in this book to consider as workarounds. A thorough Strength, Weaknesses, Opportunities, and Threads analysis (SWOT) must be done prior to any use of these alternatives. Carefully list and review the pros and cons.

1.5.5 Configuration through the SAP NetWeaver Development Studio (NWDS)

Those of you working with earlier SAP releases may remember the add-on application called Web Studio, which was used to publish the ITS services up to SAP release 4.6B. As of release 4.6C, the services were published through Transaction SE80 (ABAP Development Workbench).

But now that we are dealing with Web Dynpro Java, although not mandatory, customers are asked to set up a SAP NetWeaver Development Infrastructure (NWDI), which provides access to the SAP NetWeaver Development Studio (NWDS). In NWDS, you can also configure additional settings.

1.5.6 Configuration through the SAP NetWeaver Portal

Since the latest SAP NetWeaver Application Server (AS) release, it is possible to right-click on the portal objects and access additional configuration. This configuration is part of the personalization of the user interface (UI) and is theoretically meant for test purposes, not productive use.

1.5.7 Configuration through the Backend System

SAP also provided a myriad of user exits, classes, and BAdIs to support the self-services configuration. Although useful, they do require technical programming knowledge (ABAP) and many regression tests.

We will review these alternatives in the relevant chapters, where appropriate.

1.6   Enhancement Package Concept

An *enhancement package* (EhP) is the new channel to deliver new functionalities on top of SAP ERP 6.0. Enhancement packages are released on a frequent basis, containing new functionalities that the customer could enable as per the business requirements.

Enabling an enhancement package may provide a missing functionality or simply bring new functionalities into the HCM processes. By using the enhancement package, you are making sure that your processes are aligned with the latest offering as well as the latest technology in use.

The concept is to provide a range of added value functionalities for many processes. SAP's release strategy, as illustrated by Figure 1.2, is to deliver roughly up to three enhancement packages per year.

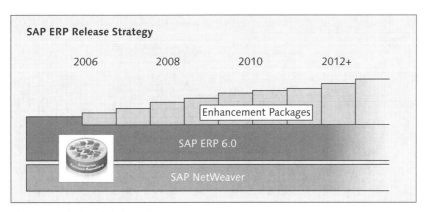

Figure 1.2   SAP ERP Release Strategy

Info

Enhancement packages are like Russian nested dolls. After you install the latest enhancement package, for example, EhP 4, it automatically includes the previous enhancement packages, in this case EhP 1, 2, and 3.

At this time, four support packages (Figure 1.3) have been delivered. The latest, EhP 4, was released in May 2009. EhP 5 is scheduled for general availability in mid-2011.

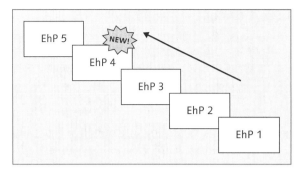

Figure 1.3 Enhancement Package Suite

Tip!

You can quickly assess the enhancement package level from your system by either using Transaction SPAM or the menu path SYSTEM • STATUS, as illustrated in Figure 1.4.

Support Package Level for Installed Software Components

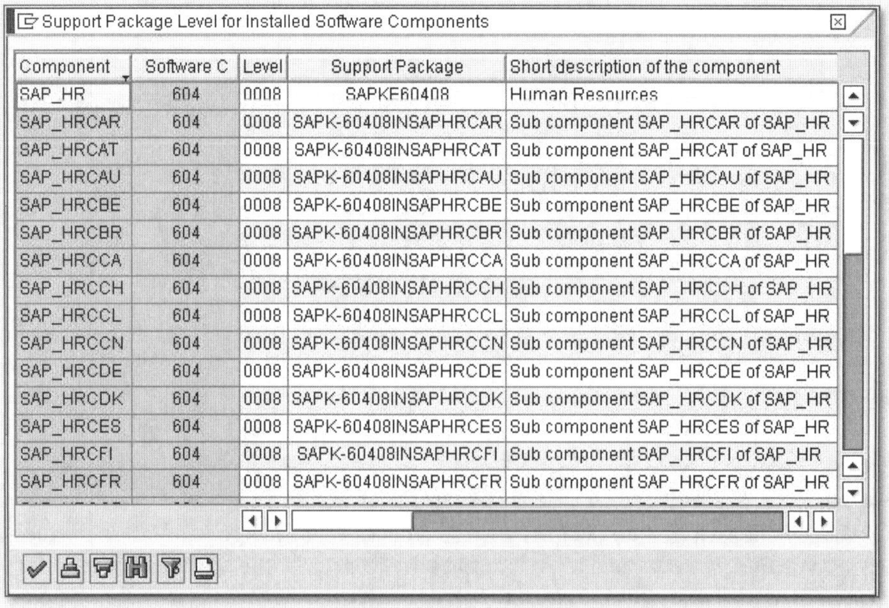

Component	Software C	Level	Support Package	Short description of the component
SAP_HR	604	0008	SAPKE60408	Human Resources
SAP_HRCAR	604	0008	SAPK-60408INSAPHRCAR	Sub component SAP_HRCAR of SAP_HR
SAP_HRCAT	604	0008	SAPK-60408INSAPHRCAT	Sub component SAP_HRCAT of SAP_HR
SAP_HRCAU	604	0008	SAPK-60408INSAPHRCAU	Sub component SAP_HRCAU of SAP_HR
SAP_HRCBE	604	0008	SAPK-60408INSAPHRCBE	Sub component SAP_HRCBE of SAP_HR
SAP_HRCBR	604	0008	SAPK-60408INSAPHRCBR	Sub component SAP_HRCBR of SAP_HR
SAP_HRCCA	604	0008	SAPK-60408INSAPHRCCA	Sub component SAP_HRCCA of SAP_HR
SAP_HRCCH	604	0008	SAPK-60408INSAPHRCCH	Sub component SAP_HRCCH of SAP_HR
SAP_HRCCL	604	0008	SAPK-60408INSAPHRCCL	Sub component SAP_HRCCL of SAP_HR
SAP_HRCCN	604	0008	SAPK-60408INSAPHRCCN	Sub component SAP_HRCCN of SAP_HR
SAP_HRCDE	604	0008	SAPK-60408INSAPHRCDE	Sub component SAP_HRCDE of SAP_HR
SAP_HRCDK	604	0008	SAPK-60408INSAPHRCDK	Sub component SAP_HRCDK of SAP_HR
SAP_HRCES	604	0008	SAPK-60408INSAPHRCES	Sub component SAP_HRCES of SAP_HR
SAP_HRCFI	604	0008	SAPK-60408INSAPHRCFI	Sub component SAP_HRCFI of SAP_HR
SAP_HRCFR	604	0008	SAPK-60408INSAPHRCFR	Sub component SAP_HRCFR of SAP_HR

Figure 1.4 Transaction SPAM Overview

Enhancement packages are not just a trend or nice to have, they provide missing functionalities and new functionalities in a timely manner. This keeps you up to date with the functionalities required by the business, meaning you can increase the satisfaction rate from the key/stakeholders or simply improve current processes.

In this evolving technological world, the enhancement packages also secure that you are using the latest UI, based on the latest technology (e.g., Web Dynpro).

Remember the following when considering installing enhancement packages:

▶ Having SAP ERP 6.0 is *not* the end of the functionalities road, there is *more* to it. Pay close attention, and raise the relevant questions when attending demos.

▶ Assess carefully which other functionalities could be added on top of the regular SAP ERP.

▶ Communicate with other teams because enhancement packages are enabled for all SAP components.

▶ Assess the technical requirements to deploy such new functionalities, and take advantage of the SAP Product Availability Matrix (PAM).

▶ Anticipate resources and mandates for enhancement packages.

▶ Monitor the next expected functionalities through the next enhancement packages to leverage and anticipate your business's needs and requirements.

▶ Challenge SAP through customer feedback channels, partners, user groups, and so on for new functionalities.

Further information regarding the strategy for SAP ERP 6.0 and more information regarding the enhancement packages can be found on the SAP Marketplace:

Description	SAP Marketplace Link (login required)
SAP ERP upgrade	*http://service.sap.com/upgrade-erp*
Enhancement package (EhP) documentation	*http://service.sap.com/erp-ehp*
Software distribution center (SWDC)	*http://service.sap.com/swdc*

This chapter shows SAP NetWeaver Portal as the central interface for all interactions within the system. Thanks to a friendly and intuitive web-based user interface and a myriad of Self-Services at the user's fingertips, SAP NetWeaver Portal web enables all SAP functionalities.

2 SAP NetWeaver Portal

Self-Services are part of the SAP end-user delivery matrix, as illustrated in Figure 2.1. As such, they are an integral part of SAP's proposed way to streamline business processes. However, after SAP ERP HCM is successfully deployed, we are facing new challenges when it comes to web enabling the Self-Services provided by SAP through the standard license. This is due to the technology necessary to provide end users with seamless and convenient access to all systems they need access to. This technology is the SAP NetWeaver Portal, together with SAP's Web Dynpro technology.

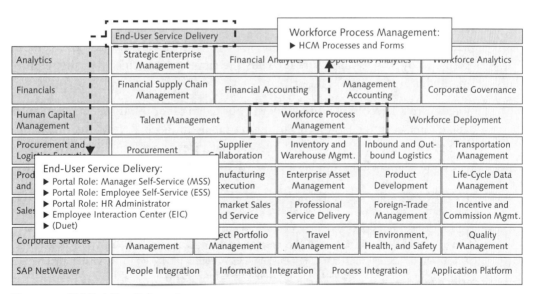

Figure 2.1 SAP End-User Delivery Scope

This chapter introduces the SAP NetWeaver Portal Content Directory (PCD), which contains the available portal objects, through the Business Packages concept, for setting up the access to the web-based functionalities.

This chapter also points out technical requirements to check before any implementation, provides a quick introduction to the standard content location, and a shows how to add additional functionalities with the portal archive file. We will take a detailed walk through the portal objects and focus on the most useful properties.

We'll also cover additional tips and tricks, such as the work protect mode and useful technical considerations.

Let's get started!

2.1   Web-Enabling HCM Self-Services through SAP NetWeaver Portal

Prior to any installation, you must check the technical requirements. With the support of the Basis team, you must assess the current release you are running against support package levels and enhancement package(s). You typically compare the functionalities expected by SAP and the current status of your systems by running a Product Availability Matrix (PAM).

After this has been duly checked, you must carefully review the standard content provided by SAP to make sure it covers the current requirements or the requirements yet to be issued.

Finally, from a technical point of view, your technical or infrastructure team must make some critical decisions regarding setting up of the SAP NetWeaver Development Infrastructure (NWDI) with SAP NetWeaver Development Studio (NWDS) and, above all, the guidelines to be applied while working in SAP NetWeaver Portal.

> **Caution**
>
> SAP ERP 6.0 does provide the basic functionalities. However, as technology keeps moving forward, you must review the enhancement packages provided by SAP for more functionalities. When deploying Self-Services functionalities, you should deploy EhP 1 through EhP 4 (EhP 5 is pending for delivery in mid-2011).

2.1.1   System Patches

You have made the right decision to web-enable the HCM self-services. Before investigating which business package and functionalities to deploy, carefully review with your infrastructure team which support package or patches should be applied to your system landscape. This applies to most environments, for example, SAP ERP, SAP NetWeaver Application Server (AS), and so on.

Upgrading your systems to the latest patch level ensures that you will not have to go through the hassle of solving known bugs or issues. Not to mention that if issues arise, SAP will (in most cases) request you to apply the latest patch before starting any troubleshooting.

Enforcing this basic rule saves valuable time and troubleshooting work days.

Online Check with the Product Availability Matrix (PAM)

A thorough check can also be done using PAM provided by SAP. This functionality can be accessed via *http://service.sap.com/pam* (User Name and Password required). This platform will help you assess which SAP release contains which functionalities and their technical requirements.

System Patches: Portal

As illustrated in Figure 2.2, the portal patch and component information can be found under your portal, assuming you have the right authorization access clearance, via the following address:

http://<yourserver>:<yourport>/sap/monitoring/ComponentInfo

System Patches: SAP ERP Backend System

As illustrated in Figure 2.3, the backend system component levels and patches can be found under Transaction SPAM (Support Package Manager), assuming you have the right authorization access clearance.

System

Software Components

Vendor	Name	Version	Provider	Location	Applied
sap.com	ADSSAP	7.01 SP5 (1000.7.01.5.0.20090825153742)	SAP AG	SAP AG	20100319194154
sap.com	BASETABLES	7.01 SP5 (1000.7.01.5.0.20090825152300)	SAP AG	SAP AG	20100319151824
sap.com	BI_MMR	7.01 SP5 (1000.7.01.5.0.20090825154303)	SAP AG	SAP AG	20100319194226
sap.com	BI_UDI	7.01 SP5 (1000.7.01.5.0.20090824190100)	SAP AG	SAP AG	20100319195134
sap.com	BP_DMSCONN	6.75 SP1 (1000.6.75.1.9.20081125093814)	SAP AG	SAP AG	20100307124237
sap.com	BP_ERP05_TALENT	1.01 SP9 (1000.1.01.9.0.20090831045527)	SAP AG	MAIN_ERP5VVAL_C	20100319201526
sap.com	BP_ERP4CSP	60.2 SP0 (1000.60.2.0.0.20041024061259)	SAP AG	SAP AG	20100307124313
sap.com	BP_ERP5ASS	1.0 SP16 (1000.1.0.16.0.20090726022823)	SAP AG	MAIN_ERP05VAL_C	20100319201531
sap.com	BP_ERP5BUA	1.0 SP16 (1000.1.0.16.0.20090726022822)	SAP AG	MAIN_ERP05VAL_C	20100319201539
sap.com	BP_ERP5BUY	1.41 SP5 (1000.1.41.5.0.20091102175101)	SAP AG	MAIN_ERP54VAL_C	20100319201551
sap.com	BP_ERP5COM	1.41 SP5 (1000.1.41.5.0.20091102175047)	SAP AG	MAIN_ERP54VAL_C	20100319201623
sap.com	BP_ERP5DCO	1.0 SP16 (1000.1.0.16.0.20090726022830)	SAP AG	MAIN_ERP05VAL_C	20100319201627
sap.com	BP_ERP5ESS	1.41 SP5 (1000.1.41.5.0.20091102175059)	SAP AG	MAIN_ERP54VAL_C	20100319201647
sap.com	BP_ERP5EXC	1.31 SP5 (1000.1.31.5.0.20090831152027)	SAP AG	MAIN_ERP53VAL_C	20100319201655
sap.com	BP_ERP5HER	1.0 SP16 (1000.1.0.16.0.20090726022815)	SAP AG	MAIN_ERP05VAL_C	20100319201659
sap.com	BP_ERP5HRA	1.41 SP5 (1000.1.41.5.0.20091102175102)	SAP AG	MAIN_ERP54VAL_C	20100319201707
sap.com	BP_ERP5INV	1.0 SP16 (1000.1.0.16.0.20090726022817)	SAP AG	MAIN_ERP05VAL_C	20100319201711
sap.com	BP_ERP5MSS	1.41 SP5 (1000.1.41.5.0.20091102175100)	SAP AG	MAIN_ERP54VAL_C	20100319201723
sap.com	BP_ERP5MTC	1.2 SP6 (1000.1.2.6.0.20090831052353)	SAP AG	MAIN_ERP52VAL_C	20100319201731
sap.com	BP_ERP5PLA	1.0 SP16 (1000.1.0.16.0.20090726022819)	SAP AG	MAIN_ERP05VAL_C	20100319201735
sap.com	BP_ERP5PRS	1.41 SP5 (1000.1.41.5.0.20091102175055)	SAP AG	MAIN_ERP54VAL_C	20100319201744
sap.com	BP_ERP5PSS	1.0 SP16 (1000.1.0.16.0.20090726022829)	SAP AG	MAIN_ERP05VAL_C	20100319201748
sap.com	BP_ERP5QIN	1.31 SP5 (1000.1.31.5.0.20090831152031)	SAP AG	MAIN_ERP53VAL_C	20100319201756
sap.com	BP_ERP5SAL	1.41 SP5 (1000.1.41.5.0.20091102175053)	SAP AG	MAIN_ERP54VAL_C	20100319201808
sap.com	BP_ERP5SUP	1.0 SP16 (1000.1.0.16.0.20090726022824)	SAP AG	MAIN_ERP05VAL_C	20100319201812
sap.com	BP_ERP7MPL	1.20 SP6 (1000.1.20.6.0.20090831052358)	SAP AG	MAIN_ERP52VAL_C	20100319201817
sap.com	BP_ERP7MSV	1.20 SP6 (1000.1.20.6.0.20090831052403)	SAP AG	MAIN_ERP52VAL_C	20100319201822
sap.com	BP_PLMWD	1.40 SP5 (1000.1.40.5.0.20091102175051)	SAP AG	MAIN_ERP54VAL_C	20100319201826
sap.com	BP_RETAIL	60.1 SP0 (1000.60.1.0.0.20051020154859)	SAP AG	SAP AG	20100307125947
sap.com	BPERP_BCS	1.30 SP5 (1000.1.30.5.0.20090831152037)	SAP AG	MAIN_ERP53VAL_C	20100319201240
sap.com	BPERP_CDM	1.41 SP5 (1000.1.41.5.0.20091102135231)	SAP AG	MAIN_ERP54VAL_C	20100319201248
sap.com	BPERP_CLC	1.30 SP5 (1000.1.30.5.0.20090831152049)	SAP AG	MAIN_ERP53VAL_C	20100319201252
sap.com	BPERP_CSM	1.20 SP6 (1000.1.20.6.0.20090831052357)	SAP AG	MAIN_ERP52VAL_C	20100319201257
sap.com	BPERP_DPM	1.41 SP5 (1000.1.41.5.0.20091102135232)	SAP AG	MAIN_ERP54VAL_C	20100319201305
sap.com	BPERP_IAT	1.41 SP5 (1000.1.41.5.0.20091102135233)	SAP AG	MAIN_ERP54VAL_C	20100319201313
sap.com	BPERP_LMT	1.20 SP6 (1000.1.20.6.0.20090831052352)	SAP AG	MAIN_ERP52VAL_C	20100319201318
sap.com	BPERP_REP	1.41 SP5 (1000.1.41.5.0.20091102135234)	SAP AG	MAIN_ERP54VAL_C	20100319201322
sap.com	BPERP_TECINF	1.41 SP5 (1000.1.41.5.0.20091104122308)	SAP AG	MAIN_ERP54VAL_C	20100319200348
sap.com	BPERP_THO	1.30 SP5 (1000.1.30.5.0.20090831152024)	SAP AG	MAIN_ERP53VAL_C	20100319201326
sap.com	BPERP_WOM	1.30 SP5 (1000.1.30.5.0.20090831160400)	SAP AG	MAIN_ERP53VAL_C	20100319201331
sap.com	BPERP_XBRL	1.30 SP5 (1000.1.30.5.0.20090831152039)	SAP AG	MAIN_ERP53VAL_C	20100319201335
sap.com	BPERPADW	1.40 SP5 (1000.1.40.5.0.20091102175046)	SAP AG	MAIN_ERP54VAL_C	20100319201141
sap.com	BPERPEIC	1.40 SP5 (1000.1.40.5.0.20091102175052)	SAP AG	MAIN_ERP54VAL_C	20100319201146
sap.com	BPERPERCAD	1.40 SP5 (1000.1.40.5.0.20091102175048)	SAP AG	MAIN_ERP54VAL_C	20100319201150
sap.com	BPERPERCRE	1.40 SP5 (1000.1.40.5.0.20091102135240)	SAP AG	MAIN_ERP54VAL_C	20100319201155
sap.com	BPERPFINMDM	1.40 SP5 (1000.1.40.5.0.20091102135243)	SAP AG	MAIN_ERP54VAL_C	20100319201159

Figure 2.2 SAP NetWeaver Portal Component Info

Component	Software C	SP-Level	Support Package	Short description of the component
EA-HR	604	0012	SAPK-60412INEAHR	SAP Enterprise Extension HR
EA-HRCAR	604	0012	SAPK-60412INEAHRCAR	Sub component EA-HRCAR of EA-HR
EA-HRCAT	604	0012	SAPK-60412INEAHRCAT	Sub component EA-HRCAT of EA-HR
EA-HRCAU	604	0012	SAPK-60412INEAHRCAU	Sub component EA-HRCAU of EA-HR
EA-HRCBE	604	0012	SAPK-60412INEAHRCBE	Sub component EA-HRCBE of EA-HR
EA-HRCBR	604	0012	SAPK-60412INEAHRCBR	Sub component EA-HRCBR of EA-HR
EA-HRCCA	604	0012	SAPK-60412INEAHRCCA	Sub component EA-HRCCA of EA-HR
EA-HRCCH	604	0012	SAPK-60412INEAHRCCH	Sub component EA-HRCCH of EA-HR
EA-HRCCN	604	0012	SAPK-60412INEAHRCCN	Sub component EA-HRCCN of EA-HR
EA-HRCDE	604	0012	SAPK-60412INEAHRCDE	Sub component EA-HRCDE of EA-HR
EA-HRCDK	604	0012	SAPK-60412INEAHRCDK	Sub component EA-HRCDK of EA-HR
EA-HRCES	604	0012	SAPK-60412INEAHRCES	Sub component EA-HRCES of EA-HR
EA-HRCFI	604	0012	SAPK-60412INEAHRCFI	Sub component EA-HRCFI of EA-HR
EA-HRCFR	604	0012	SAPK-60412INEAHRCFR	Sub component EA-HRCFR of EA-HR
EA-HRCGB	604	0012	SAPK-60412INEAHRCGB	Sub component EA-HRCGB of EA-HR

Figure 2.3   SAP ERP Backend System Component Info

2.1.2   Functionalities Provided by SAP in the Standard Product

From the beginning, SAP provided a wide range of functionalities in the standard offering, also known as the out-of-the-box solution. These functionalities were previously based on Internet Transaction Server (ITS) technology, using HTML. It was possible to use these functionalities as a standalone solution. Today, with the SAP NetWeaver Portal, they are consolidated and provided in a business package. The use of a SAP NetWeaver Portal is mandatory because self-services cannot be used as standalone services.

Business Packages Concept

The SAP business packages are predefined portal content, also known as template functionalities. They are provided either by SAP or certified partners. Business packages are great assets when web enabling SAP HCM services. All standard portal objects required to run the functionalities are already provided by SAP.

Business packages are viewed in a folder, which serves as a placeholder containing all required elements in order to web-enable SAP HCM functionalities.

Business packages must be downloaded from the SAP Marketplace by your Portal System Administrator, and uploaded into the PCD.

The following business packages are available, as illustrated in Figure 2.4:

▶ Common parts

▶ End user (Employee Self-Services)

▶ Line manager (Manager Self-Services)

Additional business packages are made available, depending on the enhancement package installed on top of the standard business packages.

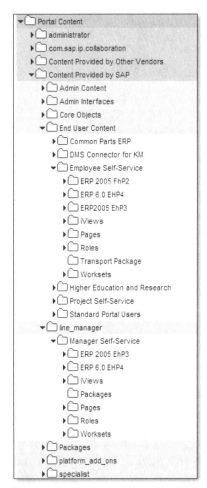

Figure 2.4 SAP NetWeaver Portal Content Directory with SAP Standard Content

Standard Content Provided

As we have seen, SAP provides standard content, such as iViews, pages, worksets, and roles, through business packages. The latest package content is stored in the PCD in the CONTENT PROVIDED BY SAP folder. Additional folders contain migrated content, which includes the earlier package releases, and enhancement packages installed, respectively.

Figure 2.4 illustrates the content provided by SAP and the migrated content as stored under the PORTAL CONTENT directory root folder.

Note

As always, it is important to notice that the standard content provided by SAP is not to be changed in any way. This is critical to preserve the PCD's consistency.

Additional Functionalities

Additional functionalities can also be uploaded by using a Portal Archive file, which bears the file extension .par.

According to the SAP definition from SAP Online Help:

> *Portal applications are packaged in PAR (Portal Archive) files. A PAR file is a standard ZIP file with a .par extension that contains a deployment descriptor, all Java classes, web resources and other files required to run the application. Within the portal, the name of the PAR file is the name of the application. The fully qualified name of any component or service defined in the PAR is the name of the PAR file, followed by a period (.) and then the name of the component or service.*

All PAR files can be accessed using a standard HTTP request with data such as the following:

- HTML, which is a set of tags and rules

- Cascading Style Sheets (CSS), which is a style sheet language used to describe the look and feel of the UI

- Images

2.2 Introduction to Portal Objects: iViews, Pages, Worksets, and Roles

The SAP NetWeaver Portal self-services are built on different objects. Picture yourself reading a newspaper. You are the reader, this is your role in the SAP NetWeaver Portal. The newspaper contains different sections such as World, Economy, Sports, and so on. These sections correspond to a workset in SAP NetWeaver Portal. Now that you have opened your newspaper, you have many pages. The same principle applies in the SAP NetWeaver Portal with many pages. Within each page, you have several articles. These articles are like the iViews in the SAP NetWeaver Portal.

When accessing the SAP NetWeaver Portal via CONTENT ADMINISTRATION, SAP provides a legend with all icons used in the PCD and related directories. They are illustrated in Figure 2.5.

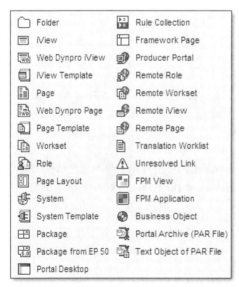

Folder	Rule Collection
iView	Framework Page
Web Dynpro iView	Producer Portal
iView Template	Remote Role
Page	Remote Workset
Web Dynpro Page	Remote iView
Page Template	Remote Page
Workset	Translation Worklist
Role	Unresolved Link
Page Layout	FPM View
System	FPM Application
System Template	Business Object
Package	Portal Archive (PAR File)
Package from EP 50	Text Object of PAR File
Portal Desktop	

Figure 2.5 Portal Icons

Note that the icon for the iView now has a "WD" on it to show that the new Web Dynpro UI is available.

The PCD contains the catalog of the functionalities available for configuration. It is located on the left side of the editor screen, as shown in Figure 2.6. It provides a centralized access point to the portal content and allows you to manage the content and adapt the hierarchy structure as required.

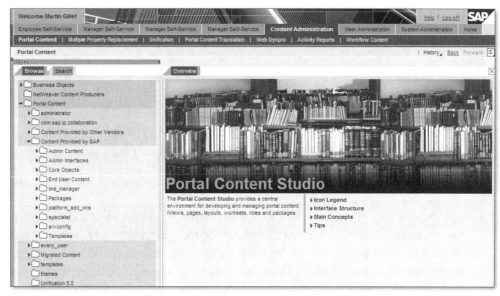

Figure 2.6 SAP NetWeaver Portal Content Directory

Next let's introduce the four portal objects: iViews, pages, worksets, and roles.

2.2.1 iViews

An *iView* is a functionality that contains an application. Each application is retrieving data from a data source, which is either from SAP or elsewhere. For example, the iView Time Registration contains the application Cross-Application Time Sheet (CATS).

2.2.2 Pages

A *page* is a placeholder that contains one or more iViews to organize the functionalities display for the end users. For example, the page Time Registration holds the iView Time Registration. Although using a page is not mandatory, as an iView could be directly linked to a workset, a page is recommended to harmonize the access path to the SAP NetWeaver Portal functionalities.

2.2.3   Worksets

A *workset* is a collection of pages or iViews that is used to organize the display to the end user, for example, worksets for personnel data or time management. Worksets are called the second level of navigation. The standard configuration is based on pages, linked to different worksets.

2.2.4   Roles

A *role* is a collection of worksets distributed in a logical sequence to the end-user role. The role is the first level of navigation.

When connecting to the SAP NetWeaver Portal, the end user is assigned a role that consolidates the UI by providing access to the worksets. (Worksets are pointing to pages, which are then pointing to the iViews.)

For example, the Employee Self-Services role will contain a series of worksets (which you might see as tabs): Overview, Employee Search, Working Time, Benefits and Payments, Career and Job, Personal Information, Purchasing, Work Environment, Travel and Expenses, Life and Work Events, and Corporate Information. These worksets will contain the different pages, which in turn will contain the relevant iView(s), as introduced earlier.

Now that you are acquainted with the portal objects, let's see how they can be set up in the PCD.

2.3   Setting Up the Portal Content Directory

The PCD contains folders. Standard folders contain the business packages as provided by SAP. Like the standard entries in SAP ERP, these standard folders should not be changed. portal administrators should provide a display role only.

In the customer dedicated folder in the PCD, you will deal mostly with the following objects:

▶ iViews

▶ Pages

▶ Worksets

▶ Roles

2.3.1 Linking Objects

All the portal objects are linked together. Although technically, you can link them however you want, a typical linking process is an iView linked to a page, a page linked to a workset, and a workset linked to the portal role.

There are two types of links:

▶ **Standard copy**
A typical copy of a standard reference object copied into a customer object. The copied object is totally independent and can be configured as needed.

▶ **Delta link copy**
A copy of a standard reference object into a *delta link* copy for a customer object. Technically, the copied object is still attached to the reference object. It is useful for technical upgrades or standard patching processes. The copied object remains totally independent in terms of configuration and can be configured as needed.

A delta link copy is always preferred.

2.3.2 Folders Setup

Because you will deploy the necessary objects, it is essential to have an unambiguous PCD structure.

We suggest a structure that is most of the time enforced, assuming that you have a multiple countries initiative (thus, a translation process also applies) with ESS, MSS, Administrator Role, and Reporting.

The country structure is only relevant for the ESS subfolder because for the other functionalities, you would take advantage of the proxy class configuration. ESS contains dedicated screens (iViews, etc.) for each supported country.

> **Caution!**
>
> Depending on the view you are using when using the PCD, folders might look like they are empty when, in fact, they contain data! Use extreme caution when deleting "empty" folders. It's an unpleasant lesson to learn—a folder deleted may equal lost work!
>
> Unlike in the SAP NetWeaver Portal Knowledge Management, which can use a "Waste Basket,"[1] it is not possible to recover Portal Objects once deleted.

Naming Convention

All objects created in the SAP NetWeaver Portal for the self-services projects must clearly be marked as customer objects to avoid any confusion or misunderstanding. The standard objects provided by SAP have the prefix ID *com.sap*. When copying standard objects or just creating your own objects or folders, enforce the following naming convention: *com.<yourcompany>*, for example, *com.sappress*. This naming convention informs SAP that these portal objects and folders belong to the customer. It also eases the search browsing when dealing with portal functionalities such as reporting or authorizations assignment.

Portal Project Structure Proposal

To ensure that all configurations belong to the project team, you must set up a dedicated portal structure containing all relevant objects and folders. It is highly recommended to structure the folders in a detailed approach to organize the long-term deployment and project maintenance.

It is crucial to set up a clear naming convention for each folder and object. If your SAP NetWeaver Portal team does not provide a naming convention, we suggest following the naming convention for the root object: *XSS—Project Self-Services*. You can then attach the following folders to the root SAP NetWeaver Portal folder:

```
Root Folder: XSS Project
      Common project parts
            iViews
            Pages
            Worksets
            Role
            Translation
```

---

1 Documentation: *http://help.sap.com/saphelp_nw70/helpdata/en/46/52f159390d3a66e10000000a114 a6b/frameset.htm*

```
Employee Self-Services
    Belgium
        iViews
        Pages
        Worksets
        Role
        Translation
    France
        iViews
        Pages
        Worksets
        Role
        Translation
    Germany
        iViews
        Pages
        Worksets
        Role
        Translation
    (more countries)
Manager Self-Services
    iViews
    Pages
    Worksets
    Role
    Translation
Administrator Role
    iViews
    Pages
    Worksets
    Role
    Translation
Reporting (Standard R.3 reporting, queries, Business Warehouse, etc.)
    iViews
    Pages
    Worksets
    Role
    Translation
Third Party links (Org Publisher, Taleo, etc.)
    iViews
    Pages
    Worksets
    Role
```

```
        Translation
    Transport
        Release 1
        Release 2
```

2.4   Object Properties

You can configure many properties for the standard objects you have copied or the objects you have created. This section describes the most useful properties to configure. We will explain the most common property settings used during a self-services project.

2.4.1   iViews

Each iView contains a handful of settings that you can easily adjust depending on the end-user requirements, as illustrated in Figure 2.7.

Figure 2.7   iView Properties Overview

As illustrated in Figure 2.8, we would normally set up, depending on the requirements, the following parameters with these return values:

▶ The HEIGHT TYPE should be set to AUTOMATIC, instead of FIXED so that the iView will adjust to the end-user screen.

▶ The INITIAL STATE of the service should be set to OPEN; otherwise, end users might be confused.

▶ Because we currently use the Homepage Framework for the navigation, INITIAL STATE OF NAVIGATION PANEL should be set by default to CLOSE.

Figure 2.8 Useful iView Properties

As illustrated in Figure 2.9, additional simple options can be configured, just by setting the radio button to YES or NO.

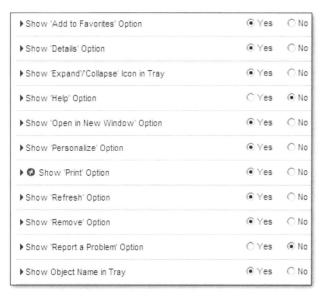

Figure 2.9 Additional Configuration Options at the iView Level

The following settings are typically used:

▶ Show 'Add to Favorites' Option: Yes because it is handy for end users.

▶ Show 'Details' Option: Yes because it is convenient for troubleshooting.

▶ Show 'Expand/Collapse' Icon in tray: Yes because end users can decide for themselves.

▶ Show 'Open in new Window' Option: Yes because it is useful for end users.

▶ Show 'Personalize' Option: No because it jeopardizes the template configured and deployed to end users. Personalization means mostly no harmonized support but rather a case-by-case situation, which the support team can't endorse.

▶ Show 'Print' Option: Yes because it is handy for end users.

▶ Show 'Refresh' Option: Yes because it allows end users to reload manually data from the system source, if updated data is available.

▶ Show 'Remove' Option: No, because it jeopardizes the template configured and deployed to end users. Personalization means mostly no harmonized support but rather a case-by-case situation, which the support team can't endorse.

▶ Show 'Report a problem' Option: No, unless your support team is ready to use that channel for communication. Most of the time, adequate issue ticketing systems are already in place for issue notifications.

▶ Show Object Name in Tray: Yes, this option displays the name of the iView in the tray.

2.4.2 Pages

Each page contains a handful of settings that you can easily adjust depending on the end-user requirements, as illustrated in Figure 2.10.

As illustrated in Figure 2.11, we would normally set up, depending on the requirements, the following parameters with these return values:

▶ The Height Type should be set to Automatic, instead of Fixed so that the page adjusts to the end-user screen.

▶ The Initial State of the service should be set to open; otherwise, end users might be confused.

▶ Because we currently use the Homepage Framework for the navigation, the Initial State of Navigation Panel should be set by default to Close.

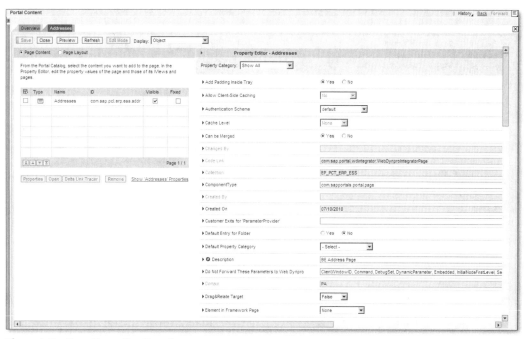

Figure 2.10 Page Properties Overview

Figure 2.11 Useful Page Properties

As illustrated in Figure 2.12, additional simple options can be configured, just by setting the radio button to YES or NO. Most of the settings are similar to the iViews settings. Unfortunately, there is no mass update tool currently available to maintain these settings.

The following settings are typically used:

▶ SHOW 'ADD TO FAVORITES' OPTION: YES because it is handy for end users.

▶ SHOW 'DETAILS' OPTION: YES because it is convenient for troubleshooting.

▶ SHOW 'EXPAND/COLLAPSE' ICON IN TRAY: YES because end users can decide for themselves.

Figure 2.12   Additional Configuration Options at the Page Level

▶ SHOW 'OPEN IN NEW WINDOW' OPTION: YES because it is useful for end users.

▶ SHOW 'PERSONALIZE' OPTION: No because it jeopardizes the template configured and deployed to end users. Personalization means mostly no harmonized support but rather a case-by-case situation, which the support team can't endorse.

▶ SHOW 'PRINT' OPTION: YES because it is handy for end users.

▶ SHOW 'REFRESH' OPTION: YES because it allows end users to reload manually data from the system source, if updated data is available.

▶ SHOW 'REMOVE' OPTION: No, just like PERSONALIZE, it jeopardizes the template configured and deployed to the end users. Personalization means mostly no harmonized support but rather a case-by-case situation, which the support team can't endorse.

▶ SHOW 'REPORT A PROBLEM' OPTION: No, unless your support team is ready to use that channel for communication. Most of the time, adequate issue ticketing systems are already in place for issue notifications.

▶ SHOW OBJECT NAME IN TRAY: Most of the time No because the name is already displayed in the iView tray. Choosing YES doubles the display name: once in the iView tray and once in the page tray. Having the name twice is not an issue; it's a "look and feel" decision.

2.4.3   Worksets

Each workset contains a handful of settings that you can easily adjust depending on the end-user requirements, as illustrated in Figure 2.13.

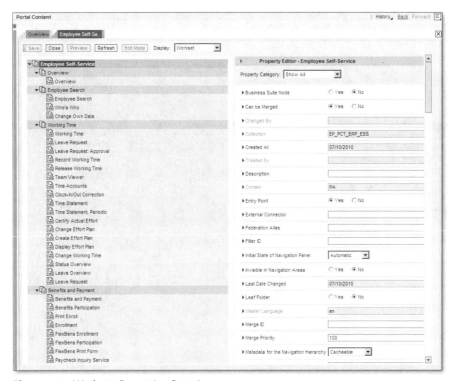

Figure 2.13   Worksets Properties Overview

Figure 2.14   Useful Workset Properties

As illustrated in Figure 2.14, worksets can also have these additional settings:

► CAN BE MERGED: YES, meaning that the workset can be merged among other worksets.

► SHOW 'ADD TO FAVORITES' OPTION: NO because the option is already made available at the iView and/or the page entry level.

▸ SORT PRIORITY: This entry should be provided by your portal administrator to set the workset sequencing correctly.

2.4.4 Roles

Each role contains a handful of settings that you can easily adjust depending on the end-user requirements, as illustrated in Figure 2.15.

Figure 2.15 Role Properties Overview

Roles can also have additional settings, as illustrated in Figure 2.16:

▸ ENTRY POINT: YES, to show up in the end-user role assignment, as illustrated in Figure 2.16. Failing to set the property to YES leave the portal role hidden from the end user.

▸ SORT PRIORITY: This entry should be provided by your portal administrator to set the roles sequencing correctly.

Figure 2.16   Useful Role Properties

2.5   Creating Quick Links

From the portal object page level each self-services functionality can be assigned a Quick Link, which end users can use.

We normally set up the Quick Link at the page entry level, within the page properties, as illustrated in the Figure 2.17.

Figure 2.17   Quick Link Address Assigned to the Page Address

A Quick Link name is assigned to the functionality, which can then be reached directly using the portal address:

http://<yourserver>:<yourport>/irj/portal/<nameofQuickLink>.

2.6   How to Transport Objects

Now that you know how to configure and set up the PCD, you may wonder how you transport all these objects from the development portal into the test system and then on to the productive system. You have two options:

▶ Manage all the transport requests from the SAP NetWeaver Development Infrastructure (NWDI).

▶ Manage the transport manually by exporting important objects from the SAP NetWeaver Portal directly.

2.6.1   Transporting with SAP NetWeaver Development Infrastructure (NWDI)

Although the NWDI is nice to have, it isn't a must-have when dealing with SAP NetWeaver Portal. Project can be implemented with and without it. Setting up

NWDI is not just for HCM self-services; it should also be part of a portal deployment strategy. However, because it requires technical skills and resources to deploy it, some customers decide not to use NWDI.

This tool provides additional transport security (and perhaps fulfills compliance requests) by enforcing versioning and standard checks for transport conflicts.

This transport topic is a legitimate question that must be raised to the portal administration team to clearly identify and set the portal transport strategy.

For now, we'll settle for a manual export and import of portal objects because this is the quickest standard way of handling these objects. However, if you run NWDI, transport will take place from within this infrastructure.

2.6.2   Transporting Manually

The quickest way to transport content from one portal to another independently, without support from a portal administrator, is to export and import from the source portal. Figure 2.18 illustrates the access path for exporting and importing portal content.

Figure 2.18   Package Export Editor

Although we recommend this solution, be sure to use extreme caution because you basically have to handle the transport versioning and potential conflict checks on your own. This might be a big gamble given the amount of hours you have spent configuring the system.

Once again, this transport topic is a legitimate question that must be raised to the portal administration team to clearly identify and set the portal transport strategy.

The transport strategy should include the following issues (this is not an exhaustive list):

▸ Content integrity and checks

▸ Content versioning

▸ Content naming conventions

▸ Release cycles for transport

2.7   Portal Layout

The standard SAP NetWeaver Portal already provides myriad portal layout and templates. It goes without saying that it might be mandatory or preferred that you adhere to the company or customer web branding, so you should check with the communication team in charge of corporate branding.

Based on the internal requirements, a dedicated portal theme can then be created in the portal configuration. Although it is easier to have one layout for all users, it is technically possible to assign a different portal theme to different portal users.

To ease the portal support and maintenance, it is recommended that the portal system administrator remove the option CHANGE PORTAL THEME from the portal user PERSONALIZE option.

2.8   Languages and Portal Translation

Languages and translation are important points when dealing with multi-language countries or international deployments. We will focus on the language and translation configuration at the system level.

Don't forget that language is also set up in the system user attributes as well as the default setting of the browser parameter. Language settings are also maintained in the SAP UserID parameter (Transaction SU01) and in the Internet browser.

2.8.1 Language

Assuming that you are deploying self-services for multiple countries, languages must be appropriately set up in the SAP ERP system as well as in the SAP NetWeaver Portal, the SAP NetWeaver Business Warehouse (BW), and other relevant systems in use.

Installed languages in the SAP ERP system can be viewed using Transaction SMLT — Language Management, as illustrated in Figure 2.19.

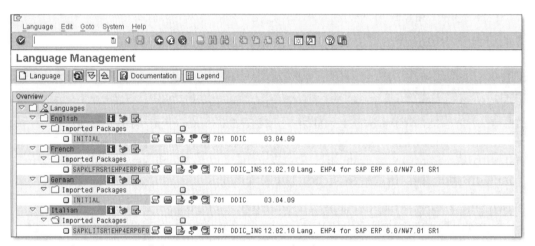

Figure 2.19 Installed Languages on SAP ERP Backend

The list of available languages can also be seen when using the translation feature from the customizing tables.

In parallel to the languages deployment on the target system, the portal must also support these languages. You must check with the infrastructure team to determine whether or not both systems' lists match.

We recommend reading the following SAP Notes for background information, even if they do not apply to your release:

▶ Note 778884 — *Central Note for the Portal Content Translation*

▶ Note 1013521 — *Configuration of Supported Languages within the Portal*

▶ Note 195442 — *Language Import and Support Packages*

▶ Note 533888 — *Example for Language Import and Error Specification*

2.8.2 Portal Translation

Assuming that the portal deployment will be done in multiple languages, proper translation must be done on the SAP NetWeaver Portal side. This can easily be achieved with the portal steps described in the following subsections.

Translating Objects with the Portal Translation Worklist

To translate the objects, follow these steps:

1. Access the portal path via PORTAL • CONTENT ADMINISTRATION • PORTAL CONTENT TRANSLATION, as illustrated in the Figure 2.20.

Figure 2.20 Translation Worklist Editor

2. Add all portal objects to be translated into the translation worklist object, as illustrated in Figure 2.21 by opening the translation worklist object and then right-clicking ADD ALL OBJECTS TO THE TRANSLATION WORKLIST from the PCD and your content.

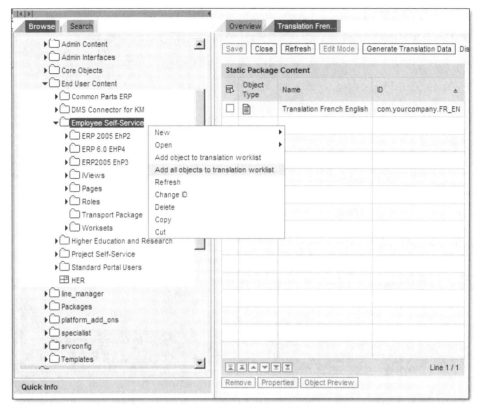

Figure 2.21 Adding Objects to Be Translated into the Translation Worklist

3. After all objects are added to the worklist, click on the icon GENERATE TRANSLA-
TION DATA, which closes the list.

4. Choose RELEASED FOR TRANSLATION to make it available for translation process-
ing. The system then issues a message: STATUS OF TRANSLATION WORKLIST IS
"RELEASED FOR TRANSLATION." IT IS NOT POSSIBLE TO ADD NEW OBJECTS TO THE
TRANSLATION WORKLIST.

5. Close the translation worklist to carry on, or cancel the release to add more
objects.

Picking Up the Transaction Worklist Package

From the WORKLIST TRANSLATION menu, pick up your transaction worklist package,
by following these steps:

1. Set the source language and the target language.

2. Load the translation worklist. A new screen appears as illustrated in Figure 2.22.

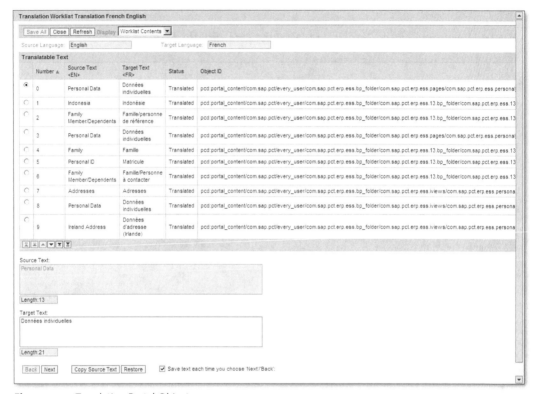

Figure 2.22 Translating Portal Objects

> **Tip**
>
> At the bottom of the screen, to avoid losing data during the process, flag the option SAVE TEXT EACH TIME YOU CHOOSE NEXT/BACK.

3. From this screen, you can sort the columns, groups, and then all the different objects bearing the same name.

4. Translate the object in the TARGET TEXT box. You can also copy the source text, if it is relevant for your translation process.

5. Repeat the translation as needed for all objects, and close the object. You return to the main screen.

6. Mark the translation worklist as translated by clicking on the icon MARK AS TRANS-LATED. The system sets the status TRANSLATED to the translation worklist.

Returning to the Translation Worklist Coordination

To go back to the translation worklist, follow these steps:

1. From your PCD, choose and open your translation worklist. The system reminds you that STATUS OF TRANSLATION WORKLIST IS "TRANSLATED." IT IS NOT POSSIBLE TO ADD NEW OBJECTS TO THE TRANSLATION WORKLIST.

2. Click on the icon PUBLISH TRANSLATION to make the translation configuration effective, as illustrated in Figure 2.23.

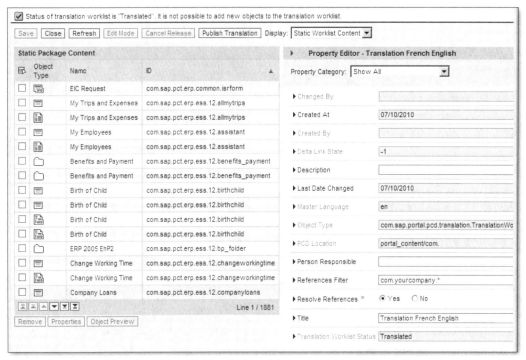

Figure 2.23 Publishing Translated Content

The translation is now effective for all the objects in scope.

You can also "force the language" from each portal object, but as stated in SAP Note 1232473 (Limitations on Usage of ForcedRequestLanguage in WD iView), it has limitations.

> **Note**
>
> Translation is done on the SAP NetWeaver Portal side and the SAP ERP configuration side, but have you taken care of the "soft configuration?" Soft configuration examples include the translation of the qualification catalog, the training catalog, or the organizational structure.

2.9   Work Protect Mode

Unlike the standard SAP ERP system, in the standard SAP NetWeaver Portal application, when a user leaves a screen (iView) or a process to go to another one, the SAP NetWeaver Portal does not always prompt the user to save or discard the current information, which can be annoying and frustrating for common users.

To bypass this, you can ask the Basis team to activate the work protect mode for all users.

Depending on the end user actions in the current business process, work protect mode will open a screen with the options shown in Figure 2.24.

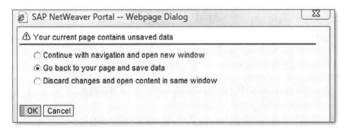

Figure 2.24   Work Protect Mode Enabled

> **Note**
>
> Refer to SAP Note 734861—WorkProtect Mode—Global Settings, for the global configuration for WorkProtect (which is available since SAP NetWeaver Portal 6.0) through the set of properties via portal service configuration. Depending on your portal version, you need admin role assigned to your portal user and/or access to the SAP NetWeaver administrator.

2.10   Other Technical Considerations

Although perhaps out of scope for this self-services configuration book, this section points out a list of other technical consideration that should also be on your portal deployment list. These considerations are meant to challenge you, whether or not the information and questions provided are relevant for you.

2.10.1   Browser in Use

It is important to assess and check with SAP Notes to determine which browser will be used to gain access to SAP NetWeaver Portal. Not all browsers are supported. Standard browsers such as Internet Explorer (IE) are enforced.

You should also read the following SAP notes, for example, depending on your SAP release:

- 1098009—Limitations for Web Dynpro ABAP
- 1223128—Adobe Interactive Forms Do Not Work with Firefox
- 960549—Portal Limitations for the Firefox Browser
- 990034—Firefox Browser for End Users
- 1347768—Web Dynpro and Microsoft Internet Explorer Version 8.0

This information regarding browser compatibility is also available on the marketplace under the Product Availability Matrix (PAM): *http://service.sap.com/PAM* (user name and password required).

2.10.2 Business Server Pages (BSP) Activation

If you still use BSP functionalities, it is important to activate the required technical services as well as the expected functionalities.

When first accessing a new SAP system and calling the BSP, the error message SERVICE CANNOT BE REACHED appears. It returns error code 403, which denies access to the functionality.

The activation can be done through SAP backend Transaction SICF — HTTP Service Hierarchy Maintenance, as illustrated in Figure 2.25.

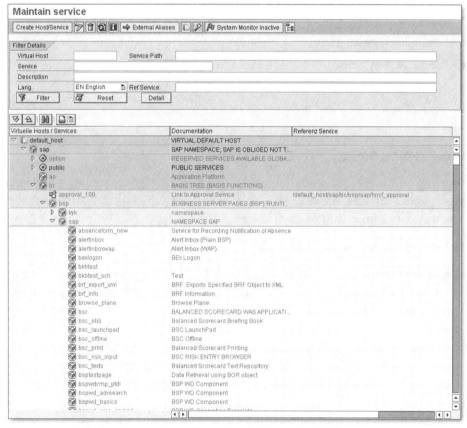

Figure 2.25 Activating Business Server Pages through Transaction SICF

Alternatively, Transaction SE80—Object Navigator can also be used to activate BSPs.

We strongly recommend the following SAP Notes:

- 517484—Inactive Services in the Internet Communication Framework
- 891232—BSP Security Relevant Changes

For example, the following technical nodes must be activated:

- */sap/bc/bsp/sap/system*
- */sap/bc/bsp/sap/public/bc*
- */sap/public/bsp/sap/public/bc*
- */sap/public/bsp/sap/system*
- */sap/public/bsp/sap/htmlb*
- */sap/public/bc*
- */sap/public/bc/ur*

2.10.3 Portal Sizing

To avoid end users from enduring a waiting experience when you are providing access to self-services, it is important to raise the question of portal sizing with the portal system administrators from the very beginning.

There are two main sizing issues:

- Identify the number of simultaneous users logged at once on the portal system. These simultaneous logged users, also known as concurrent users, determine the peak of accesses that the SAP NetWeaver Portal can handle. The concurrent user determination depends on several parameters such as the system sizing, the number of users likely to have access to the self-services functionalities, the number of functionalities, and so on. Clearly identify which parameters to apply to your project, and initiate the question to the portal system administrators.
- Check the network bandwidth because SAP NetWeaver Portal establishes a permanent dialog with the SAP ERP system to exchange data. Depending on the data volume to be considered and the network infrastructure, adjustments might be required. Raise the question to the Basis team to fully assess what is required.

2.10.4   Population in Scope

Because the self-services are meant for the whole staff, it is wise to distinguish, for example, the connected users from the disconnected users. Most of the users will be connected through their PCs. However, depending on your business activity, some personnel might also be disconnected, which raises new access requirements. Disconnected users might connect through the use of "self-services kiosks" spread among the company, smart phones, iPads, and other devices.

Identifying the population in scope right from the project start ensures that you do not run into pitfalls when going live with the self-services functionalities.

When identifying the population in scope, also clearly identify the printing requirements if you enable the self-services printing, for example, for the payslip or the time statement. Additional printing material might be required on top of the self-services kiosks.

2.10.5   Portal Help

Most projects keep the standard help functionality located on the upper-right corner in the portal (button HELP). Providing help to the end user should always bring added value, but in most cases, the HELP button takes the user to the *http://help.sap.com* website. Unless you plan to train functional users into SAP experts, or you have created a dedicated support page such as a Frequently Asked Questions (FAQ), you should ask the infrastructure team to deactivate this help link. Alternatively, replace the standard link with your customer or company link pointing to this support page, which will be much more helpful to end users.

2.10.6   Portal Troubleshooting and Debugging

Like all technology, SAP NetWeaver Portal may fail to execute certain functionalities from time to time. To help you anticipate these system failures, ask the SAP NetWeaver Portal administrators to provide a tracing tool. It is not an obligation or a must, but it will definitively be an asset portal troubleshooting. In fact, the support team will request a portal trace of all portal activity when troubleshooting.

For example, as illustrated in Figure 2.26, SAP is using the HttpWatch software, which allows many support functionalities such as issuing a portal activity trace.

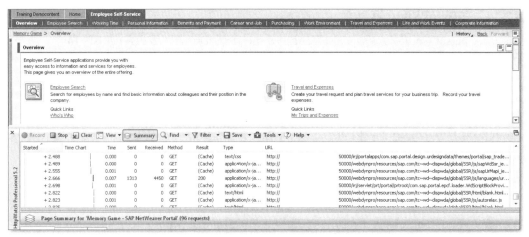

Figure 2.26 Example of Tracing tool: HttpWatch (Professional)

2.10.7 Active Component Framework (ACF)

According to the SAP standard definition:

> *The Active Component Framework (ACF) integrates active components in web-based SAP user interfaces. The present implementation contains ActiveX controls, JavaBeans, and applets that run in web browsers or in SAP NetWeaver Business Client (NWBC).*

The ACF provides the necessary infrastructure for the following scenarios:

- ▶ Processing mass data (fetch data from the backend and reset modified data)
- ▶ Displaying data in-place or outside a web browser or SAP NetWeaver Business Client (NWBC)
- ▶ Integrating components in the Web Dynpro programming model (data binding, event handling)
- ▶ Keeping the status of a component when a new page is loaded

To use, for example, the personnel change request or the processes and forms, and depending on your SAP NetWeaver Portal, you may have to request the installation of the ACF. This component is normally installed by default on the latest SAP NetWeaver Portal release.

If you don't install ACF, you'll see a blank screen with an "X" icon illustrating a potential technical issue.

Ask your SAP NetWeaver Portal administrator whether or not ACF is already installed and available for use.

2.10.8 Internet Graphical Server (IGS)

To display, for example, maps in the Travel Expenses Planning self-service functionality, you may have to request the installation of the Internet Graphics Server (IGS), which must be deployed onto SAP NetWeaver Portal. This component is normally installed by default on the latest SAP NetWeaver Portal release.

If you don't install IGS, you'll see a blank screen with an "X" icon illustrating a potential technical issue.

Ask your SAP NetWeaver Portal administrator whether or not it is already installed and available for use.

2.10.9 Adobe Document Server (ADS)

You should first ask your SAP NetWeaver Portal administrator whether Adobe Document Server (ADS) is already installed and available for use because ADS is a prerequisite to enabling change requests and/or HCM Processes and Forms into a portable document format (PDF) rendering.

ADS is also useful in the configuration of these change requests and/or HCM Processes and Forms.

2.10.10 Universal Worklist (UWL) Checklist

Although not directly managed under SAP HCM self-services, the UWL is valuable because it gathers all workflows and notifications in a central inbox.

We recommend that your read SAP Note 676253 — EP 6.0: Central Note for Universal Worklist (UWL), which is release independent. This note reviews the main points regarding UWL.

2.11 Conclusion

Through this chapter, we have seen the standard SAP NetWeaver Portal Content Directory, also known as the PCD. The PCD has a similar configuration backbone as the SAP ERP IMG. We pointed out the first important step of checking the current technical requirements also known as patches and the business package releases to be downloaded into the PCD. We identified the standard SAP placeholder containing all the standard portal objects: the business package. If you need to add additional functionalities, from a certified SAP partner or a customer-made development, a Portal Archive file (.par) can also be imported into SAP NetWeaver Portal.

We reviewed the four standard SAP NetWeaver Portal objects: iViews, pages, worksets, and roles. Within these objects, we covered the properties that you can configure to best meet the business requirements. We also discussed how to enable a Quick Link per functionality. End user will love this detailed attention for their daily tasks because they will only need to recall the Quick Link provided to access the portal functionality.

We also pointed out the strategy you must put in place regarding the SAP NetWeaver Portal objects transports. Corporate branding is always important in order to make the end user comfortable. This step can be achieved by deploying a portal theme that is either common to all users or dedicated per user groups.

Last but not least, we also listed additional technical considerations that should be part of your SAP NetWeaver Portal deployment checklist.

Now that we have discussed the SAP NetWeaver Portal in detail, let's take a deep look into the SAP ERP backend configuration settings in the next chapter.

This chapter explains how to enable SAP NetWeaver Portal self-services via SAP ERP backend configuration steps based on the Homepage Framework, Object and Data Provider (OADP), and Internal Service Request (ISR) concepts.

3 Backend Configuration

Now that we have covered the SAP NetWeaver Portal configuration in the previous chapter, before we go ahead with the detailed explanation of the ESS and MSS configuration, let's focus on the configuration also available in the SAP ERP backend system. This configuration is actually a very powerful ally when it comes to deploying self-services functionalities. This configuration deals with the Homepage Framework, which handles comprehensive user menus for ESS; the Object and Data Provider (OADP), which supports the fields data import for MSS; and the Internal Service Request (ISR), which is the technology in use up to SAP ERP 6.0 regarding the personnel change requests that a manager can trigger from the self-services.

This chapter reviews all required configuration steps for each functionality. We do recommend, however, that you read the standard documentation provided by SAP to better comprehend how it can support you in your SAP NetWeaver Portal self-services deployment.

3.1 Homepage Framework

SAP ERP 5.0 provided a new configuration functionality called Homepage Framework, which makes configuration easier for business analysts and makes navigation easier for end users.

The Homepage Framework is a straightforward configuration tool designed to organize ESS overview page and surrounding services pages. It introduces the notion of resources, headers, area group pages, and subarea group pages. All these objects are linked together with the configuration shown in Figure 3.1 and Figure 3.2.

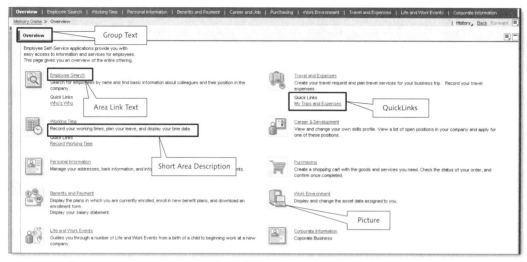

Figure 3.1 Homepage Framework Configuring in Parallel with SAP NetWeaver Portal

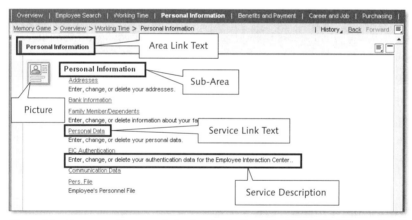

Figure 3.2 Homepage Framework Configuring in Parallel with SAP NetWeaver Portal

The Homepage Framework also provides several options such as displaying or not displaying the services, adjusting the picture (logo) of the area pages, and, most important, providing detailed documentation for each process (when the business department is requesting it). This documentation is also referred as *context information*, which helps the end user when performing a task or triggering a process as illustrated in Figure 3.3.

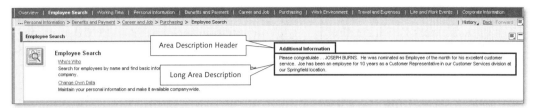

Figure 3.3 Homepage Framework with Additional Information for the End User

The Homepage Framework is provided as is as of SAP ERP 5.0. It does not require enhancement packages because it is part of the standard out-of-the-box SAP backend system.

Section 3.4, Homepage Framework Configuration, will take you through the configuration steps in the SAP ERP backend plus the one configuration in the SAP NetWeaver Portal.

The standard documentation can be reached here:

http://help.sap.com/erp2005_ehp_05/helpdata/EN/aa/9f75620a8d4a2e9181db37f2fa 2a62/frameset.htm.

3.2   Object and Data Provider (OADP)

The Object and Data Provider (OADP) is located under the configuration of MSS. However, because many customers configure their own services, based in the OADP, we have isolated this configuration block in the backend configuration.

The OADP is the standard configuration tool provided to customize and adjust the MSS screens.

Furthermore (and most important), the OADP is also the method used by SAP to supply data and business rules in standard or customers fields, for example, when illustrating the employees displayed to the Manager, which are based on the personnel development evaluation paths. The evaluation paths, which are the sum of relationships in-between personnel development objects, are often used to "feed" the fields. For example, the relationship between a person (object P) to a position (object S) linked to an organizational unit (object O) is the evaluation path O-S-P. This O-S-P access path is used by SAP to retrieve all personnel reporting directly to the manager, for example. Alternatively, if you need more flexibility to apply business rules or read customer tables, for example, the system can also empower OADP via function modules. The function module allows ABAP programming.

OADP was introduced in SAP release R/3 Enterprise (also known as 4.70). For customers who have already made configurations prior to SAP ERP 6.0, nothing is lost because SAP standard provides the (handy) program RP_OADP_MIGRATE_CUS-TOMIZING—Migration of OADP Customizing Tables (used as of SAP ERP 2005). This program can be reached using Transaction HRWPC_OADP_MIGRATION—Migration from OADP Customizing.

OADP is also used for the configuration of the HR administrator role. Section 3.5 highlights and illustrates the different configuration entries for OADP. The standard documentation can be reached here:

http://help.sap.com/saphelp_erp60/helpdata/EN/e7/947e40ec66ce62e10000000a1551 06/content.htm.

3.3   Internal Service Requests (ISR)

The MSS personnel change requests along with the ESS form for Code of Business Conduct are powered by the SAP standard Internal Service Request (ISR).

> **Note**
>
> A detailed documentation and further information is provided in the SAP Note 1049057 — ISR Documentation — "ISR Cookbook." Carefully review what is still relevant for your SAP release because all functionalities might not apply to you.

Although totally useable in SAP ERP 6.0, the ISR technology is likely to become obsolete in the next generation of SAP applications. Therefore, we also strongly advise that you look at the next generation for forms: the Human Capital Management (HCM) Processes and Forms, which are also introduced in this chapter.

Section 3.6 highlights the ISR configuration access, illustrates the ISR configuration steps and the workflow tasks available, and introduces the HCM Processes and Forms.

3.4   Homepage Framework Configuration

The configuration of the Homepage Framework is done using standard IMG steps.

For technical reasons, each configuration table contains two views:

▶ The first view contains SAP standard entries, which should never be altered.

▶ The second view contains the entries already contained in the first view. We are using the second view to make changes and adjustment.

Before we dive into the IMG and the configuration of the Homepage Framework, we would recommend the following steps.

3.4.1 Preparing for Configuration

Before you start the configuration, we strongly recommend that you make a graphical design, perhaps on a flipchart, of the areas, subareas, services, and resources you want to enable. This graphical representation makes the step-by-step configuration walkthrough easier and will be a valuable asset when it comes to the documentation because it highlights all the hierarchical links between the objects and provides an overview as illustrated in Figure 3.4 and Figure 3.5.

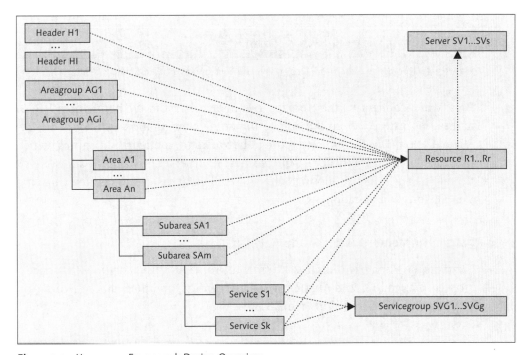

Figure 3.4 Homepage Framework Design Overview

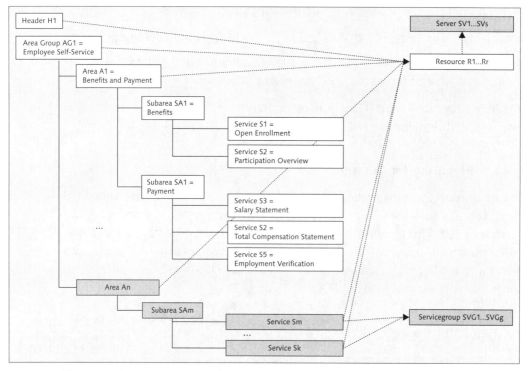

Figure 3.5 Homepage Framework Design Overview Mapped with Self-Services Values

Also, when configuring the Homepage Framework, avoid the numbering 1, 2, 3, and so on. Instead, set up the numbering in the configuration as follows: 10, 20, 30, and so on. This leaves some room in-between the configuration entries, which provides some flexibility in case the business requirements change or adjustments need to be made. It also allows you to add configuration entries without changing the previous configuration.

3.4.2 Implementation Guide Access

To access the Homepage Framework, from the root SAP CUSTOMIZING IMPLEMENTATION GUIDE, go to CROSS-APPLICATION COMPONENTS, and then choose HOMEPAGE FRAMEWORK as illustrated in Figure 3.6.

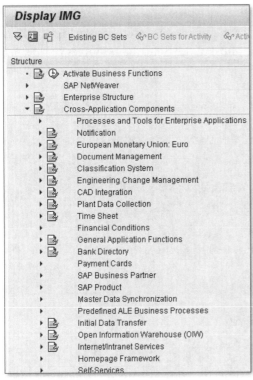

Figure 3.6 IMG Access Path to the Homepage Framework

3.4.3 Define Resources

In this configuration step, you define the resources to be used in the group pages and area pages. One of the options is to have the resources configured in another separate system; for example, for response time constraints. You also must set the server name where the resource is located. Additionally, each resource must have a set of attributes in order to be operational.

For us, the most important parts are the following:

▸ The URL parameters to pass on, such as the forced language

▸ The URL of the PCD page, which is critical because this is the link between the SAP ERP backend configuration and the SAP NetWeaver Portal

Define Server for Resources (Optional)

In this configuration step, you add the server where the resources are located. This configuration entry is optional because, most of the time, the resources are located on the same machine.

IMG Access Path	SAP Customizing Implementation Guide • Cross-Application Components • Homepage Framework • Resources • Define Server for Resources
IMG Activity	PCUI_HPF_063
Transaction Code	S_FAD_62000052
Table Name	V_T7XSSSERSDB

You make the following entries, as illustrated in Figure 3.7:

▶ Server: "CUSTOMER_NAME"

▶ Protocol: "https"

▶ Name and Port: "serverxx.com:8080"

▶ Directory Path: "etc/resourcefiles"

The system then concatenates at runtime the entries into the following URL address:

https://serverxx.com:8080/etc/resourcefiles.

Note that the system automatically adds the colon (:) and the forward slashes (//) after the protocol.

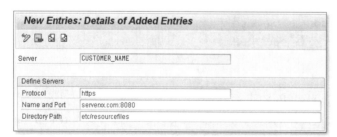

Figure 3.7 Configuring the Server for a Homepage Framework Resource

The same applies if you want to point to the customer pictures and logos. To do that, you make the following entries:

- SERVER: "CUSTOMER_NAME"
- DIRECTORY PATH: "pictures"
- URL OF RESOURCE OBJECT: "picture01.jpg"

The system then retrieves the picture from the following URL address:

https://serverxx.com:8080/etc/resourcefiles/pictures/picture01.jpg.

Define Resources

In this configuration step, you define the resources to be used in the area group pages and the area pages. Technically speaking, the system allows different types of objects as illustrated in Figure 3.8:

- Texts
- Pictures
- Hyperlinks
- Services (web applications)
- URLs

IMG Access Path	SAP CUSTOMIZING IMPLEMENTATION GUIDE • CROSS-APPLICATION COMPONENTS • HOMEPAGE FRAMEWORK • RESOURCES • DEFINE RESOURCES
IMG Activity	PCUI_HPF_065
Transaction Code	S_FAD_62000051
Standard Table Name	V_T7XSSSERRES (Add Entries)
Customer Table Name	V_T7XSSSERRESC (Change Entries)

As underlined by SAP documentation:

> *Each of these objects in question is a resource. Resources can be reused throughout the pages you define. When you define a URL for a resource, you need to provide the relevant content at the location the URL refers to.*

The relevant URL is the PCD location as identified in SAP NetWeaver Portal.

To avoid confusion when browsing from workset to workset, it is important to start the portal URL with *ROLES://* so that each time the end user is moving within the portal role allocated, the relevant workset is highlighted in SAP NetWeaver Portal. Failing to do so will lead to the proper functionality but will leave the OVERVIEW workset highlighted although the end user has moved to another workset.

Figure 3.8 Defining the Homepage Framework Resource with Working Time Page as an Example

would become

*ROLES://portal_content/com.sap.pct/specialist/com.sap.pct.compspecialist/Roles/com.sap.pct.
compspecialist.compensation_specialist/com.sap.pct.compspecialist.comp_administration/com.
sap.pct.compspecialist.comp_administration.employee_data*

It will then show the entire URL access path in the same box and not on one line, which
is handy when writing the configuration documentation.

Important!

Because ESS is country dependent (in SAP language, *Molga*), a service is provided for
each country supported by SAP. The country is determined via the personnel area of the
employee, which is linked to the country per configuration in table V_T500P—Assignment
of Personnel Area to Company Code.

3.4.4 Define Headers and Area Group Pages

Define Headers (Optional)

In this configuration step, you can configure the header brought onto the SAP
NetWeaver Portal screen, which is optional.

IMG Access Path	SAP Customizing Implementation Guide • Cross-Application Components • Homepage Framework • Headers and Area Group Pages • Define Headers
IMG Activity	PCUI_HPF_010
Transaction Code	S_FAD_62000040
Standard Table Name	V_T7XSSSERHEB (Add Entries)
Customer Table Name	V_T7XSSSERHEBC (Change Entries)

The standard entry SAPDEFAULT is "Welcome" as shown in Figure 3.9. In most
cases, per customer or client instructions, you keep the standard. If you want to
add your own text, feel free to add the entry in this configuration step. Just don't
forget to translate that entry when dealing with multiple languages.

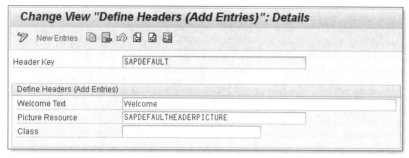

Figure 3.9 Homepage Framework: Define Headers

Define Area Group Pages

You also must configure the area group pages that will be the distinction between ESS and MSS. It is almost like a placeholder that contains further configuration.

IMG Access Path	SAP CUSTOMIZING IMPLEMENTATION GUIDE • CROSS-APPLICATION COMPONENTS • HOMEPAGE FRAMEWORK • HEADERS AND AREA GROUP PAGES • DEFINE AREA GROUP PAGES
IMG Activity	PCUI_HPF_020
Transaction Code	S_FAD_62000042
Standard Table Name	V_T7XSSSERARGB (Add Entries)
Customer Table Name	V_T7XSSSERARGBC (Change Entries)

Note that depending on the release, SAP standard applies the following naming convention:

▶ Up to SAP ERP 5.0: Entry bears the name SAPDEFAULTESS.

▶ As of SAP ERP 6.0: Entry bears the name SAPDEFAULTESS_ERP2005.

In this configuration step, you set up the following values as shown in Figure 3.10:

▶ AREA GROUP ROLE TEXT: "Overview" (it will appear in the SAP NetWeaver Portal frame).

▶ AREA GROUP TEXT: "Employee Self-Services" (it will appear in the SAP NetWeaver Portal frame).

▶ QUICK-LINK HEADING: "Quick Links" is the standard verbiage, but it's up to you to adjust this entry to a closer customer definition such as "Shortcuts."

▶ AREA GROUP LINK TYPE: In most cases, you are dealing with Web Dynpro Java Applications. If not, see Section 3.4.7, which describes the allowed types.

▶ LINK RESOURCE: Link the resources to be called (which as we have seen previously will pick up the URL address path from the PCD).

▶ AREA GROUP DESCRIPTION: This description will appear on the upper page. SAP provides the following standard description:

> *Employee Self-Service applications provide you with easy access to information and services for employees. This page gives you an overview of the entire offering.*

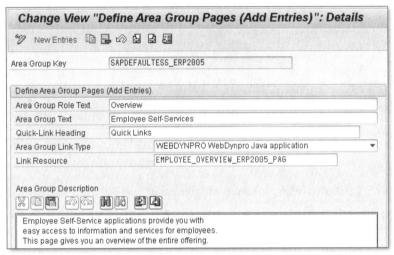

Figure 3.10 Homepage Framework Defining the Area Group Pages with the Employee Self-Services as Example

---

Note

If you create your own entries, don't forget to translate these to make them relevant for your project.

3.4.5 Define Areas

Now that we have defined the area groups page (or placeholder) for ESS and MSS, it is time to organize it into different areas that could be described as subcategories within the placeholder.

Define Areas

The SAP standard offering provides a long list of standard areas for self-services. To abide by the rules of not touching the standard, we make a copy of the relevant entries into customer-named entries. This ensures that the entries entirely belong to the customer and that no one will jeopardize the configuration when another team is demonstrating the functionalities or just setting it up for another country, for example.

IMG Access Path	SAP CUSTOMIZING IMPLEMENTATION GUIDE • CROSS-APPLICATION COMPONENTS • HOMEPAGE FRAMEWORK • AREAS • DEFINE AREAS
IMG Activity	PCUI_HPF_030
Transaction Code	S_FAD_62000043
Standard Table Name	V_T7XSSSERARB (Add Entries)
Customer Table Name	V_T7XSSSERARBC (Change Entries)

Note that depending on the release, the SAP standard applies the following naming convention:

▶ Up to SAP ERP 5.0: Entry bears, for example, the name EMPLOYEE_PERSINFO.

▶ As of SAP ERP 6.0: Entry bears, for example, the name EMPLOYEE_PERS-INFO_ERP2005; the "ERP2005" part confirms that this is the latest standard entry provided by SAP.

For example, EMPLOYEE_PERSINFO_ERP2005—Personal Information contains the following values as illustrated in Figure 3.11:

▶ AREA KEY: Unique name of the configuration entry.

▶ AREA LINK TEXT: "Personal Information" (text to be displayed in SAP NetWeaver Portal).

▶ PICTURE RESOURCE: Link to the picture resource that will display a nice thumbnail next to the area to illustrate the functionality.

▶ AREA LINK TYPE: In most cases, we are dealing with Web Dynpro Java applications; otherwise, see Section 3.4.7, which describes the allowed types.

▶ LINK RESOURCE: Link the resources to be called (which as we have seen previously will pick up the URL address path from the PCD).

▶ AREA DESCRIPTION (SUMMARY): Summary to be displayed directly under the area in the SAP NetWeaver Portal (optional).

▶ AREA DESCRIPTION HEADING: Title name to be displayed on the right side of the SAP NetWeaver Portal screen (optional).

▶ AREA DESCRIPTION (LONG TEXT): A detailed documentation regarding the functionality called (optional).

▶ AREA DESCRIPTION LONG TEXT (EXTERNAL): An access path to an external container such as a SAP NetWeaver Knowledge Management (KM) placeholder where all documentation is stored and maintained by the business (optional).

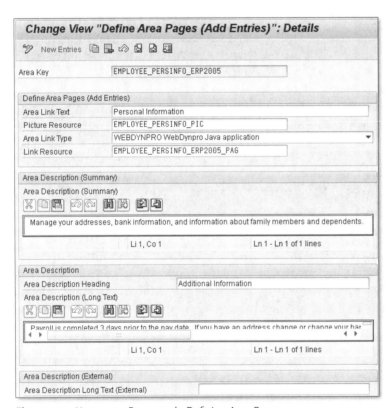

Figure 3.11 Homepage Framework: Defining Area Pages

Assign Areas to Group Pages

Now that we have identified and created the areas to be used, we must link them to the group pages so they can be displayed in SAP NetWeaver Portal.

IMG Access Path	SAP CUSTOMIZING IMPLEMENTATION GUIDE • CROSS-APPLICATION COMPONENTS • HOMEPAGE FRAMEWORK • AREAS • ASSIGN AREAS TO AREA GROUP PAGES
IMG Activity	PCUI_HPF_040
Transaction code	S_FAD_62000044
Standard Table Name	V_T7XSSSERARG (Find Entries)
Customer Table Name	V_T7XSSSERARGC (Add and Change Entries)

> **Note**
>
> As stated earlier, when configuring the Homepage Framework, avoid the numbering 1, 2, 3, and so on, and use 10, 20, 30, and so on, instead to leave some room in-between the configuration entries changes or adjustments.

In this table, against the relevant AREA GROUP KEY, allocate the AREA KEY, and assign a POSITION. Position 10 will come first, 20 then after, and so on as illustrated in Figure 3.12.

Change View "Assign Areas to Area Group Pages (Find Entries)": Overvie

New Entries

Assign Areas to Area Group Pages (Find Entries)

Area Group Key	Area Key	Position	
SAPDEFAULTESS_ERP2005	EMPLOYEE_BENEFITPAY_ERP2005	7	
SAPDEFAULTESS_ERP2005	EMPLOYEE_CAREER_ERP2005	4	
SAPDEFAULTESS_ERP2005	EMPLOYEE_CORPORATEINFO_ERP2005	10	
SAPDEFAULTESS_ERP2005	EMPLOYEE_LIFEWORKEVENTS_ERP2005	9	
SAPDEFAULTESS_ERP2005	EMPLOYEE_PERSINFO_ERP2005	5	
SAPDEFAULTESS_ERP2005	EMPLOYEE_PURCHASING_ERP2005	6	
SAPDEFAULTESS_ERP2005	EMPLOYEE_SEARCH_ERP2005	1	
SAPDEFAULTESS_ERP2005	EMPLOYEE_TRAVEL_ERP2005	2	
SAPDEFAULTESS_ERP2005	EMPLOYEE_WORKENVIRONMENT_ERP2005	8	
SAPDEFAULTESS_ERP2005	EMPLOYEE_WORKTIME_ERP2005	3	
SAPDEFAULTMSS	MSS_HCM_AREA_ATTENDANCE	1	
SAPDEFAULTMSS	MSS_HCM_AREA_HEADCOUNT	5	
SAPDEFAULTMSS	MSS_HCM_AREA_PERSONNELCHANGEREQU…	2	
SAPDEFAULTMSS	MSS_HCM_AREA_RECRUITING	3	
SAPDEFAULTMSS	MSS_HCM_AREA_REPORTING	4	

Figure 3.12 Homepage Framework: Assigning Areas to Area Group Pages

In the group pages, the areas always start from the upper-left side and then move to the right side, then on the left side under the first area, and so on.

3.4.6 Define Subareas

Each area can be subdivided into subareas, which is not mandatory. Nevertheless, each area must at least have one subarea for obvious technical reasons.

Define Subareas

In this configuration step, we define the subareas.

IMG Access Path	SAP CUSTOMIZING IMPLEMENTATION GUIDE • CROSS-APPLICATION COMPONENTS • HOMEPAGE FRAMEWORK • SUBAREAS • DEFINE SUBAREAS
IMG Activity	PCUI_HPF_050
Transaction code	S_FAD_62000045
Standard Table Name	V_T7XSSSERSARB (Add Entries)
Customer Table Name	V_T7XSSSERSARBC (Change Entries)

Note that depending on the release, SAP standard applies the following naming convention:

▶ Up to SAP ERP 5.0: Entry bears, for example, the name EMPLOYEE_PERSINFO_SUBPERSINFO.

▶ As of SAP ERP 6.0: Entry bears, for example, the name EMPLOYEE_PERSINFO_SUBPERSINFO_2005; ERP2005 confirms the latest standard entry that was provided by SAP.

For example EMPLOYEE_PERSINFO_SUBPERSINFO_2005 — Personal Information contains the following values, as illustrated in Figure 3.13:

▶ SUBAREA KEY: "EMPLOYEE_PERSINFO_SUBPERSINFO_2005" is a unique name identifying the subarea key technical name and standard area.

▶ SUBAREA TEXT: "Personal Information."

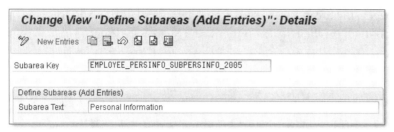

Figure 3.13 Homepage Framework: Defining Subareas

Assign Subareas to Areas

Now that we have identified and created the subareas to be used, we must link them to the areas so they can be displayed in SAP NetWeaver Portal.

IMG Access Path	SAP CUSTOMIZING IMPLEMENTATION GUIDE • CROSS-APPLICATION COMPONENTS • HOMEPAGE FRAMEWORK • SUBAREAS • ASSIGN SUBAREAS TO AREAS
IMG Activity	PCUI_HPF_060
Transaction Code	S_FAD_62000046
Standard Table Name	V_T7XSSSERAR (Find Entries)
Customer Table Name	V_T7XSSSERARC (Add and Change Entries)

> **Note**
>
> When configuring the Homepage Framework, use the 10, 20, 30, and so on numbering convention instead of 1, 2, 3, and so on, to leave some room in-between the configuration entries for later adjustments.

In this table, against the relevant AREA KEY, allocate the SUBAREA KEY and assign a POSITION. Position 10 will come first, 20 then after, and so on as illustrated in Figure 3.14.

3.4.7 Define Services

Now that we have defined all required entries for the Homepage Framework, here comes the most important part: the definition of the services. The service will be the functionality that the end user will run after accessing SAP NetWeaver Portal.

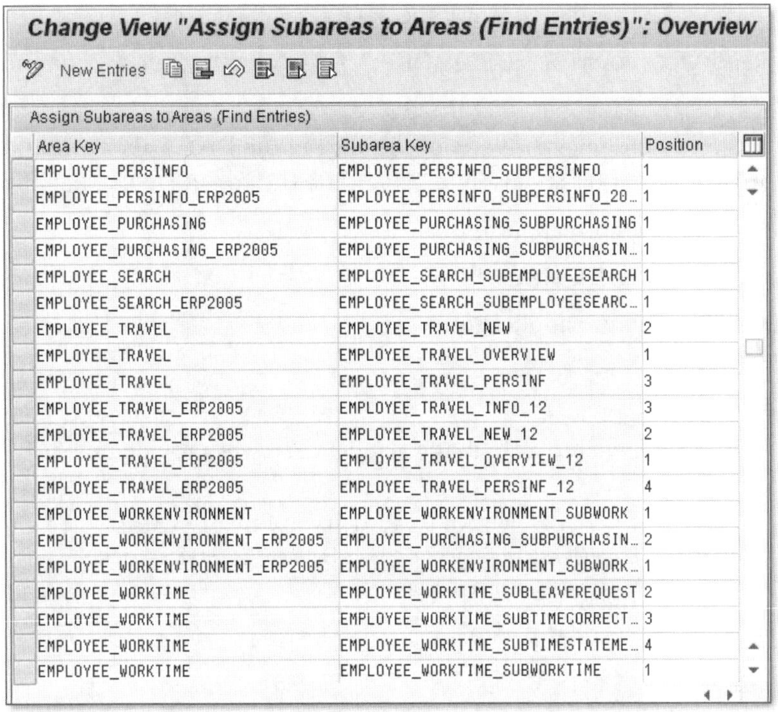

Change View "Assign Subareas to Areas (Find Entries)": Overview

New Entries

Assign Subareas to Areas (Find Entries)

Area Key	Subarea Key	Position
EMPLOYEE_PERSINFO	EMPLOYEE_PERSINFO_SUBPERSINFO	1
EMPLOYEE_PERSINFO_ERP2005	EMPLOYEE_PERSINFO_SUBPERSINFO_20...	1
EMPLOYEE_PURCHASING	EMPLOYEE_PURCHASING_SUBPURCHASING	1
EMPLOYEE_PURCHASING_ERP2005	EMPLOYEE_PURCHASING_SUBPURCHASIN...	1
EMPLOYEE_SEARCH	EMPLOYEE_SEARCH_SUBEMPLOYEESEARCH	1
EMPLOYEE_SEARCH_ERP2005	EMPLOYEE_SEARCH_SUBEMPLOYEESEARC...	1
EMPLOYEE_TRAVEL	EMPLOYEE_TRAVEL_NEW	2
EMPLOYEE_TRAVEL	EMPLOYEE_TRAVEL_OVERVIEW	1
EMPLOYEE_TRAVEL	EMPLOYEE_TRAVEL_PERSINF	3
EMPLOYEE_TRAVEL_ERP2005	EMPLOYEE_TRAVEL_INFO_12	3
EMPLOYEE_TRAVEL_ERP2005	EMPLOYEE_TRAVEL_NEW_12	2
EMPLOYEE_TRAVEL_ERP2005	EMPLOYEE_TRAVEL_OVERVIEW_12	1
EMPLOYEE_TRAVEL_ERP2005	EMPLOYEE_TRAVEL_PERSINF_12	4
EMPLOYEE_WORKENVIRONMENT	EMPLOYEE_WORKENVIRONMENT_SUBWORK	1
EMPLOYEE_WORKENVIRONMENT_ERP2005	EMPLOYEE_PURCHASING_SUBPURCHASIN...	2
EMPLOYEE_WORKENVIRONMENT_ERP2005	EMPLOYEE_WORKENVIRONMENT_SUBWORK...	1
EMPLOYEE_WORKTIME	EMPLOYEE_WORKTIME_SUBLEAVEREQUEST	2
EMPLOYEE_WORKTIME	EMPLOYEE_WORKTIME_SUBTIMECORRECT...	3
EMPLOYEE_WORKTIME	EMPLOYEE_WORKTIME_SUBTIMESTATEME...	4
EMPLOYEE_WORKTIME	EMPLOYEE_WORKTIME_SUBWORKTIME	1

Figure 3.14 Homepage Framework: Assign Subareas to Areas

Allowed Service Types

Because we are dealing with multiple technologies, the services can call different types. The Homepage Framework supports the following service types and expects entries in this view as indicated:

- Business Server Page (BSP): Service built with BSP.
- Directory Path: No entry.
- Object Name: BSP-Application/BSP-Page.
- Internet Transaction Server (ITS): ITS-based service.
- Directory Path: No entry.
- Object Name: ITS-Application.
- PORTALPAGE: Call a portal page (located in the PCD).
- Directory Path: No entry.
- Object Name: No entry.

▸ URL OF PCD PAGE: The absolute URL of the page.

▸ UNIFORM RESOURCE LOCATOR (URL): Direct URL launched in a separate window.

You can either enter the relevant parts of the URL in the DIRECTORY PATH and OBJECT NAME fields or enter an absolute URL in the URL OF PCD PAGE field.

▸ WEBDYNPRO: Web Dynpro application.

▸ DIRECTORY PATH: Vendor/DC-Name.

▸ OBJECT NAME: Web Dynpro application.

Define Services

In this configuration step, we can find all the standard services provided by SAP.

IMG Access Path	SAP CUSTOMIZING IMPLEMENTATION GUIDE • CROSS-APPLICATION COMPONENTS • HOMEPAGE FRAMEWORK • SERVICES • DEFINE SERVICES
IMG Activity	PCUI_HPF_070
Transaction Code	S_FAD_62000047
Standard Table Name	V_T7XSSSERSRV (Add Entries)
Customer Table Name	(Select CHANGE ENTRIES)

Note that depending on the release, SAP standard applies the following naming convention as illustrated in Figure 3.15:

▸ Up to SAP ERP 5.0: Entry bears, for example, the name EMPLOYEE_PERSINFO_BANK.

▸ As of SAP ERP 6.0: Entry bears, for example, the name EMPLOYEE_PERS-INFO_BANK05; 05 confirms the latest standard entry provided by SAP.

For example EMPLOYEE_PERSINFO_ADDRESS05 — Addresses contains the following values as illustrated in Figure 3.16:

▸ SERVICE KEY: Enter a unique identifier for the service; in this case, the standard entry is "EMPLOYEE_PERSINFO_ADDRESS05."

Figure 3.15 Homepage Framework: Excerpt of Services with Their Naming Convention

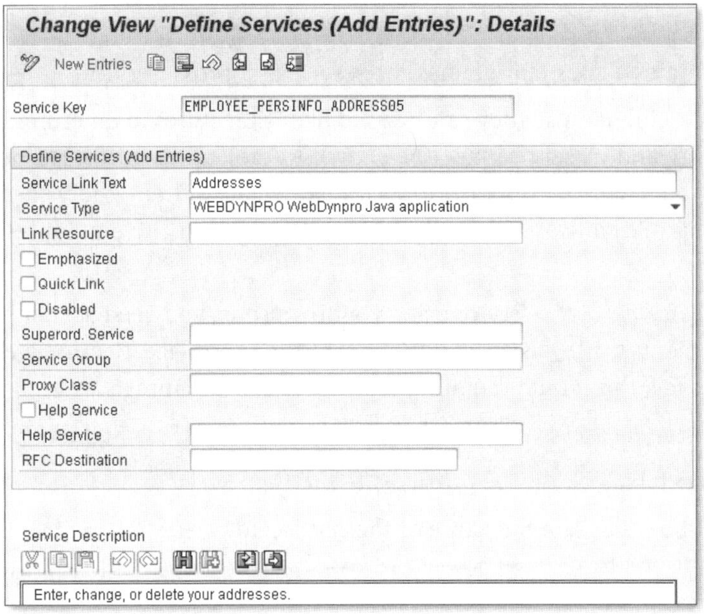

Figure 3.16 Homepage Framework: Defining a Service with the Address as an Example

- SERVICE LINK TEXT: Enter the title of the service, in this case, "Addresses."

- SERVICE TYPE: In most cases, you are dealing with Web Dynpro Java applications; otherwise, see the allowed service types in Section 3.4.7.

- LINK RESOURCE: Normally you link the resource identifier. However, when dealing with ESS, the resource is country dependent and thus automatically determined. The system will identify the personnel area of the employee and identify through table V_T500P the country (Molga) assigned to it.

- EMPHASIZED: Tick this box if you want to make the entry appear in bold.

- QUICK LINK: Tick this box if you want to enable this service as a Quick Link.

- DISABLED: Tick this box if you want to deactivate the service. The service will still appear on the screen but will not be activate. For example, it could be useful for appraisal review to deactivate when the appraisal period is closed. Just removing the entry would cause too many tickets raised by end users for support.

- SUPERORD. SERVICE: Set the information for the superordinate service.

- SERVICE GROUP: Contains the service group to which a service belongs. If you want to group a service with other services in a service group on an area page, enter the relevant service group here.

  You can define service groups in the V_T7XSSSERSRVG and V_T7XSSSERSRVGC views.

- PROXY CLASS: Contains a class that defines the service as a proxy service.

  Proxy classes are useful because they can be used like HR features to determine which functionality and/or service must be shown to the end user. Instead of creating myriad roles, you can use a proxy class to let the system know that this service is only relevant for active workers, and the rest of the employees should not see it.

  To influence the behavior of the service using your own code, you need to create a class that implements the IF_XSS_SER_PROXY_SERVICE interface. Because we deal with ABAP code, this would require a little bit of programming.

  The Class Builder can be accessed through Transaction SE24—Class Builder.

- HELP SERVICE checkbox: Tick this box to activate the Help Service.

- HELP SERVICE textbox: Allocate the name of the service key area.

▶ RFC DESTINATION: Assign the logical remote function call destination if relevant; otherwise, leave blank.

▶ SERVICE DESCRIPTION: Enter the relevant service description.

Define Country Specific Services

In this configuration step, you maintain services for each individual supported country (Molga in SAP terminology).

IMG Access Path	SAP CUSTOMIZING IMPLEMENTATION GUIDE • CROSS-APPLICATION COMPONENTS • HOMEPAGE FRAMEWORK • SERVICES • DEFINE COUNTRY-SPECIFIC SERVICES
IMG Activity	PCUI_HPF_080
Transaction Code	S_FAD_62000048
Standard Table Name	V_T7XSSSERSRVCG (Add Entries)
Customer Table Name	V_T7XSSSERSRVCGC (Change Entries)

Note that depending on the release, the SAP standard applies the following naming convention:

▶ Up to SAP ERP 5.0: Entry bears, for example, the name EMPLOYEE_PERSINFO_ADDRESS.

▶ As of SAP ERP 6.0: Entry bears, for example, the name EMPLOYEE_PERSINFO_ADDRESS; 05 confirms the latest standard entry provided by SAP.

For example, EMPLOYEE_PERSINFO_ADDRESS—Addresses contains the following values as illustrated in Figure 3.17 and Figure 3.18 (closeup):

▶ SERVICE KEY: Name of the service as previously defined.

▶ COUNTRY GROUPING ID: For example 01 for Germany, 10 for the USA, 12 for Belgium, and so on.

▶ LINK RESOURCE: Link to the resource as previously defined (which points to the relevant application per country).

In this table, against the SERVICE KEY SHORT, allocate the COUNTRY GROUPING and the LINK RESOURCE.

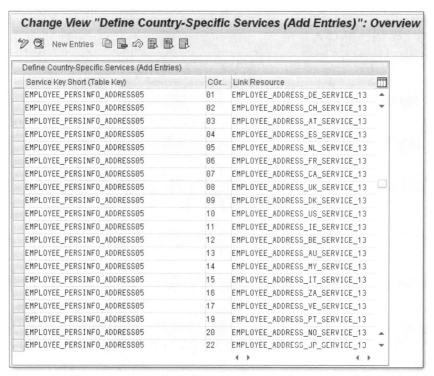

Figure 3.17 Homepage Framework: Defining Country Specific Services with the Address Service as an Example

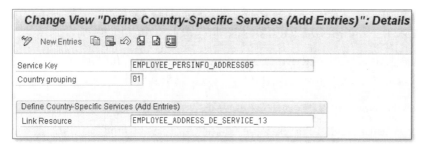

Figure 3.18 Homepage Framework: Defining Country-Specific Services with the Address Service as an Example (Closeup)

Assign Services to Subareas

In this configuration step, you assign the services to the subareas.

IMG Access Path	SAP CUSTOMIZING IMPLEMENTATION GUIDE • CROSS-APPLICATION COMPONENTS • HOMEPAGE FRAMEWORK • SERVICES • ASSIGN SERVICES TO SUBAREAS
IMG Activity	PCUI_HPF_090
Transaction Code	S_FAD_62000049
Standard Table Name	V_T7XSSSERSAR (Find Entries)
Customer Table Name	V_T7XSSSERSARC (Add and Change Entries)

Against each relevant SUBAREA KEY, allocate the SERVICE KEY SHORT and its POSITION as illustrated in Figure 3.19.

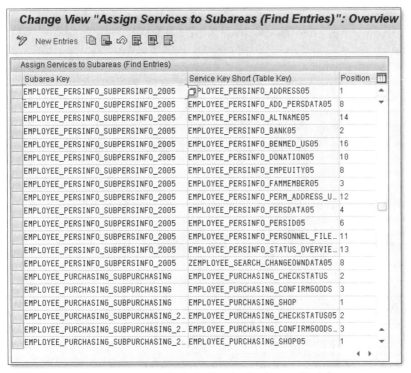

Figure 3.19 Homepage Framework: Assigning the Services to the Subareas

> **Note**
>
> When configuring the Homepage Framework, use the 10, 20, 30, and so on numbering convention instead of 1, 2, 3, and so on, to leave some room in-between the configuration entries for later adjustments.

Define Service Groups (Optional)

As we have seen in the definition of the service, the service group can be handy in the configuration step, although not mandatory. This service group is useful if you want to group a service with other services in a service group on an area page. Here you define the relevant service group.

IMG Access Path	SAP CUSTOMIZING IMPLEMENTATION GUIDE • CROSS-APPLICATION COMPONENTS • HOMEPAGE FRAMEWORK • SERVICES • DEFINE SERVICE GROUPS
IMG Activity	PCUI_HPF_100
Transaction Code	S_FAD_62000050
Standard Table Name	V_T7XSSSERSRVG (Add Entries)
Customer Table Name	V_T7XSSSERSRVGC (Change Entries)

Define the SERVICE GROUP KEY along with the SERVICE GROUP TEXT as illustrated in Figure 3.20.

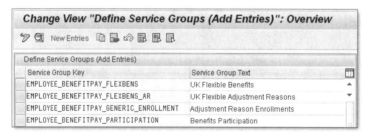

Figure 3.20   Homepage Framework: Define Service Groups (Optional)

Define Links on the Confirmation Page

In this configuration step, you are determining which link(s) to show at the end of a process.

IMG Access Path	SAP CUSTOMIZING IMPLEMENTATION GUIDE • CROSS-APPLICATION COMPONENTS • HOMEPAGE FRAMEWORK • SERVICES • DEFINE LINKS ON CONFIRMATION PAGE
IMG Activity	PCUI_HPF_106
Transaction Code	S_S7B_68000051
Standard Table Name	V_T7XSSSERLNK

For example, after the employee submits a leave request, we have instructed the system to display the following links as illustrated in Figure 3.21:

▶ SHOW HOMEPAGE LINK (optional text possible)

▶ SHOW AREAPAGE LINK (optional text possible)

▶ SHOW RESTART LINK (optional text illustrated in the figure)

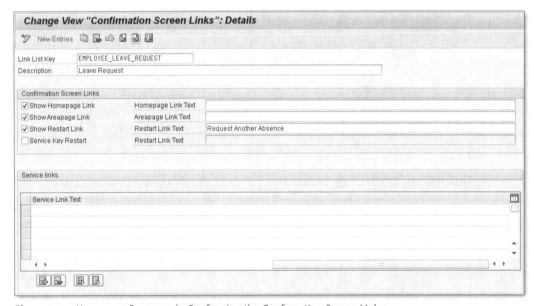

Figure 3.21 Homepage Framework: Configuring the Confirmation Screen Links

This configuration step is not necessary but will make navigation through the different self-services easier for end users.

3.4.8 Mapping between SAP ERP and SAP NetWeaver Portal Configuration

We have seen previously that thanks to the resource URL of the PCD, we are making the connection from the SAP ERP system to the SAP NetWeaver Portal.

You may be wondering how SAP NetWeaver Portal knows which configuration to pick. (For this issue, we won't use the SAP standard offering.)

To answer this question, a tiny configuration setting must be done in the SAP NetWeaver Portal page properties:

1. Connect to the SAP NetWeaver Portal.
2. From the PCD, call the properties of the Employee Self-Service Overview iView, for example, as illustrated in Figure 3.22.

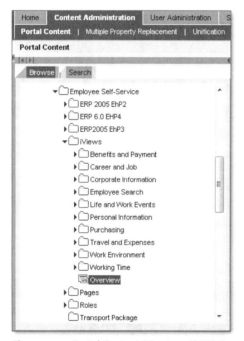

Figure 3.22   Portal Content Directory (PCD) Overview iView

3. From the PCD, call up the Employee Self-Service Overview iView.
4. Double-click on the object to open the properties.

In the WEB DYNPRO properties, look for the APPLICATION PARAMETER as illustrated in Figure 3.23. (The standard string is the following: *sap.xss. menuargrp=SAPDEFAULTESS_ERP2005&sap.xss.menuhdr=SAPDEFAULT.*)

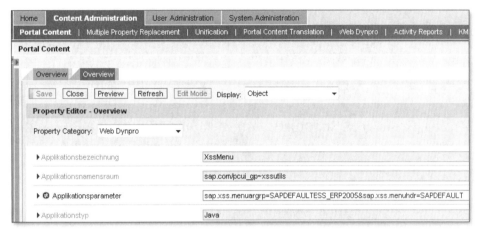

Figure 3.23 Application Parameter for the iView Overview from the Portal Content Directory (PCD)

5. If you have created your own entries, such as a copy of the standard, paste your parameter string here, like this one:

sap.xss.menuargrp=ZSAPDEFAULTESS_ERP2005&sap.xss.menuhdr=ZSAPDEFAULT

This ensures that SAP NetWeaver Portal is picking up and retrieving your Homepage Framework configuration.

3.5   Object and Data Provider (OADP) Configuration

This section highlights the steps for configuring the OADP. Let's first locate the IMG path, and then reveal the transfer program for existing configuration into the latest SAP ERP 6.0 release.

Following that, we will focus on the Object Provider and the Data Provider, as well as the organizational views.

3.5.1   Implementation Guide Access

To access the OADP, you have two options:

▶ Call the SAP Customizing Implementation Guide and go to the bottom of the IMG: Integration with Other mySAP.com Components • Business Packages/ Functional Packages • Manager Self-Service (mySAP ERP) • Object and Data Provider.

Note

The Manager Self-Service (mySAP ERP) is the latest placeholder for functionalities, whereas the Manager Self-Service was the placeholder for earlier functionalities in SAP ERP 5.0 and before.

▶ Call up Transaction SIMG_SPORT—IMG Business/Functional Packages. This transaction is handy because it points directly to the integration with other SAP component and avoids fastidious browsing through the IMG.

3.5.2   Transfer Existing Customizing Settings

As we have seen in the introduction, customers who have already configured OADP can still use their customizing. To move on with the latest release, this configuration step launches the program RP_OADP_MIGRATE_CUSTOMIZING—Migration of OADP Customizing Tables (used as of SAP ERP 2005).

IMG Access Path	Integration with Other mySAP.com Components • Business Packages/Functional Packages • Manager Self-Service (mySAP ERP) • Object and Data Provider • Transfer Existing Customizing Settings
IMG Activity	PORT_MAN_OADP_001
Transaction Code	S_AXC_91000008

This program can also be reached directly using Transaction HRWPC_OADP_ MIGRATION—Migration from OADP Customizing. This program is only meant for customers still using the SAP release under SAP ERP 6.0. It is meant to transfer smoothly current configuration to the new SAP system.

You can either select all views and views groups, which gathers the whole configuration, or you can select manually the view group(s) and view(s) to be migrated (this is the preferred choice because it avoids "spamming" the configuration in the IMG).

To avoid any configuration inconsistencies, we strongly recommend you do the following:

▶ Run documentation provided with the program.

▶ Run this program in TEST RUN in a test system.

▶ Read about and be aware of some inconsistencies detected by SAP, which were corrected thanks to the SAP Note 1060699—MSS: Inconsistencies w/Report RP_OADP_MIGRATE_CUST.

3.5.3 Object Provider

Now that we have introduced the OADP, located the IMG access path, and revealed the transfer program, let's take a closer look at the configuration options.

Define a Rule for Object Selection

In this step, per the user requirements, you can create a rule for object selection. Normally you would first review the standard entries provided and then, if necessary, create a copy of a standard entry to adjust it as illustrated in Figure 3.24. This rule for object selection is a placeholder for the configuration to be done.

IMG Access Path	INTEGRATION WITH OTHER MYSAP.COM COMPONENTS • BUSINESS PACKAGES/FUNCTIONAL PACKAGES • MANAGER SELF-SERVICE (MYSAP ERP) • OBJECT AND DATA PROVIDER • OBJECT PROVIDER • DEFINE RULES FOR OBJECT SELECTION
IMG Activity	PORT_MAN_OADP_100
Transaction Code	S_AXC_91000009
Table Name	V_TWPC_OBJSELRUL

For example, in the standard, the selection rule MSS_ECM_SEL_RU5—Employees of an Organizational Unit is calling all the employees belonging to an organizational unit.

The configuration available in this configuration step is the following (see Figure 3.24):

► EVALUATION PATH: In this case, the evaluation path "O-P" is used. The evaluation path is the sum of relationships between personnel development objects. For example, the object O is the organizational unit, and P is the person. Standard evaluation paths can be viewed in the table T77AT—Evaluation Path Texts.

► DEPTH OF STRUCTURE: This field should be set if you want to limit the depth of the structure. Depending on the size of the organizational structure, this could be quite important regarding the response time.

► FUNCTION MODULE: If you have complex business requirements or just need more flexibility than the use of an evaluation path, you can also use a function module. This function module requires some programming and therefore the help of a developer.

► DELETE DUPLICATES: Tick this box if you want to enable the system filtering for duplicates.

► EXCLUDE MANAGERS: Tick this box if you want to disable the display of managers in the data returned on the screen.

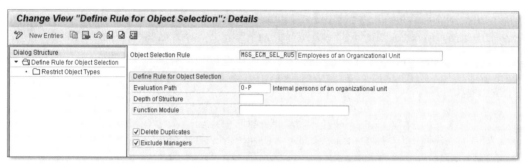

Figure 3.24 Object and Data Provider, Defining the Rule for Object Selection

Additional configuration is always available per object types. In the standard, because we deal mainly with object P for person, this object is set up in this configuration entry as illustrated in Figure 3.25.

Other relevant objects include the following:

► US: SAP UserID

► BP: Business partner

► H: External person

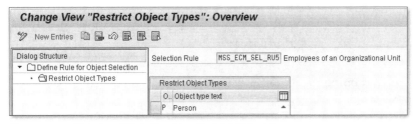

Figure 3.25 Object and Data Provider: Restrict Object Type

Business Add-Ins

Naturally, SAP is quite flexible and provides several Business Add-Ins (BAdIs) to enhance the standard configuration. You can also take advantage of the BAdIs to exclude managers from the data provider in case managers should not be maintained directly (e.g., in the compensation process) by their n+1 manager but by the executive committee or the Chief Financial Officer (CFO), or if managers should not influence the navigation objects.

The use and setup of BAdIs requires the support of a developer as a little programming is involved.

BAdI: OADP: Exclude Managers	
IMG Access Path	INTEGRATION WITH OTHER MYSAP.COM COMPONENTS • BUSINESS PACKAGES/FUNCTIONAL PACKAGES • MANAGER SELF-SERVICE (MYSAP ERP) • OBJECT AND DATA PROVIDER • OBJECT PROVIDER • BUSINESS ADD-INS (BADIS) • BADI: OADP: EXCLUDE MANAGERS
IMG Activity	PORT_MAN_OADP_110
Transaction Code	S_AXC_91000010

Additional programming needs to be defined in BAdI builder HRWPC_EXCL_MANAGERS.

BAdI: OADP: Modification of Navigation Objects	
IMG Access Path	INTEGRATION WITH OTHER MYSAP.COM COMPONENTS • BUSINESS PACKAGES/FUNCTIONAL PACKAGES • MANAGER SELF-SERVICE (MYSAP ERP) • OBJECT AND DATA PROVIDER • OBJECT PROVIDER • BUSINESS ADD-INS (BADIS) • BADI: OADP: MODIFICATION OF NAVIGATION OBJECTS

IMG Activity	PORT_MAN_OADP_120
Transaction Code	S_AXC_91000011

Additional programming needs to be defined in BAdI builder HRWPC_MOD_NAVOBJECTS.

Group Parameters for Object Search

In this configuration step, you create a parameter to group a set of configuration options for a dedicated entry.

IMG Access Path	INTEGRATION WITH OTHER MYSAP.COM COMPONENTS • BUSINESS PACKAGES/FUNCTIONAL PACKAGES • MANAGER SELF-SERVICE (MYSAP ERP) • OBJECT AND DATA PROVIDER • OBJECT PROVIDER • GROUP PARAMETERS FOR OBJECT SEARCH
IMG Activity	PORT_MAN_OADP_130
Transaction Code	S_AXC_91000012
Table Name	V_TWPC_PARAMGRP

For example, the standard entry parameter group MSS_ECM_EESRCH—Parameters for Employee Search contains a set of values only for this parameter group as illustrated in Figure 3.26.

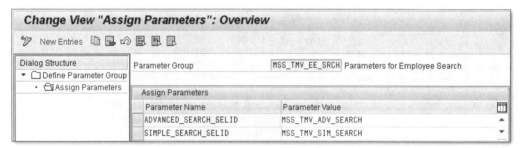

Figure 3.26 Object and Data Provider: Assigning Parameters

This parameter group contains the parameter names that are allocated a return parameter value.

You could compare this to a SAP UserID system parameter that returns default values when the system is running a functionality.

Define Object Selections

Now that we've defined the rules, we must assign them to the object selection to restrict or narrow down the entries returned to the manager's list.

IMG Access Path	INTEGRATION WITH OTHER MYSAP.COM COMPONENTS • BUSINESS PACKAGES/FUNCTIONAL PACKAGES • MANAGER SELF-SERVICE (MYSAP ERP) • OBJECT AND DATA PROVIDER • OBJECT PROVIDER • DEFINE OBJECT SELECTIONS
IMG Activity	PORT_MAN_OADP_140
Transaction Code	S_AXC_91000013
Table Name	V_TWPC_OBJSEL

For example, the standard entry MSS_ATO_SEL1 — Direct Reports contains the settings as illustrated in Figure 3.27. We are assigning the object selection name along with the rules for object selection, based on the customer naming convention. These entries will be used in the forthcoming configuration steps.

RULES FOR OBJECT SELECTION defines the rule for root objects with rule for target objects.

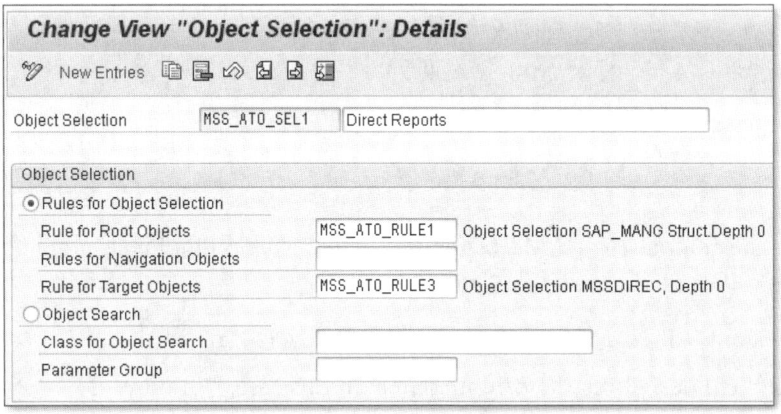

Figure 3.27 Object and Data Provider: Object Selection

Alternatively, additional flexibility is provided by the search class CL_HRWPC_ SEARCH_VIA_SELID. Additional programming is required as well as the support of a developer.

This additional flexibility is achieved in the configuration by enabling OBJECT SEARCH and setting the CLASS FOR OBJECT SEARCH.

3.5.4 Data Provider

Now that we have defined rules, the object selection, and their respecting parameters, we can focus on setting up the screen displays. The Data Provider is the configuration step where you adjust the display and the content provided in the fields in standard SAP functionalities such as MSS or personnel change requests.

These configuration steps are widely used because they are the backbone for the configuration of each dedicated business scenario and provide great flexibility.

Define Columns

In this step, for each dedicated process, such as the personnel change requests, the performance appraisal process, the enterprise compensation management process, and so on, we define the configuration of the columns.

IMG Access Path	INTEGRATION WITH OTHER MYSAP.COM COMPONENTS • BUSINESS PACKAGES/FUNCTIONAL PACKAGES • MANAGER SELF-SERVICE (MYSAP ERP) • OBJECT AND DATA PROVIDER • DATA PROVIDER • DEFINE COLUMNS
IMG Activity	PORT_MAN_OADP_220
Transaction Code	S_AXC_91000036
Table Name	V_TWPC_COL_ERP

For example, the column AP_NAME (Appraisal—Field Name) Employee contains the following values as illustrated in Figure 3.28:

▶ COLUMN NAME: "AP_NAME" for Appraisal—(Employee) Name.

▶ NAME: Text field describing the column name, in this case, "Employee."

▶ FOR GENERIC USE: Flag this box if you want to enable the selected column as displayable in any column groups.

- ALIGNMENT: Just like in your text application, choose the relevant alignment. Most of the time, we choose the LEFT-JUSTIFIED.

- CONVERS. ROUT.: Set a conversion routine, based on standard function module templates provided by SAP: CONVERSION_EXIT_xxxxx_INPUT and CONVERSION_EXIT_xxxxx_OUTPUT. The INPUT module performs the conversion from display format to internal format. The OUTPUT module performs the conversion from internal format to display format.

- FM FOR COLUMN CONTENTS: Set the function module that will be used to populate the data into the field. In this case, we are using the standard function module HRWPC_CB_NAME.

- FM FOR COLUMN FRAMEWORK: Additional function module you can use when building the column framework.

- SERVICE KEY: The data provided in this column leads to a service. For example, the column AP_NAME could lead to the personal information service. Set the service name as provided in the Homepage Framework configuration.

- EVENT-LINK: Tick this box to activate the hyperlink and allow the end user to navigate to the service provided.

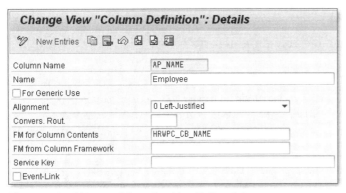

Figure 3.28 Object and Data Provider: Define Column

Define Coherence Relationships

Because you are dealing with personnel development objects and master data, you must enforce a check of coherence in the object relationships.

This configuration step allows you to define the coherence for the relationships as illustrated in Figure 3.29.

IMG Access Path	INTEGRATION WITH OTHER MYSAP.COM COMPONENTS • BUSINESS PACKAGES/FUNCTIONAL PACKAGES • MANAGER SELF-SERVICE (MYSAP ERP) • OBJECT AND DATA PROVIDER • DATA PROVIDER • DEFINE COHERENCE RELATIONSHIPS
IMG Activity	PORT_MAN_OADP_260
Transaction Code	S_AXC_91000038
Table Name	V_TWPC_FRIEND

For example, the standard entries in this configuration table identify the VALIDITY PERIOD and the RELATIONSHIP PERIOD.

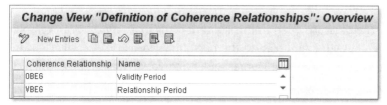

Figure 3.29   Object and Data Provider: Definition of Coherence Relationships

Define Column Groups

In this step, you define the column groups to be used at a later stage in the configuration.

IMG Access Path	INTEGRATION WITH OTHER MYSAP.COM COMPONENTS • BUSINESS PACKAGES/FUNCTIONAL PACKAGES • MANAGER SELF-SERVICE (MYSAP ERP) • OBJECT AND DATA PROVIDER • DATA PROVIDER • DEFINE COLUMN GROUPS
IMG Activity	PORT_MAN_OADP_230
Transaction Code	S_AXC_91000037

Create Customer-Specific Column Groups

This step allows you to create customer-specific column groups by providing a column group identifier and a name (description). You simply add a column group name and description. Do not forget to abide by the customer naming convention.

Table Name	V_TWPC_ARRAYTP

Check Standard Assignment of Column to Column Group

In this critical step, you are configuring the following information as shown in Figure 3.30:

▶ POSITION: The position of the column.

▶ VISIBLE: Tick this box if the column should be visible.

▶ DO NOT DISPLAY: Tick this box if you want the column to be hidden from basic display but nonetheless made available in the available fields for a display variant.

▶ INVISIBLE: Tick this box if you want the column to be hidden at all times. Display and display variant are then not providing this column.

▶ COHERENCE: Assign the coherence as defined previously.

Table Name	V_TWPC_ACOL

Change View "Put Columns Together in a Column Group": Overview

New Entries

Column Group	Name	Column Name	Name of the Column	Position	Visible	Do Not Display	Invisible	Coherence
ECMBONUS	ECM Bonus	EC_BSSAL	Calc. Base	6	☑	☐	☐	
ECMBONUS	ECM Bonus	EC_BUDGET	Budget	5	☑	☐	☐	
ECMBONUS	ECM Bonus	EC_CURRENCY	Curr.	9	☑	☐	☐	OBEG
ECMBONUS	ECM Bonus	EC_EFFDA	Effective	10	☑	☐	☐	
ECMBONUS	ECM Bonus	EC_NAME	Employee	1	☑	☐	☐	
ECMBONUS	ECM Bonus	EC_NOTES	Notes	11	☐	☐	☐	VBEG
ECMBONUS	ECM Bonus	EC_PERCENT	Percentage	8	☑	☐	☐	
ECMBONUS	ECM Bonus	EC_POSITION	Position	3	☐	☐	☐	
ECMBONUS	ECM Bonus	EC_STATE	Status	12	☑	☐	☐	
ECMBONUS	ECM Bonus	EC_SUMMARY	Overview	4	☐	☐	☐	
ECMLTI	ECM LTI	EC_APPREJ	Approve / Reject	2	☑	☐	☐	
ECMLTI	ECM LTI	EC_BUDGET	Budget	5	☑	☐	☐	
ECMLTI	ECM LTI	EC_EFFDA	Effective	7	☑	☐	☐	
ECMLTI	ECM LTI	EC_NAME	Employee	1	☑	☐	☐	
ECMLTI	ECM LTI	EC_NOTES	Notes	8	☐	☐	☐	
ECMLTI	ECM LTI	EC_NUMBER	Number	6	☑	☐	☐	
ECMLTI	ECM LTI	EC_POSITION	Position	3	☐	☐	☐	
ECMLTI	ECM LTI	EC_STATE	Status	9	☑	☐	☐	
ECMLTI	ECM LTI	EC_SUMMARY	Overview	4	☐	☐	☐	
ECMSALADJ	ECM Salary Adjustment	EC_AMOUNT	Amount	7	☑	☐	☐	
ECMSALADJ	ECM Salary Adjustment	EC_APPRAISAL	Appraisal Score	16	☑	☐	☐	

Figure 3.30 Object and Data Provider: Column with Column Groups Overview

Create or Change Assignment of Column to Column Group

In this step, we regroup the columns into a column group. This grouping will be useful in later configuration, as illustrated in Figure 3.31.

Table Name	V_TWPC_ACOL_C

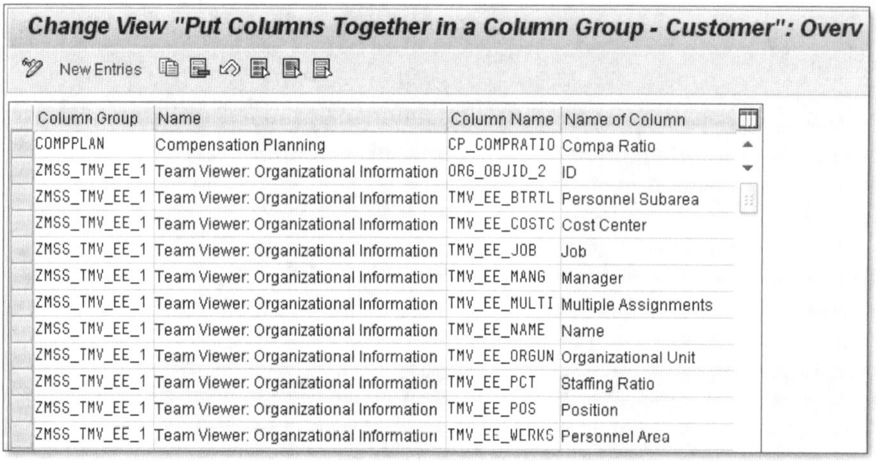

Change View "Put Columns Together in a Column Group - Customer": Overv

New Entries

Column Group	Name	Column Name	Name of Column
COMPPLAN	Compensation Planning	CP_COMPRATIO	Compa Ratio
ZMSS_TMV_EE_1	Team Viewer: Organizational Information	ORG_OBJID_2	ID
ZMSS_TMV_EE_1	Team Viewer: Organizational Information	TMV_EE_BTRTL	Personnel Subarea
ZMSS_TMV_EE_1	Team Viewer: Organizational Information	TMV_EE_COSTC	Cost Center
ZMSS_TMV_EE_1	Team Viewer: Organizational Information	TMV_EE_JOB	Job
ZMSS_TMV_EE_1	Team Viewer: Organizational Information	TMV_EE_MANG	Manager
ZMSS_TMV_EE_1	Team Viewer: Organizational Information	TMV_EE_MULTI	Multiple Assignments
ZMSS_TMV_EE_1	Team Viewer: Organizational Information	TMV_EE_NAME	Name
ZMSS_TMV_EE_1	Team Viewer: Organizational Information	TMV_EE_ORGUN	Organizational Unit
ZMSS_TMV_EE_1	Team Viewer: Organizational Information	TMV_EE_PCT	Staffing Ratio
ZMSS_TMV_EE_1	Team Viewer: Organizational Information	TMV_EE_POS	Position
ZMSS_TMV_EE_1	Team Viewer: Organizational Information	TMV_EE_WERKS	Personnel Area

Figure 3.31 Object and Data Provider: Setting Columns into Column Groups

Define Hierarchical Column Groups

This step is optional if you have created customer column(s) and group(s). In this step, you are defining the hierarchy of the different column groups.

IMG Access Path	Integration with Other mySAP.com Components • Business Packages/Functional Packages • Manager Self-Service (mySAP ERP) • Object and Data Provider • Data Provider • Define Hierarchical Column Groups
IMG Activity	PORT_MAN_OADP_240
Transaction Code	S_AXC_91000039

Check Hierarchical Column Groups in the Standard SAP System

In this optional step, you could group together single columns into a column group. This table is the standard table view.

Table Name	V_TWPC_HIERATP

Create or Change Hierarchical Column Groups

In this optional step, you could group together single columns into a column group. This table is the customer table view.

Table Name	V_TWPC_HIERATP_C

Redefine Column Headers

When dealing with different languages or just to meet business requirements, you must adjust the column headers into the different target language descriptions. These different configuration steps allow you to do that. Although not mandatory, we recommend checking the standard translation to avoid any communication inconsistencies in the end-user interface.

IMG Access Path	INTEGRATION WITH OTHER MYSAP.COM COMPONENTS • BUSINESS PACKAGES/FUNCTIONAL PACKAGES • MANAGER SELF-SERVICE (MYSAP ERP) • OBJECT AND DATA PROVIDER • DATA PROVIDER • REDEFINE COLUMN HEADERS
IMG Activity	PORT_MAN_OADP_250
Transaction Code	S_AXC_91000040

Create Customer-Specific Header Types

In this step, you have the option to create customer-specific header types for the columns. This is quite handy if you have the alternative to name the columns according to business requirements.

Table Name	V_TWPC_COLHTYP

Simply provide the column HEADER TYPE as illustrated in Figure 3.32.

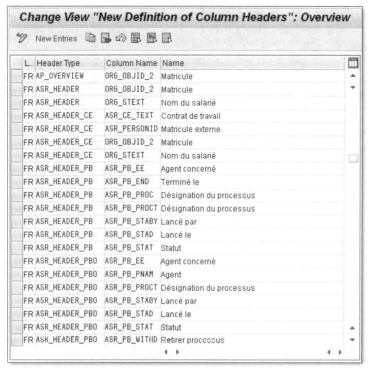

Figure 3.32 Object and Data Provider: Definition of Translated Column Headers

Check Column Headers for Standard Header Types

In this step, you translate the header type into the target language, for example, translation into French.

| Table Name | V_TWPC_COLHEAD |

Create or Change Column Headers

This step is the same step as previously illustrated but, in this case, it is done in the customer table view.

| Table Name | V_TWPC_COLHEAD_C |

Define Data Views

In this configuration step, you create a data view that will hold the value for the column groups and the column header type.

IMG Access Path	INTEGRATION WITH OTHER MYSAP.COM COMPONENTS • BUSINESS PACKAGES/FUNCTIONAL PACKAGES • MANAGER SELF-SERVICE (MYSAP ERP) • OBJECT AND DATA PROVIDER • DATA PROVIDER • DEFINE DATA VIEWS
IMG Activity	PORT_MAN_OADP_200
Transaction Code	S_AXC_91000014
Table Name	V_TWPC_DATAVW

For example, data view MSS_ASR_ORG_1 — Organizational Information contains the following values:

▶ COLUMN GROUP (as defined earlier): MSS_ASR_ORG_1 — Org. Overview: Organizational Info

▶ COLUMN HEADER TYPE (as definer earlier): MSS_TMV_ORG

This data views will be useful in upcoming configuration.

Group Data Views

In this configuration step, you are assigning the different data views that will be provided to the dropdown options in the functional screens for the end users.

IMG Access Path	INTEGRATION WITH OTHER MYSAP.COM COMPONENTS • BUSINESS PACKAGES/FUNCTIONAL PACKAGES • MANAGER SELF-SERVICE (MYSAP ERP) • OBJECT AND DATA PROVIDER • DATA PROVIDER • GROUP DATA VIEWS
IMG Activity	PORT_MAN_OADP_210
Transaction Code	S_AXC_91000015
Table Name	V_TWPC_DATAVWGRP

For example, the standard entry for MSS and the creation of a requisition MSS_REQ_CR — Display End User Functionality contains the following data views with their respective positioning (see Figure 3.33):

▸ MSS_REQ_DV_ALL: All Sent Requisition Requests (Position 1)

▸ MSS_REQ_DV_EXT: Sent Extended Requisition Requests (Position 3)

▸ MSS_REQ_DV_SIM: Sent Simple Requisition Requests (Position 2)

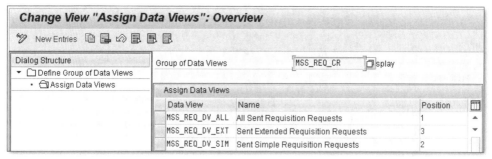

Figure 3.33 Object and Data Provider: Assign Data Views

3.5.5 Define Organizational Structure Views

This configuration node depicts how important the organizational structure is in the system. Assuming that the organizational structure is maintained, you do need to provide the relevant employees to the managers by using the OADP, which can be configured with the customizing steps described in this section.

Define Organizational Structure Views

In this configuration step, you assign the configuration achieved into an organizational structure view.

IMG Access Path	Integration with Other mySAP.com Components • Business Packages/Functional Packages • Manager Self-Service (mySAP ERP) • Object and Data Provider • Organizational Structure Views • Define Organizational Structure Views
IMG Activity	PORT_MAN_OADP_300
Transaction Code	S_AXC_91000016
Table Name	V_TWPC_ORGVW

For example, the standard organizational structure view MSS_ASR_ORG_SUB—
Organizational Structure contains the following values as illustrated in Figure
3.34:

▶ OBJECT SELECTION: "MSS_TMV_ORG_SUB"—ORG.UNITS IN ORG.STRUCTURE TO
  LEVEL 2

▶ GROUPS OF DATA VIEWS: "MSS_ASR_ORG"—DISPLAY

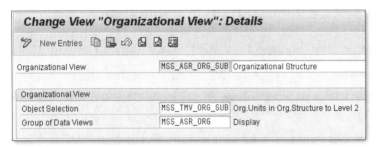

Figure 3.34 Object and Data Provider: Define Organizational View

Group Organizational Structure Views

In this configuration step, you assign the different views allowed and their respective positioning to the group organizational views.

IMG Access Path	INTEGRATION WITH OTHER MYSAP.COM COMPONENTS • BUSINESS PACKAGES/FUNCTIONAL PACKAGES • MANAGER SELF-SERVICE (MYSAP ERP) • OBJECT AND DATA PROVIDER • ORGANIZATIONAL STRUCTURE VIEWS • GROUP ORGANIZATIONAL STRUCTURE VIEWS
IMG Activity	PORT_MAN_OADP_310
Transaction Code	S_AXC_91000017
Table Name	V_TWPC_ORGVWG_P

For example, the standard value MSS_ECM_SEL—Employee Selection for Manager
Self Service Enterprise Compensation Management (ECM) contains the following
values:

▶ MSS_ECM_SEL_DIR: DIRECTLY SUBORDINATE EMPLOYEES (POSITION 3)

▶ MSS_ECM_SEL_LIS: EMPLOYEES FROM ORGANIZATIONAL UNITS (POSITION 1)

- ▶ MSS_ECM_SEL_SEA: Employee Search (Position 4)
- ▶ MSS_ECM_SEL_TRE: Employees from Organizational Structure (Position 2)

These values will be provided in the dropdown list when the end user is calling the different options made available.

3.6   Internal Service Request (ISR) Configuration

As stated earlier, the Internal Service Request (ISR) is the technology used to enable the personnel change requests (also called personnel change notifications).

This section introduces the configuration of the ISR and highlights the relevant standard templates provided for the HR processes.

These personnel change requests will be further described in Chapter 6.

3.6.1   Implementation Guide Access

To access the ISR from the root IMG, choose SAP Customizing Implementation Guide go to Cross-Application Components • Internet/Intranet Services • Internal Service Request (ISR).

3.6.2   Definition of Scenarios with Specific Customizing

Because the scenarios are used for multiple components, we will first highlight the standard templates relevant for HR processes.

Relevant Scenarios for the Human Resources

SAP provides templates as examples. Note that these are examples and not ready-to-use forms. The layout provided would be totally inadequate for customer requirements, and the form content contains only a few fields—not enough to answer and meet all business requirements.

Regarding the HR scenarios, following are the relevant entries made available for testing and example purposes:

- SPEG: Change Employee Group and Subgroup in InfoType 0001: Organizational Management
- SPPA: Change Personnel Area and Subarea in InfoType 0001: Organizational Management
- SPPD: Request for Internal Transfer (Enhanced)
- SPPM: Request for Promotion
- SPPS: Request for Internal Transfer
- SPR1: Regular Employment—Long Form
- SPR2: Regular Employment—Short Form
- SPR3: Contingent Employment Form
- SPR4: Extended Employment Form
- SPS1: Request to Change Project
- SPSD: Request for Separation (Enhanced)
- SPSE: Request for Separation
- SPSP: Request for Special Payment in InfoType 0015 Additional Payments
- SPTD: Request for Transfer (Enhanced)
- SPTR: Request for Transfer
- SPWT: Change of Working Time in InfoType 0007 Working Time

The standard naming convention starts with SPXX for HR.

Request for Master Data Change

This configuration step leads to a major customizing step: the definition of a custom scenario when requesting the change of master data.

IMG Access Path	In the SAP CUSTOMIZING IMPLEMENTATION GUIDE, go to CROSS-APPLICATION COMPONENTS • INTERNET/INTRANET SERVICES • INTERNAL SERVICE REQUEST (ISR) • DEFINITION OF SCENARIOS WITH SPECIFIC CUSTOMIZING • REQUEST FOR MASTER DATA CHANGE

Define Own Scenarios for Request to Change Master Data

This configuration node provides the "business card" of the selected scenario.

IMG Access Path	In the SAP CUSTOMIZING IMPLEMENTATION GUIDE, go to CROSS-APPLICATION COMPONENTS • INTERNET/INTRANET SERVICES • INTERNAL SERVICE REQUEST (ISR) • DEFINITION OF SCENARIOS WITH SPECIFIC CUSTOMIZING • REQUEST FOR MASTER DATA CHANGE • DEFINE OWN SCENARIOS FOR REQUEST TO CHANGE MASTER DATA
IMG Activity	COOMCCA_VC_SCENARIO
Transaction Code	S_ALR_87100748
Table Name	VC_SCENARIO

The standard template SPSP—Special Payment with Version 0 illustrates this customizing entry. This template contains the following configuration settings, as illustrated in Figure 3.35:

▶ THE VERSION IS CALLED: The version identifier, in this case, we deal with release "0."

▶ THIS SCENARIO VERSION IS ACTIVE: This flag is switched on, which means the form can be used.

▶ VALID FROM/TO: As always when dealing with configuration, a start and end date must be enforced.

▶ DESCRIPTION: Provide a description for the form.

▶ ENTER A LONG TEXT HERE: If applicable, provide a long text to further describe the scenario.

▶ APPLICATION: By default, this is left blank as STANDARD APPLICATION.

▶ NOTIFICATION TYPE: In this case, value "57" means that the personnel change requests do not require an approval step. Alternatively, set value "56" to require an approval step.

▶ ENTRY TYPE IN WEB: Determines the rendering on the screen, for example, a PDF or a Java Server Page (JSP). In this case, we opt for the PDF option: A-ENTRY USING ADOBE PDF.

▶ FORM: This is the form name. Either set a form name per your customer naming guidelines and conventions, or let the system generate automatically the name. In this standard example, the system generated the name: ISR_FORM_SPSP.

To edit the form, click on the icon with the pencil, which leads you to the Form Designer.

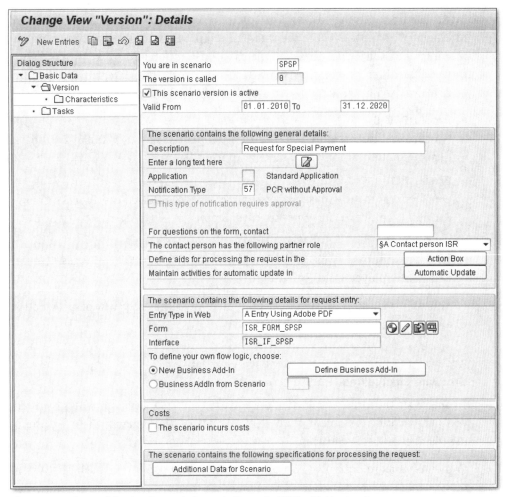

Figure 3.35 Internal Service Request: Scenario Example SPSP with Version 0

If you want to define your own logic, you can also use the SAP-provided BAdIs QISR—Internal Service Request: Programming Interface Forms, which provides different interfaces to meet your business requirements.

Available Workflow Templates for Personnel Change Requests

When dealing with personnel change requests, standard workflow templates are provided as listed in this section. You can use them as they are by copying the task into a customer naming convention. You then start the configuration as illustrated in Chapter 9. Alternatively, if the standard templates do not meet your criteria or requirements, simply use these templates for inspiration and adjust the configuration and the different workflow steps, such as the agent rule determination, within your own workflow task. Following are the standard templates:

▶ **ProcessPCR_0**
No approval step required is based on template task WS 50000042 – Process Change Request Employee Data (No Approval Step).

▶ **ProcessPCR_1**
One-step approval is based on template task WS50000041 – Process Change Request Employee Data (One Approval Step).

▶ **ProcessPCR_2**
Two-step approval is based on template task WS50000031 – Process Change Request Employee Data (Two Approval Step).

Further information regarding workflows and a typical setup will be provided in Chapter 9.

**Additional Configuration: Maintenance View for
Grouping Change Request Scenarios**

To deactivate the forms provided to the end user, no fancy development is required, you simply configure table V_WPC_PCR_GROUPS – Maintenance View for Grouping Change Request Scenarios.

Copy the standard entry and edit the end date with a date in the past. The system then changes the end date for the employee grouping for change requests. The result will be the nondisplay on the end user SAP NetWeaver Portal screen as illustrated in Figure 3.36.

Alternatively, as always, you can take advantage of the BAdI HRWPC_PCR_EEGRP (Adjustment: Assignment Employee – Employee Grouping) where you can create customer-specific employee groups for change requests.

Repeat this step for each relevant change request scenario.

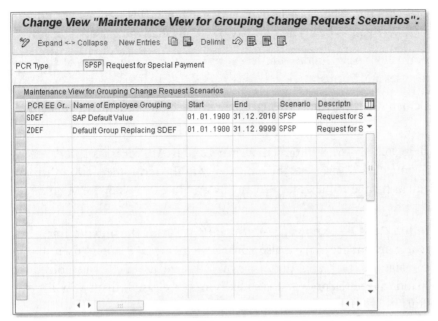

Figure 3.36 Internal Service Request: Maintenance View for Grouping Change Requests

3.6.3 HCM Processes and Forms

The ISR technology used up to SAP ERP 6.0 is included and meets most requirements. However, if you currently use the ISR and migrate to the latest SAP ERP 6.0 release or just start in this release, you might consider the use of HCM Processes and Forms as illustrated in Figure 3.37.

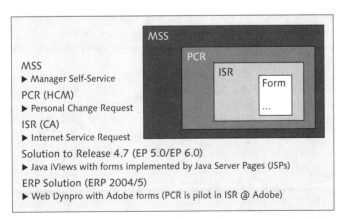

Figure 3.37 Technical Overview When Dealing with Forms in Self-Services

This topic is wide enough to have its own dedicated book. This section is introduced here in order for you to be aware of the two options that you currently have.

Transaction SFP—Form Builder will lead you into the configuration of the new HCM Processes and Forms.

We recommend starting your investigation journey by reading the following SAP Notes:

▶ **SAP Note 952693—MSS: Interactive Forms and HCM Processes and Forms**
In this note, SAP Clearly sets the direction with the recommendation that you implement change requests for Release mySAPERP 2005 using HCM Processes and Forms.

▶ **SAP Note 1258649—Composite SAP Note: HCM Forms Documentation**
For your convenience, I have also consolidated "my SAP notes" used during implementations, regarding the forms in SAP Note 1258649. This note is for information purposes only and is unlikely to be released, that's why it bears the status In Process.

Comparison Personnel Change Requests versus HCM Processes and Forms

This whole topic could actually fit into a book only dealing with this functionality. As the use of these functionalities are quite a challenging assessment, the following is a summary from SAP standard documentation, comparing the two technologies as illustrated in Table 3.1.

	Personnel Change Request	HCM Processes and Forms
Function	Gather data using an interactive form (in the portal), update HR data in the backend (manually).	Gather data and automatically update HR data directly from the interactive form.
Process flow, role integration	Started by manager, two or three process steps, update only in the final process step.	Unlimited number of steps, loops, and branches are possible; each standard or customer-specific portal role can be assigned to any step.

Table 3.1 Comparing Technologies

	Personnel Change Request	HCM Processes and Forms
Technology	Interactive form, BAdI, workflow (three templates).	Interactive form, table customizing, BAdI (optional), workflow with specific library.
Implementation	Customer-specific process can only be implemented with coding (BAdI implementation).	Customer-specific process can be implemented without coding using standard InfoType logic (input helps, checks, mandatory fields, update operations, etc.).
Example 1	Input helps are defined by means of BAdI implementations.	Input helps are automatically available when the relevant fields are used (customizing for tables).
Example 2	Checks/business logic are defined by means of BAdI implementations.	Business logic for the backend as standard, or customer-specific business logic via BAdI.
Tracking and analyses	Status overview only for managers and only for personnel change requests that have not yet been completed.	Operational level: Process browser for the HR administrator role, process status for all roles involved. Analyses: Predefined key figures and queries.
Integration in digital personnel file	Standard examples and framework do not allow for automatic saving in the backend.	Automatic saving of data in the backend (update InfoTypes). You can determine when data is saved to the backend (not only in the final step).
Process templates	Approximately 10–15.	Approximately 20 (including newly implemented versions of personnel change requests).

Table 3.1 Comparing Technologies (Cont.)

3.7 Conclusion

This chapter introduced the configuration of the Homepage Framework, which is more than just a nice to have feature to configure the frontend user interface. This configuration also allows extra flexibility thanks to the BAdIs and the proxy class that you can set up in the services.

We also reviewed the Object and Data Provider (OADP) and its configuration. Do not become overwhelmed by the myriad options available via customizing, rather be glad you have the standard entries from the system that you can tweak. If you need new customer entries, follow a standard entry, and carefully copy each configuration step.

Finally, this chapter briefly introduced the notion of forms, either powered by Internal Service Requests (ISRs), which enable the personnel change requests, or powered by the next generation, also known as the Human Capital Management (HCM) Processes and Forms. It goes without saying that an assessment and further investigation will be required from your side to decide which technology to choose.

Be sure to respect in all circumstances the naming convention either enforced by SAP or required by the customer guidelines.

Also carefully assess where your configuration must take place; most of the time, the appropriate placeholder is the standard table (with an adequate naming convention) or in the customer view of the standard table. The table can be easily identified as ending with a "C."

Last but not least, do not forget to translate where appropriate.

Now that we have covered the backend configuration, let's continue the journey with the ESS and MSS configuration in the next chapter.

Before venturing on a configuration project for ESS and MSS, we need to clarify a few aspects of both functionalities: The recent changes in technology, the available business packages, and also the existing release are worth being considered.

4 Background Information on Self-Services Configuration

Since its introduction in 1998, self-services were put in place to extend access to functionalities through a web-based UI. These self-services were meant to make employee access to their personal details easier, without chasing the information or contacting other colleagues such as the HR department.

In this chapter, we discuss some background information and necessary preparatory work for the configuration of Employee Self-Services (see Section 4.1) and Manager Self-Services (see Section 4.2).

4.1 Introduction to Employee Self-Services Configuration

To let the HR department focus on the core HR processes and decrease the HR workload, SAP introduced the motto "Let's empower the employees." Employees were empowered to access their data (and change where applicable and duly authorized) while at the same time decreasing the information requests workload from the HR side. HR remains a contact point in case of further questions, but the primary access to information remains in the hands of the employee because, for example, who knows better than the employee if a bank account changes?

4.1.1 Download Business Packages

You might think that the standard package contains all functionalities. Although it is certainly true for the basic information and functionalities, when deploying an SAP NetWeaver Portal system, the Portal Content Directory (PCD) might look desperately empty. This is not a bug!

As explained in Chapter 1, Section 1.6, business packages must be downloaded when you kick off the self-services deployment. You will download the business package that is relevant for your SAP ERP release.

The same applies when deploying enhancement packages. Additional business packages are then available in the PCD.

Figure 4.1 illustrates the ESS Business Package 1.0 (which is relevant for backend release SAP ERP 6.0), along with the business packages for EhP 1 through EhP 4.

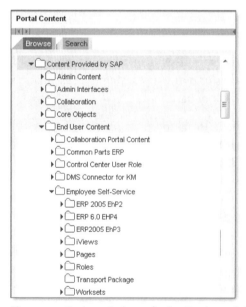

Figure 4.1 Business Packages for the Employee Self-Services

4.1.2 From Internet Transaction Server (ITS) to Web Dynpro

From the beginning, self-services were written in standard HTML. Self-services were in release 4.6B released through an application called SAP Web Studio. As of release 4.6C, release of services was available in Transaction SE80 — Object Navigator (ABAP Workbench), which finally got rid of the external application.

As of SAP ERP 5.0, Internet Transaction Server (ITS) services were migrated into Web Dynpro Java. Not only were the services using the latest sweet UI but they were also using Java (and some "good old" function modules) as programming language.

SAP Note 870126: ITS-Based ESS Services in SAP ERP 2005

This note highlights which ITS services can be used with the latest releases. There are some major restrictions. Carefully read the note and assess which service(s) you can use.

For example, I have used in-between projects such as the installation of SAP Learning Management System (LMS) called Learning Solution (LSO), the service PV7I Training Center (see Figure 4.2), and the service PV8I My Bookings (see Figure 4.3).

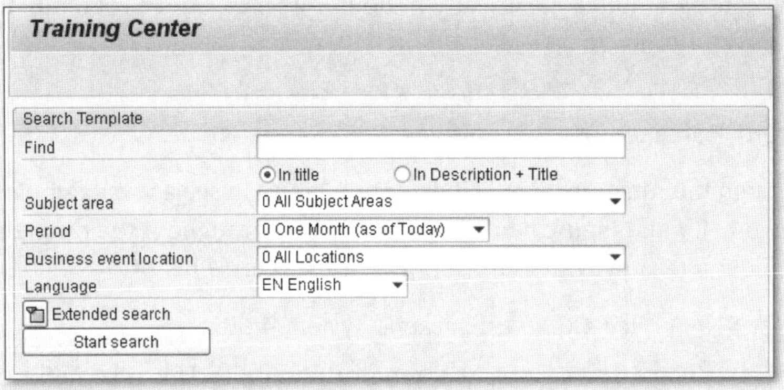

Training Center

Search Template

Find	
	⦿ In title ◯ In Description + Title
Subject area	0 All Subject Areas ▾
Period	0 One Month (as of Today) ▾
Business event location	0 All Locations ▾
Language	EN English ▾
📁 Extended search	
Start search	

Figure 4.2 ITS Service PV7I: Training Center

My Bookings

My Bookings

No bookings could be found. If you want to make bookings for business events, choose 'To search' or 'To basket'.

Business Event	Start	End	Location	Status

To Search	To Shopping Basket

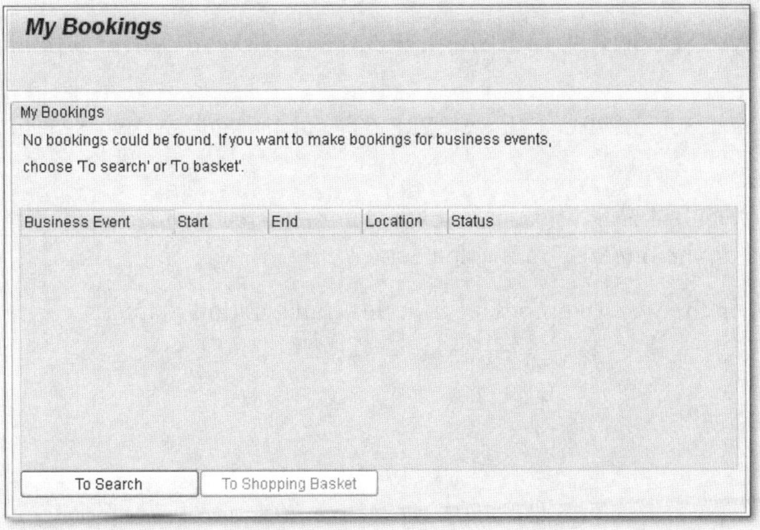

Figure 4.3 ITS Service PV8I: My Bookings

This is only a short-term solution because these ITS services will not be supported in the future.

These Java Web Dynpros are provided with this technology until SAP ERP 6.04 (standard SAP ERP 6.0 release up to EhP 4).

As of EhP 5, all self-services will be converted to ABAP Web Dynpros. The current EhP 5 release date for General Availability (GA) is expected for June 2011.

Although the UI remains (almost) the same, ABAP is now the technology powering self-services. This seems to be a plus for customers and consultants because, most of the time, ABAP programmers are already in-house, whereas Java programmers are a bit more difficult to find.

4.1.3 Different Releases from Employee Self-Services

As we walk through the functionalities' UI evolution, you can see a few examples, illustrated in Figure 4.4 and Figure 4.5, of functionalities throughout the different releases. The following list provides an overview of the release history:

▶ SAP Employee Self-Service 4.6B with backend system 4.6B

▶ SAP Employee Self-Service 4.6C with backend system 4.6C. This release introduced the workplace sort of ancestor from the SAP NetWeaver Portal

▶ SAP Employee Self-Service 4.7 with backend system 4.7

▶ SAP Employee Self-Service with SAP ERP 5.0 and backend system SAP ERP 5.0

▶ SAP Employee Self-Service with SAP ERP 6.0 and backend system SAP ERP 6.0

Figure 4.4 and Figure 4.5 show examples of the internet screen rendering for some services based on the Internet Transaction Server.

We will focus on the Web Dynpro screens in this configuration chapter.

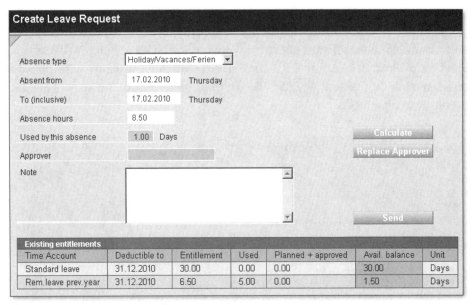

Figure 4.4 ITS: Trigger a Leave Request

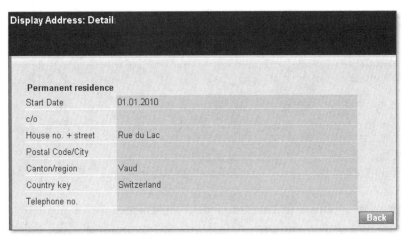

Figure 4.5 ITS: Maintain Address

4.1.4 Past Configuration Options

As we now deal with SAP ERP 6.0 (the latest release), most configuration options that you use to deal with have become obsolete.

For example, table V_T588M_ESS (the counterpart of the well-known backend configuration table T588M—InfoType Screen Control), which used to be maintained when using ITS self-services, is not relevant anymore with Web Dynpro self-services. Figure 4.6 illustrates service EHD21—Self Services for Germany, with options for screen 0200 in table V_T588M_ESS. In this older version, it was possible, for example, to hide ESS fields.

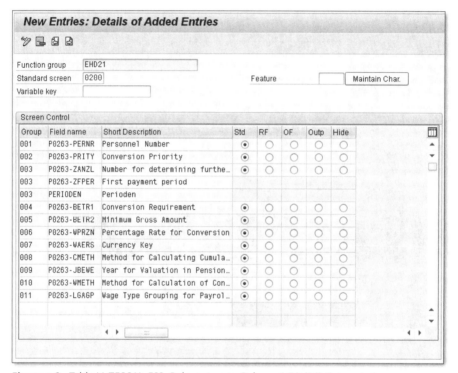

Figure 4.6 Table V_T588M_ESS: Relevant up to Release 4.70 (R/3 Enterprise)

These configuration options discussed throughout this chapter are highlighted in the Background Information and Important Tables section in Chapter 5, Section 5.12, and in Chapter 5, Section 5.19.

4.1.5   Self-Services (New) Functionalities

Since the beginning with ITS services, SAP provided myriad services. Since technology shifted to Web Dynpro Java (and soon ABAP), SAP also offers (a few) new self-services.

Clock-In/Out Web Dynpro

A new self-service is now available for clock in and out corrections, if you have forgotten to clock in during the working hours.

Cross-Application Time Sheet (CATS) Approval Screen

The Cross-Application Time Sheet (CATS) approval screen is now (finally) available as a Web Dynpro with the out-of-the-box solution and the basic self-service business packages.

You can now proudly tell the business department that they can drop the web GUI approval screen, which was just the web-enabled SAP transaction. It wasn't very nice inside the SAP NetWeaver Portal and likely led to some heavy discussions with the SAP NetWeaver Portal branding and/or communication team.

4.1.6 Access to the Employee Self-Services Configuration

You can access the configuration for self-services from the IMG via the path PERSONNEL MANAGEMENT • EMPLOYEE SELF-SERVICE • SERVICE SPECIFIC SETTINGS.

The IMG is divided into different steps to configure the functionalities provided by SAP.

The standard functionalities are made available without any technical settings. However, as new functionalities have been introduced through enhancement packages, you might need to activate additional functionalities through Transaction SFW5—Switch Framework Customizing.

For example, in regards to the self-services, in EhP 3, a new functionality in personal information allows the maintenance of the employee home address in a different country from the one he is currently working in.

We are assuming that all required customizing in the relevant fields has been done. For example, in the PERSONNEL ADMINISTRATION, PERSONNEL DEVELOPMENT, PERSONNEL TIME, and PAYROLL fields, the assumption is that the configuration is already ready for attendances and absences types, personnel areas and subareas, wage types, and so on.

Self-service configuration comes on top of standard functionalities configured.

Prior to the start of the configuration, you should read the standard documentation provided online by SAP. The online documentation for SAP ERP 6.0 with EhP 4 is available at the following address:

http://help.sap.com/erp2005_ehp_04/helpdata/EN/6a/5bc8a009d54fcaa8e06c826a57 253b/frameset.htm

4.2 Introduction to Manager Self-Services Configuration

Since its introduction in late 2004, self-services were put in place to extend access to functionalities through a web-based UI for managers.

These self-services were meant to make it easier for managers to access their team members' personal details and all relevant data — such as performance appraisal results, compensation management, payroll data, development plans, training plans, and qualifications — without chasing the information or contacting other colleagues such as the HR department.

MSS also unleashes many reports, either from the SAP ERP backend system or from Business Intelligence (BI) such as SAP NetWeaver Business Warehouse (BW) or SAP BusinessObjects.

Although we won't likely ever get rid of all paper-based processes, MSS also empowers managers to trigger and fill in online forms. SAP provides a range of templates that customers can customize or get inspiration from. Customers can also create their own forms.

The following standard templates are available, for example:

▶ Request for transfer

▶ Request for special payment

▶ Request for separation

▶ Request for changing working time

As stated in a previous chapter, to let HR focus on the core HR processes and decrease the workload, SAP introduced the motto "Let's empower the employees" with ESS back in 1998. It took awhile, but SAP responded to the increasing requests to enable such functionalities for managers as well. Late in 2004, customer wishes were granted as SAP release the first Human Resources Extension Set for Manager Self-Services in SAP Release 4.7 (R/3 Enterprise).

By empowering the managers, a win-win relationship was reinforced with the HR department, enabling managers to access their team data (and change where applicable and duly authorized). The purpose was also to decrease the information requests workload from the HR side. HR remains a contact point for further questions, but the primary access remains in the hands of the employee.

4.2.1 Download Business Packages

You might think that the standard MSS contains all functionalities. Although this is true for the basic information and functionalities, when deploying an SAP NetWeaver Portal system, the Portal Content Directory (PCD) might look desperately empty. This is not a bug!

As explained in Chapter 1, Section 1.6, business packages must be downloaded when kicking off the self-services deployment. You will end up with the MSS business package, which matches your SAP ERP release. The same applies when deploying enhancement packages; additional business package will then be available in the PCD.

Figure 4.7 illustrates the Manager Self-Services Business Package 1.0 (which is relevant for backend release SAP ERP 6.0), along with the business packages for EhP 1 through EhP 4.

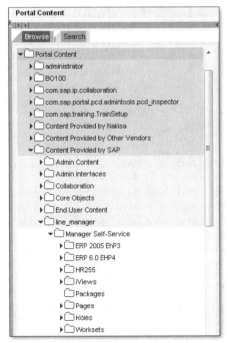

Figure 4.7 SAP NetWeaver Portal objects for the Manager Self-Services in the Portal Content Directory

4.2.2 Manager Self-Services and the Enhancement Packages

Concerning the enhancement package concept, you should carefully assess which additional functionality can be enabled with the enhancement packages.

Standard MSS is already part of the out-of-the-box system, but it can be enriched. For example, further business functions as listed here and illustrated in Figure 4.8 can also be enabled for MSS:

▶ HCM_MSS_ERC_CI_1: HCM, MSS for SAP E-Recruiting

▶ HCM_OSA_CI_1: HCM, Performance Management 01

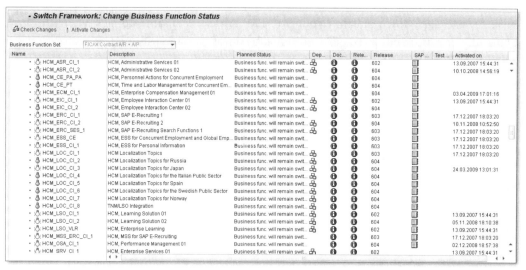

Figure 4.8 Enhancement Package Business Functions for Manager Self-Services

Standard MSS does not require enhancement packages because they are provided with the SAP ERP release.

4.2.3 Different Releases from Manager Self-Services

From the early beginning in 1998, only ESS was providing online self-services. Managers were left alone in the backend system with a many functionalities, especially reporting. SAP was aware of that fact, and managers were a frustrated by having to go through these multiple transactions and feeling like they were wandering in the application.

SAP listened and introduced in 2004 a central placeholder for all managerial activities in SAP 4.5B. This centralized functionalities placeholder was named Manager's Desktop (MDT), which was and can still be accessed using Transaction PPMDT (Manager's Desktop) in SAP.

This central functionality provides an easy UI, as illustrated in Figure 4.9, with drag-and-drop functionalities that enable managers to "drop" organizational objects onto the selected report to get the results list.

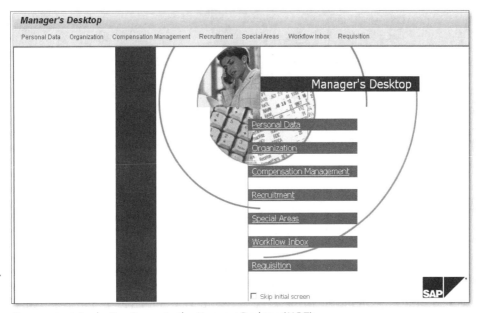

Figure 4.9 Introduction Screen to the Manager Desktop (MDT)

The MDT actually set the foundation for later development of the online MSS. In fact, as you will see in Chapter 7, part of MSS is still based on the MDT configuration to enable online reporting.

MDT is divided in different areas, which are configurable. Following are the standard MDT areas:

▶ Personal Data (as illustrated in Figure 4.10)

▶ Organization

▶ Compensation Management

▶ Recruitment

▶ Special Areas

▶ Workflow Inbox

▶ Requisition

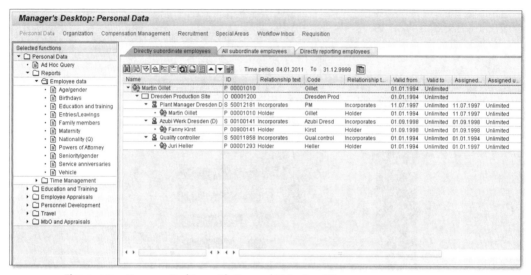

Figure 4.10 Manager Desktop with Personal Data Area View

As of release R/3 Enterprise, also known as release 4.7, MSS was born. MSS was activated thanks to two extension sets, as illustrated in Figure 4.11 (extension sets were a kind of enhancement package concept way before its time). Functional areas were migrated into online self-services, and MSS was divided into a Personnel Administration side (Extension set 1.10) and a Financials side (Extension set 2.00). These two sides were called the SAP NetWeaver Portal workset (tab) My Staff and My Budget.

Where the Personnel Administration side deals with all personnel administration, personnel development, personnel time management, and payroll functions, the Financials side deals with all the cost-related matters such as budgeting and personnel cost planning.

MSS is also powerful due to its many reporting options, either backend reports or Business Intelligence (BI), such as SAP NetWeaver Business Warehouse (BW) and forms.

Appl.	Active	Text
EA-FIN	☑	Financials Extension
EA-FS	☑	Financial Services
EA-GLT	☑	Global Trade
EA-HR	☑	Human Resources Extension
EA-ICM	☑	Incentive & Commission Mgmt
EA-PLM	☑	PLM Extension
EA-RET	☐	Retail
EA-SCM	☑	SCM Extension
EA-TRV	☑	Travel Management Extension
IS-PS	☑	Public Services
JVA	☐	Joint Venture Accounting

Figure 4.11 Activation Switch for SAP R/3 Enterprise Extension Set

As of SAP ERP 5.0, MSS was not discontinued and is still included in the self-services offering.

The Workflow inbox also got promoted to the SAP NetWeaver Portal Universal Worklist (UWL), which enabled access to workflow notifications directly in SAP NetWeaver Portal.

The requisition process was further developed with the introduction of the Talent processes and SAP e-Recruitment.

Like ESS, MSS functionalities were mainly translated to Web Dynpro as of SAP ERP 5.0. As of SAP ERP 6.0, these Web Dynpro translations got upgraded to native Web Dynpro Java.

SAP also provided some enhancements:

▶ Role-based control and work centers

▶ New scenarios for Talent Management: Maintain Position requirements

▶ New scenarios for Time Management: Cross-Application Time Sheet (CATS) mass approval

▶ Integration to HCM processes and forms

4.2.4 Access to the Manager Self-Services Configuration

The configuration for MSS is reachable from the IMG under the following path illustrated in Figure 4.12: SAP CUSTOMIZING IMPLEMENTATION GUIDE • INTEGRATION WITH OTHER MYSAP.COM COMPONENTS • BUSINESS PACKAGES/FUNCTIONAL PACKAGES • MANAGER SELF-SERVICE (MYSAP ERP).

> **Note:**
>
> Because we are dealing with the latest SAP ERP 6.0 release, we are using the configuration folder MANAGER SELF-SERVICE (MYSAP ERP), which is meant for the SAP ERP 6.0. The configuration folder MANAGER SELF-SERVICE was meant for the earlier SAP ERP 5.0 release.

Alternatively, you can access IMG directly through Transaction SIMG_SPORT — IMG Business/Functional Packages, as illustrated in Figure 4.12, which provides a handy shortcut to avoid long browsing through the standard IMG.

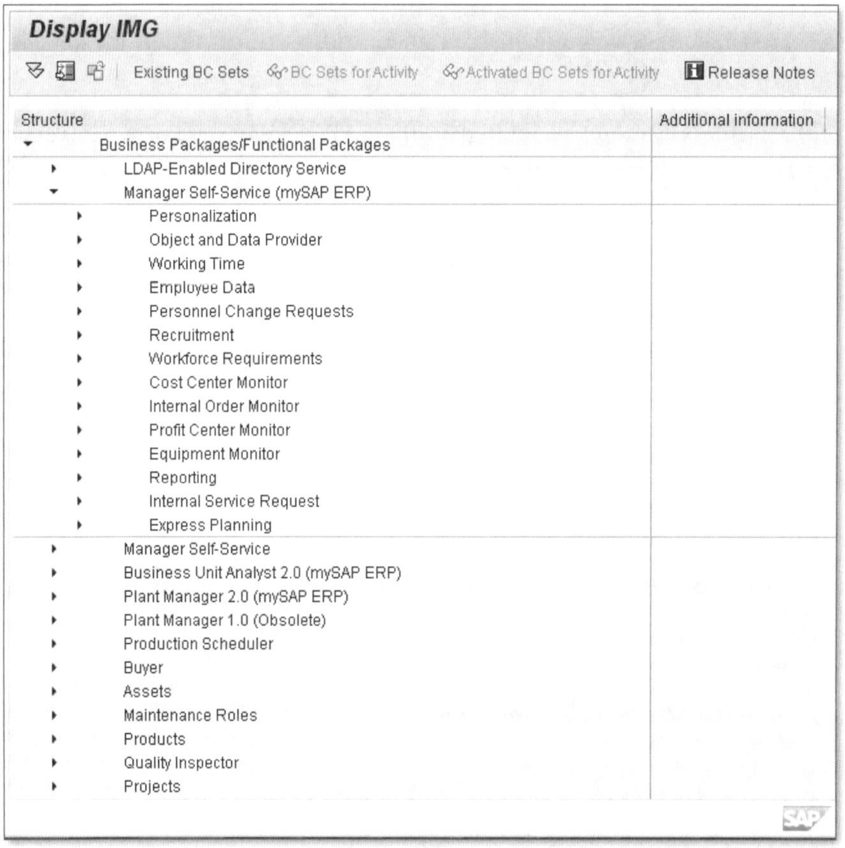

Figure 4.12 Implementation Guide Configuration Access for MSS via Transaction SIMG_SPORT

To shorten the IMG access path provided in this configuration chapter, the access described here is taken from Transaction SIMG_SPORT.

The IMG is divided into different steps to configure the functionalities provided by SAP (see Figure 4.12):

- Personalization
- Object and Data Provider (OADP)
- Working Time
- Employee Data
- personnel change requests
- Recruitment
- Workforce Requirements
- Cost Center Monitor
- Internal Order Monitor
- Profit Center Monitor
- Equipment Monitor
- Reporting
- Internal Service Request (ISR)
- Express Planning

We assume that prior to the start of the configuration, you have read the standard documentation as provided online by SAP. The online documentation for SAP ERP 6.0 with EhP 5 is available at the following address:

http://help.sap.com/erp2005_ehp_05/helpdata/EN/2f/d7844205625551e10000000a 1550b0/frameset.htm

Employee Self-Services (ESS) empowers employees to access all relevant human resources (HR) information. ESS also enables end users to trigger HR processes when needed without overloading the HR department. This chapter explains the configuration in detail.

5 Employee Self-Services Configuration

Now let's dive into the core configuration of the self-services. Where relevant and available, I have also provided some personal project experience, SAP Notes, and pitfalls/known issues with their solution.

5.1 Address Book: Who's Who

Most customers already have phone directories stored in different places, perhaps external to SAP. But did you know that SAP provides a standard phone directory known as Who's Who?

This Who's Who service enables two functionalities:

- ▶ Search employees
- ▶ Change our own data

This self-service provides consolidated data from several InfoTypes:

- ▶ InfoType 0105—Communication, for example, the email address (subtype 0010)
- ▶ InfoType 0032—Internal Data
- ▶ Organizational structure data

This self-service provides an easy way to identify, for example, the superior of a colleague, find contact details such as telephone number, email address, car licence plate, or add a face (a picture) to a name.

The following configuration steps help you set up the Who's Who self-service.

5.1.1   Selection and Output

The fields provided in the SAP NetWeaver Portal screen are handled through an
InfoSet. This configuration step enables you to select the selection and output fields.
Assess whether the standard InfoSets are meeting the requirements; otherwise,
adjust the configuration where necessary.

IMG Access Path	PERSONNEL MANAGEMENT • EMPLOYEE SELF-SERVICE • SERVICE SPECIFIC SETTINGS • ADDRESS BOOK • WHO'S WHO • WHO'S WHO (ESS): SELECTION AND OUTPUT
IMG Activity	OHIXIAC0020
Transaction Code	S_P7H_77000022
Table Name	T77WWW_WHO

Figure 5.1   IMG Step: ESS Who's Who: Maintenance Screen for Settings

Although configuration is quite easy, some limitations do apply. Note that text fields cannot be used for data selection (with the exception of the fields ORGANIZATIONAL UNIT, POSITION NAME, and JOB NAME).

Each country (also known as Molga) has its own configuration. This allows extra flexibility for national legal requirements, for example. Figure 5.1 illustrates the configuration for the United States, which is country 10.

Although part of the standard SAP reporting option, known as the SAP Queries, let's introduce some background information on the standard InfoSet /SAPQUERY/ HR_XX_PA_ESS, which is used by default when dealing with the self-service Who's Who. XX stands for the country number.

This InfoSet is contained in the standard cross-client global query area. It contains standard default fields for the selection and the output, as illustrated in Figure 5.2.

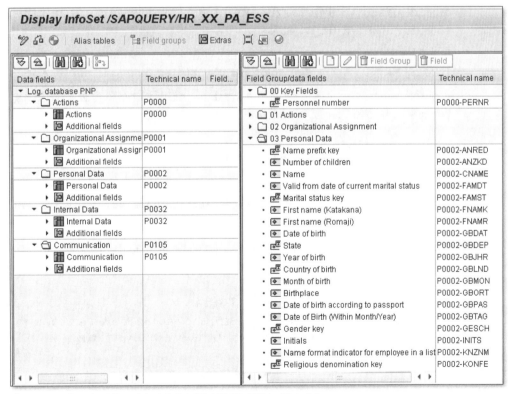

Figure 5.2 Standard Template InfoSet HR_XX_PA_ESS in Global Area

You can easily copy this standard InfoSet /SAPQUERY/HR_XX_PA_ESS into a customer Z _CUSTOMER_HR_01_PA_ESS.

To do so, follow these steps:

1. Go to Transaction SQ02 — SAP Query: Maintain InfoSet.
2. Verify that you are in the GLOBAL QUERY AREA. (This area is delivered by SAP and should not be touched because it is cross client.)
3. From the menu, go to ENVIRONMENT • QUERY AREA. Verify that you are in the GLOBAL QUERY AREA.
4. Copy the standard InfoSet /SAPQUERY/HR_XX_PA_ESS from the GLOBAL QUERY AREA (cross clients) to the standard area (client specific). Use the icon X, which calls the program RSAQR3TR.
5. Select COPY GLOBAL AREA TO STANDARD AREA. Remove the test run.
6. Select TRANSPORT INFOSETS with import option REPLACE. Provide the standard original name, "/SAPQUERY/HR_XX_PA_ESS," and the destination name, "Z_CUSTOMER_HR_01_PA_ESS."
7. From the STANDARD AREA (client specific), choose the customer InfoSet Z_CUSTOMER_HR_01_PA_ESS. Edit the content where relevant. Save and generate.
8. Adjust the configuration by replacing the standard InfoSet /SAPQUERY/HR_XX_PA_ESS with customer "Z_CUSTOMER_HR_01_PA_ESS."

5.1.2 Determine the Document Type

Assuming that you have already set up the availability of the employee's photo throughout the SAP system, you can also enable the photo for the Who's Who service.

This step is used to determine the document type if you want to display the employee photo, which is optional.

IMG Access Path	PERSONNEL MANAGEMENT • EMPLOYEE SELF-SERVICE • SERVICE SPECIFIC SETTINGS • ADDRESS BOOK • WHO'S WHO • WHO'S WHO (ESS): DETERMINE DOCUMENT TYPE

IMG Activity	OHIXIAC0010
Transaction Code	S_P7H_77000023

This configuration step, illustrated in Figure 5.3, is actually an excerpt from the SAP HR switches table. From this table, you set the value for the GROUP "ADMIN" and the semantic abbreviation (SEM. ABBR.) for the document type for (passport) "PHOTO" (the standard value) in HR.

Figure 5.3   Define Document Type

A detailed step-by-step procedure "Upload a Photo in SAP HR" for enabling pictures can be found in the online blog entry at the following address:

http://it.toolbox.com/wiki/index.php/Upload_a_photo_in_SAP_HR

5.1.3   Maintain Settings

Additional settings are provided to narrow the options enabled for the end user. These settings are similar to what was available in the ITS service PZ50 Who's Who. It consists of configuration options enabled by a tick box. If you need to disable them, simply untick the relevant box.

IMG Access Path	PERSONNEL MANAGEMENT • EMPLOYEE SELF-SERVICE • SERVICE SPECIFIC SETTINGS • ADDRESS BOOK • WHO'S WHO • WHO'S WHO (ESS): MAINTAIN SETTINGS
IMG Activity	OHIXIAC0100
Transaction Code	S_P7H_77000024

The following options are available, as illustrated in Figure 5.4:

▶ DISPLAY EMPLOYEE PHOTOGRAPH: No, if no configuration is yet in place for providing the employee's photo.

▶ ALLOW DIRECT TELEPHONE DIALING: No, if no dialing device or technology is currently in place at the customer or at the Employee Interaction Center (EIC).

▶ ALLOW ACCESS TO CALENDAR: This option enables access to the employee's calendar, and is only relevant if the calendar is already maintained.

▶ ALLOW ACCESS TO "ORGANIZATIONAL ENVIRONMENT": If you select this, beware of the SAP NetWeaver Portal response time.

▶ ALLOW OWN DATA TO BE MAINTAINED: Select this option to let employees change their own data.

▶ ALLOW OWN EMPLOYEE PHOTOGRAPH TO BE MAINTAINED: For example, selecting this option to let employees change their own photo might be useful but you may wan to reconsider letting them change their own photo. For consistency and to avoid inappropriate uploads, you should set up a control procedure internally.

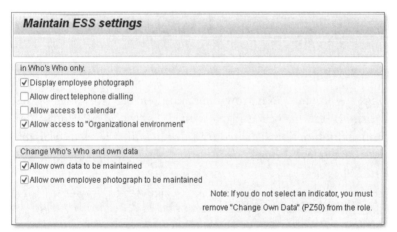

Figure 5.4 Maintain ESS Settings

5.1.4 Refine Employee Search

Naturally, when a company has a lot of personnel, it might be useful to narrow the scope of employees to be shown when performing a search. For example, you might refine the employee search to the active employees only. No fancy development is required to do this, you just adjust the configuration settings.

IMG Access Path	PERSONNEL MANAGEMENT • EMPLOYEE SELF-SERVICE • SERVICE SPECIFIC SETTINGS • ADDRESS BOOK • WHO'S WHO • WHO'S WHO (ESS): REFINE EMPLOYEE SEARCH
IMG Activity	OHIXIAC0050
Transaction Code	S_P7H_77000025

This configuration step, as illustrated in Figure 5.5, is actually another excerpt from the SAP HR switches table (T77SO). From this table, you set the value for the GROUP as "ESS" and the semantic abbreviation (SEM. ABBR.) value as "STAT2." The possible return values are the following:

▶ 0: Employee is not with the company.

▶ 1: Employee is with the company but not active.

▶ 2: Employee is with the company but retired.

▶ 3: Employee is active in the company.

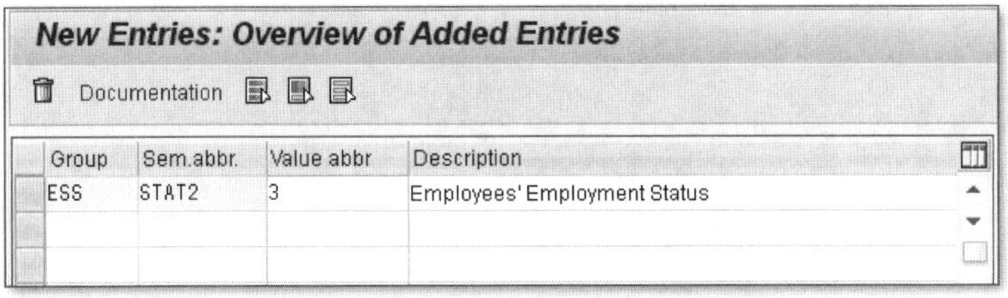

Figure 5.5 Refine Employee Search with STAT2 Semantic Abbreviation

It goes without saying that you can combine the values as required. For example, to only allow the display of active employees, you set the value "3" in the VALUE ABBR. field. To allow only active and pensioners, you set the value "23" in the VALUE ABBR. field.

5.1.5 Portal iView Who's Who

Figure 5.6 illustrates the iViews located in the SAP NetWeaver PCD regarding the Who's Who functionality.

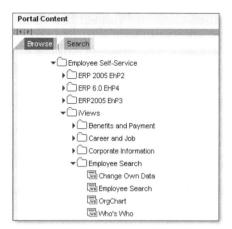

Figure 5.6 Who's Who iViews Located in the PCD

Figure 5.7 depicts the Who's Who iView as the end user sees it in the SAP NetWeaver Portal.

Figure 5.7 Who's Who Rendering for the End User in the SAP NetWeaver Portal

5.2 Working Time: Leave Request

Working time self-services are the quick win functionalities you can enable. Getting rid of the paper flow is perhaps a myth, but with SAP standard you can web-enable the leave request procedure and perhaps even empower the procedure with an approval workflow.

The first quick win in HR is the leave request that you can enable without heavy configuration in SAP NetWeaver Portal.

5.2.1 Processing Processes

In this configuration step, Processing Processes, we will go through the different configuration steps for enabling the leave request.

Create Rule Groups

In this step, we are creating groupings in order to have different "placeholders," which will enable the application of different business rules.

IMG Access Path	Personnel Management • Employee Self-Service • Service Specific Settings • Working Time • Leave Request • Processing Processes • Create Rule Groups
IMG Activity	PCUI_ESS_PT_LRQ_030
Transaction Code	S_FAD_62000011

This IMG activity is devided in two steps:

1. Create rule groups.

    Table name: V_HRWEB_RULE_GRP

    In this step, you first create the relevant entries, as illustrated in Figure 5.8, to distinguish the different group of employees and workers that you can have in the business requirements. Later in the configuration, this will help provide different sets of data or dedicate specific controls to each group.

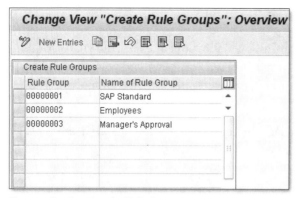

Figure 5.8 Creating the Rule Groups

2. Adjust feature WEBMO—Define Rule Group for Customizing Tables in Web Environment.

In this step, you must advise the system when and for whom the groups are relevant. To do so, you use the decision tree feature (illustrated in Figure 5.9).

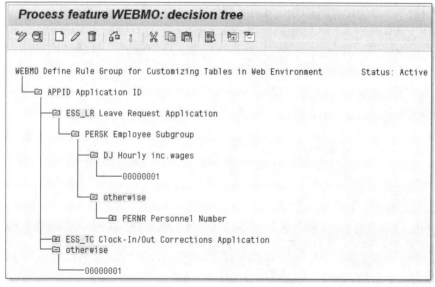

Figure 5.9 Feature (Decision Tree) WEBMO

Define Processing Processes for Each Rule Group

In this configuration step, you are making the mapping between the processing processes against each rule group that you just configured.

IMG Access Path	PERSONNEL MANAGEMENT • EMPLOYEE SELF-SERVICE • SERVICE SPECIFIC SETTINGS • WORKING TIME • LEAVE REQUEST • PROCESSING PROCESSES • DEFINE PROCESSING PROCESSES FOR EACH RULE GROUP
IMG Activity	PCUI_ESS_PT_LRQ_032
Transaction Code	S_AEN_10000452
Table Name	V_PTARQ_TPROCESS

As illustrated in Figure 5.10, the following options are available:

▸ RECORD PARTIAL-DAY/ABSENCES IN: HOURS AND/OR CLOCK TIMES

▸ TAKE ACCOUNT OF ONGOING REQUESTS

  ▸ CHECK INCLUDES UNPOSTED REQUESTS: If you tick this box, the system also checks new requests that are still open, change requests, and cancellations that have not yet been stored in the InfoTypes and have the status "approved" or "sent" in the document database.

  ▸ REMAINING LEAVE WITHOUT UNPOSTED REQUESTS: If you tick this box, the system will not include requests that have not yet been posted when it calculates the time account statuses. The requests that have not been posted have the status "approved," "sent," or "error" in the document database.

▸ IT 2001/2002 AUTHORIZATION CHECK

  ▸ EMPLOYEES: DEACTIVATE AUTHORIZATION CHECK: If you tick this box, the system checks the employee's read authorization for the absences (2001) and attendances (2002) InfoTypes when the employee is using the leave request or team calendar web application.

  ▸ MANAGERS: DEACTIVATE AUTHORIZATION CHECK: If you tick this box, the system checks the manager's read authorization for the absences (2001) and attendances (2002) InfoTypes when the manager is using the leave request or team calendar web application.

  ▸ DETERMINE NEXT AGENT: You set up how the next agent of a leave request or clock-in/out correction is to be determined.

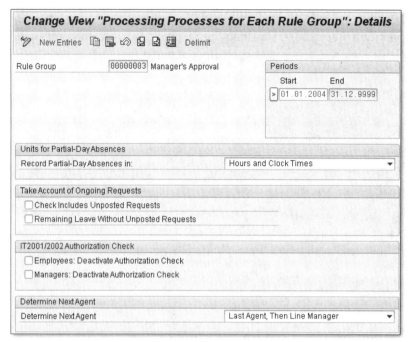

Figure 5.10 Processing Processes for Each Rule Group

Specify Processing Processes for Types of Leave

In this step, you define the processing processes per type of leave. The assumption is that Time Management is already in place and that the absences and attendances types have already been defined.

IMG Access Path	PERSONNEL MANAGEMENT • EMPLOYEE SELF-SERVICE • SERVICE SPECIFIC SETTINGS • WORKING TIME • LEAVE REQUEST • PROCESSING PROCESSES • SPECIFY PROCESSING PROCESSES FOR TYPES OF LEAVE
IMG Activity	PCUI_ESS_PT_LRQ_050
Transaction Code	S_FAD_62000013

These attendance and absence types are defined in the Time Management table T554S—Attendance and Absence Types. As this table has many views, you can use table T554S to view the full overview of this table.

Step 1 is to define absences and to process processes. You do that in table V_T554S_ WEB. Here, you are setting up the following values, as illustrated in Figure 5.11:

▶ RULE GROUP: Assign the rule group ID as defined earlier.

▶ PS GROUPING: Assign the personnel subarea grouping for attendance and absence types.

▶ SORT NUMBER: If needed, by default, the sorting number is 001 to begin with.

▶ START and END date: Set the validity start date for this configuration entry.

▶ START DATE IN THE PAST:

   ▶ PROCESSING PERMITTED TO RECALCULATION LIMIT: Select this radio button for the system to check the periods in which employees are permitted to create, change, or delete an absence of this type retroactively, when the start date of the absence is in the past.

   ▶ PROCESSING NOT PERMITTED: Select this radio button if you want to disable the start date in the past.

   ▶ RETROACTIVE PROCESSING PERMITTED IN PERIOD: Select this radio button to enable the retroactive processing permission for a period you determine.

▶ START DAY IS THE CURRENT DAY:

   ▶ PROCESSING IS PERMITTED: If the start day is the current day, select this radio button.

   ▶ PROCESSING IS NOT PERMITTED: Select this radio button to prohibit starting on the current day.

▶ START DATE IN THE FUTURE:

   ▶ UNRESTRICTED PROCESSING IS PERMITTED: Select this radio button to enable unconditional leave request in the future.

   ▶ PROCESSING NOT PERMITTED: Select this radio button to prohibit a start date in the future.

   ▶ PROCESSING PERMITTED WITHIN PERIOD: Select this radio button to allow the start date in the future within a period you determine.

- Workflow template:

  - Process Request Using Workflow: Flag this checkbox if you want to enable the workflow between the leave requester and the approver. Set the workflow IDs to be used. Upon activating this workflow option, the system will provide additional fields where you can set the Workflow IDs to be used in this process.

- User Interface elements: The options in this section allow you to customize the UI. Tick each box to enable or disable the functionality:

  - Display field for next agent: Let the user decide who is the next agent. Yes or No? Or not required?

  - Use Notes: Enable Notepad in the Leave Request screen.

  - Field selection for additional data: The system allows the display of additional fields for each attendance/absence type in the web application.We can set the additional field to be displayed to the end users in this section.

  - Explanation of Absence Type: Assign a detailed description for the explanation for the absence type.

- System response:

  - Requests have to be approved: Tick this box if the approval process has to be enabled.

  - EEs Not permitted to submit requests: Tick this box to prohibit employees from submitting requests.

  - No changes to Leave permitted: Tick this box to specify that the system checks for each type of leave whether employees are permitted to change absences that are stored in the Absences InfoType (2001).

  - No deletion of Leave permitted: Tick this box to specify that the system checks for each type of leave whether employees are permitted to delete absences that are stored in the Absences InfoType (2001).

In Step 2, you create explanatory texts for absences. If needed, you can create long text explanations for the absences to provide clear communication content to the end user.

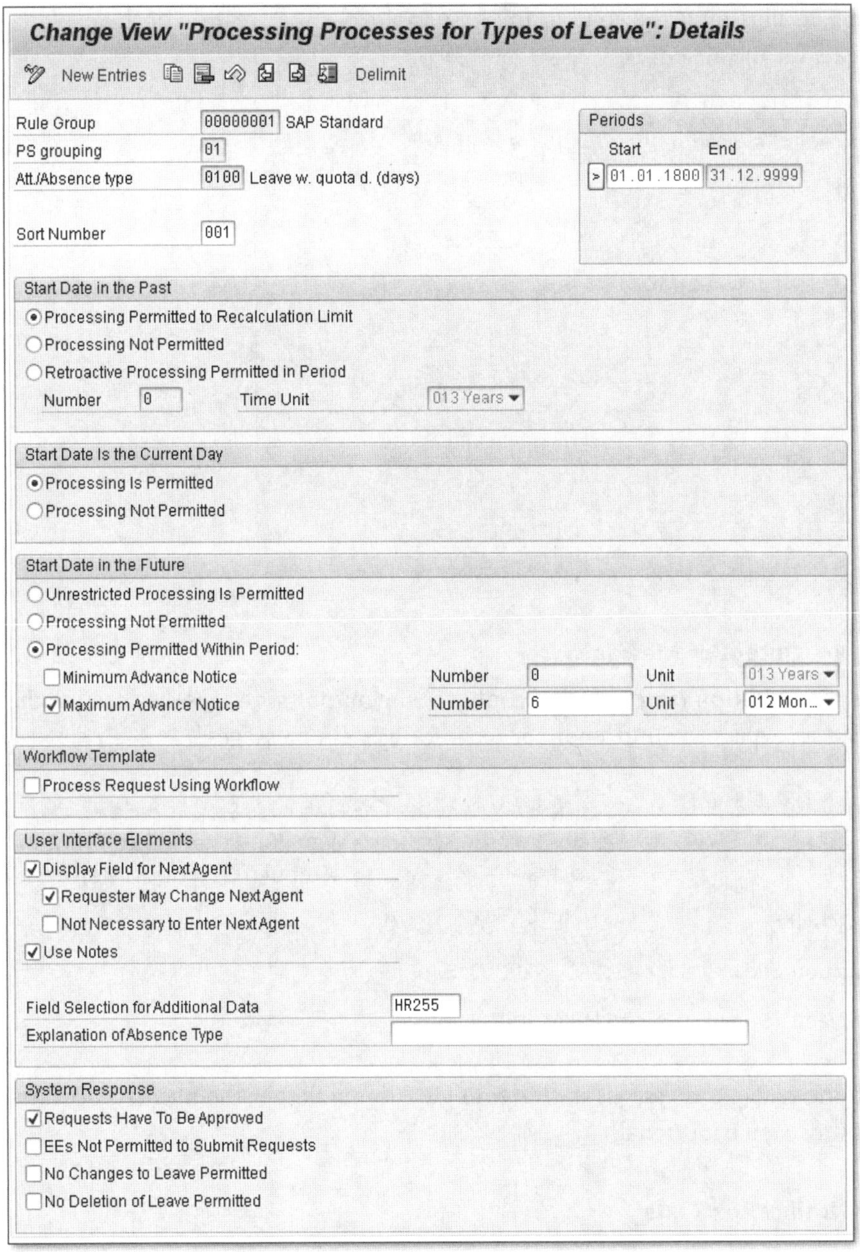

Change View "Processing Processes for Types of Leave": Details

New Entries   Delimit

Rule Group	00000001 SAP Standard
PS grouping	01
Att./Absence type	0100 Leave w. quota d. (days)
Sort Number	001

Periods

Start	End
> 01.01.1800	31.12.9999

Start Date in the Past
- ● Processing Permitted to Recalculation Limit
- ○ Processing Not Permitted
- ○ Retroactive Processing Permitted in Period
  - Number 0   Time Unit 013 Years ▼

Start Date Is the Current Day
- ● Processing Is Permitted
- ○ Processing Not Permitted

Start Date in the Future
- ○ Unrestricted Processing Is Permitted
- ○ Processing Not Permitted
- ● Processing Permitted Within Period:
  - ☐ Minimum Advance Notice   Number 0   Unit 013 Years ▼
  - ☑ Maximum Advance Notice   Number 6   Unit 012 Mon... ▼

Workflow Template
- ☐ Process Request Using Workflow

User Interface Elements
- ☑ Display Field for Next Agent
  - ☑ Requester May Change Next Agent
  - ☐ Not Necessary to Enter Next Agent
- ☑ Use Notes

Field Selection for Additional Data	HR255
Explanation of Absence Type	

System Response
- ☑ Requests Have To Be Approved
- ☐ EEs Not Permitted to Submit Requests
- ☐ No Changes to Leave Permitted
- ☐ No Deletion of Leave Permitted

Figure 5.11 Processing Process for Types of Leave

Figure 5.12 illustrates the configuring entry point for the creation of the explanatory texts for the absences.

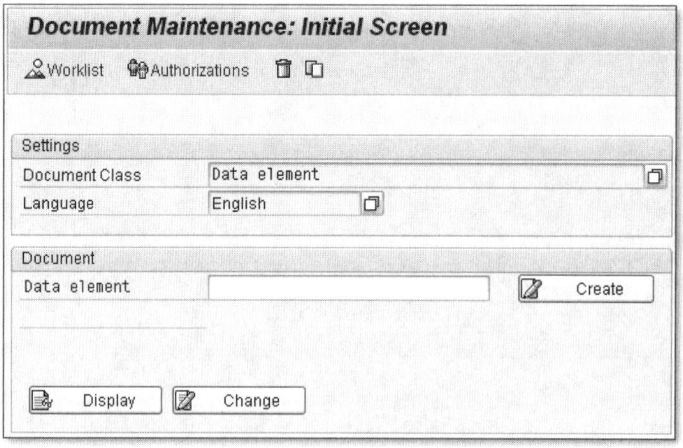

Figure 5.12   Create Explanatory Texts for Absences

Configure Output of Messages

In this configuration table, you can configure the output messages disclosed to the end user to bypass the unfriendly or technical system messages.

IMG Access Path	PERSONNEL MANAGEMENT • EMPLOYEE SELF-SERVICE • SERVICE SPECIFIC SETTINGS • WORKING TIME • LEAVE REQUEST • PROCESSING PROCESSES • CONFIGURE OUTPUT OF MESSAGES
IMG Activity	PCUI_ESS_PT_LRQ_070
Transaction Code	S_FAD_62000015
Table Name	V_HRWEB_TRS_MESS

Assign the relevant messages in this configuration table per the business requirements (this step is optional).

Write Notification Texts

This configuration step allows you to write the notification texts as required (this step is optional).

IMG Access Path	PERSONNEL MANAGEMENT • EMPLOYEE SELF-SERVICE • SERVICE SPECIFIC SETTINGS • WORKING TIME • LEAVE REQUEST • PROCESSING PROCESSES • WRITE NOTIFICATION TEXTS
IMG Activity	PCUI_ESS_PT_LRQ_083
Transaction Code	S_SLN_44000029

Define Report Variants and Background Processing

In this step, as required by the business requirements, you must first create the selection variant(s) for the following programs:

▶ PTARQEMAIL (Leave Requests: Send Emails)

▶ RPTARQLIST (Leave Requests: Check)

▶ RPTARQERR (Leave Requests: Process Clock In/Out Corrections)

You must then schedule the following programs as background jobs using Transaction SE36—Schedule Background Job:

▶ RPTARQEMAIL (Leave Requests: Send Emails)

▶ RPTARQPOST (Leave Requests: Post)

▶ RPTARQSTOPWF (Leave Requests: Complete Current Workflows)

IMG Access Path	PERSONNEL MANAGEMENT • EMPLOYEE SELF-SERVICE • SERVICE SPECIFIC SETTINGS • WORKING TIME • LEAVE REQUEST • PROCESSING PROCESSES • DEFINE REPORT VARIANTS AND BACKGROUND PROCESSING
IMG Activity	PCUI_ESS_PT_LRQ_082
Transaction Code	S_SLN_44000027

Workflow: Define Method to Execute Universal Worklist Items

In this table, you set the task against the visualization type available, linking the workflow tasks and the applications that are to be launched when a workflow item is executed in the Universal Worklist (UWL):

▶ BSP standard

▶ BSP blueprint

▶ iView

▶ Portal component

▶ Portal page

▶ ABAP Web Dynpro

▶ Java Web Dynpro

IMG Access Path	PERSONNEL MANAGEMENT • EMPLOYEE SELF-SERVICE • SERVICE SPECIFIC SETTINGS • WORKING TIME • LEAVE REQUEST • PROCESSING PROCESSES • WORKFLOW: DEFINE METHOD TO EXECUTE UNIVERSAL WORKLIST ITEM
IMG Activity	PCUI_ESS_PT_LRQ_091
Transaction Code	S_XEN_65000002
Table Name	SWFVT
	Caution: This table is cross client.

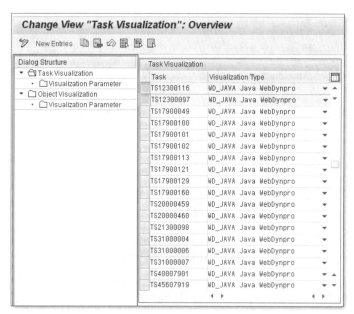

Figure 5.13 Table SWFVT: Tasks Visualization

Regarding the leave request (application *sap.com/ess~lea*), you have two standard tasks, illustrated in Figure 5.13:

▶ TS12300116 LeaveRequest

▶ TS12300097 LeaveRequest Approver

5.2.2 Layout of the Web Application

You can adjust the web application layout according to the business requirements, which helps provide the most user-friendly interface.

IMG Access Path	PERSONNEL MANAGEMENT • EMPLOYEE SELF-SERVICE • SERVICE SPECIFIC SETTINGS • WORKING TIME • LEAVE REQUEST • LAYOUT OF THE WEB APPLICATION

Specify How Leave Is Displayed and Default Values

In this step, as illustrated in Figure 5.14, for each rule group, you configure the following information, besides the obvious start and end date:

▶ DISPLAY PREVIOUS LEAVE IN ABSENCE OVERVIEW UP TO MAXIMUM:

    ▶ START OF PERIOD: By default, the value AS OF START OF CURRENT CALENDAR PERIOD is set.

    ▶ DISPLAY OF LEAVE: Set the value in years.

▶ DEFAULT VALUES:

    ▶ DEFAULT NEXT ABSENCE DAY: By default, the next calendar day is set.

    ▶ SELECTION DATE FOR OVERVIEW OF ABSENCES: By default, START OF THE YEAR is set.

▶ CALENDAR DISPLAY:

    ▶ COLOR DISPLAY OF STATUS OF LEAVE REQUESTS: Tick this box to enable highlighting in different colors.

IMG Access Path	PERSONNEL MANAGEMENT • EMPLOYEE SELF-SERVICE • SERVICE SPECIFIC SETTINGS • WORKING TIME • LEAVE REQUEST • LAYOUT OF THE WEB APPLICATION • SPECIFY HOW LEAVE IS DISPLAYED AND DEFAULT VALUES
IMG Activity	PCUI_ESS_PT_LRQ_040
Transaction Code	S_FAD_62000012
Table Name	V_PTARQ_TCONSTR

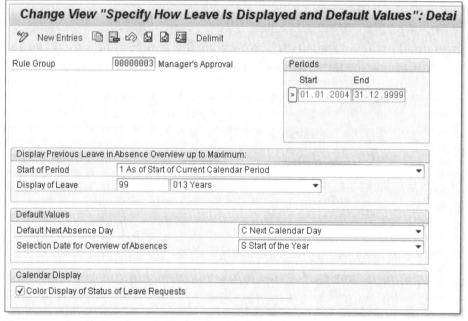

Figure 5.14 Specify How Leave Is Displayed and Default Values

Define Field Selection

Although this step is optional, you can define additional fields to be shown in the leave request process. Make the relevant entry in table V_PT_FIELD_SEL as illustrated in Figure 5.15.

IMG Access Path	PERSONNEL MANAGEMENT • EMPLOYEE SELF-SERVICE • SERVICE SPECIFIC SETTINGS • WORKING TIME • LEAVE REQUEST • LAYOUT OF THE WEB APPLICATION • DEFINE FIELD SELECTION
IMG Activity	PCUI_ESS_PT_LRQ_055
Transaction Code	S_AEN_10000316

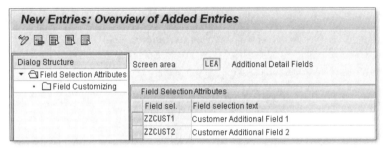

Figure 5.15 Additional Field Definition

Adjust the customizing for these fields as required (see Figure 5.16).

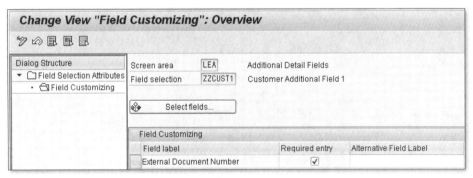

Figure 5.16 Customizing for Additional Fields

The final step is to assign the field selection to types of leave as shown previously.

Specify Display of Absence Quotas

Assuming that all relevant absence quotas have been maintained in the Time Management component, not all of them are relevant for display in the LEAVE REQUEST OVERVIEW OF QUOTAS. Some quotas might be used for technical summary reasons or as cumulative fields.

In this step, you enable the absence quotas to be displayed in the leave request process as illustrated in Figure 5.17.

IMG Access Path	PERSONNEL MANAGEMENT • EMPLOYEE SELF-SERVICE • SERVICE SPECIFIC SETTINGS • WORKING TIME • LEAVE REQUEST • LAYOUT OF THE WEB APPLICATION • SPECIFY DISPLAY OF ABSENCE QUOTAS
IMG Activity	PCUI_ESS_PT_LRQ_060
Transaction Code	S_FAD_62000014
Table Name	V_T556A_WEB

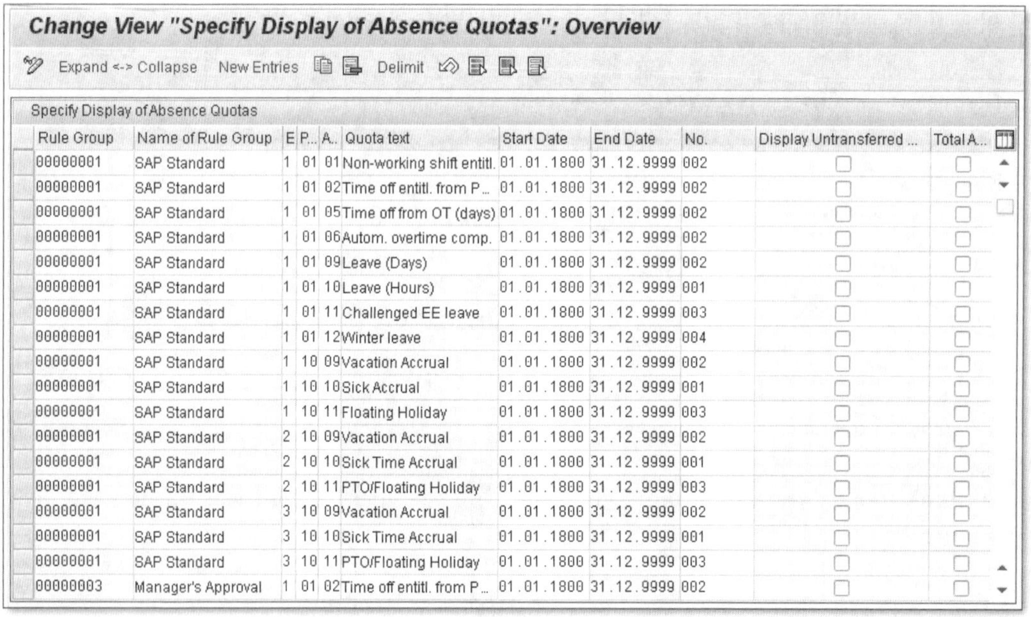

Change View "Specify Display of Absence Quotas": Overview

Expand <-> Collapse   New Entries   Delimit

Specify Display of Absence Quotas

Rule Group	Name of Rule Group	E	P..	A..	Quota text	Start Date	End Date	No.	Display Untransferred ...	Total A...
00000001	SAP Standard	1	01	01	Non-working shift entitl.	01.01.1800	31.12.9999	002	☐	☐
00000001	SAP Standard	1	01	02	Time off entitl. from P...	01.01.1800	31.12.9999	002	☐	☐
00000001	SAP Standard	1	01	05	Time off from OT (days)	01.01.1800	31.12.9999	002	☐	☐
00000001	SAP Standard	1	01	06	Autom. overtime comp.	01.01.1800	31.12.9999	002	☐	☐
00000001	SAP Standard	1	01	09	Leave (Days)	01.01.1800	31.12.9999	002	☐	☐
00000001	SAP Standard	1	01	10	Leave (Hours)	01.01.1800	31.12.9999	001	☐	☐
00000001	SAP Standard	1	01	11	Challenged EE leave	01.01.1800	31.12.9999	003	☐	☐
00000001	SAP Standard	1	01	12	Winter leave	01.01.1800	31.12.9999	004	☐	☐
00000001	SAP Standard	1	10	09	Vacation Accrual	01.01.1800	31.12.9999	002	☐	☐
00000001	SAP Standard	1	10	10	Sick Accrual	01.01.1800	31.12.9999	001	☐	☐
00000001	SAP Standard	1	10	11	Floating Holiday	01.01.1800	31.12.9999	003	☐	☐
00000001	SAP Standard	2	10	09	Vacation Accrual	01.01.1800	31.12.9999	002	☐	☐
00000001	SAP Standard	2	10	10	Sick Time Accrual	01.01.1800	31.12.9999	001	☐	☐
00000001	SAP Standard	2	10	11	PTO/Floating Holiday	01.01.1800	31.12.9999	003	☐	☐
00000001	SAP Standard	3	10	09	Vacation Accrual	01.01.1800	31.12.9999	002	☐	☐
00000001	SAP Standard	3	10	10	Sick Time Accrual	01.01.1800	31.12.9999	001	☐	☐
00000001	SAP Standard	3	10	11	PTO/Floating Holiday	01.01.1800	31.12.9999	003	☐	☐
00000003	Manager's Approval	1	01	02	Time off entitl. from P...	01.01.1800	31.12.9999	002	☐	☐

Figure 5.17 Absence Quotas Display for the Leave Request

You have two options in regards to the quotas display:

▶ DISPLAY UNTRANSFERRED QUOTAS: Tick this box to specify whether the Leave Request web application cumulates existing accrual entitlements in addition to exising entitlements. Accrual entitlements have not yet been transferred to the Absence Quota InfoType (2006).

▶ TOTAL BY ABSENCE QUOTA TYPE: Tick this box to specify that all existing data records of a quota type are to be totaled in the web application.

Specify Display of Attendance Quotas

Assuming that all relevant attendance quotas have been maintained in the Time Management component, not all of them are relevant for display in the LEAVE REQUEST OVERVIEW OF QUOTAS. Some quotas might be used for technical summary reasons or just as cumulative fields.

In this step, you enable the attendance quotas to be displayed in the leave request process, as illustrated in Figure 5.18.

IMG Access Path	PERSONNEL MANAGEMENT • EMPLOYEE SELF-SERVICE • SERVICE SPECIFIC SETTINGS • WORKING TIME • LEAVE REQUEST • LAYOUT OF THE WEB APPLICATION • SPECIFY DISPLAY OF ATTENDANCE QUOTAS
IMG Activity	PCUI_ESS_PT_LRQ_065
Transaction Code	S_PLN_62000236
Table Name	V_T556P_WEB

Change View "Specify Display of Attendance Quotas": Overview

Expand <-> Collapse   New Entries   Delimit

Specify Display of Attendance Quotas

Rule Group	Name of Rule Group	ESG	PSGpg	QType	Quota text	Start Date	End Date	No.	Total AttQuotaType
00000001	SAP Standard	1	01	01	Approved overtime	01.01.1800	31.12.9999	001	☐
00000001	SAP Standard	1	01	04	Approved attendance	01.01.1800	31.12.9999	001	☐
00000001	SAP Standard	1	99	04	Training course	01.01.1800	31.12.9999	001	☐

Figure 5.18 Attendance Quotas Display for the Leave Request

The additional option, if required, is to tick the box TOTAL BY ATTENDANCE QUOTA TYPE. It specifies that all existing data records of a quota type are to be totaled in the web application.

5.2.3 Business Add-Ins (BAdIs)

As always, standard SAP functionalities can be enriched and/or enhanced thanks to BAdIs. Several BAdIs are available for the leave request process. The next subsections describe two useful BAdIs that you can configure through the IMG.

> **Tip**
>
> Regarding colors in the UI, read the SAP Note 897623—User Exits and BADIs in the Personnel Time Area, which deals with all the BAdIs. This is quite handy as a documentation starting point.

BAdI: Control Processing Processes for Time Management Web Applications

You can use this BAdI to control the processing processes of the ESS applications for Personnel Time Management.

IMG Access Path	PERSONNEL MANAGEMENT • EMPLOYEE SELF-SERVICE • SERVICE SPECIFIC SETTINGS • WORKING TIME • LEAVE REQUEST • BUSINESS ADD-INS (BADIS) • BADI: CONTROL PROCESSING PROCESSES FOR TIME MANAGEMENT WEB APPLICATIONS
IMG Activity	PCUI_ESS_TIMCOR_006
Transaction Code	S_PLN_62000023
BAdI Implementation	PT_GEN_REQ

The BAdI contains the following standard methods:

▸ Check whether an employee is absent

▸ Read substitute

▸ Find next processor

▸ Check selected processor

▸ Determine default approver and person responsible for employee

▶ Start workflow

▶ Determine email address

▶ Get table with email lists

▶ Filter next agent

▶ Change messages from backend system

BAdI: Control Processing of Leave Requests

You can use this BAdI to enhance and control the processing of the attendances and absences component in many web applications, including the following:

▶ **Leave Request**
To control processing of leave requests.

▶ **Team Calendar**
To set the layout of the team calendar in MSS and ESS.

▶ **Time Accounts (ESS)**
To determine time accounts.

▶ **Attendance Overview (MSS)**
To adjust the legend.

IMG Access Path	PERSONNEL MANAGEMENT • EMPLOYEE SELF-SERVICE • SERVICE SPECIFIC SETTINGS • WORKING TIME • LEAVE REQUEST • BUSINESS ADD-INS (BADIS) • BADI: CONTROL PROCESSING OF LEAVE REQUESTS
IMG Activity	PCUI_ESS_PT_LRQ_080
Transaction Code	S_FAD_62000016
BAdI Implementation	CL_PT_ARQ_REQ

5.3   Working Time: Team Calendar

Now that we have covered the configuration for the leave request, let's move on to the team calendar configuration. SAP is consistent in its approach, so many of the web application configuration tables are the same as for the leave request.

5.3.1 Create Rule Groups

This is the same configuration as illustrated for the leave request, but it is now effective for the team calendar.

IMG Access Path	PERSONNEL MANAGEMENT • EMPLOYEE SELF-SERVICE • SERVICE SPECIFIC SETTINGS • WORKING TIME • TEAM CALENDAR • CREATE RULE GROUPS
IMG Activity	PCUI_ESS_PT_LRQ_030
Transaction Code	S_FAD_62000011

5.3.2 Specify Absences to Be Displayed

This is the same configuration as illustrated for the leave request, but it is now effective for the team calendar.

IMG Access Path	PERSONNEL MANAGEMENT • EMPLOYEE SELF-SERVICE • SERVICE SPECIFIC SETTINGS • WORKING TIME • TEAM CALENDAR • SPECIFY ABSENCES TO BE DISPLAYED
IMG Activity	PCUI_ESS_MSS_PT_ABS
Transaction Code	S_XEN_65000035

5.3.3 Specify Color Display of Absences

In this configuration step, as illustrated in Figure 5.19 and similar to the leave request setup, you set the following information:

▶ START OF PERIOD: Choose when the period starts.

▶ DISPLAY OF LEAVE: Choose how the leave should be displayed.

▶ COLOR DISPLAY OF STATUS OF LEAVE REQUESTS: Tick this box to reveal the colors in the team calendars.

IMG Access Path	PERSONNEL MANAGEMENT • EMPLOYEE SELF-SERVICE • SERVICE SPECIFIC SETTINGS • WORKING TIME • TEAM CALENDAR • SPECIFY COLOR DISPLAY OF ABSENCES
IMG Activity	PCUI_ESS_PT_LRQ_051
Transaction Code	S_P7H_77000003
Table Name	V_PTARQ_TCONSTR

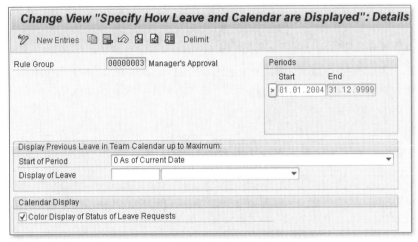

Figure 5.19 Specify How Leave and Calendar Are Displayed

5.3.4 Select Employees

In this step, as illustrated in Figure 5.20, you determine which team members are to be displayed in the team calendar based on the rule groups greated previously.

IMG Access Path	PERSONNEL MANAGEMENT • EMPLOYEE SELF-SERVICE • SERVICE SPECIFIC SETTINGS • WORKING TIME • TEAM CALENDAR • SELECT EMPLOYEES
IMG Activity	PCUI_ESS_LRQ_085
Transaction Code	S_PLN_62000260
Table Name	V_PTREQ_TEAM

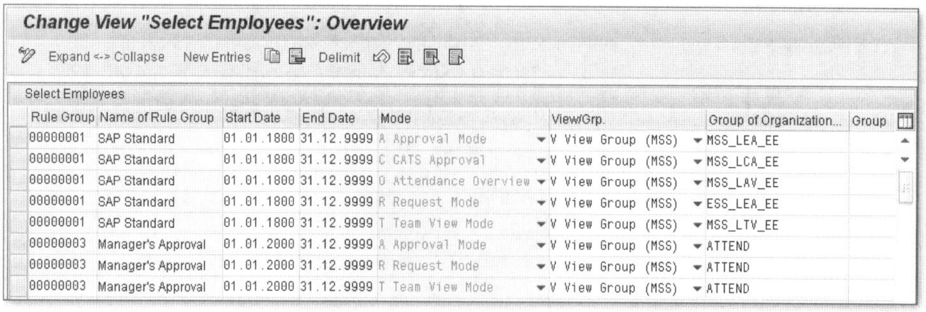

Change View "Select Employees": Overview

Expand <-> Collapse New Entries Delimit

Select Employees

Rule Group	Name of Rule Group	Start Date	End Date	Mode	View/Grp.	Group of Organization...	Group
00000001	SAP Standard	01.01.1800	31.12.9999	A Approval Mode	V View Group (MSS)	MSS_LEA_EE	
00000001	SAP Standard	01.01.1800	31.12.9999	C CATS Approval	V View Group (MSS)	MSS_LCA_EE	
00000001	SAP Standard	01.01.1800	31.12.9999	O Attendance Overview	V View Group (MSS)	MSS_LAV_EE	
00000001	SAP Standard	01.01.1800	31.12.9999	R Request Mode	V View Group (MSS)	ESS_LEA_EE	
00000001	SAP Standard	01.01.1800	31.12.9999	T Team View Mode	V View Group (MSS)	MSS_LTV_EE	
00000003	Manager's Approval	01.01.2000	31.12.9999	A Approval Mode	V View Group (MSS)	ATTEND	
00000003	Manager's Approval	01.01.2000	31.12.9999	R Request Mode	V View Group (MSS)	ATTEND	
00000003	Manager's Approval	01.01.2000	31.12.9999	T Team View Mode	V View Group (MSS)	ATTEND	

Figure 5.20 Select Employees

5.3.5 Define Layout of Team Calendar

In this configuration step, as illustrated in Figure 5.21, you define the cache validity for each rule group; the default setting is "1," which means the following according to SAP documentation:

> *The system reads the data from the database of requests only once a day for each employee. If a user chooses Refresh in the Web application, the system reads the data from the database of requests again.*

You also set up the number of rows to be displayed on one page of the team calendar, which means the number of employee's data to be displayed on one page.

IMG Access Path	Personnel Management • Employee Self-Service • Service Specific Settings • Working Time • Team Calendar • Define Layout of Team Calendar
IMG Activity	PCUI_ESS_LRQ_080
Transaction Code	S_PLN_62000259
Table Name	V_PTARQ_TCALE

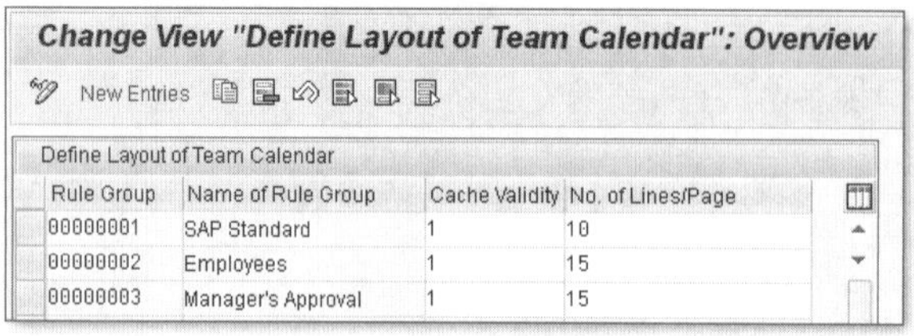

Change View "Define Layout of Team Calendar": Overview

New Entries

Define Layout of Team Calendar

Rule Group	Name of Rule Group	Cache Validity	No. of Lines/Page
00000001	SAP Standard	1	10
00000002	Employees	1	15
00000003	Manager's Approval	1	15

Figure 5.21 Define the Layout of the Team Calendar

5.3.6 BAdI: Control Processing of Leave Requests

This BAdI is the same as the Enhancement for Leave Request BAdI illustrated for the leave request.

IMG Access Path	PERSONNEL MANAGEMENT • EMPLOYEE SELF-SERVICE • SERVICE SPECIFIC SETTINGS • WORKING TIME • TEAM CALENDAR • BADI: CONTROL PROCESSING OF LEAVE REQUESTS
IMG Activity	PCUI_ESS_PT_LRQ_080
Transaction Code	S_FAD_62000016
BAdI Name	Enhancement for Leave Request

5.4 Working Time: Time Accounts

Among the Working Time self-services, you can also provide access to the employee's time accounts. These configuration steps allow you to control which accounts are shown on the screen.

IMG Access Path	PERSONNEL MANAGEMENT • EMPLOYEE SELF-SERVICE • SERVICE SPECIFIC SETTINGS • WORKING TIME • TIME ACCOUNTS.

5.4.1 Create Rule Groups

This is the same configuration as illustrated for the leave request, but it is now configured for the time accounts. Repeat the configuration as needed.

IMG Access Path	PERSONNEL MANAGEMENT • EMPLOYEE SELF-SERVICE • SERVICE SPECIFIC SETTINGS • WORKING TIME • TIME ACCOUNTS • CREATE RULE GROUPS
IMG Activity	PCUI_ESS_PT_LRQ_030
Transaction Code	S_FAD_62000011

5.4.2 Specify Display of Absence Quotas

This is the same configuration as illustrated for the leave request, but it is now configured for the time accounts. Repeat the configuration as needed.

IMG Access Path	PERSONNEL MANAGEMENT • EMPLOYEE SELF-SERVICE • SERVICE SPECIFIC SETTINGS • WORKING TIME • TIME ACCOUNTS • SPECIFY DISPLAY OF ABSENCE QUOTAS
IMG Activity	PCUI_ESS_PT_LRQ_060
Transaction Code	S_FAD_62000014
Table Name	V_T556A_WEB

5.4.3 Specify Display of Attendance Quotas

This is the same configuration as illustrated for the leave request, but it is now configured for the time accounts. Repeat the configuration as needed.

IMG Access Path	PERSONNEL MANAGEMENT • EMPLOYEE SELF-SERVICE • SERVICE SPECIFIC SETTINGS • WORKING TIME • TIME ACCOUNTS • SPECIFY DISPLAY OF ATTENDANCE QUOTAS
IMG Activity	PCUI_ESS_PT_LRQ_065
Transaction Code	S_PLN_62000236
Table Name	V_T556P_WEB

5.4.4 Specify Calculation of Remaining Leave

Although a different access path, this is the same table V_PTARQ_TPROCESS as illustrated for the leave request in Section 5.2 under the heading "Define Processing Processes for Each Rule Group." Thus, it is the same configuration as illustrated for the leave request but now configured for the time accounts. Repeat the configuration as needed.

IMG Access Path	PERSONNEL MANAGEMENT • EMPLOYEE SELF-SERVICE • SERVICE SPECIFIC SETTINGS • WORKING TIME • TIME ACCOUNTS • SPECIFY CALCULATION OF REMAINING LEAVE
IMG Activity	PCUI_ESS_PT_TQT_010

Transaction Code	S_PEN_05000395
Table Name	V_PTARQ_TPROCESS

5.4.5 Define Variant for Time Evaluation

First, you must define the variant for the time evaluation in the program RPTIME00. Call the program through Transaction SE38 — ABAP Editor, for example, and then maintain and save the dedicated variant.

The second step is to maintain and adjust the feature LLREP — Variants for Reports through the configuration step or by calling Transaction PE03 — HR: Features (see Figure 5.22), and then add the SIMF parameter in the Time Evaluation variant.

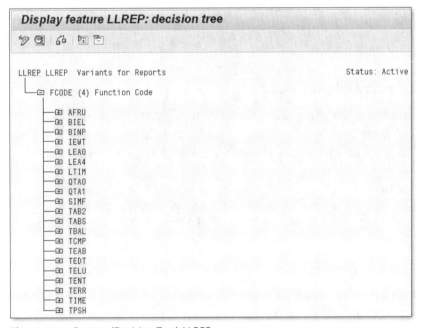

Figure 5.22 Feature (Decision Tree) LLREP

IMG Access Path	PERSONNEL MANAGEMENT • EMPLOYEE SELF-SERVICE • SERVICE SPECIFIC SETTINGS • WORKING TIME • TIME ACCOUNTS • DEFINE VARIANT FOR TIME EVALUATION

IMG Activity	PCUI_ESS_PT_TQT_011
Transaction Code	S_XEN_65000037

5.4.6 Configure Output of Messages

This is the same configuration as illustrated for the leave request, but it is now configured for the time accounts. Repeat the configuration as needed.

IMG Access Path	PERSONNEL MANAGEMENT • EMPLOYEE SELF-SERVICE • SERVICE SPECIFIC SETTINGS • WORKING TIME • TIME ACCOUNTS • CONFIGURE OUTPUT OF MESSAGES
IMG Activity	PCUI_ESS_PT_LRQ_070
Transaction Code	S_FAD_62000015
Table Name	V_HRWEB_TRS_MESS

5.4.7 Business Add-Ins (BAdIs)

Further flexibility for handling time accounts can be enabled using the BAdIs provided by SAP. These BAdIs will serve as placeholders to hold the customer additional code reflecting the business requirements not covered by the configuration.

IMG Access Path	PERSONNEL MANAGEMENT • EMPLOYEE SELF-SERVICE • SERVICE SPECIFIC SETTINGS • WORKING TIME • TIME ACCOUNTS • BUSINESS ADD-INS (BADIS)

BAdI: Control Processing Processes for Time Management Web Applications

This is the same BAdI as illustrated for the leave request. This BAdI can also contain the time accounts enhancements.

IMG Access Path	PERSONNEL MANAGEMENT • EMPLOYEE SELF-SERVICE • SERVICE SPECIFIC SETTINGS • WORKING TIME • TIME ACCOUNTS • BUSINESS ADD-INS (BADIS) • BADI: CONTROL PROCESSING PROCESSES FOR TIME MANAGEMENT WEB APPLICATIONS

IMG Activity	PCUI_ESS_TIMCOR_006
Transaction Code	S_PLN_62000023
BAdI Implementation	PT_GEN_REQ

BAdI: Control Processing of Leave Requests

This is the same BAdI as illustrated for the leave request. This BAdI can also contain the time accounts enhancements.

IMG Access Path	PERSONNEL MANAGEMENT • EMPLOYEE SELF-SERVICE • SERVICE SPECIFIC SETTINGS • WORKING TIME • TIME ACCOUNTS • BUSINESS ADD-INS (BADIS) • BADI: CONTROL PROCESSING OF LEAVE REQUESTS
Transaction Code	S_FAD_62000016
BAdI Implementation	CL_PT_ARQ_REQ

5.5 Record Working Time

Recording time entries is one of the self-services best sellers because it enables time recording through a centralized screen for all SAP components dealing with labor time (except for Production Planning because it deals with machine time).

IMG Access Path	PERSONNEL MANAGEMENT • EMPLOYEE SELF-SERVICE • SERVICE SPECIFIC SETTINGS • WORKING TIME • RECORD WORKING TIME

The standard functionality is the Cross-Application Time Sheet (CATS). CATS can either be used in the SAP NetWeaver Portal or online through the self-services.

This section describes the configuration for web-enabling the time registration process.

Tip

For further information regarding CATS, read the following books:

- ► *Integrating CATS* by Martin Gillet describes all standard configuration steps for enabling CATS (SAP PRESS, 2nd ed. 2009).

- ► *Configuring and Using CATS* by Manuel Gallardo provides insight into the technical details, including all enhancements for CATS (SAP PRESS 2008).

In this step, you set up all of the required configuration regarding the time sheet profile to use when entering time entries. Although it might look redundant, do not be misled, because you are dealing with the record working times configuration steps, so you start with the first main functionality: recording working times, also known as the time registration process or the time sheet.

IMG Access Path	PERSONNEL MANAGEMENT • EMPLOYEE SELF-SERVICE • SERVICE SPECIFIC SETTINGS • WORKING TIME • RECORD WORKING TIME • RECORD WORKING TIME

5.5.1 Set Up Data Entry Profiles

In this configuration step, you define all required configurations for the Data Entry Profile. The Data Entry Profile is the placeholder that contains all information such as the general settings, time settings, workflow, cost accounting variant, default values, worklist, and data entry checks.

IMG Access Path	PERSONNEL MANAGEMENT • EMPLOYEE SELF-SERVICE • SERVICE SPECIFIC SETTINGS • WORKING TIME • RECORD WORKING TIME • RECORD WORKING TIME • SET UP DATA ENTRY PROFILES
IMG Activity	PCUI_ESS_CATS_001
Transaction Code	S_FAD_62000063 or CAC1
Table Name	TCATST

As you deal with the online version of CATS, also referred to as CATS regular, some configuration options or user exits might not apply. Be sure to carefully test, test, and retest processes that are working fine in R/3 but are not working on the ESS Working Time service.

In SAP NetWeaver Portal, the GUID value is not passed, and therefore the display texts are not shown. When calling the user from the Web Dynpro Working Time self-service, only the values of the different columns, which are configured in Transaction CAC2—Time Sheet: Field Selection are passed to the user exit. The GUID and all other values are not passed.

In the initialization phase of the Web Dynpro application, all the columns that are visible in Transaction CAC2—Time Sheet: Field Selection are read! The data for all these columns are read and passed onto the user exit. The values from the remaining columns are not considered. SAP states that the Web Dynpro application is designed in this way.

The only solution to this issue is to adjust and change the code provided within the user exit. Test and check the behavior of the user exit from the portal side, and then check the user exit interface to monitor which values are passed.

For example, the display text for the web interface is likely not supported. Refer to SAP Note 1241169—ESS CATS: Heading for DISPTEXT1 and DISPTEXT2. For previous users with the ITS service CATW, also read SAP Note 376188—Supported User Exits from CATS in CATW Service.

Furthermore, the user parameter CVR—CATS: Variant for Time Recording must also be set up in the end user SAP UserID. The value for this parameter is the default data entry profile to be used in the CATS.

If this parameter is missing from the end user SAP UserID parameters, the system picks up the default data entry profile ESS—ESS Profile.

By default, CATS regular provides two tabs in the CROSS-APPLICATION TIME SHEET SAP NetWeaver Portal screen: a daily view and a weekly view.

Even if you edit the time settings in the configuration settings for the data entry profile, this does not impact the rendering on the screen because, unfortunately, it is hard-coded by SAP.

Unlike ITS service CATW—Record Time Entries, which enabled the selection of data entry profiles, this is not possible anymore with the Web Dynpro version.

Figure 5.23 illustrates this configuration step.

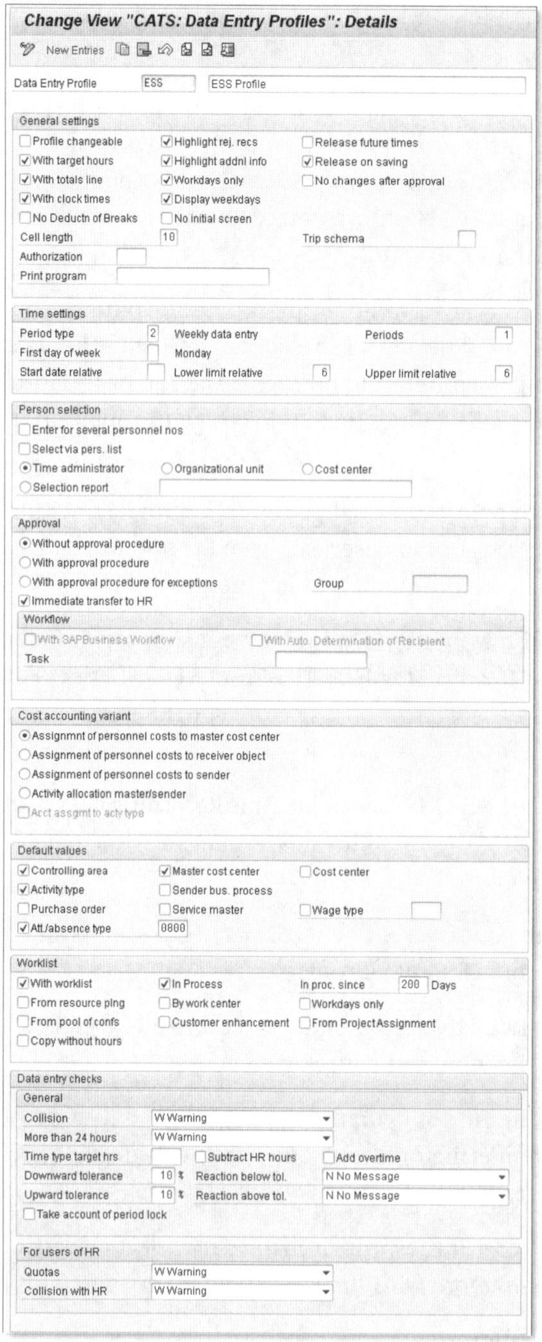

Figure 5.23 Set Up Data Entry Profiles

5.5.2 Define Field Selection

Now that the data entry profile is set up, the system still doesn't know which fields to enable for the Web Dynpro screen. This configuration step is illustrated in Figure 5.24.

IMG Access Path	PERSONNEL MANAGEMENT • EMPLOYEE SELF-SERVICE • SERVICE SPECIFIC SETTINGS • WORKING TIME • RECORD WORKING TIME • RECORD WORKING TIME • DEFINE FIELD SELECTION
IMG Activity	PCUI_ESS_CATS_004
Transaction Code	S_FAD_62000066 or CAC2

From the configuration transaction, select INFLUENCING, and indicate the data entry profile to be configured. In this example, the data entry profile is "ESS."

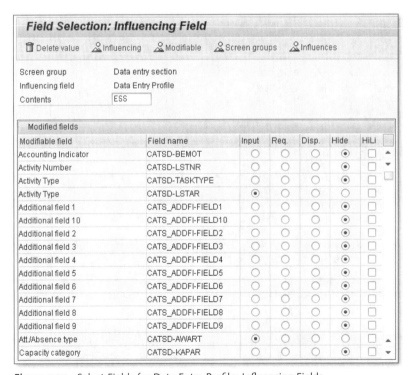

Figure 5.24 Select Fields for Data Entry Profile: Influencing Fields

Disable the fields as needed by clicking on the radio button HIDE.

When entering the configuration step, it is important to use the INFLUENCING step. Otherwise, you will change the standard reference screen and jeopardize other configurations for the time sheet.

5.5.3   Select Allowed Absence Types

Assuming that all absences types have been defined during the Time Management project, some of them might not be relevant for the time registration process. This configuration table enables you to deactivate the absence types by just flagging the entry DEACTIVATE, as illustrated in Figure 5.25.

PSG	A/AType	A/A type text	End Date	Deact	
1	0100	Leave w. quota d. (days)	31.12.1998	☐	
1	0100	Leave w. quota d. (days)	31.12.9999	☐	
1	0101	Leave w. quota d. (hours)	31.12.9999	☐	
1	0102		31.12.9999	☑	
1	0110	Leave 1/2 day	31.12.1998	☐	
1	0110	Leave 1/2 day	31.12.9999	☐	
1	0120	Seniority leave	31.12.9999	☑	
1	0130	Challenged persons lea…	31.12.9999	☐	
1	0148	SSS Sick Leave	31.12.9999	☑	
1	0149	SSS Maternity Leave	31.12.9999	☑	
1	0190	Educational leave	31.12.9999	☐	
1	0200	Illness with certificate	31.12.9999	☐	
1	0210	Illness w/o certificate	31.12.9999	☐	
1	0220	Health cure	31.12.9999	☐	
1	0221	Health cure, reduced pay	31.12.1998	☑	
1	0222	Cure, full pay for leave	31.12.1998	☑	
1	0223	Health cure, leave ded.ER	31.12.1998	☑	
1	0230	Doctor's appointment	31.12.9999	☑	
1	0240	Illness with reduced pay	31.12.1998	☑	

Change View "ESS: Deactivation of attendance/absence types": Overview

Figure 5.25   Select Allowed Absence Types

IMG Access Path	PERSONNEL MANAGEMENT • EMPLOYEE SELF-SERVICE • SERVICE SPECIFIC SETTINGS • WORKING TIME • RECORD WORKING TIME • RECORD WORKING TIME • SELECT ALLOWED ABSENCE TYPES

IMG Activity	PCUI_ESS_CATS_003
Transaction Code	S_FAD_62000065
Table Name	V_T554S_ESSEX

Tip

Although not shown in the IMG, a similar table, V_T512Z_ESSEX—ESS: Deactivate Wage Types per InfoType, exists.

This table doesn't impact the CATS process in the search help restriction.

Instead, use the user exit CATS0003—CATS: Validate Recorded Data.

5.5.4 Record Working Time for Concurrent Employment

The concurrent employment functionality was introduced in the SAP R/3 Enterprise (4.70). Concurrent Employment is finally enabled thanks to EhP 3. As a result, EhP 3 or higher must be enabled to benefit from this functionality.

IMG Access Path	PERSONNEL MANAGEMENT • EMPLOYEE SELF-SERVICE • SERVICE SPECIFIC SETTINGS • WORKING TIME • RECORD WORKING TIME • RECORD WORKING TIME • RECORD WORKING TIME FOR CONCURRENT EMPLOYMENT

Make sure to enable the business function HCM_ESS_CE—HCM, ESS for Concurrent Employment and Global Employment via Transaction SFW5—Switch Framework Customizing.

Generate a Data Entry Profile for Each Employment Relationship

In this configuration step, you enable the data entry profile for recording working times with the Web Dynpro Java for concurrent employment persons, as illustrated in Figure 5.26.

IMG Access Path	PERSONNEL MANAGEMENT • EMPLOYEE SELF-SERVICE • SERVICE SPECIFIC SETTINGS • WORKING TIME • RECORD WORKING TIME • RECORD WORKING TIME • RECORD WORKING TIME FOR CONCURRENT EMPLOYMENT • GENERATE DATA ENTRY PROFILE FOR EACH EMPLOYMENT RELATIONSHIP

IMG Activity	HRCATS_PROFILE_BY_PE
Transaction Code	S_PRN_53000823
BAdI Name	HRCATS_PROFILE_BY_PERNR—BAdI Definition for Profile by PERNR

This step actually uses BAdI HRCATS_PROFILE_BY_PERNR—BAdI Definition for Profile by PERNR with enhancement spot PRFL_TMPLT_BY_PERNR.

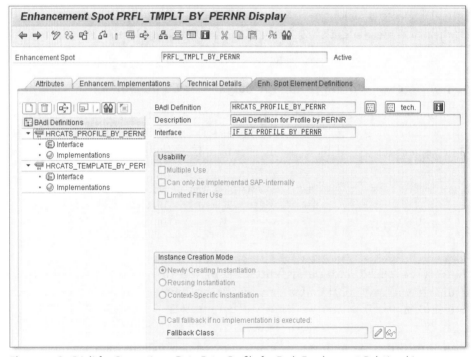

Figure 5.26 BAdI for Generating a Data Entry Profile for Each Employment Relationship

Generate Personal Templates for Each Employment Relationship

In this configuration step, you enable the template(s) to be made available for recording the working times with Java Web Dynpro for concurrent employment persons, as illustrated in Figure 5.27.

IMG Access Path	Personnel Management • Employee Self-Service • Service Specific Settings • Working Time • Record Working Time • Record Working Time • Record Working Time for Concurrent Employment • Generate Personal Templates for Each Employment Relationship
IMG Activity	PRFL_TMPLT_BY_PERNR
Transaction Code	S_PRN_53000822
BAdI Name	HRCATS_TEMPLATE_BY_PERNR—BAdI Enhancement Spot for Profile/Template by PERNR

This step actually uses BAdI HRCATS_TEMPLATE_BY_PERNR—BAdI Enhancement Spot for Profile/Template by PERNR, with enhancement spot PRFL_TMPLT_BY_PERNR.

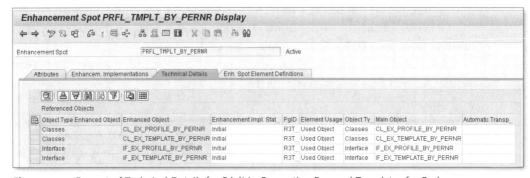

Figure 5.27 Excerpt of Technical Details for BAdI in Generating Personal Templates for Each Employment Relationship

5.5.5 Approve Working Time

The following configuration entries are described and explained in Chapter 6 because the approval process is part of the Manager's tasks.

▶ Define Approval Views

▶ Define Field Selection for Individual Approval View

▶ Define Field Selection for Detail View

▶ Define Profiles and Assign to Views

▶ Select Employees

▶ CREATE RULE GROUPS

▶ SELECT EMPLOYEES FOR APPROVAL

▶ BAdI: Refine Settings for Approval

IMG Access Path	PERSONNEL MANAGEMENT • EMPLOYEE SELF-SERVICE • SERVICE SPECIFIC SETTINGS • WORKING TIME • RECORD WORKING TIME • APPROVE WORKING TIME

5.6　Working Time: Clock-In/Out Corrections

This new self-service is now available for clock in and out corrections, if you have forgotten to clock in during the working hours. This new functionality is designed and provided for correction purposes, not to replace plant data collection (PDC) or the time administrator that also deals with the Time Manager's Workplace (Transaction PTMW) for the time corrections. The prerequisite is to use the time events as used in InfoType 2011 — Time Events. Time evaluation must be in use and set up. A valid SAP UserID must be assigned to the personnel number through InfoType 0105 — Communication, subtype 0001 — SAP UserID.

IMG Access Path	PERSONNEL MANAGEMENT • EMPLOYEE SELF-SERVICE • SERVICE SPECIFIC SETTINGS • WORKING TIME • RECORD WORKING TIME • CLOCK IN/OUT CORRECTIONS

If you want to use the program to send notifications, program RPTARQEMAIL — Leave Requests: Send Emails to Send Clock-In/Out Corrections, a valid email address must also be available in InfoType 0105 — Communication, subtype 0010 — Email.

The following is the process flow for the clock-in/out:

1. The time evaluation RPTIME00 runs and triggers some errors.

2. Program RPTCORTMAIL — Clock-In/Out Corrections: Request Correction of Errors is triggered and notifies employees for corrections.

   The employee connects in the ESS Clock-In/Out and makes the corrections.

3. Program RPTCORPOST — Clock-In/Out Corrections: Post is used to post the changes into the time events table TEVEN.

4. At any time, program RPTCORLIST—Clock-In/Out Corrections: Check Corrections can be used to retrieve a list of corrections and get an overview of the current process.

5. Time administrators can also use the program RPTCORERR—Clock-In/Out Corrections: Process Errors in Entries to monitor the entries in error status that require attention.

5.6.1 Processing Processes

In the next configuration steps, we will identify the different processes and learn how to process them.

Create Rule Groups

As in the SAP HR master data, you have many groupings. In this step, you create a rule for a dedicated group. For example, you could make distinctions among employees, workers, and managers. Along with the clock-in/out corrections, this rule group is also use for the leave request, the time calendar and the time sheet approval in MSS. In this example, a placeholder for group 00000004—Clock-In/Out Corrections has been created and will be used from this point on.

IMG Access Path	PERSONNEL MANAGEMENT • EMPLOYEE SELF-SERVICE • SERVICE SPECIFIC SETTINGS • WORKING TIME • CLOCK-IN/OUT CORRECTIONS • PROCESSING PROCESSES • CREATE RULE GROUPS
IMG Activity	PCUI_ESS_TIMCOR_001
Transaction Code	S_PLN_62000016

Because we've already created the groups for the leave request, you now review this same configuration table for the MANAGER'S APPROVAL entry.

1. Create rule groups as illustrated in Figure 5.28.

   Table Name: V_HRWEB_RULE_GRP

   In this step, you create the relevant entries to distinguish the different group with the grouping for the manager and the clock-in/out correction. Later in the configuration, this will provide different sets of data or provide dedicate specific controls to each group.

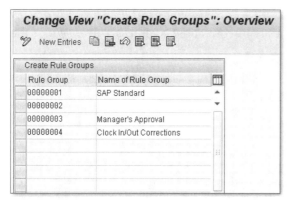

Figure 5.28   Create Rule Groups for Clock-In/Out Corrections

2. Adjust feature WEBMO—Define Rule Group for Customizing Tables in Web Environment as illustrated in Figure 5.29.

   In this step, you must advise the system when and for whom the groups are relevant by using the decision tree. In the example provided, when dealing with the clock-in/out corrections, the system calls up group 00000004—Clock-In/Out Corrections, which will then base all business process handling on the configuring done under that group.

3. Do not forget to save and activate the feature after it is adjusted.

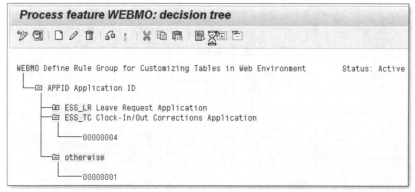

Figure 5.29   Adjust Feature (Decision Tree) WEBMO—Define Rule Group for Customizing Tables in Web Environment for Clock-In/Out Corrections

Define Periods for Clock-In/Out Corrections

In this step, you are setting the allowed time frame for the employees, as illustrated in Figure 5.30.

In this configuration screen, you set the start date and end date.

IMG Access Path	PERSONNEL MANAGEMENT • EMPLOYEE SELF-SERVICE • SERVICE SPECIFIC SETTINGS • WORKING TIME • CLOCK-IN/OUT CORRECTIONS • PROCESSING PROCESSES • DEFINE PERIODS FOR CLOCK-IN/OUT CORRECTIONS
IMG Activity	PCUI_ESS_TIMCOR_002
Transaction Code	S_PLN_62000019
Table Name	V_PTCOR_TCONSTR

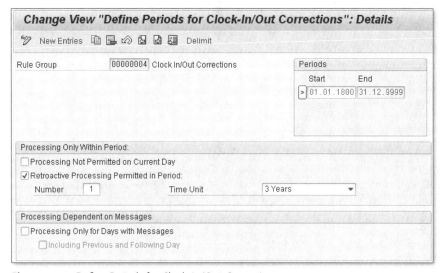

Figure 5.30 Define Periods for Clock-In/Out Corrections

Depending on the business requirements, you could allow processing on the current day. You must therefore not flag the field PROCESSING NOT PERMITTED ON CURRENT DAY. It is a best practice to allow end users to make corrections on the present day; otherwise, by the day after, they may have forgotten.

You can also allow retro processing in the past; for example, in the figure, we have set one year permissibility. In real life, we would rather opt for a time frame of one or two weeks. Changes required later in the past are made by the time administrator.

The last option is the only one that enables processing corrections for days that are triggered by the time evaluation. This option might be safe because it prevents the end user from being able to change all entries. End users can only change the faulty entries as identified by time evaluation rules.

Define Processing Processes

In this configuration step, as illustrated in Figure 5.31, you are setting the usual start and end date.

Figure 5.31 Define Processing Processes

IMG Access Path	PERSONNEL MANAGEMENT • EMPLOYEE SELF-SERVICE • SERVICE SPECIFIC SETTINGS • WORKING TIME • CLOCK-IN/OUT CORRECTIONS • PROCESSING PROCESSES • DEFINE PROCESSING PROCESSES
IMG Activity	PCUI_ESS_TIMCOR_003
Transaction Code	S_PLN_62000020
Table Name	V_PTCOR_WFATTR

You can activate additional process attributes, such as the following:

▶ USE SAP BUSINESS WORKFLOW: Although nice to have, it is a quick win to enable the automatic notification to persons in charge when corrections are performed.

▶ CORRECTIONS HAVE TO BE APPROVED: It is best practice to request an approval for any time corrections because time corrections will impact payroll.

▶ NO NEW CLOCK-IN/OUT TIMES CAN BE ENTERED: This option is rather exclusive because it means that end users can only correct faulty entries done previously through plant data collection (PDC). However, if they have forgotten to clock in, you need them to create a new clock-in entry. You then do not activate this restriction in this configuration step.

▶ CLOCK-IN/OUT ENTRIES CANNOT BE DELETED: This option is useful to safeguard the data used in corrections processes. However, bear in mind that end user can still make mistakes and create entries for a wrong date. Using this option requires another person to do the deletion, perhaps the time administrator, for example.

▶ CLOCK-IN/OUT ENTRIES CANNOT BE CHANGED: This option means that the end user gets read-only access to the clock-in/out entries, which may be counterproductive because this functionality is meant for end user to make corrections.

▶ TIME EVALUATION RUN DIRECTLY ON SAVING (RESPONSE TIMES): If you enable this option, the system automatically runs the time evaluation (program RPTIME00) for the personnel number for whom you made the correction. In most cases, you won't activate this option because first you probably need the line manager approval before the information gets validated, and also you need to consider system response time. Time evaluation and payroll programs are always run in the background during off-hours instead of productive business hours.

► DISPLAY FIELD FOR NEXT AGENT: Do you allow the end user to see the person who will be in charge of the approval? It is always useful to enable this because it is part of the communication channel between the end user and the approver.

► EMPLOYEE IS PERMITTED TO CHANGE AGENT: Flag this option if the employee can change the approval agent. In most cases, as you run the organizational management, the approval persons are already clearly identified among the structure. To avoid misuse or fraud, you should not use this option.

► NOT NECESSARY TO ENTER NEXT AGENT: The end user does not need to enter the next agent who is responsible in the process. This is automatically identified, thanks to the configuration.

► USE NOTES: Do you want to enable the end user to enter a few words? In most cases, it is handy because end users can justify the correction and why, for example, they are late or forgot to clock in.

► DETERMINE NEXT AGENT: The system looks for this value to push the approval process. In this case, the system looks for the line manager, which makes sense according to the organizational structure customers have in place.

Specify Minimum Interval Between Time Events

As illustrated in Figure 5.32, in this configuration step, you are setting the minimum interval between time events. It means, for example, that thanks to this configuration step, we are not letting the end user create a second clock in correction, as the intial clock is still under process.

IMG Access Path	PERSONNEL MANAGEMENT • EMPLOYEE SELF-SERVICE • SERVICE SPECIFIC SETTINGS • WORKING TIME • CLOCK-IN/OUT CORRECTIONS • PROCESSING PROCESSES • SPECIFY MINIMUM INTERVAL BETWEEN TIME EVENTS
IMG Activity	PCUI_ESS_TIMCOR_011
Transaction Code	S_AEN_10000363
Table Name	V_T705B

This configuration is done within each relevant personnel grouping of the personnel subareas defined by the Time Management team.

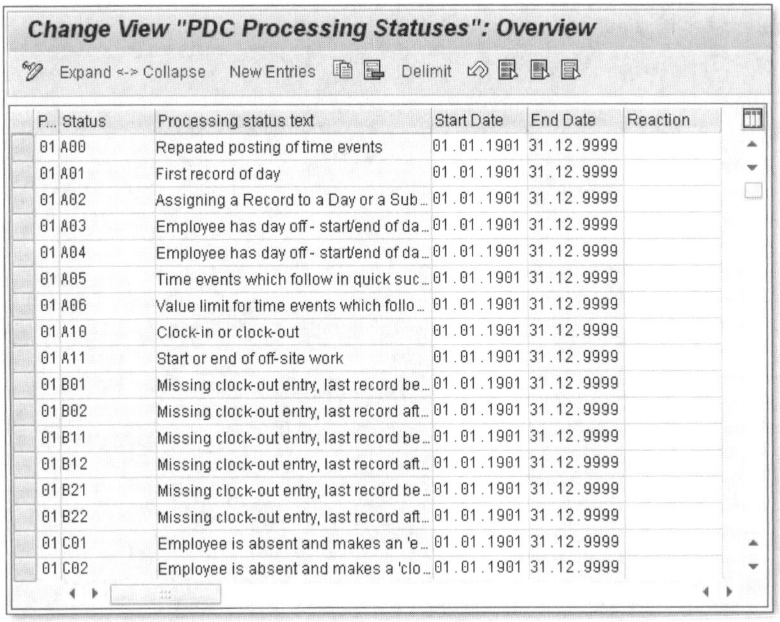
Change View "PDC Processing Statuses": Overview
Expand <-> Collapse New Entries Delimit
P... Status Processing status text Start Date End Date Reaction
01 A00 Repeated posting of time events 01.01.1901 31.12.9999
01 A01 First record of day 01.01.1901 31.12.9999
01 A02 Assigning a Record to a Day or a Sub... 01.01.1901 31.12.9999
01 A03 Employee has day off - start/end of da... 01.01.1901 31.12.9999
01 A04 Employee has day off - start/end of da... 01.01.1901 31.12.9999
01 A05 Time events which follow in quick suc... 01.01.1901 31.12.9999
01 A06 Value limit for time events which follo... 01.01.1901 31.12.9999
01 A10 Clock-in or clock-out 01.01.1901 31.12.9999
01 A11 Start or end of off-site work 01.01.1901 31.12.9999
01 B01 Missing clock-out entry, last record be... 01.01.1901 31.12.9999
01 B02 Missing clock-out entry, last record aft... 01.01.1901 31.12.9999
01 B11 Missing clock-out entry, last record be... 01.01.1901 31.12.9999
01 B12 Missing clock-out entry, last record aft... 01.01.1901 31.12.9999
01 B21 Missing clock-out entry, last record be... 01.01.1901 31.12.9999
01 B22 Missing clock-out entry, last record aft... 01.01.1901 31.12.9999
01 C01 Employee is absent and makes an 'e... 01.01.1901 31.12.9999
01 C02 Employee is absent and makes a 'clo... 01.01.1901 31.12.9999

Figure 5.32 Specify Minimum Intervals between Time Events

Define Variant for Time Evaluation

In the clock-in/out corrections process, you must tell the system which time evaluation must be updated on saving. As this is a new functionality, SAP has enhanced the decision tree LLREP—VARIANT FOR REPORTS as illustrated in Figure 5.33. This decision tree uses the function code TIME, which points to the variant to be used for time evaluation. In the following example, the system is called up the variant DEFAULT.

IMG Access Path	PERSONNEL MANAGEMENT • EMPLOYEE SELF-SERVICE • SERVICE SPECIFIC SETTINGS • WORKING TIME • CLOCK-IN/OUT CORRECTIONS • PROCESSING PROCESSES • DEFINE VARIANT FOR TIME EVALUATION
IMG Activity	PCUI_ESS_TIMCOR_015
Transaction Code	S_AEN_10000389 or PE03
Feature Name	LLREP—Variant for Reports

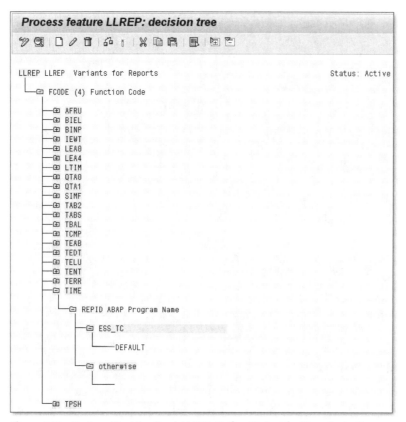

Figure 5.33 Feature (Decision Tree) LLREP: Define Variant for Time Evaluation

Do not forget to save and activate the feature after it is adjusted.

Configure Output of Messages

One of the flexible options that you have in the system is to overwrite the system message provided to the end user. You can configure the system to provide less technical and more user-friendly messages for the end users.

Prior to executing the configuration step to configure the output message, customers must first create their message class(es) and their respective customer message.

Create a Customer Message Class

As illustrated in Figure 5.34 and Figure 5.35, through table T100, you are creating a customer message class, for example, ZHR_XSS—Self-Service Customer Message

Class. This customer message class will contain all messages you could provide to the end user (for an example, see Figure 5.36).

Transaction Code	SM31—Maintain Table
Table Name	T100

When creating the customer message class, make sure to respect the customer naming convention and to translate the message(s) into the different target languages if required.

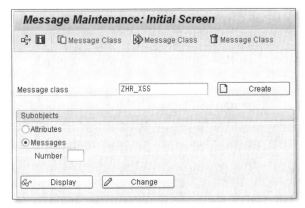

Figure 5.34 Maintain Customer Message Class

Message Maintenance: Change Message Class

Message class	ZHR_XSS	Activ

Attributes / Messages

Package	$TMP
Last changed by	MAGIL
Changed on	11.01.2011	Last changed at	17:30:31

Attributes

Original lang.	EN English
Person respons.	ADMIN_XSS
Short text	Self Services Customer Message Class

Figure 5.35 Maintain Customer Class Attributes

Configure Output of Messages

Now that you have customer messages available, you can configure the system to render that particular customer message instead of the standard message.

IMG Access Path	PERSONNEL MANAGEMENT • EMPLOYEE SELF-SERVICE • SERVICE SPECIFIC SETTINGS • WORKING TIME • CLOCK-IN/OUT CORRECTIONS • PROCESSING PROCESSES • CONFIGURE OUTPUT OF MESSAGES
IMG Activity	PCUI_ESS_PT_LRQ_070
Transaction Code	S_FAD_62000015
Table Name	V_HRWEB_TRS_MESS

From the customizing entry, choose the RULE GROUP FOR CUSTOMIZING tab for 00000004 — Clock-In/Out Corrections.

Within the configuration table, as illustrated in Figure 5.36, assign the standard message that SAP normally triggers. Next to the standard message, assign the customer message and its message type (warning, error, message on next screen, cancel, or information).

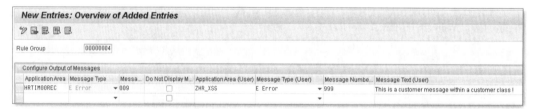

Figure 5.36 Configure Output of Messages

Notification Texts

To configure the output of messages, in this configuration step, you write the notification texts (see Figure 5.37 and Figure 5.38).

IMG Access Path	PERSONNEL MANAGEMENT • EMPLOYEE SELF-SERVICE • SERVICE SPECIFIC SETTINGS • WORKING TIME • CLOCK-IN/OUT CORRECTIONS • PROCESSING PROCESSES • WRITE NOTIFICATION TEXTS

IMG Activity	PCUI_ESS_TIMCOR_008
Transaction Code	S_PLN_62000039

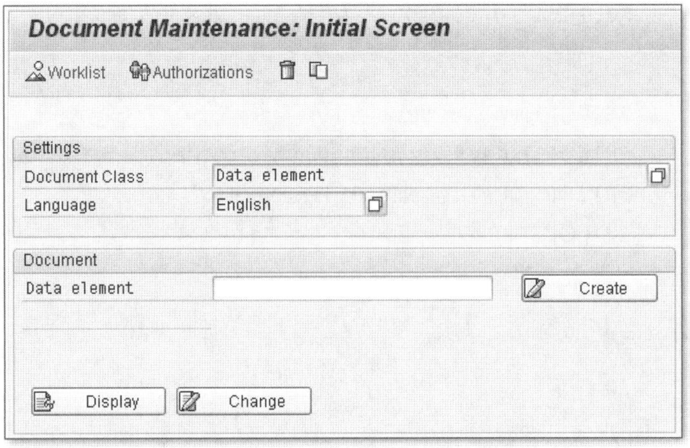

Figure 5.37 Write Notification Texts

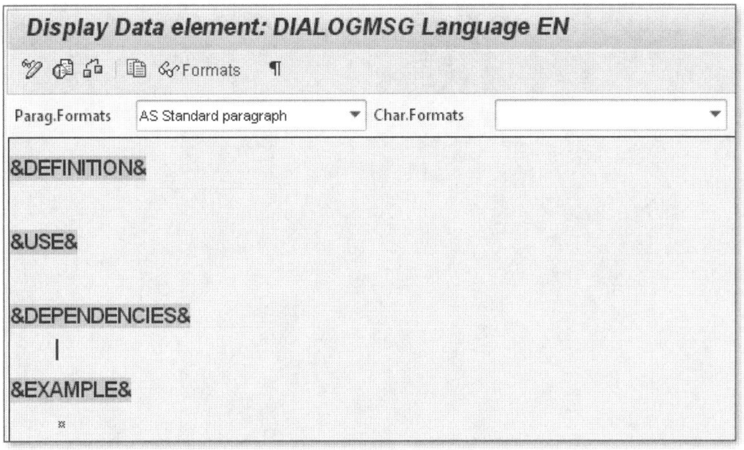

Figure 5.38 Sample Text for Dialog Messages

Define Report Variants and Background Processing

As illustrated in Figure 5.39 through Figure 5.41, this configuration step creates the selection variant for the clock-in/out reports by calling the respective programs listed in this section. This variant will be the placeholder to default values such as the time slot or the personnel selection.

IMG Access Path	Personnel Management • Employee Self-Service • Service Specific Settings • Working Time • Clock-In/Out Corrections • Processing Processes • Define Report Variants and Background Processing
IMG Activity	PCUI_ESS_TIMCOR_009
Transaction Code	S_PLN_62000137
Programs Names	RPTCORTMAIL as illustrated in Figure 5.39
	RPTCORLIST as illustrated in Figure 5.40
	RPTCORERR as illustrated in Figure 5.41
	RPTCORSTOPWF as illustrated in Figure 5.42

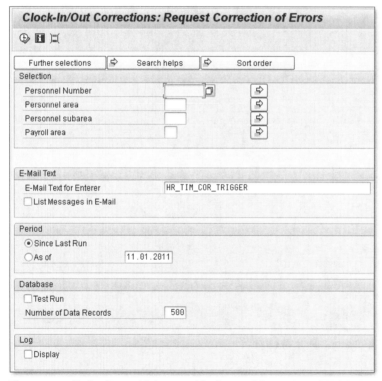

Figure 5.39 Define Report Variants and Background Processing—RPTCORTMAIL

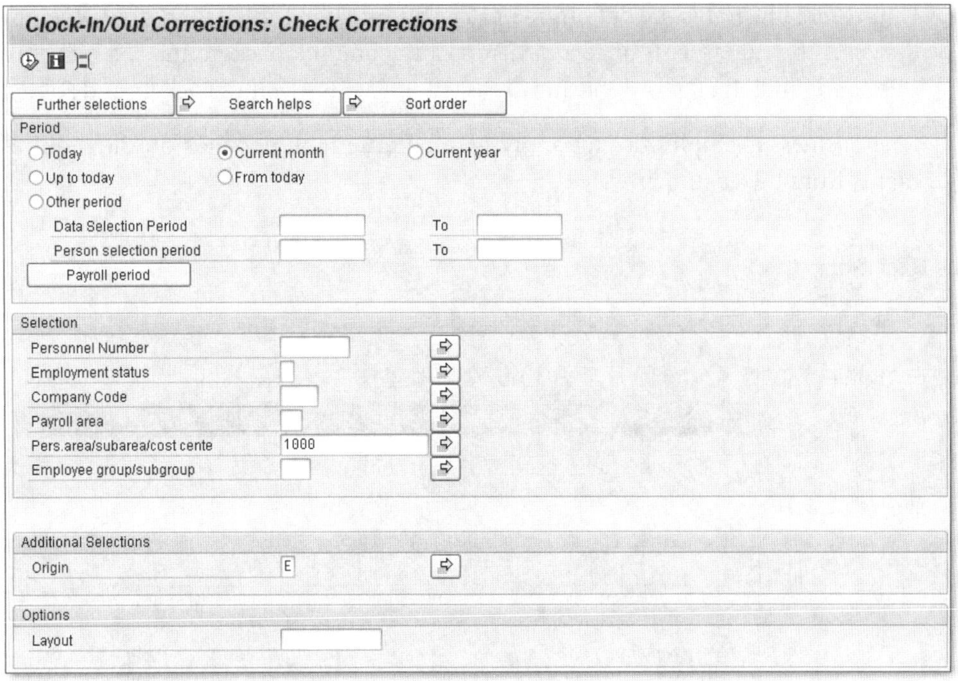

Clock-In/Out Corrections: Check Corrections

⊕ 🔳 🗙

| Further selections | ⇨ | Search helps | ⇨ | Sort order |

Period

○ Today   ⦿ Current month   ○ Current year
○ Up to today   ○ From today
○ Other period

Data Selection Period		To	
Person selection period		To	
Payroll period			

Selection

Personnel Number		⇨
Employment status		⇨
Company Code		⇨
Payroll area		⇨
Pers.area/subarea/cost cente	1000	⇨
Employee group/subgroup		⇨

Additional Selections

| Origin | E | ⇨ |

Options

| Layout | |

Figure 5.40 Define Report Variants and Background Processing—RPTCORLIST

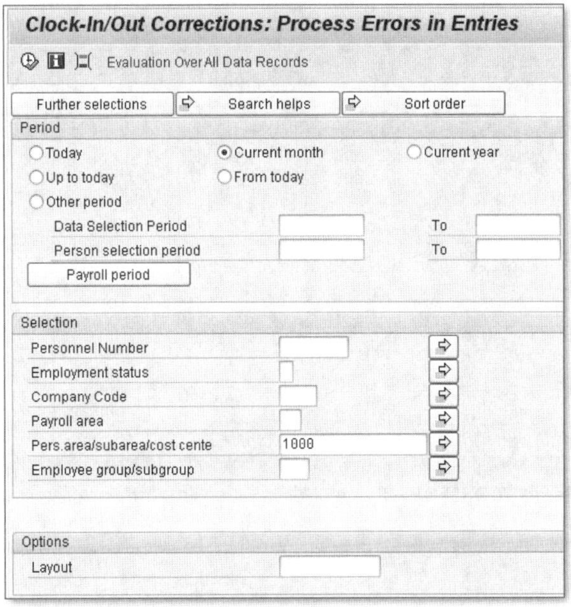

Clock-In/Out Corrections: Process Errors in Entries

⊕ 🔳 🗙   Evaluation Over All Data Records

| Further selections | ⇨ | Search helps | ⇨ | Sort order |

Period

○ Today   ⦿ Current month   ○ Current year
○ Up to today   ○ From today
○ Other period

Data Selection Period		To	
Person selection period		To	
Payroll period			

Selection

Personnel Number		⇨
Employment status		⇨
Company Code		⇨
Payroll area		⇨
Pers.area/subarea/cost cente	1000	⇨
Employee group/subgroup		⇨

Options

| Layout | |

Figure 5.41 Define Report Variants and Background Processing—RPTCORERR

Figure 5.42 illustrates the definition of a background job for the workflow program that must be run at least once a day. You can define the background job by using this configuration step or by using Transaction SM36—Define Background Job.

Real business examples do not apply here because it all depends on the requirements from the customer.

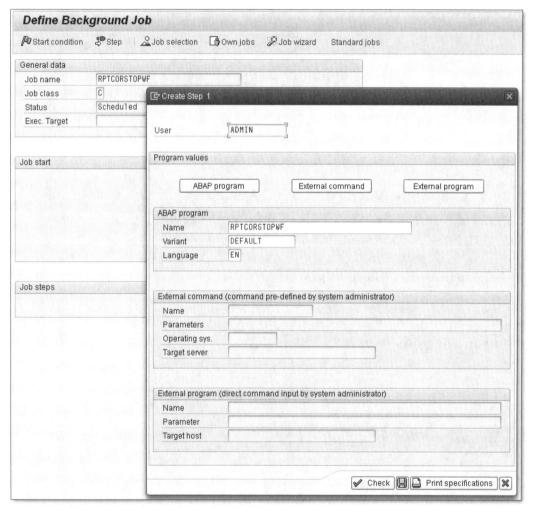

Figure 5.42 Define Background Job for RPTCORSTOPWF

Workflow: Define Tasks for Universal Worklist

This configuration step is rather technical, and it's mandatory if you use SAP Business Workflow and the Universal Worklist (UWL).

IMG Access Path	PERSONNEL MANAGEMENT • EMPLOYEE SELF-SERVICE • SERVICE SPECIFIC SETTINGS • WORKING TIME • CLOCK-IN/OUT CORRECTIONS • PROCESSING PROCESSES • WORKFLOW: DEFINE TASKS FOR UNIVERSAL WORKLIST
IMG Activity	PCUI_ESS_TIMCOR_23
Transaction Code	S_XEN_65000005
Table Name	SWFVT Caution: Cross client.

As illustrated in Figure 5.43, in this step, you copy task TS12300116—Process Leave Request by Employee into customer TS92300116. This task determines the visualization type to be used for the clock-in/out correction when dealing with workflow and notifications. In this example, it calls a Web Dynpro Java.

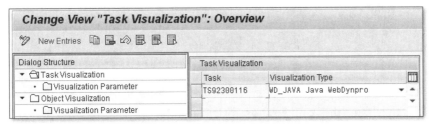

Figure 5.43 Workflow: Define Tasks for Universal Worklist—Customer Tasks TS92300116

Now that the leave request task has been copied, you must adjust the visualization parameter (attributes) so that it applies for the correct application, in this case, the clock-in/out corrections.

In the visualization parameter, as illustrated in Figure 5.44, set the following technical values:

▶ APPLICATION: "WTimeCor"

▶ PACKAGE: *"sap.com/ess~wtcor"*

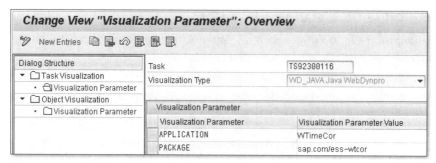

Figure 5.44 Workflow: Define Tasks for Universal Worklist—Task TS92300116 Visualization Parameter

5.6.2 Layout of the Web Application

Now that we have dealt with the configuration of the processing processes for the correction of clock-in/out, let's deal with the layout rendering of the web application. These standard configuration steps, although not mandatory, can be useful to adjust the UI for end users. Carefully review the standard entries and assess what should be changed or adjusted in the UI, for example, additional fields.

IMG Access Path	PERSONNEL MANAGEMENT • EMPLOYEE SELF-SERVICE • SERVICE SPECIFIC SETTINGS • WORKING TIME • CLOCK-IN/OUT CORRECTIONS • LAYOUT OF THE WEB APPLICATION

Configure Calendar

Figure 5.45 illustrates the configuration for group 00000004—Clock-In/Out Corrections. This configuration step indicates the following information:

▶ FIRST DAY OF THE WEEK: Sets the first day of the week (theoretically Monday for most of us, but it might be different when dealing with staff working on shifts).

▶ CAL. SCALE: Sets the time scale of the calendar; in this case, we have chosen the "60" minutes time block for each cell.

▶ TIME FRAME TYPE: Setting FIXED TIME FRAME means that the calendar shown is fixed. Alternatively, the TIME FRAME option sets the time frame according to the work schedule, if required by the business requirements.

▶ 1ST TIME: Sets the first time slot of the day, in this example, 8:00 am.

- NO. ROWS: Sets the number of rows for each day. In the standard scenario, you set 25. You might consider fewer rows according to the business needs to avoid empty or just overwhelming screens.

- TIME PAIR: Lets the system retrieve the information from the InfoType 2011- Time Events and then display it onto the UI.

- ATT/ABS: Lets the system retrieve the information from the InfoType 2001—Absences and InfoType 2002—Attendance and display these onto the UI.

IMG Access Path	PERSONNEL MANAGEMENT • EMPLOYEE SELF-SERVICE • SERVICE SPECIFIC SETTINGS • WORKING TIME • CLOCK-IN/OUT CORRECTIONS • LAYOUT OF THE WEB APPLICATION • CONFIGURE CALENDAR
IMG Activity	PCUI_ESS_TIMCOR_007
Transaction Code	S_PLN_62000024
Table Name	V_PTCOR_CALE

Figure 5.45 Configure the Calendar

Define Field Selection

In this step, you can add additional fields in the team calendar.

IMG Access Path	PERSONNEL MANAGEMENT • EMPLOYEE SELF-SERVICE • SERVICE SPECIFIC SETTINGS • WORKING TIME • CLOCK-IN/OUT CORRECTIONS • LAYOUT OF THE WEB APPLICATION • DEFINE FIELD SELECTION
IMG Activity	PCUI_ESS_TIMCOR_013
Transaction Code	S_AEN_10000844

This configuration step is divided into four configuration steps:

1. Make an overview of time event types.

   In this step, you create a list of all the time event types; the list is provided by the Time Management team to display in the clock-in/out corrections UI.

   Figure 5.46 illustrates the basic standard list that you have created with the different time event types. Time event types can vary according to the time event group created by the Time Management team.

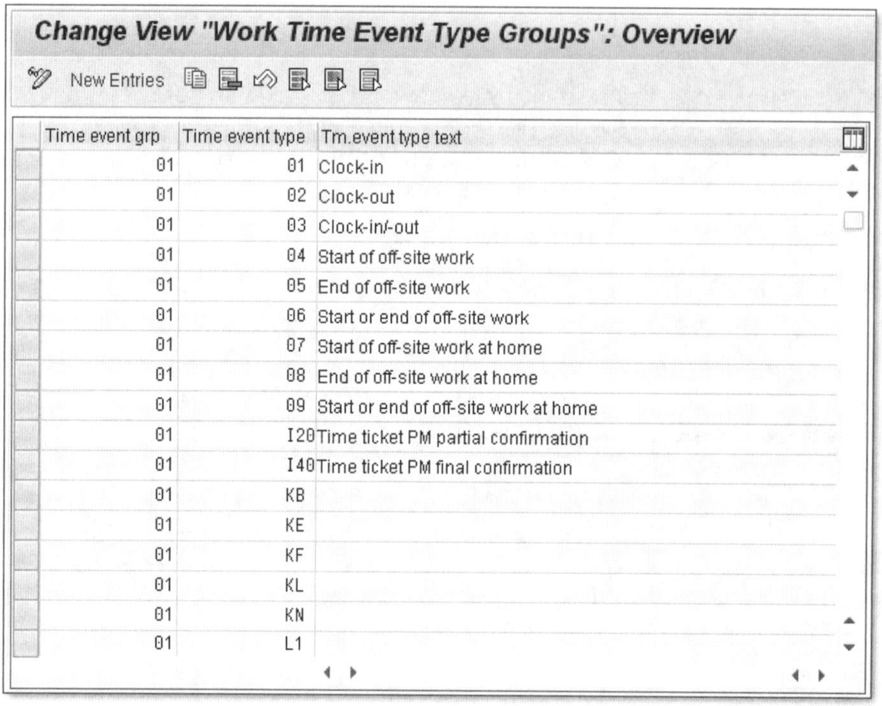

Change View "Work Time Event Type Groups": Overview

New Entries

Time event grp	Time event type	Tm.event type text
01	01	Clock-in
01	02	Clock-out
01	03	Clock-in/-out
01	04	Start of off-site work
01	05	End of off-site work
01	06	Start or end of off-site work
01	07	Start of off-site work at home
01	08	End of off-site work at home
01	09	Start or end of off-site work at home
01	I20	Time ticket PM partial confirmation
01	I40	Time ticket PM final confirmation
01	KB	
01	KE	
01	KF	
01	KL	
01	KN	
01	L1	

Figure 5.46 Define Field Selection: Overview of Time Types

2. Define the field selection.

   Table Name: V_PT_FIELD_SEL

   In this step, as illustrated in Figure 5.47, you set a new field. Set a name and a description, for example, TIMEDAT—Additional Time Data. Save your entries. Select the entry, and double-click on FIELD CUSTOMIZING on the left side of your screen. Move to the next configuration step.

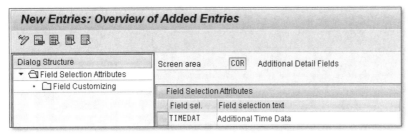

Figure 5.47 Define Field Selection: Define Field Selection Attributes

3. Define field customizing.

   Table Name: V_PT_FIELD_SEL_C

   In this configuration step, as illustrated in Figure 5.48, you check the field label and set, if required, the field as mandatory. Try to avoid mandatory fields because they might just block the end user from moving on with the process. You can also set an alternative field label, in this case, "Reason."

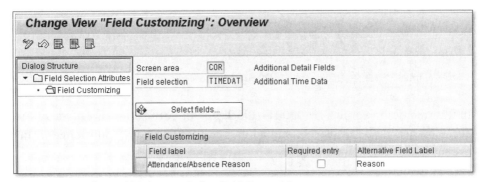

Figure 5.48 Define Field Selection: Define Field Customizing

4. Assign time event types to field selection.

   Table Name: V_PTCOR_TTYPE

   In this configuration step, as illustrated in Figure 5.49, you assign the customer field to the time event type so that it will be shown to end users on their UI. Repeat the past configuration steps for all additional fields you want to enable and assign to the group 00000004—Clock-In/Out Corrections.

Figure 5.49 Define Field Selection: Assign Time Event Types to Field Selection

Specify Absences to Be Displayed

Just like in the team calendar configuration that we covered earlier in this chapter, you must tell the system which absences to display, as illustrated in Figure 5.50. All time absences customizing entries might not be relevant for display.

IMG Access Path	PERSONNEL MANAGEMENT • EMPLOYEE SELF-SERVICE • SERVICE SPECIFIC SETTINGS • WORKING TIME • CLOCK-IN/OUT CORRECTIONS • LAYOUT OF THE WEB APPLICATION • SPECIFY ABSENCES TO BE DISPLAYED
IMG Activity	PCUI_ESS_TIMCOR_016
Transaction Code	S_PEN_05000403
Table Name	V_T554S_WEB

In this step, for the group 00000004—Clock-In/Out Corrections, assign the difference absences to be displayed, and adjust the configuration as illustrated in the team calendar configuration step.

New Entries: Overview of Added Entries

Expand <-> Collapse   New Entries   Delimit

Processing Processes for Types of Leave

Rule Group	Name of Rule Group	PSG	A/AType	Att./abs. type text	Start Date	End Date
00000004	Clock In/Out Corrections	01	0100	Leave w. quota d. (days)	01.01.1800	31.12.9999
00000004	Clock In/Out Corrections	01	0110	Leave 1/2 day	01.01.1800	31.12.9999
00000004	Clock In/Out Corrections	01	0190	Educational leave	01.01.1800	31.12.9999

Figure 5.50 Specify Absences to Be Displayed

Specify Display of Partial-Day Absences

In this configuration step for group 00000004 — Clock-In/Out Corrections, you tell the system the units to be used for the display of the partial-day absence(s) within a valid time range (see Figure 5.51). You can choose from CLOCK TIMES, HOURS, or HOURS AND CLOCK TIMES.

IMG Access Path	PERSONNEL MANAGEMENT • EMPLOYEE SELF-SERVICE • SERVICE SPECIFIC SETTINGS • WORKING TIME • CLOCK-IN/OUT CORRECTIONS • LAYOUT OF THE WEB APPLICATION • SPECIFY DISPLAY OF PARTIAL-DAY ABSENCES
IMG Activity	PCUI_ESS_TIMCOR_017
Transaction Code	S_PEN_05000402
Table Name	V_PTARQ_TPROCESS

For your convenience, the easiest setting for the end user is HOURS AND CLOCK TIMES (see Figure 5.51).

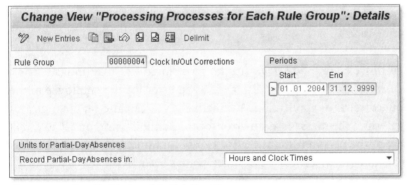

Figure 5.51 Specify Display of Partial-Day Absences

Define Messages to Be Displayed

Depending on the grouping of personnel subareas for time recording, you set the different messages to be displayed, as illustrated in Figure 5.52.

IMG Access Path	PERSONNEL MANAGEMENT • EMPLOYEE SELF-SERVICE • SERVICE SPECIFIC SETTINGS • WORKING TIME • CLOCK-IN/OUT CORRECTIONS • LAYOUT OF THE WEB APPLICATION • DEFINE MESSAGES TO BE DISPLAYED

IMG Activity	PCUI_ESS_TIMCOR_004
Transaction Code	S_PLN_62000021
Table Name	V_T555E

The system generates quite a few messages, so to avoid an overflow for the end user, you decide which messages are relevant for display.

You list the different messages to be displayed along with the following information:

► MAIL: The MAIL indicator communicates errors to the end users. Enter indicator "1" to trigger once the error message notification to the end user.

Caution

According to SAP documentation:

> The SAP system downloads a mail indicator to the subsystem regardless of whether you enter one in this field. If the field is blank or contains a 0, the system downloads mail indicator 0 to the subsystem.

See SAP Note 87232—Mail Indicator When Downloading KK1 for more information on this default setting.

► LIST ID: In this example, we have set the most logical display indicator "3," which means that the message is displayed as an error for the employee in the clock-in/out corrections application. Alternatively, you can also set the indicator to "1" to interpret the message as an error for the administrator, or "2" to direct the message at the person responsible for IT. The administrator merely receives a note to the effect that a message of this type has occurred.

Tip

You can use the report RPTERR00—Time Management: Error Handling to query these entries.

► BALANCE: If you enter a balance indicator when an error occurs, then the balance displayed at the time recording terminal (PDC) is deleted.

► GENERATE ONCE: If flagged, it advise the system to only process the message once, even if time evaluation is recalculated.

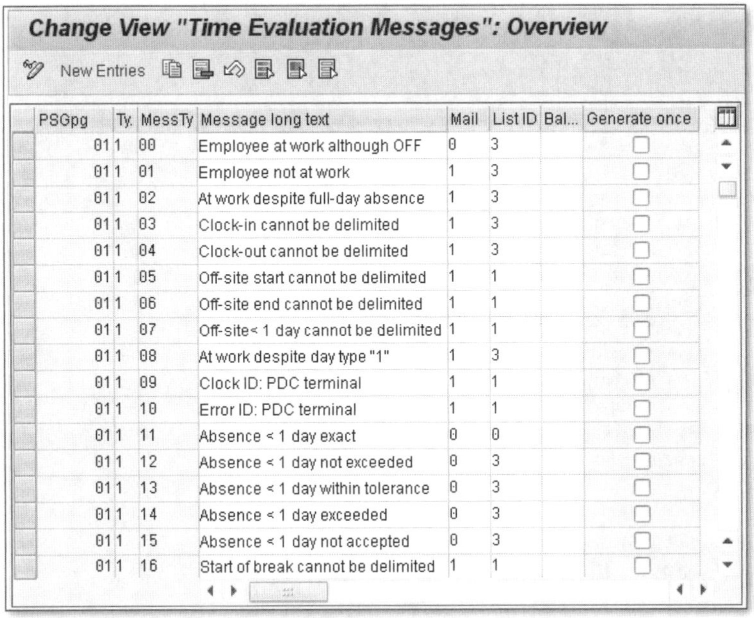

PSGpg	Ty.	MessTy	Message long text	Mail	List ID	Bal...	Generate once
01	1	00	Employee at work although OFF	0	3		☐
01	1	01	Employee not at work	1	3		☐
01	1	02	At work despite full-day absence	1	3		☐
01	1	03	Clock-in cannot be delimited	1	3		☐
01	1	04	Clock-out cannot be delimited	1	3		☐
01	1	05	Off-site start cannot be delimited	1	1		☐
01	1	06	Off-site end cannot be delimited	1	1		☐
01	1	07	Off-site< 1 day cannot be delimited	1	1		☐
01	1	08	At work despite day type "1"	1	3		☐
01	1	09	Clock ID: PDC terminal	1	1		☐
01	1	10	Error ID: PDC terminal	1	1		☐
01	1	11	Absence < 1 day exact	0	0		☐
01	1	12	Absence < 1 day not exceeded	0	3		☐
01	1	13	Absence < 1 day within tolerance	0	3		☐
01	1	14	Absence < 1 day exceeded	0	3		☐
01	1	15	Absence < 1 day not accepted	0	3		☐
01	1	16	Start of break cannot be delimited	1	1		☐

Figure 5.52 Define Messages to Be Displayed

Check Time Balances to Be Displayed

Employees can view their time balances by checking the balance overview in the SAP NetWeaver Portal, so in this configuration step, you tell the system whether or not the time balances specified for download to the terminal are also suitable for the clock-in/out corrections process (see Figure 5.53).

IMG Access Path	Personnel Management • Employee Self-Service • Service Specific Settings • Working Time • Clock-In/Out Corrections • Layout of the Web Application • Check Time Balances to Be Displayed
IMG Activity	PCUI_ESS_TIMCOR_005
Transaction Code	S_PLN_62000022
Table Name	V_T555I

You adjust the information field with one of the values such as "DATE" (date of the last day for which payroll was run) or the quota information. You also can let the system convert the hours into minutes if the Hrs-min box is ticked.

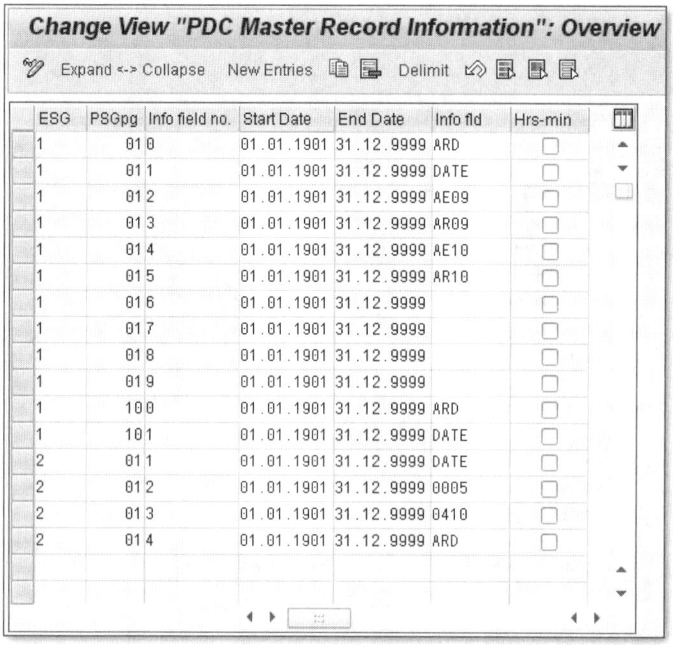

ESG	PSGpg	Info field no.	Start Date	End Date	Info fld	Hrs-min
1	01	0	01.01.1901	31.12.9999	ARD	☐
1	01	1	01.01.1901	31.12.9999	DATE	☐
1	01	2	01.01.1901	31.12.9999	AE09	☐
1	01	3	01.01.1901	31.12.9999	AR09	☐
1	01	4	01.01.1901	31.12.9999	AE10	☐
1	01	5	01.01.1901	31.12.9999	AR10	☐
1	01	6	01.01.1901	31.12.9999		☐
1	01	7	01.01.1901	31.12.9999		☐
1	01	8	01.01.1901	31.12.9999		☐
1	01	9	01.01.1901	31.12.9999		☐
1	10	0	01.01.1901	31.12.9999	ARD	☐
1	10	1	01.01.1901	31.12.9999	DATE	☐
2	01	1	01.01.1901	31.12.9999	DATE	☐
2	01	2	01.01.1901	31.12.9999	0005	☐
2	01	3	01.01.1901	31.12.9999	0410	☐
2	01	4	01.01.1901	31.12.9999	ARD	☐

Figure 5.53 Check Time Balances to Be Displayed

5.6.3 Business Add-Ins (BAdIs)

As always, throughout the system, SAP provides BAdIs to enhance the standard functionality. In the clock-in/out process, you can take advantage of the two BAdIs listed in the following subsections. These BAdIs can help you meet the business requirements if not all of them are met in standard. However, it would require the support of a developer.

IMG Access Path	Personnel Management • Employee Self-Service • Service Specific Settings • Working Time • Clock-In/Out Corrections • Business Add-Ins

BAdIs can be accessed through Transaction SE18—Business Add-Ins: Definitions, or directly from the customizing. The class and the method can be viewed using Transaction SE24—Class Builder.

BAdI: Control Processing Processes for Time Management Web Applications

This BAdI contains additional coding regarding the handling of the controls operated in the UI when processing the clock-in/out process. It is a placeholder for further programming to adjust the system behavior per the user requirements.

IMG Access Path	PERSONNEL MANAGEMENT • EMPLOYEE SELF-SERVICE • SERVICE SPECIFIC SETTINGS • WORKING TIME • CLOCK-IN/OUT CORRECTIONS • BUSINESS ADD-INS • BADI: CONTROL PROCESSING PROCESSES FOR TIME MANAGEMENT WEB APPLICATIONS
IMG Activity	PCUI_ESS_TIMCOR_006
Transaction Code	S_PLN_62000023
BAdI Name	PT_GEN_RE—BAdI: Control Processing Processes for Web Applications
Class	CL_DEF_IM_PT_GEN_REQ
Methods	▶ IF_EX_PT_GEN_REQ~CHECK_IF_ACTOR_ABSENT: Check Whether an Employee Is Absent ▶ IF_EX_PT_GEN_REQ~GET_ACTOR_SUBSTITUTES: Read Substitute ▶ IF_EX_PT_GEN_REQ~SEARCH_FOR_NEXT_PROCESSOR: Find Next Agent ▶ IF_EX_PT_GEN_REQ~CHECK_SELECTED_NEXT_PROCESSOR: Check Selected Agent ▶ IF_EX_PT_GEN_REQ~FIND_RESP_AND_DEFAULT_NEXT_PRC: Determine Default Approver and Supervisor for Employee ▶ IF_EX_PT_GEN_REQ~START_WF: Start Workflow ▶ IF_EX_PT_GEN_REQ~GET_EMPLOYEE_COMMUNICATION: Determine Email Address ▶ IF_EX_PT_GEN_REQ~GET_ADMINS: Get Table with Email Lists ▶ IF_EX_PT_GEN_REQ~FILTER_NEXT_PROCESSOR: Filter Next Agent ▶ IF_EX_PT_GEN_REQ~MODIFY_APPLICATION_MESSAGES: Change Messages from Backend System

BAdI: Control Clock-In/Out Corrections

This BAdI contains additional coding regarding the handling of the controls operated in the processing of the clock-in/out process. It is a placeholder for further programming to adjust the system behavior per the user requirements.

IMG Access Path	PERSONNEL MANAGEMENT • EMPLOYEE SELF-SERVICE • SERVICE SPECIFIC SETTINGS • WORKING TIME • CLOCK-IN/OUT CORRECTIONS • BUSINESS ADD-INS • BADI: CONTROL CLOCK-IN/OUT CORRECTIONS
IMG Activity	PCUI_ESS_TIMCOR_010
Transaction Code	S_PLN_62000278
BAdI Name	PT_COR_REQ—Enhancements for Clock-In/Out Corrections
Class	CL_DEF_IM_PT_COR_REQ
Methods	▸ IF_EX_PT_COR_REQ~SIMULATE_VIA_BLOP: Simulate Clock-In/Out Corrections with BLP
	▸ IF_EX_PT_COR_REQ~POST_VIA_BLOP: Post Clock-In/Out Corrections with BLP
	▸ IF_EX_PT_COR_REQ~CHECK_TIME_CONSTRAINTS: Check Dates of Request

5.7 Working Time: Time Statement

Along with the payslip, the time statement is an important employee document to review employee locations and time entries at work. The time statement not only provides the current or past information but also an opportunity to become more sustainable. Providing the time statement in a PDF saves paper and money.

IMG Access Path	PERSONNEL MANAGEMENT • EMPLOYEE SELF-SERVICE • SERVICE SPECIFIC SETTINGS • WORKING TIME • TIME STATEMENT

SAP provides two services:

▸ EMPLOYEE_WORKTIME_TIMESTATEMENTPER: Time Statement

▸ EMPLOYEE_WORKTIME_TIMESTATEMENT: Time Statement with Freely Definable Period

Bear in mind that accessing the time statement also requires authorization for the object P_PCLX HR: Clusters and the cluster B2 for time information.

5.7.1 Enter the Name of HR Form for Time Statement

Although this configuration is part of the Time Management component, when it comes to the self-services, you have to set the name of the HR form to be used for the time statement. This piece of information is set in an HR feature: HRFOR HR Forms. This is a decision tree that we have already covered in previous sections. As a return value, the name of the form is set in the feature directly, as illustrated in Figure 5.54, with report category T for Time.

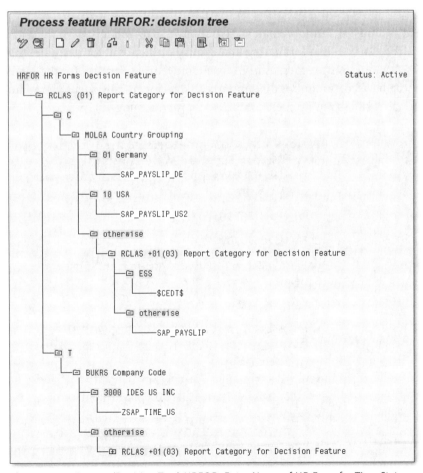

Figure 5.54 Feature (Decision Tree) HRFOR: Enter Name of HR Form for Time Statement

IMG Access Path	PERSONNEL MANAGEMENT • EMPLOYEE SELF-SERVICE • SERVICE SPECIFIC SETTINGS • WORKING TIME • TIME STATEMENT • ENTER NAME OF HR FORM FOR TIME STATEMENT
IMG Activity	PCUI_ESS_TMSTMT_003
Transaction Code	S_FAD_62000074 or PE03
Feature Name	HRFOR

Do not forget to activate the feature after it has been adjusted.

5.7.2 BAdI: Make Settings for Time Statement

If you need to adjust the time statement layout or the data rendering on the time statement form, such as the formatting and display of the total, for example, the BAdI XSS_TIM_PER_INT Business Add-In for Employee Self-Services for the Time Statement can be used. It requires the support of a developer, however, to translate the additional business requirements into ABAP programming.

IMG Access Path	PERSONNEL MANAGEMENT • EMPLOYEE SELF-SERVICE • SERVICE SPECIFIC SETTINGS • WORKING TIME • TIME STATEMENT • BUSINESS ADD-INS • BADI: MAKE SETTINGS FOR TIME STATEMENT
IMG Activity	PCUI_ESS_TMSTMT_001
Transaction Code	S_FAD_62000070
BAdI Name	XSS_TIM_PER_INT—Business Add-In for ESS Time Statement
Class	CL_EX_XSS_TIM_PER_INT
Methods	▶ IF_EX_XSS_TIM_PER_INTERFACE~PROVIDE_OVERVIEW_LINE: Public Formatting of a Row in the Overview Table ▶ IF_EX_XSS_TIM_PER_INTERFACE~PROVIDE_DROPDOWN_ENTRIES: Fill Dropdown List Box ▶ IF_EX_XSS_TIM_PER_INTERFACE~PROVIDE_OVERVIEWTAB_FIELDCAT: Field Catalog for Overview Table

> - IF_EX_XSS_TIM_PER_INTERFACE~PROVIDE_PERIOD_
>   TABLE: Create Table of All Periods That Can Be
>   Displayed
> - IF_EX_XSS_TIM_PER_INTERFACE~PROVIDE_DEFAULT_
>   DATE_RANGE: Default Value for Display of Date

Based on past project implementations, you should walk through SAP Note 897623, which provides an overview of all the BAdIs in the Personnel Time Management area.

SAP Note 897623—User Exits and BADIs in the PT Area

This SAP Note contains all the enhancements for Personnel Time Management. It's a must have and a must read to fully comprehend the product's capabilities to meet business requirements.

5.8   Benefits and Payments: Semiretirement Simulation

Most companies provide benefits and payments to their personnel. The following sections describe the configuration for enabling benefits and displaying payments results in ESS.

Some of the configuration provided here might not be relevant for all countries because some of the implementation steps are, for example, specific to Germany or the United States.

Before enabling the semiretirement simulation, you have to meet some prerequisites in the system:

- The HR Funds and Position Management (PM) simulation code in the feature Determine Payroll Program Variant for Payroll Simulation (PM004) must be in use.

- The payroll report RPCALCXX (XX standing for your country, for example, RPCALCB0 for Belgium) must be called and use the report variant FPM0001.

- Decision tree DAT01—Default Value for Semiretirement InfoType must be set up and active.

IMG Access Path	PERSONNEL MANAGEMENT • EMPLOYEE SELF-SERVICE • SERVICE SPECIFIC SETTINGS • BENEFITS AND PAYMENT • SEMIRETIREMENT SIMULATION

5.8.1　Set Up a Semiretirement Model

As illustrated in Figure 5.55, when you create a name for the semiretirement model, make sure you abide by the naming convention of the customer or of the legal requirements.

IMG Access Path	PERSONNEL MANAGEMENT • EMPLOYEE SELF-SERVICE • SERVICE SPECIFIC SETTINGS • BENEFITS AND PAYMENT • SEMIRETIREMENT SIMULATION • SET UP SEMIRETIREMENT MODEL
IMG Activity	PAY_DE_AT_010
Transaction Code	S_PH9_46000001
Table Name	V_T5DA1

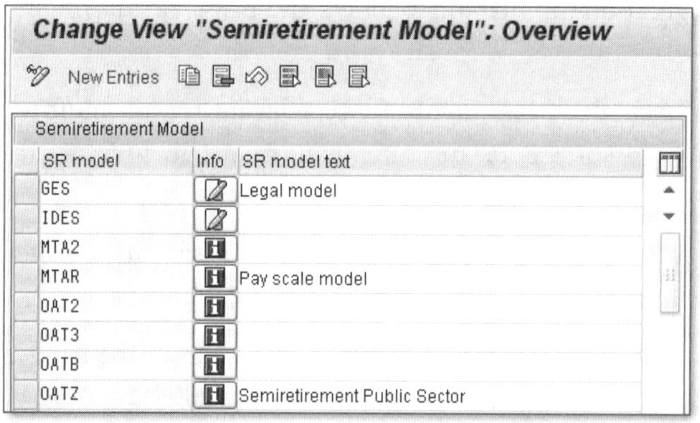

Figure 5.55　Set Semiretirement Model

As illustrated in Figure 5.56, you set the different attributes for the semiretirement plans that you have created. These attributes are provided by the business team or the legal documentation. In this example, we have chosen the "GES" — LEGAL MODEL.

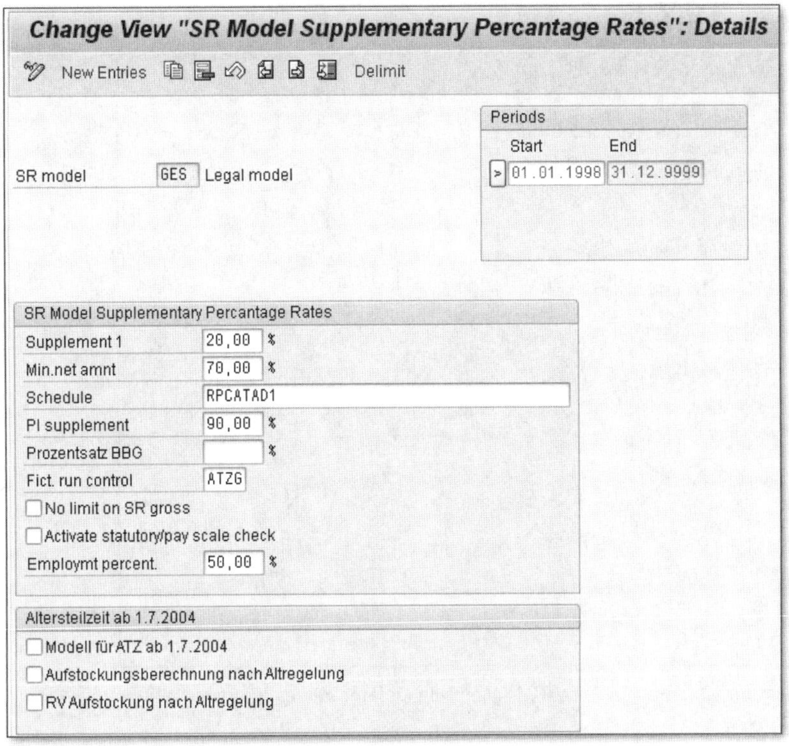

Figure 5.56 Semiretirement Model: Supplementary Percentage Rates

5.8.2 Maintain Default Values for Semiretirement InfoType (Germany)

In the Semiretirement InfoType (0521), you can allocate a semiretirement model and specify the semiretirement phase in which the employee belongs.

IMG Access Path	PERSONNEL MANAGEMENT • EMPLOYEE SELF-SERVICE • SERVICE SPECIFIC SETTINGS • BENEFITS AND PAYMENT • SEMIRETIREMENT SIMULATION • MAINTAIN DEFAULT VALUES FOR SEMIRETIREMENT INFOTYPE (GERMANY)
IMG Activity	PAY_DE_AT_050
Transaction Code	S_PH9_46000603 or PE03
Feature Name	DAT01—DEFAULT VALUE FOR SEMI-RETIREMENT INFOTYPE

The feature DAT01—DEFAULT VALUE FOR SEMI-RETIREMENT INFOTYPE, as illustrated in Figure 5.57, provides the default values to be returned by the system.

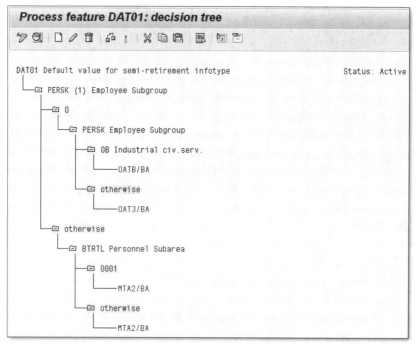

Figure 5.57 Feature (Decision Tree) DAT01: Maintain Default Values for Semi-Retirement InfoType (Germany)

5.8.3 Enter Variant for Payroll Program

This configuration step, as illustrated in Figure 5.58, determines the simulation variant to be used in the payroll program (program RPCALCXX; XX stands for your country).

IMG Access Path	Personnel Management • Employee Self-Service • Service Specific Settings • Benefits and Payment • Semiretirement Simulation • Enter Variant for Payroll Program
IMG Activity	PCUI_ESS_PAPADE_PY02
Transaction Code	S_P3H_97000001 or PE03
Feature Name	PM004—Determining the Simulation Variant for the Payroll Program

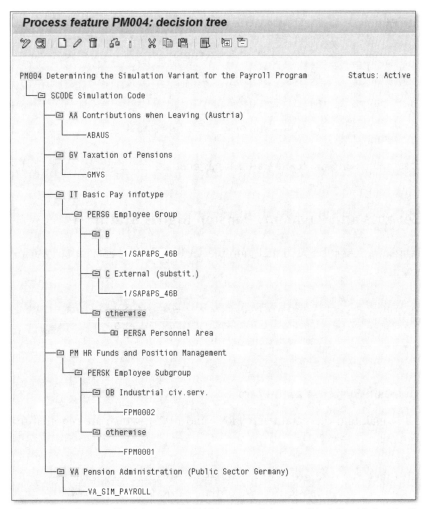

Figure 5.58 Feature (Decision Tree) PM004: Determining the Simulation Variant for the Payroll Program

5.8.4 Enter HR Form Name

This piece of information is also set in an HR feature (as you have seen in previous configuration steps): HRFOR HR Forms Decision feature. As a return value, the name of the form is set in the feature.

IMG Access Path	PERSONNEL MANAGEMENT • EMPLOYEE SELF-SERVICE • SERVICE SPECIFIC SETTINGS • BENEFITS AND PAYMENT • SEMIRETIREMENT SIMULATION • ENTER HR FORM NAME
IMG Activity	PCUI_ESS_PAPADE_PY01
Transaction Code	S_PLN_62000458
Feature Name	HRFOR—HR FORMS DECISION FEATURE

Do not forget to activate the feature after it has been adjusted.

5.9   Benefits and Payment: Pension Rights Status

In this configuration section, you maintain the settings for the ESS scenario Value of Entitlements.

IMG Access Path	PERSONNEL MANAGEMENT • EMPLOYEE SELF-SERVICE • SERVICE SPECIFIC SETTINGS • BENEFITS AND PAYMENT • PENSION RIGHT STATUS

5.9.1   Maintain System Parameters

You must first maintain the parameters PRNT and BWST, which are required for the ESS scenario.

IMG Access Path	PERSONNEL MANAGEMENT • EMPLOYEE SELF-SERVICE • SERVICE SPECIFIC SETTINGS • BENEFITS AND PAYMENT • PENSION RIGHT STATUS • MAINTAIN SYSTEM PARAMETERS CPS
IMG Activity	OHADBAV000C
Transaction Code	S_L9C_94000137
Table Name	V_5DCY_A

As illustrated in Figure 5.59, you add the required entries here.

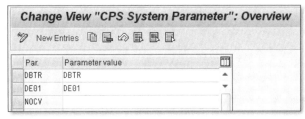

Figure 5.59 Maintain System Parameters Company Pension Scheme (CPS)

5.9.2 Statements

In the statements configuration steps, you determine the system settings required for the automatic creation of statements in the customer pension scheme.

IMG Access Path	PERSONNEL MANAGEMENT • EMPLOYEE SELF-SERVICE • SERVICE SPECIFIC SETTINGS • BENEFITS AND PAYMENT • PENSION RIGHT STATUS • STATEMENTS

Set Up Functional Areas

You choose the country grouping, and then maintain the required functional areas for further customizing steps.

IMG Access Path	PERSONNEL MANAGEMENT • EMPLOYEE SELF-SERVICE • SERVICE SPECIFIC SETTINGS • BENEFITS AND PAYMENT • PENSION RIGHT STATUS • STATEMENTS • GENERAL SETTINGS • SET UP FUNCTIONAL AREA
IMG Activity	OHADBAV920
Transaction Code	S_PH0_48000019
Table Name	V_T5DF5

As illustrated in Figure 5.60, check and maintain the relevant functional areas for the statements.

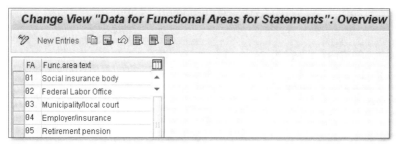

Figure 5.60 Set Up Functional Areas

Assign First Signatory

In this configuration step, you list the first signatories with their contact details. This table looks similar to the administrators table (table T526) in InfoType 0001 — Organizational Assignment.

IMG Access Path	PERSONNEL MANAGEMENT • EMPLOYEE SELF-SERVICE • SERVICE SPECIFIC SETTINGS • BENEFITS AND PAYMENT • PENSION RIGHT STATUS • STATEMENTS • GENERAL SETTINGS • ASSIGN FIRST SIGNATORY
IMG Activity	OHADBAV925
Transaction Code	S_PH0_48000024
Table Name	T522G

Figure 5.61 illustrates the assignment of the first signatory for the documents.

Change View "First Signatory for Statements": Overview

New Entries

User	Long text	Name	Tel.no.	
KNOLLA	Mrs	Astrid Rosbach	1234567	
LIMPERT	Mrs	Susanne Limpert	31 22	
MAGIL		Martin Gillet	026746611	
PILCHW	Mrs	Walburga Pilch	06227 7 4567	

Figure 5.61 Assign First Signatory

Assign Second Signatory

In this configuration step, you list the second signatories with their contact details.

IMG Access Path	PERSONNEL MANAGEMENT • EMPLOYEE SELF-SERVICE • SERVICE SPECIFIC SETTINGS • BENEFITS AND PAYMENT • PENSION RIGHT STATUS • STATEMENTS • GENERAL SETTINGS • ASSIGN SECOND SIGNATORY
IMG Activity	OHADBAV926
Transaction Code	S_PH0_48000083
Table Name	V_513A_D

Figure 5.62 illustrates the assignment of the second signatory for the documents.

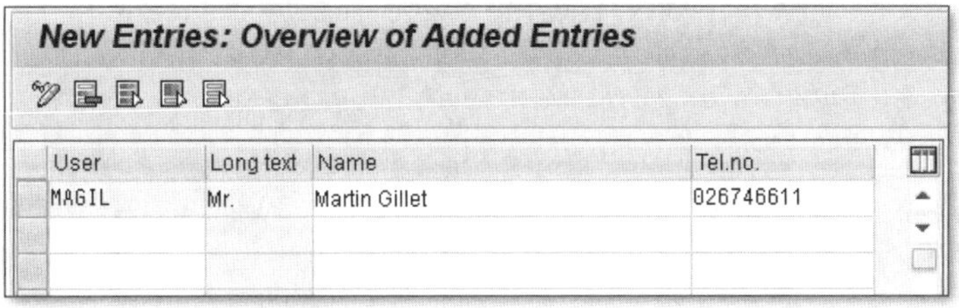

Figure 5.62 Assign Second Signatory

Archiving

Thanks to Transaction SARA—Archive Administration, you can store most statements from HR for each employee. SAP standard optical archiving can be used to meet this requirement.

The standard object type CERTIFPAYD and the document type HROBWFORM have been provided to archive the statements.

SAP Enhancements

As always, SAP provides several enhancements to improve the standard functionalities. The following section describes the options available for further configuration.

Set Up Statement Types

The data used in a pension calculation run is classified by the statement type and is stored in a cluster. In the standard system, SAP provides the following models:

► P0 Application form without data

► P1 Individual pension

► P2 Surviving dependants' pension

► P3 Pension entitlement

► P4 Pension adjustment

► P5 Vested entitlement

► P6 Reimbursement

► P7 Invalidity pension

IMG Access Path	PERSONNEL MANAGEMENT • EMPLOYEE SELF-SERVICE • SERVICE SPECIFIC SETTINGS • BENEFITS AND PAYMENT • PENSION RIGHT STATUS • STATEMENTS • SAP ENHANCEMENTS • SET UP STATEMENT TYPES
IMG Activity	OHADBAV945
Transaction Code	S_PH0_48000041
Table Name	V_5DC7_E

Adjust or copy the relevant entries per the business requirements.

Figure 5.63 illustrates the setting up of the statement types.

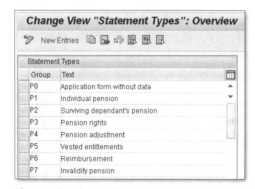

Figure 5.63 Set Up Statement Types

Set Up Statement Tables

As illustrated in Figure 5.64, you can identify which statement tables can be used when statements are based on a form.

Table	Info	Name for permitted tables	Type	St.ID	
P0000	H	Actions	*	☐	▲
P0001	H	Organizational assignment	*	☐	▼
P0002	H	Personal data	*	☐	
P0006	H	Addresses	*	☐	
P0007	H	Planned working time		☐	
P0008	H	Basic pay	*	☐	
P0009	H	Bank details	*	☐	
P0010	H	Capital formation		☐	
P0012	H	Tax data		☐	
P0013	H	Social insurance		☐	
P0020	H	DEUEV		☐	
P0029	H	Workers' compensation association		☐	
P0041	H	Date specifications	*	☐	
P0049	H	Reduced hours / winter compensation		☐	
P0051	H	PSG: ASI/SPF data		☐	
P0079	H	Supplementary social insurance		☐	
P0111	H	Garnishment/Cession D		☐	
P01CCV	H	Cyclical pension rights	B	☐	
P01C_AVB...	H		B	☐	
P01C_BAL...	H	Surviving dependant payments and difference amounts	B	☐	
P01C_BBA...	H		B	☐	
P01C_BCT...	H	Processing information	B	☐	
P01C_BDA...	H	Vested payments	B	☐	
P01C_BDA...	H	Vested entitlements	B	☐	
P01C_BFA...	H	Family members and dependants	B	☐	
P01C_BKA...	H	Funded pension rights	B	☐	
P01C_BMA...	H	General employee data	B	☐	
P01C_BRC...	H	Calculated reimbursements	B	☐	
P01C_BRE...	H	Pension until leaving date	B	☐	▲
P01C_BRE...	H	Data for proportional reduction	B	☐	▼

Figure 5.64 Set Up Statement Tables

IMG Access Path	PERSONNEL MANAGEMENT • EMPLOYEE SELF-SERVICE • SERVICE SPECIFIC SETTINGS • BENEFITS AND PAYMENT • PENSION RIGHT STATUS • STATEMENTS • SAP ENHANCEMENTS • SET UP STATEMENT TABLES
IMG Activity	OHADBAV950

Transaction Code	S_PH0_48000004
Table Name	V_T5DF9

If required, customer statement tables that are needed when printing the form must be specified here. You can use the standard entries provided by SAP for inspiration. SAP delivers the following model entries for the company pension scheme (CPS):

- ▶ Statement tables in statement cluster
  - ▶ P01C_BALLA Surviving dependants' pensions and difference amounts
  - ▶ P01C_BCTRL Processing information
  - ▶ P01C_BDAGP Vested payments
  - ▶ P01C_BDAUA Vested entitlements
  - ▶ P01C_BFAMI Family dependants and surviving dependants
  - ▶ P01C_BKAAN Capitalized entitlements
  - ▶ P01C_BMADA General employer data
  - ▶ P01C_BRCAL Calculated reimbursements
  - ▶ P01C_BREBA Pension until leaving date
  - ▶ P01C_BREMN Data for proportional reduction
  - ▶ P01C_BRERE Pension from basic pension payments
  - ▶ P01C_BREZW Pension increase
  - ▶ P01C_BRPAY Effected reimbursements
  - ▶ P01C_BZUAB Payments/deductions
- ▶ InfoTypes
  - ▶ P0000 Actions
  - ▶ P0001 Organizational Assignment
  - ▶ P0002 Personal Data
  - ▶ P0006 Addresses
  - ▶ P0009 Bank Details
  - ▶ P0041 Date Specifications

- ▶ Other tables
  - ▶ LADRS Address of benefits provider
  - ▶ OADRS Address of enterprise
  - ▶ OADRS1 Enterprise data
  - ▶ PADRS Address of employee
  - ▶ SACHP Administrator

Set Up Statement Functions

Statement functions enable the customer to change the process flow of the statement driver. Within the customer include RPCAVZD0, you can adjust the process flow. Figure 5.65 illustrates the standard entries when determining the statement functions.

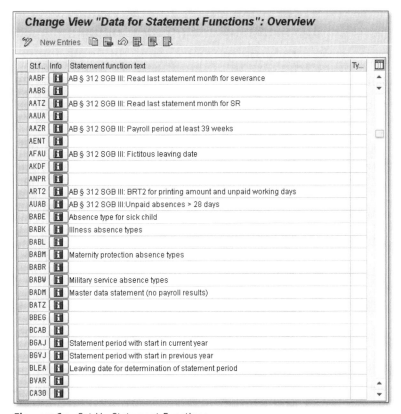

Figure 5.65   Set Up Statement Functions

IMG Access Path	PERSONNEL MANAGEMENT • EMPLOYEE SELF-SERVICE • SERVICE SPECIFIC SETTINGS • BENEFITS AND PAYMENT • PENSION RIGHT STATUS • STATEMENTS • SAP ENHANCEMENTS • SET UP STATEMENT FUNCTIONS
IMG Activity	OHADBAV955
Transaction Code	S_PH0_48000043
Table Name	V_T5DF8

Set Up Statements

In these configuration steps, you create the attributes of the statements, also known as the form identifier.

IMG Access Path	PERSONNEL MANAGEMENT • EMPLOYEE SELF-SERVICE • SERVICE SPECIFIC SETTINGS • BENEFITS AND PAYMENT • PENSION RIGHT STATUS • STATEMENTS • SET UP STATEMENTS

Maintain Standard Texts

In this configuration step, you set up the different standard texts to be used in the statements.

IMG Access Path	PERSONNEL MANAGEMENT • EMPLOYEE SELF-SERVICE • SERVICE SPECIFIC SETTINGS • BENEFITS AND PAYMENT • PENSION RIGHT STATUS • STATEMENTS • SET UP STATEMENTS • MAINTAIN STANDARD TEXTS
IMG Activity	OHADBAV972
Transaction Code	S_PH0_48000102 or SO10—SAPscript: Standard Texts

Figure 5.66 illustrates Transaction SO10 with the standard TEXT ID "PAMA" for the mail to employees and the handling of applicant master data.

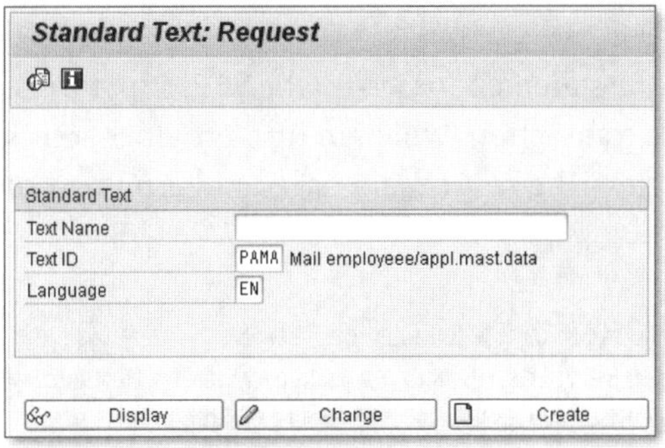

Figure 5.66 Maintain Standard Texts

Copy Statement

This configuration step is relevant for the German statements only.

IMG Access Path	Personnel Management • Employee Self-Service • Service Specific Settings • Benefits and Payment • Pension Right Status • Statements • Set Up Statements • Copy Statement
IMG Activity	OHADBAV979
Transaction Code	S_AL0_96000311 or PM22
Program Name	RPUFRMDA

This standard program is used to copy and delete the SAPscripts entries, as illustrated in Figure 5.67.

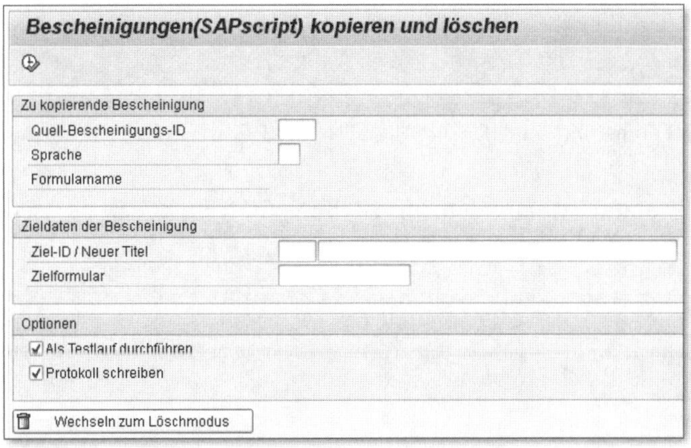

Figure 5.67 Copy Statement for German Statements

Set Up SAPscript Forms

In this configuration step you maintain the statement based on the SAPscript forms. Figure 5.68 illustrates how to access the transaction, which in turn provides access to the form attributes including the name, the source language, and a myriad of other options.

IMG Access Path	PERSONNEL MANAGEMENT • EMPLOYEE SELF-SERVICE • SERVICE SPECIFIC SETTINGS • BENEFITS AND PAYMENT • PENSION RIGHT STATUS • STATEMENTS • SET UP STATEMENTS • SET UP SAPSCRIPT FORMS
IMG Activity	OHADBAV973
Transaction Code	S_PH0_48000103 or SE71

Figure 5.68 Set Up SAPscript Forms with Sample Form HR_BEN_CONF

Figure 5.69 illustrates the standard sample form HR_BEN_CONF that can be used as a starting point when designing customer forms.

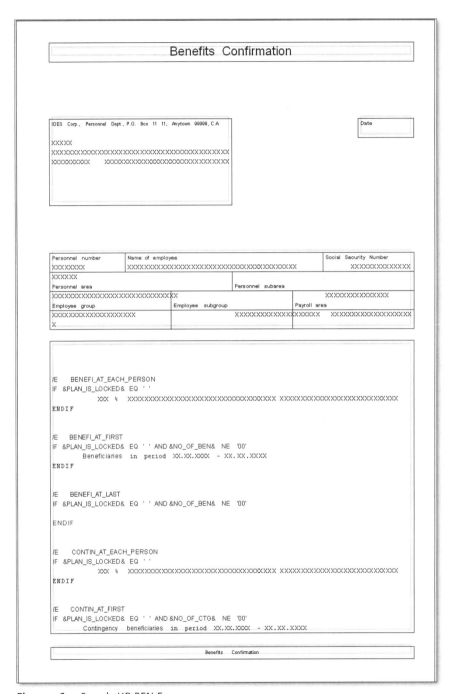

Figure 5.69 Sample HR BEN Form

Assign Standard Texts to Forms

In this configuration step, you assign the standard texts previously defined to the forms with a sample AREA BAV COMPANY PENSION SCHEME (see Figure 5.70).

IMG Access Path	PERSONNEL MANAGEMENT • EMPLOYEE SELF-SERVICE • SERVICE SPECIFIC SETTINGS • BENEFITS AND PAYMENT • PENSION RIGHT STATUS • STATEMENTS • SET UP STATEMENTS • ASSIGN STANDARD TEXTS TO FORMS
IMG Activity	OHADBAV974
Transaction Code	S_PH0_48000256
Table Name	V_T50F0_B

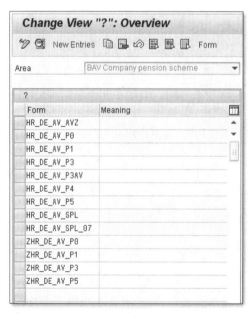

Figure 5.70 Assign Standard Texts to Forms

Set the Archiving Indicator

In this configuration step, as illustrated in Figure 5.71, you tick the box ARCHIVE to enable the archiving of the form.

IMG Access Path	PERSONNEL MANAGEMENT • EMPLOYEE SELF-SERVICE • SERVICE SPECIFIC SETTINGS • BENEFITS AND PAYMENT • PENSION RIGHT STATUS • STATEMENTS • SET UP STATEMENTS • SET ARCHIVING INDICATOR
IMG Activity	OHADBAV977
Transaction Code	S_AL0_96000312
Table Name	V_T50F0_C

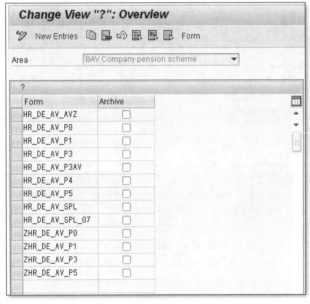

Figure 5.71 Set Archiving Indicator

Set Up Statement Parameters

In these configuration steps, you assign the different attributes configured previously on the form. Figure 5.72 illustrates the overview of the configuration table.

IMG Access Path	PERSONNEL MANAGEMENT • EMPLOYEE SELF-SERVICE • SERVICE SPECIFIC SETTINGS • BENEFITS AND PAYMENT • PENSION RIGHT STATUS • STATEMENTS • SET UP STATEMENTS • SET UP STATEMENT PARAMETERS
IMG Activity	OHADBAV975
Transaction Code	S_PH0_48000042
Table Name	V_T5DF0_B

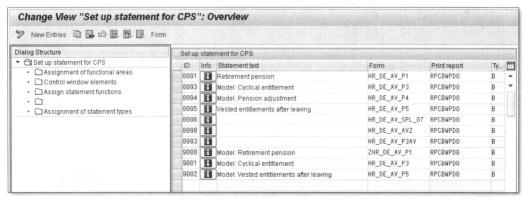

Figure 5.72 Set Up Statement Parameters for Company Pension Scheme (CPS): Overview

Figure 5.73 shows the assignment to the functional locations, Figure 5.74 shows the control of the window elements, Figure 5.75 shows the assignment of the statement functions, and Figure 5.76 shows the assignment of the assignment types.

Review the configuration in the previous steps, and review the attributes in this configuration step. You can also get inspiration from the SAP standard entries.

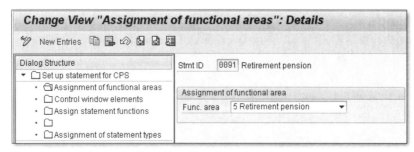

Figure 5.73 Assignment of Functional Locations

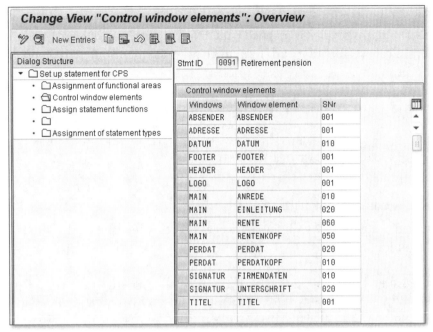

Figure 5.74   Control Window Elements

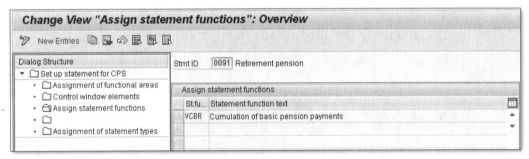

Figure 5.75   Assignment Statement Functions

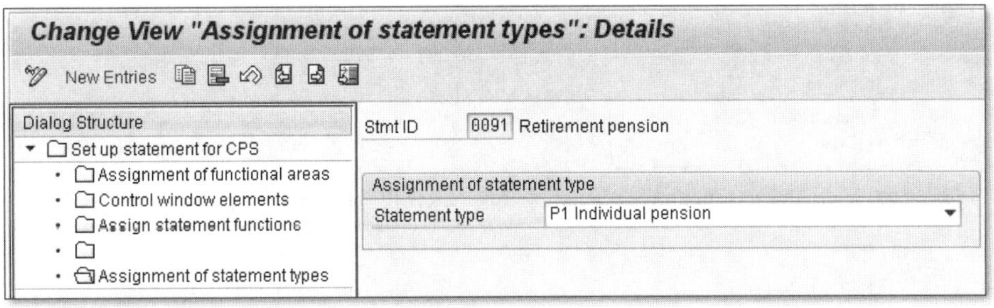

Change View "Assignment of statement types": Details

Figure 5.76   Assignment of Statement Types

Form Printing for Several Benefits Providers

If the customer pension plan is mapped with different benefits providers, you can maintain the data required for each form to be provided to the different group of people.

IMG Access Path	PERSONNEL MANAGEMENT • EMPLOYEE SELF-SERVICE • SERVICE SPECIFIC SETTINGS • BENEFITS AND PAYMENT • PENSION RIGHT STATUS • STATEMENTS • FORM PRINTING FOR SEVERAL BENEFITS PROVIDERS

Address Information for Benefits Providers

As illustrated in Figure 5.77 with the German examples, you maintain the pension organization for the CPS.

IMG Access Path	PERSONNEL MANAGEMENT • EMPLOYEE SELF-SERVICE • SERVICE SPECIFIC SETTINGS • BENEFITS AND PAYMENT • PENSION RIGHT STATUS • STATEMENTS • FORM PRINTING FOR SEVERAL BENEFITS PROVIDERS • ADDRESS INFORMATION FOR BENEFITS PROVIDERS
IMG Activity	OHADBAV984
Transaction Code	S_PH0_48000152
Table Name	V_T5DC3

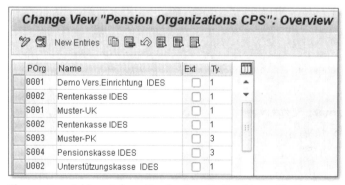

Figure 5.77 Address Information for Benefits Providers with German Examples

Statement Data for Benefits Providers

In this configuration step, as illustrated in Figure 5.78, you gather all the required information for building up the statement data for the benefits providers.

IMG Access Path	PERSONNEL MANAGEMENT • EMPLOYEE SELF-SERVICE • SERVICE SPECIFIC SETTINGS • BENEFITS AND PAYMENT • PENSION RIGHT STATUS • STATEMENTS • FORM PRINTING FOR SEVERAL BENEFITS PROVIDERS • STATEMENT DATA FOR BENEFITS PROVIDERS
IMG Activity	OHADBAV985
Transaction Code	S_PH0_48000099
Table Name	V_5DW3_2

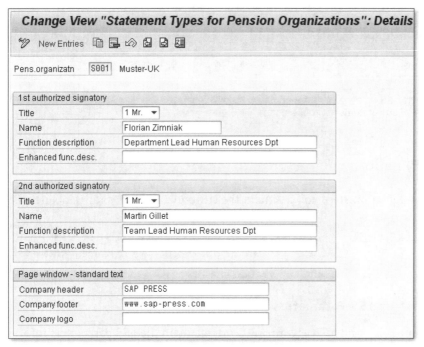

Figure 5.78 Statement Data for Benefits Providers

237

Form Statement Groups

As illustrated in Figure 5.79, you allocate the form statement groups to be used in the benefit providers process.

IMG Access Path	PERSONNEL MANAGEMENT • EMPLOYEE SELF-SERVICE • SERVICE SPECIFIC SETTINGS • BENEFITS AND PAYMENT • PENSION RIGHT STATUS • STATEMENTS • FORM PRINTING FOR SEVERAL BENEFITS PROVIDERS • FORM STATEMENT GROUPS
IMG Activity	OHADBAV995
Transaction Code	S_PH0_48000046
Table Name	V_T5DWS

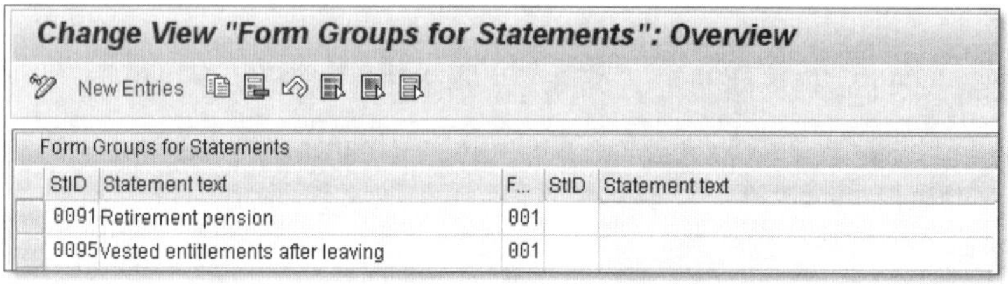

Change View "Form Groups for Statements": Overview

New Entries

Form Groups for Statements

StID	Statement text	F...	StID	Statement text
0091	Retirement pension	001		
0095	Vested entitlements after leaving	001		

Figure 5.79 Form Statement Groups

5.10 Benefits

In this configuration step, you maintain the customizing entries for the benefits.

IMG Access Path	PERSONNEL MANAGEMENT • EMPLOYEE SELF-SERVICE • SERVICE SPECIFIC SETTINGS • BENEFITS AND PAYMENT • BENEFITS

5.10.1 Set Up ESS Parameters

In this step, as illustrated in Figure 5.80, you maintain the ESS parameters for the benefits. This configuration step gathers the attributes for the benefits entry. The example illustrated shows the BENEFIT AREA "10" USA, which is a placeholder to hold different configuration options such as payroll simulation as ESS and the control parameters for the display rendering.

IMG Access Path	PERSONNEL MANAGEMENT • EMPLOYEE SELF-SERVICE • SERVICE SPECIFIC SETTINGS • BENEFITS AND PAYMENT • BENEFITS • SET UP ESS PARAMETERS
IMG Activity	PCUI_ESS_BEN_PARA_01
Transaction Code	S_FAD_62000017
Table Name	V_5UB3_ESS_1

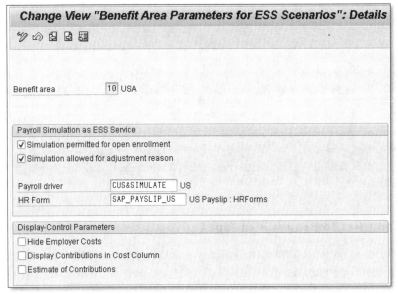

Figure 5.80 Set Up ESS Parameters (USA Example)

5.10.2 Define URLs

In this configuration step, you create the relevant entries for the URL, pointing to the different providers involved in the benefits process. For example, the provider DKV with its relevant website addresses is illustrated in Figure 5.81.

IMG Access Path	PERSONNEL MANAGEMENT • EMPLOYEE SELF-SERVICE • SERVICE SPECIFIC SETTINGS • BENEFITS AND PAYMENT • BENEFITS • DEFINE URLs
IMG Activity	PCUI_ESS_BEN_URLS_01
Transaction Code	S_FAD_62000018
Table Name	V_T74HP

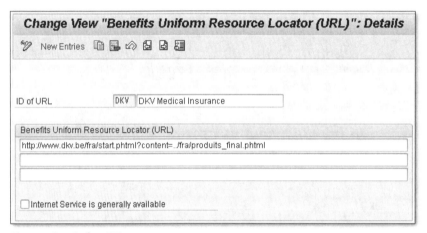

Figure 5.81 Define URLs

5.10.3 Assign URLs to Benefit Plan Types

In this configuration step, you map the URLs previously created into the benefit plans, as illustrated in Figure 5.82.

IMG Access Path	PERSONNEL MANAGEMENT • EMPLOYEE SELF-SERVICE • SERVICE SPECIFIC SETTINGS • BENEFITS AND PAYMENT • BENEFITS • ASSIGN URLs TO BENEFIT PLAN TYPES
IMG Activity	PCUI_ESS_BEN_URLS_02
Transaction Code	S_FAD_62000019
Table Name	V_5UB1_ESS

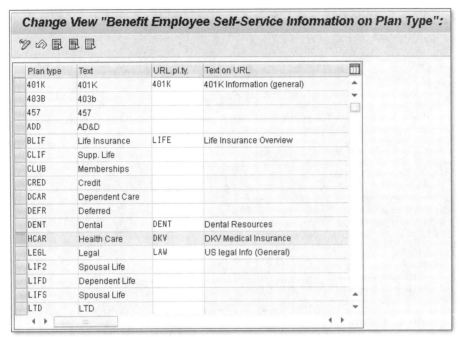

Figure 5.82 Assign URLs to Benefit Plan Types

5.10.4 Assign URLs to Benefit Plans

As illustrated in Figure 5.83, you assign the URLs previously created to the benefit plans.

IMG Access Path	PERSONNEL MANAGEMENT • EMPLOYEE SELF-SERVICE • SERVICE SPECIFIC SETTINGS • BENEFITS AND PAYMENT • BENEFITS • ASSIGN URLs TO BENEFIT PLANS
IMG Activity	PCUI_ESS_BEN_URLS_03
Transaction Code	S_FAD_62000020
Table Name	V_5UBA_ESS

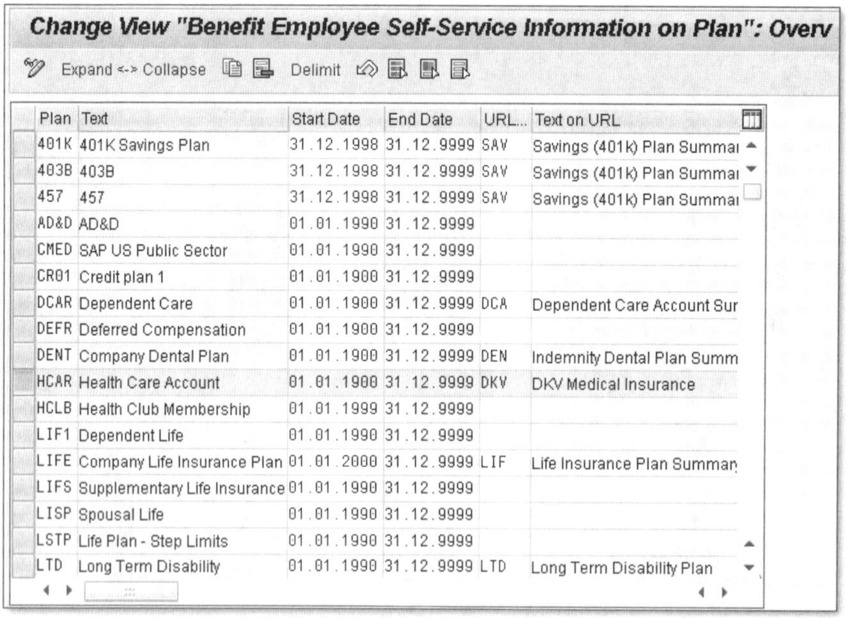

Change View "Benefit Employee Self-Service Infomation on Plan": Overv

Expand <-> Collapse Delimit

Plan	Text	Start Date	End Date	URL...	Text on URL
401K	401K Savings Plan	31.12.1998	31.12.9999	SAV	Savings (401k) Plan Summai
403B	403B	31.12.1998	31.12.9999	SAV	Savings (401k) Plan Summai
457	457	31.12.1998	31.12.9999	SAV	Savings (401k) Plan Summai
AD&D	AD&D	01.01.1990	31.12.9999		
CMED	SAP US Public Sector	01.01.1990	31.12.9999		
CR01	Credit plan 1	01.01.1900	31.12.9999		
DCAR	Dependent Care	01.01.1900	31.12.9999	DCA	Dependent Care Account Sur
DEFR	Deferred Compensation	01.01.1900	31.12.9999		
DENT	Company Dental Plan	01.01.1900	31.12.9999	DEN	Indemnity Dental Plan Summ
HCAR	Health Care Account	01.01.1900	31.12.9999	DKV	DKV Medical Insurance
HCLB	Health Club Membership	01.01.1999	31.12.9999		
LIF1	Dependent Life	01.01.1990	31.12.9999		
LIFE	Company Life Insurance Plan	01.01.2000	31.12.9999	LIF	Life Insurance Plan Summar
LIFS	Supplementary Life Insurance	01.01.1990	31.12.9999		
LISP	Spousal Life	01.01.1990	31.12.9999		
LSTP	Life Plan - Step Limits	01.01.1990	31.12.9999		
LTD	Long Term Disability	01.01.1990	31.12.9999	LTD	Long Term Disability Plan

Figure 5.83 Assign URLs to Benefit Plans

5.10.5 Assign URLs to Investments

As illustrated in Figure 5.84, you assign the URLs previously created to the investments.

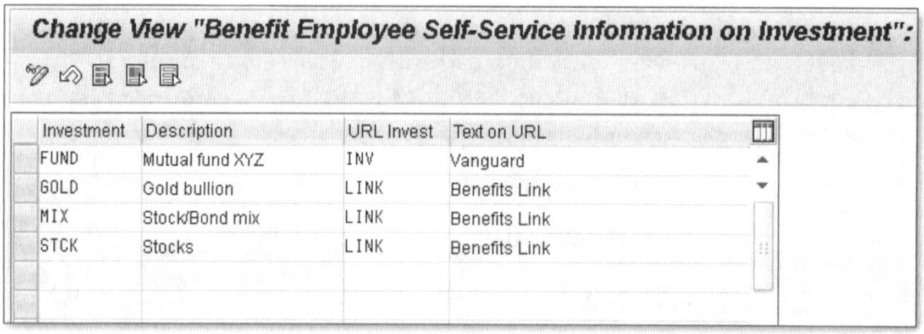

Change View "Benefit Employee Self-Service Infomation on Investment":

Investment	Description	URL Invest	Text on URL
FUND	Mutual fund XYZ	INV	Vanguard
GOLD	Gold bullion	LINK	Benefits Link
MIX	Stock/Bond mix	LINK	Benefits Link
STCK	Stocks	LINK	Benefits Link

Figure 5.84 Assign URLs to Investments

IMG Access Path	PERSONNEL MANAGEMENT • EMPLOYEE SELF-SERVICE • SERVICE SPECIFIC SETTINGS • BENEFITS AND PAYMENT • BENEFITS • ASSIGN URLS TO INVESTMENTS

IMG Activity	PCUI_ESS_BEN_URLS_04
Transaction Code	S_FAD_62000021
Table Name	V_5UBN_ESS

5.10.6 Implement Customer Enhancement for Estimating Contributions

In this configuration step, SAP provides additional flexibility thanks to BAdIs that can be used to estimate the employees' contributions. The use of this BAdI requires the support of a developer.

IMG Access Path	PERSONNEL MANAGEMENT • EMPLOYEE SELF-SERVICE • SERVICE SPECIFIC SETTINGS • BENEFITS AND PAYMENT • BENEFITS • IMPLEMENT CUSTOMER ENHANCEMENT FOR ESTIMATING CONTRIBUTIONS
IMG Activity	PCUI_ESS_BEN_BADI_01
Transaction Code	S_FAD_62000022
BAdI Name	HRBEN00ESS0001 — Benefits ESS: Customer Enhancement for Estimating Contributions
Class	CL_EX_HRBEN00ESS0001
Methods	▸ IF_EX_HRBEN00ESS0001~ESTIMATE_CONTRIBUTION_SAVING: Estimation of Contributions for Savings Plans ▸ IF_EX_HRBEN00ESS0001~ESTIMATE_CONTRIBUTION_MISCEL: Estimation of Contributions for Miscellaneous Plans ▸ IF_EX_HRBEN00ESS0001~ESTIMATE_CONTRIBUTION_STOCKP: Estimation of Contributions for Stock Purchase Plans

5.10.7 Implement Customer Enhancement for Filling the Costs and Remarks

This BAdI enables the customer to add the business requirement handling logic for filling costs and handling remarks.

IMG Access Path	PERSONNEL MANAGEMENT • EMPLOYEE SELF-SERVICE • SERVICE SPECIFIC SETTINGS • BENEFITS AND PAYMENT • BENEFITS
IMG Activity	PCUI_ESS_BEN_BADI_02
Transaction Code	S_FAD_62000023
BAdI Name	HRBEN00ESS0002 — Benefits ESS: Customer Enhancement for Filling Costs/Remarks
Class	CL_EX_HRBEN00ESS0002
Method	IF_EX_HRBEN00ESS0002~FILL_PLAN_COST_INFO: Filling of Costs and Remarks Columns

5.11   Salary Statement

When it comes to the salary statement, customers must also make the technology assessment because several options exist in the system as described in the following list. As we have plenty of options to choose from when dealing with the salaray statement and the forms in general, we must assess the in-house customer skills that we have and the rendering that we would like to provide to the end user, ranging from a basic form to the ultimate PDF (Portable Document Format) file.

▶ **Form Using HR Forms Workplace (HRFORMS)**
The first option is to use the HR forms. These template forms can be accessed through Transaction HRFORMS — HR Forms Workplace.

▶ **Form Using HR Forms Editor (PE51)**
The second option is to use Transaction PE51 — HR Form Editor, which is a bit older but still provides the requirement form online.

▶ **Former ITS service PZ11_PDF — Remuneration Statement**
If you want to create your own form, you can get inspiration from the former Internet Transaction Service PZ11_PDF — Remuneration Statement. This former service renders a nice remuneration statement into a PDF.

Alternatively, you can also point out the program RSTXPDFT4 — Converting SAPscript (OTF) or ABAP List Spool Job to PDF to your development team. This standard program converts spool requests into a PDF. This program might also inspire the developers when creating a customer form and, in this case, a remuneration statement.

IMG Access Path	PERSONNEL MANAGEMENT • EMPLOYEE SELF-SERVICE • SERVICE SPECIFIC SETTINGS • BENEFITS AND PAYMENT • SALARY STATEMENT

5.12 Own Data

The maintenance of the employee's own data is perhaps the best quick win to enable because it empowers users to maintain their personal data where relevant and appropriate.

IMG Access Path	PERSONNEL MANAGEMENT • EMPLOYEE SELF-SERVICE • SERVICE SPECIFIC SETTINGS • OWN DATA

Reaching out to employees with self-services will decrease the HR department workload and allow them to focus on more added-value tasks.

Before we get to the different configuration steps and options, let's consider some background information as well as important tables.

5.12.1 Background Information and Important Tables

Before jumping ahead into the personal employee own data, carefully review this important information concerning background and tables.

> **SAP Note 818958—ESS PersInfo Important Configuration Tables**
>
> This SAP Note is a must read because it sheds some light on the tables to be used as of SAP ERP 6.0 and SAP ERP 5.0.
>
> Many of the tables that you used to maintain with ITS are now obsolete or not supported with Web Dynpro.

SAP Note 818958 ESS PersInfo Important Configuration Tables is important. For your convenience, we have included the use of the following tables from the SAP Note:

▶ **T7XSSPERSUBTYPE**

This table is used to configure the Use Case and Time Constraint of subtypes. Subtypes that are configured in this table will be made available to the user on the Overview screen. Subtypes that are not configured in this table will not be made available to the user on the Overview screen.

Table entries for this table are predelivered.

Changes to this table only need to be made in the case of the following:

▶ Adding a previously unsupported subtype

▶ Changing the Use Case of a configured subtype

▶ Removing a standard subtype (this will have the result of records of this subtype no longer appearing on the ESS Overview screen)

> **SAP Note 818957—ESS PersInfo: Guide for Configuration of Use Cases**
>
> For detailed information on how to configure this table, refer to SAP Note 818957—ESS PersInfo: Guide for Configuration of Use Cases.

▶ **T588MFPROPS and T588MFPROPC**

These tables define properties (e.g., Required Field) of fields used in a service. These properties are used in the background at the Business Logic stage of verification (i.e., after a user clicks Next on the Detail screen); they do not control appearance or behavior of fields on the Detail screen itself.

▶ Table entries for T588MFPROPS are predelivered.

▶ Table entries in T588MFPROPC can be added for country-specific or customer-specific changes to standard behavior.

This table is *not* self-services specific.

▶ **T582ITVCHCK and T582ITVCLAS**

These tables control the verification class used by a given scenario. In other words, it points to the ABAP class where the Infotype Business Logic is stored. T582ITVCLAS is generic across an InfoType; T582ITVCHCK can be configured to a finer granularity for each InfoType and country.

This table is *not* ESS specific.

Table entries for these tables are predelivered.

▶ **T582ITVERS**

This is the entity table for InfoType versions. For a country version to be supported, the IT version (country) must be recorded in a table.

This table is *not* ESS specific.

Table entries for this table are pre-delivered.

▶ **T591A**

This table defines IT subtype characteristics. For subtypes that utilize the object id or OBJPS (i.e., the child subtype of IT0002 Family Members), it is necessary for the subtype to be flagged in this table. As this table is used for all SAP HR Master Data, it is very unlikely that a change to this table would be required.

This table is *not* ESS specific.

Table entries for this table are pre-delivered.

▶ **T588IT_SCREEN**

This table makes the assignment of UI structures to UI class. For a Personal Information service to be supported, the structure used by this service must have a corresponding UI class configured in this table.

This table is also used to configure the technical Data Dictionnary Structure (DDIC) structure used by services in the R/3-based Remote Function Calls (RFCs).

This table is *not* ESS specific.

Table entries for this table are predelivered.

Note

Only for SAP ERP 5.0: In release SAP ERP 5.0 only, table T588IT_SCREEN—Assignment of UI Structures is used.

▶ **T588UICONVCLAS**

As of SAP ERP 6.0, table T588UICONVCLAS—Assignment UI Structures and UI Conversion Classes is used instead of table T588IT_SCREEN—Assignment of UI Structures.

Thanks to SAP Communities (SDN) member Markus Klein, a detailed example of "Employee Self-Services Personal Information User Interface Enhancement Without Modification" is available as a WIKI entry:

http://wiki.sdn.sap.com/wiki/display/profile/ESS+Personal+Information+UI+enhancement+without+modification

Only as of release SAP ERP 6.0: This table replaces table T588IT_SCREEN as of release 6.0.

5.12.2 Determine Active Subtypes and Make Settings

ESS allows the employee to create, edit, or maintain the following InfoTypes:

- 0002 – Personal Data
- 0006 – Address
- 0009 – Bank Details
- 0021 – Family Members

This configuration step is country dependent (in SAP terms MOLGA dependent). In the selection popup screen, choose the country grouping first, for example, "01" for Germany.

Because each InfoType could have different subtypes, you enable the subtypes to be shown in the end user rendering.

IMG Access Path	PERSONNEL MANAGEMENT • EMPLOYEE SELF-SERVICE • SERVICE SPECIFIC SETTINGS • OWN DATA • DETERMINE ACTIVE SUBTYPES AND MAKE SETTINGS
IMG Activity	PCUI_ESS_PERSINFO1
Transaction Code	S_E34_98000018
Table Name	V_T7XSSPERSUBTY

Figure 5.85 illustrates the overview of the configuration table Determine Active Subtypes and Make Settings.

Figure 5.86 shows a detailed view of the configuration of the active subtypes and its settings. The available settings are listed here:

- VALIDITY PERIOD FOR DATA CAN BE SET: Enables a validity period for the InfoType and its subtype.

▶ NEW BUTTON ALWAYS AVAILABLE ON OVERVIEW SCREEN: Enables the NEW button on the end user screen.

▶ DATA MUST BE AVAILABLE AT ALL TIMES: Enables the mandatory existence of data at all times.

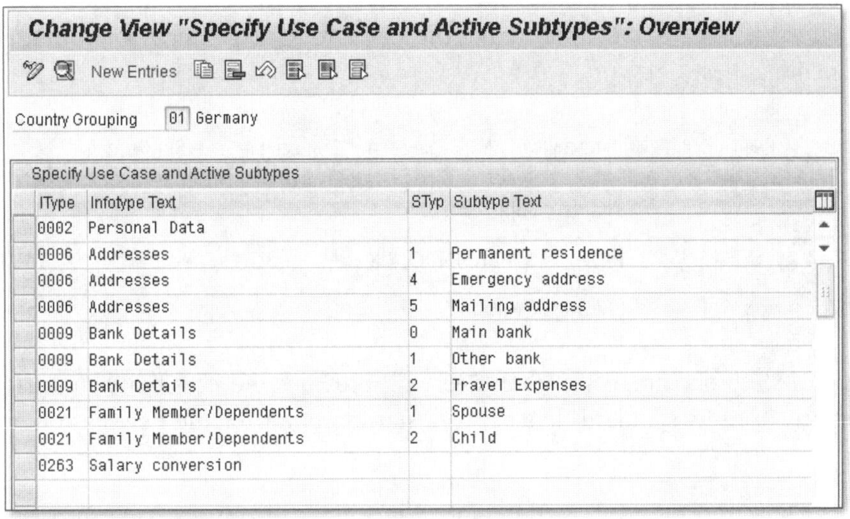

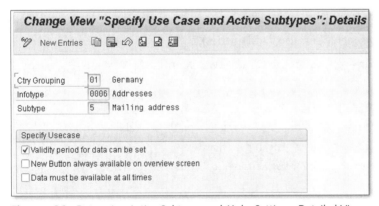

Figure 5.85 Determine Active Subtypes and Make Settings: Overview

Figure 5.86 Determine Active Subtypes and Make Settings: Detailed View

SAP Note 818957 — ESS PersInfo: Guide for Configuration of Use Cases also sheds some light on this functionality for the standard SAP ERP 6.0 release (not containing enhancement packages), featuring the standard tables V_T7XSSPERSUBTY and V_T7XSSPERSUBTYP.

5.12.3 Reuse Country-Specific Applications

SAP provides its standard functionalities for more than 30 countries. However, some countries that are not supported in the standard package might want to use such functionalities.

IMG Access Path	PERSONNEL MANAGEMENT • EMPLOYEE SELF-SERVICE • SERVICE SPECIFIC SETTINGS • OWN DATA • REUSE COUNTRY-SPECIFIC APPLICATIONS
IMG Activity	PCUI_ESS_PERSINFO_CX
Transaction Code	S_E34_98000019

To extend ESS to nonsupported countries, SAP provides the possibility to reuse applications from its standard delivery as a starting point for the new customer application.

To achieve that, you must follow these four steps:

1. Reuse the screen structure for the new country version.

2. Specify use case and active subtypes.

3. Define country-specific services (add entries).

4. Specify fields for bizcards on the OVERVIEW screen.

> **Note**
>
> Read the following SAP Notes for more information on this reusability functionality:
> ▶ Note 936179 Reuse of Country-Specific Services
> ▶ Note 953852 Best Fit Selection for Reusing Country-Specific Services

5.12.4 Change Default Start Date

In the real world, often the start date of an employee is foreseen several weeks before the actual start date. This is due mainly to the user ID and workplace allocation process. For security reasons mainly, you can set up another start date for the employee in the self-services.

IMG Access Path	PERSONNEL MANAGEMENT • EMPLOYEE SELF-SERVICE • SERVICE SPECIFIC SETTINGS • OWN DATA • CHANGE DEFAULT START DATE
IMG Activity	PCUI_ESS_PERSINFO_BD
Transaction Code	S_P7H_34000001
BAdI Name	HRXSS_PER_BEGDA—ESS: Change Default Begin Date to Customer Selected Date
Class	CL_EX_HRXSS_PER_BEGDA
Method	IF_EX_HRXSS_PER_BEGDA~DEFAULT_DATE: Determine Default Start Date

SAP provides BAdI HRXSS_PER_BEGDA to handle the ESS and its begin date based in the customer business requirements.

Customers can also take advantage of the user exit HRESSW2—HR: Check Start Date for ESS, which is used when checking the start date for employees using the self-services.

5.12.5 Determine Fields for Business Cards on the Area Page

Based on the backend configuration, you can also configure the SAP NetWeaver Portal information screens thanks to the following configuration options.

IMG Access Path	PERSONNEL MANAGEMENT • EMPLOYEE SELF-SERVICE • SERVICE SPECIFIC SETTINGS • OWN DATA • CUSTOMIZING OF PERSONAL INFORMATION SCREENS • DETERMINE FIELDS FOR BUSINESS CARD ON AREA PAGE
IMG Activity	PCUI_ESS_PERSINFO_BC
Transaction Code	S_AER_95000338
Table Name	V_T7XSSPERBIZFLC

In this configuration step, as illustrated in Figure 5.87, you specify the fields for the bizcard displayed on the ESS personal data screen, in this example, for the

InfoType 0006—Address. It determines the field technical name, its label, and its position in the screen.

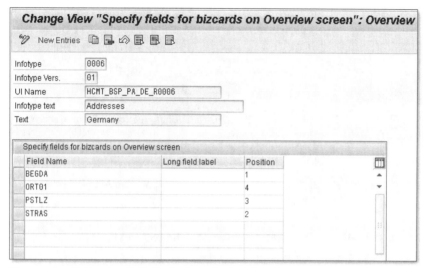

Figure 5.87 Determine Fields for Business Card on Area Page

5.12.6 Foreign Address Settings

This functionality is a favorite because it solves a critical business requirement. For example, because I live in Belgium, I could be working in surrounding countries such as Luxemburg or Germany. This functionality was not supported by SAP until EhP 3, which caused some frustration within the business team. This section deals with the configuration of the foreign address as of EhP 3. It also provides the sample code for customers who have not reached this enhancement package level yet.

Foreign Address Settings

IMG Access Path	PERSONNEL MANAGEMENT • EMPLOYEE SELF-SERVICE • SERVICE SPECIFIC SETTINGS • OWN DATA • FOREIGN ADDRESS SETTINGS

As of EhP 3, if required, you can activate through Transaction SFW5—Switch Framework Customizing, and the business function HCM_ESS_CI_1 can be activated.

This functionality solves a functional issue that we have been coping with for a long time. Prior to EhP 3, it was not technically possible to have a different home address than the country in which the employee was hired.

In fact, the country assignment is done at the personnel area level in table V_T500P — Assignment of Personnel Area to Company Code. Assume you are working in Switzerland in Basel (very) close to the French border. You work in Basel, Switzerland, but you are living in Saint Louis, France, which is next door to Basel. In SAP HR, because you belong to the Personnel Area CH01 — Switzerland Basel, the system is requiring your address(es) from InfoType 0006 to belong to the country allocated to your personnel area.

Not a big deal if you work in the United States but, in Europe, where you can drive across three countries or more in less than two hours (France, Belgium, Luxemburg, the Netherlands, Germany, etc.), this was a major burden for HR.

SAP now provides, thanks to EhP 3, a standard configuration point to maintain an address that can differ from the employment country.

Documentation regarding this functionality can be found at the following address:

http://help.sap.com/erp2005_ehp_03/helpdata/EN/7E/881E4E84B9457A84067DB0A 535C824/frameset.htm

Determine Countries for Foreign Address Entry and Make Settings

In this configuration node, you select first the subtypes as already configured for InfoType 0006 — Address under PERSONNEL MANAGEMENT • PERSONNEL ADMINISTRATION • PERSONAL DATA • ADDRESSES • CREATE ADDRESS TYPES: TABLE V_T591A — SUBTYPE CHARACTERISTICS.

IMG Access Path	PERSONNEL MANAGEMENT • EMPLOYEE SELF-SERVICE • SERVICE SPECIFIC SETTINGS • OWN DATA • FOREIGN ADDRESS SETTINGS • DETERMINE COUNTRIES FOR FOREIGN ADDRESS AND MAKE SETTINGS
IMG Activity	PCUI_ESS_PERSINFO_FA
Transaction Code	S_AER_95000339
Table Name	V_T7XSSPERFORADD

For example, as illustrated in Figure 5.88, we want to enable Belgians to have their PERMANENT RESIDENCE (subtype 1) in Germany, France, and Switzerland.

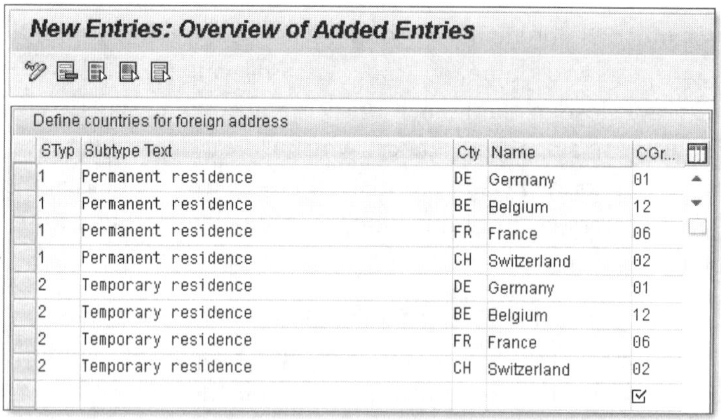

New Entries: Overview of Added Entries

Define countries for foreign address

STyp	Subtype Text	Cty	Name	CGr...	
1	Permanent residence	DE	Germany	01	
1	Permanent residence	BE	Belgium	12	
1	Permanent residence	FR	France	06	
1	Permanent residence	CH	Switzerland	02	
2	Temporary residence	DE	Germany	01	
2	Temporary residence	BE	Belgium	12	
2	Temporary residence	FR	France	06	
2	Temporary residence	CH	Switzerland	02	

Figure 5.88 Determine Countries for Foreign Address and Make Settings

Also, depending on your support package level, you might want to check SAP Note 1253136—Fix for ESS Foreign Address Country Dropdown Field because there was a bug in the functionality: The COUNTRY dropdown field was not getting filled with the countries.

Symptoms are described by SAP:

> While using the Foreign address ESS functionality, the country dropdown was not getting filled with the countries, i.e., it was empty even if there are entries in the customizing table.

Specify Countries for Foreign Address Entry

If you have more complex business requirements and fall short with the standard configuration options provided by SAP, you can always take advantage of BadI HRXSS_PER_FOREIGN_ADDRESS: Definition for Foreign Address (Interface IF_EX_HRXSS_PER_FOREIGN_ADDR). The method GET_FOREIGN_ADDRESS_VALUES will be used.

IMG Access Path   PERSONNEL MANAGEMENT • EMPLOYEE SELF-SERVICE • SERVICE SPECIFIC SETTINGS • OWN DATA • FOREIGN ADDRESS SETTINGS • SPECIFY COUNTRIES FOR FOREIGN ADDRESS ENTRY

IMG Activity	PCUI_ESS_ADDRESS
Transaction Code	S_PRN_53000813
BAdI Name	HRXSS_PER_FOREIGN_ADDRESS—BAdI Definition for Foreign Address

5.13   Additional Useful Information Regarding the Self-Services

This section includes additional important information, gathered during project implementations, which can be helpful when dealing with the personal information self-service.

5.13.1   Emergency Address

When dealing with the emergency contact, you can either maintain the emergency contact subtype for InfoType 0006—Address or maintain the emergency contact subtype for InfoType 0021—Family Member/Dependents.

Some self-service Web Dynpros for emergency contacts are available in the SAP NetWeaver Portal; for example, for Belgium, we have *ess/be/emergency*.

SAP Note 1049110—ESS Emergency Contact

Caution! SAP Note 1049110—ESS Emergency Contact, states the following: "With SAP ERP 6.0, some Web Dynpro Java objects are delivered for internal test purposes only. These Web Dynpro objects are not released by SAP and are never tested by SAP."

This note also contains the exhaustive list of emergency contact Web Dynpros technically available but not released for general use.

5.13.2   Country Field Set to Display Only

When dealing with the personal information address scenario, the COUNTRY field is set to display only to secure the consistency between the name of the country and the country-specific checks triggerred for that country.

This is available since support package 08 for SAP ERP 6.0.

> **SAP Note 987549—ESS PersInfo Address Scenario: Country Field**
>
> Be sure to carefully review SAP Note 987549—ESS PersInfo Address Scenario: Country Field.

5.13.3 Delete Button Not Working in Self-Service

It has been reported that in some self-service screens, the Delete button is not working at all. This bug has been reported for several countries. So far, SAP released SAP Notes for France, Spain, Hong Kong, and Norway.

You must update to Stack 5 for EhP 3 if not already done.

If you have a similar behavior for other countries, inspire yourself in your communication with SAP Support with the following SAP Notes:

▶ 1356835 (France) ESS FR: Delete Function Is Not Working in Address Scenario

▶ 1353844 (Spain) ESS: Delete Function Is Not Working in ES Address Data

▶ 1350256 (Hong Kong) ESS: Delete Function Is Not Working in HK Address Data

▶ 1345981 (Norway) ESS: Delete Button Is Not Working in Norway Personal Data

5.13.4 Additional Fields and Subtypes for the United States Family/ Dependents InfoType

It has been reported that the entries for subtypes Domestic Partner and Child of Domestic Partner of InfoType Family/Dependents for the United States are not present in the subtype table T7XSSPERSUBTYPE.

Also some of the fields of structure Hcmt_Bsp_Pa_Us_R0021 are not added in the frontend Web Dynpro application views.

> **SAP Note 988053—Additional Fields and Subtypes in US Family/Dependents**
>
> Review SAP Note 988053—Additional Fields and Subtypes in US Family/Dependents, which solves the issue.
>
> Be aware that the corrections are both backend and frontend.

5.13.5 Multiple Data Record and Date Handling Enhancements

When SAP developed and designed the Web Dynpro for Personal Information self-services, the intention was to provide a simple user experience. Therefore, the system only displayed the most recent information. At the time, it refrained from the complexity of dealing with validity periods.

However, because validity periods are important and a main feature in HR, SAP enhanced the functionalities and the validity period for data records.

The validity changes are now enabled thanks to the Usecase setting for the scenario. Detailed documentation regarding these new configuration options—now part of the standard—can be found in SAP Note 965324, which you should review for more information.

5.13.6 Past Date Handling

Also note that in the standard package it was not possible to change data retroactively, which was quite a burden. For example, let's say you moved from one address to another address in January. This has an impact on your payroll because the firm pays a fee depending on the distance between your home and your work location. In November, you want to finally update your address record. You do not want to "hassle" the HR department or send an email to request a master data change, so you want to use the self-service for the address.

Unfortunately, in SAP ERP 6.0 with EhP 2, it was not possible to do this. The workaround was to maintain a BAdI provided by SAP. The customer maintained the BAdI and wrote the code, which could be quite frustrating and tough to "sell" to the project team when you bought a standard product.

The following SAP Notes shed some light on this issue:

▶ Note 947172 ESS PersInfo: Retroactive Data Maintenance
▶ Note 982586 ESS PersInfo: Retroactive Data Maintenance

Sample Code for Retroactive Change

The following code provides the technical handling to enable the retroactive change in Self-Services. This code is provided in the standard delivery as of ERP 6.03 (ERP 6.0 release with Enhancement Package 3 or higher).

```
METHOD IF_EX_HRXSS_PER_BEGDA~DEFAULT_DATE.
  CLASS CL_EXIT_MASTER DEFINITION LOAD.
  DATA: EXIT_OBJ_TAB TYPE SXRT_EXIT_TAB.

  DATA: exitintf TYPE REF TO IF_EX_HRXSS_PER_BEGDA,
        wa_flt_cache_line TYPE REF TO sxrt_flt_cache_struct,
        flt_name TYPE FILTNAME.

  FIELD-SYMBOLS:
    <exit_obj>       TYPE SXRT_EXIT_TAB_STRUCT,
    <flt_cache_line> TYPE sxrt_flt_cache_struct.

  READ TABLE INSTANCE_FLT_CACHE
        WITH KEY flt_name    = flt_name
                 method_name = 'DEFAULT_DATE'
        TRANSPORTING NO FIELDS.
  IF sy-subrc NE 0

    CREATE DATA wa_flt_cache_line TYPE sxrt_flt_cache_struct.
    ASSIGN wa_flt_cache_line->* TO <flt_cache_line>.
    <flt_cache_line>-flt_name    = flt_name.
    <flt_cache_line>-method_name = 'DEFAULT_DATE'.

      LOOP AT INSTANCE_BADI_TABLE ASSIGNING <exit_obj>
          WHERE METHOD_NAME  = 'DEFAULT_DATE'.
        APPEND <exit_obj> TO EXIT_OBJ_TAB.
      ENDLOOP.
      IF sy-subrc ne 0.
        CALL METHOD CL_EXIT_MASTER=>CREATE_OBJ_BY_INTERFACE_FILTER
            EXPORTING
                CALLER      = me
                INTER_NAME  = 'IF_EX_HRXSS_PER_BEGDA'
                METHOD_NAME = 'DEFAULT_DATE'

                delayed_instance_creation  = sxrt_true
            IMPORTING
                exit_obj_tab = exit_obj_tab.

        APPEND LINES OF exit_obj_tab TO INSTANCE_BADI_TABLE.
      ENDIF.
```

```
        <flt_cache_line>-valid = sxrt_false.

    LOOP at exit_obj_tab ASSIGNING <exit_obj>
        WHERE ACTIVE   = SXRT_TRUE.

      <flt_cache_line>-valid = sxrt_true.

      <flt_cache_line>-obj =
          CL_EXIT_MASTER=>instantiate_imp_class(
                  CALLER      = me
                  imp_name  = <exit_obj>-imp_name
                  imp_class = <exit_obj>-imp_class ).
        MOVE <exit_obj>-imp_class to <flt_cache_line>
                  imp_class.
        MOVE <exit_obj>-imp_switch to <flt_cache_line>
                  imp_switch.
        MOVE <exit_obj>-order_num to <flt_cache_line>
                  order_num.
        INSERT <flt_cache_line> INTO TABLE
INSTANCE_FLT_CACHE.

    ENDLOOP.
    IF <flt_cache_line>-valid = sxrt_false.
      INSERT <flt_cache_line> INTO TABLE INSTANCE_FLT_CACHE.
    ENDIF.
  ENDIF.

  LOOP AT INSTANCE_FLT_CACHE ASSIGNING <flt_cache_line>
      WHERE flt_name    = flt_name
        AND valid       = sxrt_true
        AND method_name = 'DEFAULT_DATE'.

    CALL FUNCTION 'PF_ASTAT_OPEN'
      EXPORTING
        OPENKEY = 'H5jloEYnMulX00002a94X0'
        TYP     = 'UE'.

    CASE <flt_cache_line>-imp_switch.
      WHEN 'VSR'.
        DATA: exc        TYPE sfbm_xcptn,
"#EC NEEDED
              data_ref   TYPE REF TO DATA.
```

```
            IF <flt_cache_line>-eo_object is initial.
              CALL METHOD ('CL_FOBU_METHOD_EVALUATION')=>load
                   EXPORTING
                      im_class_name     = <flt_cache_line>
                                                    imp_class
                      im_interface_name = 'IF_EX_HRXSS_PER_BEGDA'
                      im_method_name    = 'DEFAULT_DATE'
                   RECEIVING
                      re_fobu_method    = <flt_cache_line>
                                                    eo_object
                   EXCEPTIONS
                      not_found         = 1
                      OTHERS            = 2.
              IF sy-subrc = 2.
                MESSAGE ID sy-msgid TYPE sy-msgty NUMBER sy-msgno
                     WITH sy-msgv1 sy-msgv2 sy-msgv3 sy
msgv4.
              ENDIF.
              CHECK sy-subrc = 0.
            ENDIF.

            CLEAR data_ref.
            GET REFERENCE OF MOLGA INTO data_ref.
            CALL METHOD <flt_cache_line>-eo_object->set_parameter(
                im_parmname = 'MOLGA'
                im_value    = data_ref ).

            CLEAR data_ref.
            GET REFERENCE OF PERNR INTO data_ref.
            CALL METHOD <flt_cache_line>-eo_object->set_parameter(
                im_parmname = 'PERNR'
                im_value    = data_ref ).

            CLEAR data_ref.
            GET REFERENCE OF INFTY INTO data_ref.
            CALL METHOD <flt_cache_line>-eo_object->set_parameter(
                im_parmname = 'INFTY'
                im_value    = data_ref ).

            CLEAR data_ref.
            GET REFERENCE OF SUBTY INTO data_ref.
```

```
      CALL METHOD <flt_cache_line>-eo_object->set_parameter(
          im_parmname = 'SUBTY'
          im_value    = data_ref ).

      CLEAR data_ref.
      GET REFERENCE OF BEGDA INTO data_ref.
      CALL METHOD <flt_cache_line>-eo_object->set_parameter(
          im_parmname = 'BEGDA'
          im_value    = data_ref ).

      CALL METHOD <flt_cache_line>-eo_object->evaluate
          IMPORTING
             ex_exception    = exc
          EXCEPTIONS
             raise_exception = 1
             OTHERS          = 2.
      IF sy-subrc = 2.
        MESSAGE ID sy-msgid TYPE sy-msgty NUMBER sy-msgno
                   WITH sy-msgv1 sy-msgv2 sy-msgv3 sy-msgv4.

      ENDIF.
    WHEN OTHERS.
      EXITINTF?= <flt_cache_line>-OBJ.
      CALL METHOD EXITINTF->DEFAULT_DATE
          EXPORTING
            MOLGA = MOLGA
            PERNR = PERNR
            INFTY = INFTY
            SUBTY = SUBTY
          CHANGING
            BEGDA = BEGDA.

  ENDCASE.

  CALL FUNCTION 'PF_ASTAT_CLOSE'
      EXPORTING
          OPENKEY = 'H5jloEYnMulX00002a94X0'
          TYP     = 'UE'.
  ENDLOOP.

ENDMETHOD.
```

5.14   Career and Job

The Talent Management suite provided by SAP would be the "cherry on top" when it comes to career and job management, but, from the standard solutions, SAP already provides (basic) functionalities in the field of career and jobs.

IMG Access Path	PERSONNEL MANAGEMENT • EMPLOYEE SELF-SERVICE • SERVICE SPECIFIC SETTINGS • CAREER AND JOB

5.14.1   Qualification Catalog

We assume that the qualification catalog, which is dealing with Objects "Q"— Qualification and "QK"—Qualification Groups is already maintained. You can check the qualification catalog by calling Transaction PPQD—Display Qualifications Catalog.

If the qualification catalog is empty, you can maintain the catalog using the IMG access path: PERSONNEL MANAGEMENT • PERSONNEL DEVELOPMENT • MASTER DATA • EDIT QUALIFICATION CATALOG.

To access your qualification catalog, use functional Transaction OOQA—Change Qualifications Catalog.

5.14.2   Skills Profile

In this configuration step, you set the root qualification catalog node to be used when dealing with the skills profile in ESS.

IMG Access Path	PERSONNEL MANAGEMENT • EMPLOYEE SELF-SERVICE • SERVICE SPECIFIC SETTINGS • CAREER AND JOB • SKILLS PROFILE

Make Settings for the Skills Profile Service

This configuration step, as illustrated in Figure 5.89, is an excerpt from the main HR switches table T77S0. It is used to adjust the display of information in the self-service skills profile Web Dynpro.

IMG Access Path	PERSONNEL MANAGEMENT • EMPLOYEE SELF-SERVICE • SERVICE SPECIFIC SETTINGS • CAREER AND JOB • SKILLS PROFILE • MAKE SETTINGS FOR SKILLS PROFILE SERVICE
IMG Activity	PCUI_ESS_PAPD_001
Transaction Code	S_FAD_62000030
Table Name	T77S0

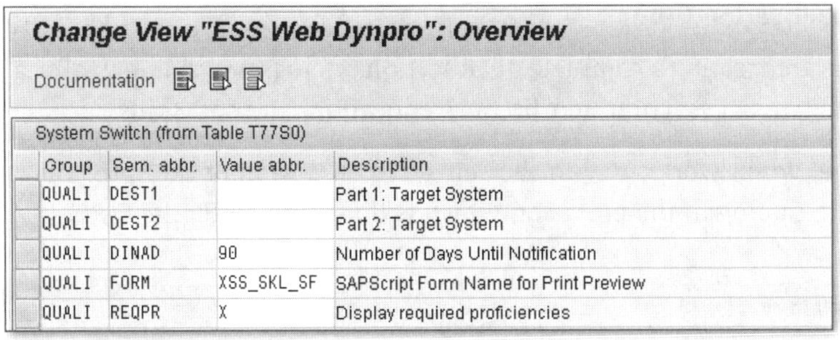

Change View "ESS Web Dynpro": Overview

Documentation 🗒 🗒 🗒

System Switch (from Table T77S0)

Group	Sem. abbr.	Value abbr.	Description
QUALI	DEST1		Part 1: Target System
QUALI	DEST2		Part 2: Target System
QUALI	DINAD	90	Number of Days Until Notification
QUALI	FORM	XSS_SKL_SF	SAPScript Form Name for Print Preview
QUALI	REQPR	X	Display required proficiencies

Figure 5.89 Make Settings for the Skills Profile Service

It deals with the switch group QUALI for the following semantic abbreviations as shown in Figure 5.89:

▸ DEST1 <set the Target system here> PART 1: TARGET SYSTEM

▸ DEST2 <set the Target system here> PART 2: TARGET SYSTEM

Destination 1 and 2 are only relevant if you host the qualification catalog in another system, reached via an RFC as defined in the Basis Transaction SM59—RFC Destinations (Display/Maintain).

You set the value, maximum 20 characters, of the target system here.

▸ DINAD 90 NUMBER OF DAYS UNTIL NOTIFICATION

Set the number of days until the notification will be triggered.

▸ FORM XSS_SKL_SF SAPSCRIPT FORM NAME FOR PRINT PREVIEW

Set the name of the form to be called when triggering a skills profile print preview.

The standard form XSS_SKL_SF is defaulted here. Customers can copy and adjust the standard form or just create their own form using Transaction SE71 — SAPscript form.

▶ REQPR X DISPLAY REQUIRED PROFICIENCIES

The value "X" (standard setting) means that the required proficiencies for a position are to be displayed in the self-services. Customers can deactivate this feature by removing the "X" (Active) value and leaving the field blank.

Define Root Qualification Group

Often, customers are creating a complete qualification catalogs, providing qualification groups from languages, computer literacy, education, and soft skills.

Most of the time, when working with the self-services, customer do not want to display the entire catalog to the end user, which is illustrated in Figure 5.90.

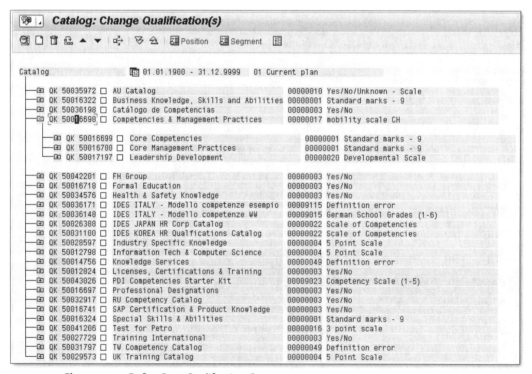

Figure 5.90 Define Root Qualification Group

This configuration step, illustrated in Figure 5.91, allows you to restrict the view on the qualification catalog and to set a root qualification group to be used. This root qualification group is used as a filter. In fact, it only displays all qualification groups and qualifications that are maintained under the root qualification group.

IMG Access Path	PERSONNEL MANAGEMENT • EMPLOYEE SELF-SERVICE • SERVICE SPECIFIC SETTINGS • CAREER AND JOB • SKILLS PROFILE • DEFINE ROOT QUALIFICATION GROUP
IMG Activity	SIMG_CFMENUOHP2OOQES
Transaction Code	S_PH0_48000271
Table Name	T77S0

Perhaps, to proceed with this step, you do need to create an additional qualification group as a placeholder in the qualification catalog. Otherwise, make sure this potential requirement is addressed when deploying the qualification catalog in the company.

▶ GROUP: "QUALI"

▶ SEM. ABBR.: "ESSST"

▶ VALUE ABBR.: "50012345" (sample data)

▶ ESS: "Initial skills group for profile maintenance"

Value "50016698" is the qualification root object that will be used, as illustrated from a real test qualification catalog.

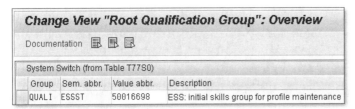

Figure 5.91 Define Root Qualification Group

Be aware that the qualification catalog content might differ from development, test, and production systems, so be sure to identify the correct value.

The technical name of the qualification group can be reached using Transaction PPQD — Display Qualifications Catalog. After you are in the catalog, from the menu, go to VIEW • KEY ON. This will enable the key (technical ID) of the object "QK" qualification group.

5.15 Equipment Overview

The equipment overview allows you to display the content of InfoType 0040 — Objects on Loan.

IMG Access Path	PERSONNEL MANAGEMENT • EMPLOYEE SELF-SERVICE • SERVICE SPECIFIC SETTINGS • EQUIPMENT OVERVIEW

Further information regarding the Work Environment can be accessed under the Marketplace with the following address:

http://help.sap.com/erp2005_ehp_04/helpdata/EN/43/1896d907f12be8e10000000a1553f7/frameset.htm.

5.15.1 Edit Views

As illustrated in Figure 5.92, in this configuration step, you identify the different equipment types to be shown on the self-services end user screen.

IMG Access Path	PERSONNEL MANAGEMENT • EMPLOYEE SELF-SERVICE • SERVICE SPECIFIC SETTINGS • EQUIPMENT OVERVIEW • EDIT VIEWS
IMG Activity	FPB_MAN_EQUIP_001
Transaction Code	S_ALN_01002601
Table Name	V_FCOM_EQMVIEW_C

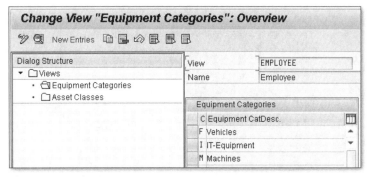

Figure 5.92 Edit Views

5.15.2 Specify the RFC Connection to the HCM System

If you deal with separate systems, one dedicated for HR and one for the other components, you need to set the RFC system to be used (see Figure 5.93).

IMG Access Path	PERSONNEL MANAGEMENT • EMPLOYEE SELF-SERVICE • SERVICE SPECIFIC SETTINGS • EQUIPMENT OVERVIEW • SPECIFY RFC CONNECTION TO HCM SYSTEM
IMG Activity	FPB_MAN_EQUIP_002
Transaction Code	S_ALN_01002616
Table Name	V_FCOM_EQMHCM_C

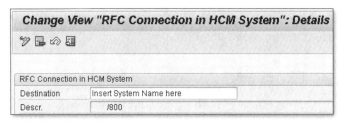

Figure 5.93 Specify the RFC Connection to the HCM System

5.15.3 Business Add-Ins

When dealing with the display of the equipment, you can also use BAdIs to extend SAP flexibility when it comes to meeting the business requirements.

IMG Access Path	PERSONNEL MANAGEMENT • EMPLOYEE SELF-SERVICE • SERVICE SPECIFIC SETTINGS • EQUIPMENT OVERVIEW • BUSINESS ADD-INS (BADIS)

BAdI: Change Equipment Monitor

This BAdI enables customer to further adjust the content and layout of the equipment display.

IMG Access Path	PERSONNEL MANAGEMENT • EMPLOYEE SELF-SERVICE • SERVICE SPECIFIC SETTINGS • EQUIPMENT OVERVIEW • BUSINESS ADD-INS (BADIS) • BADI: CHANGE EQUIPMENT MONITOR
IMG Activity	FCOM_EQM_CHANGE
BAdI Name	FCOM_EQM_CHANGE—BAdI: Change Equipment Monitor
Class	CL_EX_FCOM_EQM_CHANGE
Methods	IF_EX_FCOM_EQM_CHANGE~CHANGE_CONTENT: Change Contents IF_EX_FCOM_EQM_CHANGE~CHANGE_LAYOUT: Change Layout

BAdI: Assignment of Equipment to Users

This BAdI enables customer to enhance the business process and rules when it comes to handling the assignment of equipment to users.

IMG Access Path	PERSONNEL MANAGEMENT • EMPLOYEE SELF-SERVICE • SERVICE SPECIFIC SETTINGS • EQUIPMENT OVERVIEW • BUSINESS ADD-INS (BADIS) • BADI: ASSIGNMENT OF EQUIPMENT TO USERS
IMG Activity	FCOM_EQM_EQUI_USER
BAdI Name	FCOM_EQM_EQUI_USER—BAdI: Assignment of Equipment to Users

Class	CL_EX_FCOM_EQM_EQUI_USER
Methods	IF_EX_FCOM_EQM_EQUI_USER~GET_EQUI_4_USER: Determine Equipment for User
	IF_EX_FCOM_EQM_EQUI_USER~GET_USER_4_EQUIS: Determine User for Equipment

5.16   Travel Management

Travel Management functionalities were introduced quite early in SAP releases. Travel Management started out in the Financial component, then moved to the HR component, and today is back to the Financial component. SAP also introduced the additional functionalities in regards to Travel Planning.

5.17   Company Information

The company information is an internal document belonging to the company. This document describes legal and internal rules regarding working conditions and what is expected from employees.

SAP delivers standard scenario SECC (Code of Business Conduct) as a sample example (see Figure 5.94). Customers and companies must adjust the layout and the content where appropriate. By default, the form is set as an ENTRY USING ADOBE PDF. Using a PDF is a quick win because it enables the end user to save the file locally and print it on demand in a professionnal manner. Printing a web form from Internet Explorer wouldn't provide enough professional rendering in terms of layout. As for the authorization team, it also allows them to lock the PDF file in read-only mode and perhaps even add a bar code to authenticate the document.

SAP powers this functionality through ISR.

This ISR will be covered in more detail in the Chapter 6 because this is in fact part of the technology used in the personnel change requests.

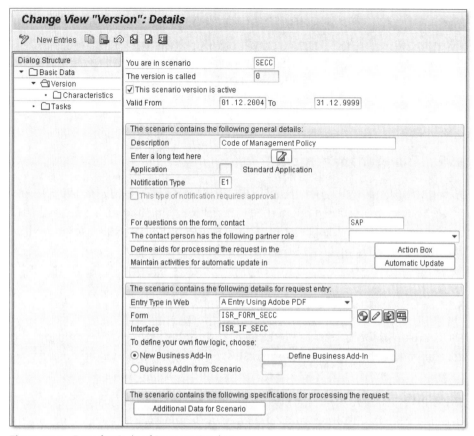

Figure 5.94 Form for Code of Business Conduct

5.18 Employee Self-Services User Exits

As illustrated in Figure 5.95, SAP also provides several user exits when it comes to ESS. These user exits can be an asset when deploying the self-services. The user exits require the support of a developer because they involve ABAP programming.

Exit name	Short text
HRESSW1	HR-ESS: Internet Scenario Who's Who
HRESSW2	HR: Check Start Date for ESS
HRESSW3	HR: Propose Start Date for ESS
HRESSW4	HR: Password Assignment/User Code for ESS User

Figure 5.95 Employee Self-Services User Exits

▶ **HRESSW1 HR-ESS: Internet Scenario Who's Who**
User Exit: HRESSW1
Function Module: EXIT_SAPLRH65_001: Search String Enhancement

This user exit allows customer to adjust the ESS for the Who's Who application and the search rule.

▶ **HRESSW2 HR: Check Start Date for ESS**
User Exit: HRESSW2
Function Module: EXIT_SAPLEHSS_001: Check Start Date for ESS

This user exit allows customer to check further the start date for the ESS users.

▶ **HRESSW3 HR: Propose Start Date for ESS**
User Exit: HRESSW3
Function Module: EXIT_SAPLEHSS_002: Propose Start Date for ESS

This user exit allows customer to set and/or propose a default start date for the ESS user.

▶ **HRESSW4 HR: Password Assignment/User Code for ESS User**
User Exit: HRESSW4
Function Module: EXIT_SAPLEHUS_001 — Enter Password/User ID for ESS User

When going live with hundreds of thousands of SAP users, we do not want (plus security rules will prohibit it) to let all users start with an initial password of "initpass." SAP provides the user exit HRESSW4 to enable customers to create and assign their own algorithm for the initial password to ensure that all users are starting with a different password.

5.19 Alternatives and Additional Configuration

As we have seen, standard self-service configuration is straightforward. However, let's highlight some alternative configuration. These handy workarounds might become very useful when dealing with business requirements. We do, however, strongly advise you to weigh the pros and cons as well as heavily test all the workarounds and alternatives described in this section.

Bear in mind that some of the workarounds are provided by SAP for testing purposes only. Therefore, the use of these workarounds in productive environments is not recommended. Nevertheless, if you need to use these alternatives as the last remaining course of action, carefully test, test, and retest, and at the same time assess collateral damages.

5.19.1 SAP NetWeaver Development Studio (NWDS)

As we have seen, self-service configuration is not complicated, but it might leave some gaps with the business requirements received.

Along with backend configuration, the SAP NetWeaver Development Infrastructure (NWDI)—the SAP NetWeaver Portal technical landscape—also includes the SAP Netweaver Development Studio (NWDS). NWDI is not mandatory when using SAP NetWeaver Portal and self-services. Customers make this choice. Deploying the NWDI requires a bit more support from the Basis team, but it makes self-services deployment easier. Experience has shown the following quick wins:

▶ Faster access and troubleshooting of Java Web Dynpros

▶ Faster reaction time to apply corrections locally direclty in the NWDS instead of waiting for support packages and SAP Notes, which might take months

▶ More grasp on SAP NetWeaver Portal content transport integrity

▶ Additional configuration options for self-services (most important)

5.19.2 Configuration as Alternative through SAP NetWeaver Development Studio (NWDS)

The additional and optional configuration discussed in the following subsections is available through NWDS.

In regards to adjusting standard screens, it is a vast debate between companies' principles and internal rules. This is your decision, but technically you can achieve these adjustments if you choose to.

Change the Display Attribute of a Field

We have learned that the old table V_T588M_ESS—Control of Screen Fields for ESS Scenarios, used for ITS services, is not relevant anymore with the Java-based Web Dynpros.

Another alternative to the procedure described by Markus Klein (*http://wiki.sdn. sap.com/wiki/display/profile/ESS+Personal+Information+UI+enhancement+without+ modification*) is to use the configuration step in the NWDS that allows you to change the attribute of a field in most cases.

For example, you might want to change the field PAYEE for the bank details from EDIT to DISPLAY so that the employee name cannot be edited.

Caution

The self-service ADDRESS and the DISPLAY ONLY field for the country, although technically possible, is not supported nor working if you edit the field properties. As we have seen, the current standard solution is to deploy the standard functionality provided in EhP 3.

Change the Sequence of Existing Fields

Sometimes in an effort to simplify, business requirements want to change the sequence of fields as provided in the standard screens. For example, you might want the postal code to come before the city name.

Adjusting standard screens is your decision, but technically, thanks to the NWDS, you can edit the sequence of fields.

Add a Field to a View

In addition to the Markus Klein SDN Wiki entry (*http://wiki.sdn.sap.com/wiki/dis- play/profile/ESS+Personal+Information+UI+enhancement+without+modification*), you can also add the additional fields in the NWDS. You might think you don't have additional fields, but in most cases, you will because customers have maintained in some InfoTypes the Customer Include allowing them to add additional field(s) to existing InfoTypes.

Therefore, most of the time, these fields are web enabled as well on the self-services screens.

Add a Text Box to the Screen for User Assistance

Another quick win that you can enable with NWDS is the addition of a text box to the self-service screen to assist the end user.

Most of the time, documentation and assistance are provided to a separate Knowledge Management (KM) system. Therefore, customers are trying to limit this configuration step to the bare minimum.

Add a Dynamic Event to the Screen Display

In some cases, you might want to enable a dynamic event. For example, you might want the field SINCE (DATE) to appear only if you select a value other than SINGLE, such as MARRIED, in the PERSONAL DATA self-service screen. NWDS lets you achieve that and clean up the screens.

Change the Delivered Text Element of a Service

Since we began working on SAP, we all should know the golden rule, which is not to touch the SAP standard. This also applies to avoiding renaming SAP elements.

However, in certain circumstances raised in the business requirements, it might be useful to adjust and change the delivered text element of a service to ensure that you are using the customer language and vocabulary.

Be extra careful when dealing with several languages because you might need to repeat this step in the target languages.

5.19.3 Configuration through Portal Personalization

As of SAP NetWeaver 7.0, SAP provides the Portal Personalization. This Portal Personalization is accessed by pressing `Ctrl` and then right-clicking.

This functionality can be accessed from the end user screen and from the portal administrator, directly from the PCD.

This last remaining course of action should only be used if the customer falls short on other configurations or other alternatives illustrated and introduced earlier in this chapter.

This alternative does not substitute for enabling or disabling subtypes for the self-services because we do have a configuration table in the backend to achieve that.

When playing around with this alternative, we strongly recommend that you test this configuration in full.

Bear in mind that this configuration is likely not to be transportable and has to be read-justed in the productive system directly, including when deploying support packages.

At this stage, it is still not clear if this is fully supported by SAP as a standard functionality. This is the reason why it is introduced as the last remaining course of action.

On the other hand, if you do not have NWDS and you are falling short on configuration tables, you don't have much choice but to use this alternative.

More information regarding portal personalization can be found with the following address:

http://help.sap.com/saphelp_nw04s/helpdata/en/42/ed3ce7f8593eebe10000000a1553f7/frameset.htm.

End User View for Configuration

If not deactivated, the end user can reset or adjust the screen currently shown. Figure 5.96 illustrates the personalization options for the self-service address.

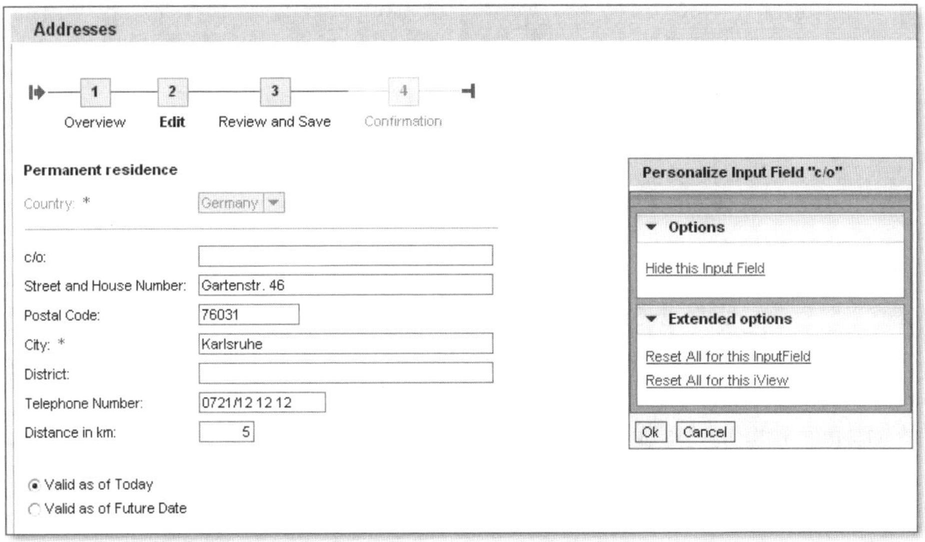

Figure 5.96 Portal Personalization End User for iView Address

In real life, this is one of the first things checked when performing an audit. You should only let the administrator personalize the screen, and you should deactivate the end user personalization as illustrated in the next steps.

Configuration View from the Portal Content Directory (PCD)

Portal administrators can launch directly from the PCD in preview mode and adjust the screen. For example, you can rearrange the order of the columns, map additional fields, or just rename them.

Figure 5.97 illustrates the Portal Personalization with the portal administrator view.

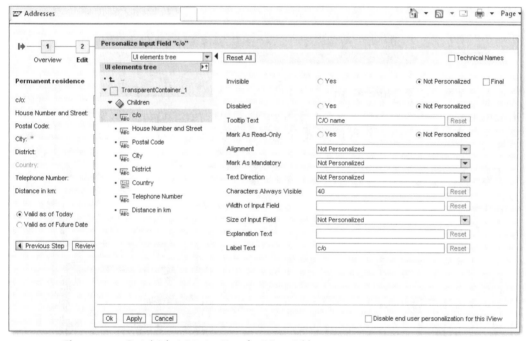

Figure 5.97 Portal Administrator User for iView Address

When performing this configuration, the portal administrator must have a valid personnel number mapped to his SAP UserID, thanks to the InfoType 0105 Communication, subtype 0001—System User Name (SY-UNAME).

Deactivating This Configuration Option in the Production System

To deactivate the end user personalization, from the portal administrator view mark the box DISABLE END USER PERSONALIZATION FOR THIS iVIEW at the bottom of the screen as shown in Figure 5.97. This will ensure that end users cannot reset nor adjust the end user screen.

5.20   Conclusion

Throughout this chapter, we have seen that SAP delivers several functionalities for the ESS. Most of these functionalities can be deployed quickly and enable quick wins for both the company and the employees.

Despite the fact that the standard functionalities are easy to set up, they do challenge us in many ways due to employees' expectations or business requirements. This chapter illustrated the standard configuration steps as well as the known pitfalls or questions that might be raised during a project.

We also introduced optional and additional alternatives to best meet the business requirements. Although not mandatory, these workarounds can be further investigated and at least raised as alternatives, if available on your current systems.

These alternatives solutions should not be preferred to standard configuration in the backend system, if available. Prioritize the configuration as follows:

▶ Backend configuration

▶ BAdI and backend user exits

▶ Portal configuration through iView parameters

▶ Portal Personalization

▶ SAP NetWeaver Development Studio (NWDS)

Now that we have walked through the Employee Self-Services, let's move to the Manager Self-Services, which empowers line and project managers.

Manager Self-Services (MSS) empowers managers to access all relevant HR information regarding their team members. MSS enables end users to trigger HR processes when needed, at their convenience, without overloading the HR department.

6   Manager Self-Services Configuration

This chapter covers the configuration of the MSS functionalities as provided in the latest SAP ERP 6.0 release backend system and also highlights the configuration required in the SAP NetWeaver Portal objects.

Additional configuration is also illustrated regarding a generic iView that you can reuse as a template for displaying data in MSS.

Bear in mind that MSS does not replace master data or other configurations that must exist, for example, configuration for components such as Time Management, Personnel Administration, Personnel Development, Payroll, and so on. SAP's strength lies in the fact that we don't duplicate these configuration settings. Carefully assess and check with the relevant colleagues what has already been done to identify any gaps or missing configuration.

Some MSS functionalities, such as the performance appraisal, SAP e-Recruiting integration, SAP Learning Solution (LSO) integration, and Enterprise Compensation Management (ECM), do require a lot of configuration. For that reason, these functionalities have been covered in depth with detailed configuration in additional SAP PRESS books (see Appendix).

Let's jump into the core configuration of MSS. Where relevant and available, I have also provided some personal project experience, SAP Notes, and common pitfalls/known issues with their solution.

6.1   Object and Data Provider (OADP)

The configuration of the Object and Data Provider (OADP) is explained in Chapter 3. It reviews the configuration steps to customize it.

IMG Access Path	BUSINESS PACKAGES/FUNCTIONAL PACKAGES • MANAGER SELF-SERVICE (MYSAP ERP) • OBJECT AND DATA PROVIDER

6.2   Working Time

Working time is quite critical for most managers because they can oversee their team members' whereabouts thanks to the team calendar. They can also view and maintain, if needed, their team members' absences and attendance, as well as the time registration.

Last but not least, they are also involved in the approval process when dealing with the leave request or the time entries, for example.

IMG Access Path	BUSINESS PACKAGES/FUNCTIONAL PACKAGES • MANAGER SELF-SERVICE (MYSAP ERP) • WORKING TIME

6.2.1   Team Calendar

This configuration step deals with the team calendar configuration for MSS. SAP is faithful to its motto "not to duplicate configuration." As a result, unless stated, the configuration steps might be using the same configuration step as already explained in ESS—Working Time IMG.

IMG Access Path	BUSINESS PACKAGES/FUNCTIONAL PACKAGES • MANAGER SELF-SERVICE (MYSAP ERP) • WORKING TIME • TEAM CALENDAR

To avoid redundant explanations and screenshots, kindly refer to Chapter 5 when noted in the text.

The SAP NetWeaver Portal TEAM CALENDAR rendering is illustrated in Figure 6.1.

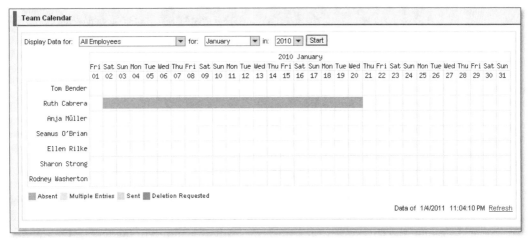

Figure 6.1 Team Calendar Rendering in MSS

Create Rule Groups

Create the relevant grouping for MSS. This grouping configuration step is the same as already illustrated in the ESS team calendar configuration step.

IMG Access Path	BUSINESS PACKAGES/FUNCTIONAL PACKAGES • MANAGER SELF-SERVICE (mySAP ERP) • WORKING TIME • TEAM CALENDAR • CREATE RULE GROUPS
IMG Activity	PCUI_ESS_PT_LRQ_030
Transaction Code	S_FAD_62000011
Table Name	V_HRWEB_RULE_GRP

Adjust the feature WEBMO—Define Rule Group for Customizing Tables in Web Environment as needed.

Specify Absences to Be Displayed

This configuration step specifies the absences to be displayed. Define the relevant absences/processing processes for MSS and adjust the explanatory texts for absences if needed. This step is the same as already illustrated in the ESS team calendar configuration step.

IMG Access Path	BUSINESS PACKAGES/FUNCTIONAL PACKAGES • MANAGER SELF-SERVICE (MYSAP ERP) • WORKING TIME • TEAM CALENDAR • SPECIFY ABSENCES TO BE DISPLAYED
IMG Activity	PCUI_ESS_MSS_PT_ABS
Transaction Code	S_XEN_65000035
Table Name	V_T554S_WEB

Specify Color Display of Absences

This configuration step specifies the color(s) to be displayed for the absences. Define the relevant configuration for MSS, and enable the color display of statuses in the leave request. This step is the same as already illustrated in the ESS team calendar configuration step.

IMG Access Path	BUSINESS PACKAGES/FUNCTIONAL PACKAGES • MANAGER SELF-SERVICE (MYSAP ERP) • WORKING TIME • TEAM CALENDAR • SPECIFY COLOR DISPLAY OF ABSENCES
IMG Activity	PCUI_ESS_PT_LRQ_051
Transaction Code	S_P7H_77000003
Table Name	V_PTARQ_TCONSTR

Select Employees

This configuration step specifies the selection of employees. Define the relevant configuration for MSS and the manager's approval. It is the same as already illustrated in the ESS team calendar configuration step.

IMG Access Path	BUSINESS PACKAGES/FUNCTIONAL PACKAGES • MANAGER SELF-SERVICE (MYSAP ERP) • WORKING TIME • TEAM CALENDAR • SELECT EMPLOYEES
IMG Activity	PCUI_ESS_LRQ_085
Transaction Code	S_PLN_62000260
Table Name	V_PTREQ_TEAM

Define Layout of Team Calendar

This configuration defines the layout for the team calendar. Define the relevant configuration for MSS and the manager's approval. It is the same as already illustrated in the ESS team calendar configuration step.

IMG Access Path	BUSINESS PACKAGES/FUNCTIONAL PACKAGES • MANAGER SELF-SERVICE (MYSAP ERP) • WORKING TIME • TEAM CALENDAR • DEFINE LAYOUT OF TEAM CALENDAR
IMG Activity	PCUI_ESS_LRQ_080
Transaction Code	S_PLN_62000259
Table Name	V_PTARQ_TCALE

BAdI: Control Processing of Leave Requests

This configuration step defines the control processing for the leave request through the means of Business Add-Ins (BAdIs). The BAdI called is CL_PT_ARQ_REQ— Enhancement for Leave Request. This step is the same as already illustrated in the ESS team calendar configuration step.

IMG Access Path	BUSINESS PACKAGES/FUNCTIONAL PACKAGES • MANAGER SELF-SERVICE (MYSAP ERP) • WORKING TIME • TEAM CALENDAR • BADI: CONTROL PROCESSING OF LEAVE REQUESTS
IMG Activity	PCUI_ESS_PT_LRQ_080
BAdI Name	CL_PT_ARQ_REQ

6.2.2   Attendance Overview

The attendance overview is quite important because it also enables the manager to follow up and check attendances entries as maintained in the Personnel Time Management component.

IMG Access Path	BUSINESS PACKAGES/FUNCTIONAL PACKAGES • MANAGER SELF-SERVICE (MYSAP ERP) • WORKING TIME • ATTENDANCE OVERVIEW

Once again, SAP is reusing configuration tables already maintained for the working time in the ESS and the team calendar for MSS.

Create Rule Groups

This grouping configuration creates the relevant grouping for MSS. This step is the same as already illustrated in the ESS team calendar configuration step.

IMG Access Path	BUSINESS PACKAGES/FUNCTIONAL PACKAGES • MANAGER SELF-SERVICE (MYSAP ERP) • WORKING TIME • ATTENDANCE OVERVIEW • CREATE RULE GROUPS
IMG Activity	PCUI_ESS_PT_LRQ_030
Transaction Code	S_FAD_62000011
Table Name	V_HRWEB_RULE_GRP

Adjust the feature WEBMO—Define Rule Group for Customizing Tables in Web Environment as needed.

Select Employees

This configuration step selects employees. Although bearing a different IMG activity for MSS, this step has a similar IMG activity PCUI_ESS_LRQ_085 in ESS. These two IMG activities are pointing to the same configuration table V_PTREQ_TEAM.

IMG Access Path	BUSINESS PACKAGES/FUNCTIONAL PACKAGES • MANAGER SELF-SERVICE (MYSAP ERP) • WORKING TIME • ATTENDANCE OVERVIEW • SELECT EMPLOYEES
IMG Activity	PCUI_MSS_PT_ATT_001
Transaction Code	S_XEN_65000029
Table Name	V_PTREQ_TEAM

As illustrated in Chapter 5, adjust the configuration, this time for the manager's approval entry.

BAdI: Control Processing of Leave Requests

Also already mentioned previously, this configuration step defines the control processing for the leave request through the means of BAdIs. It is the same as already illustrated in the ESS team calendar configuration step. The BAdI called is CL_PT_ARQ_REQ—Enhancement for Leave Request.

IMG Access Path	BUSINESS PACKAGES/FUNCTIONAL PACKAGES • MANAGER SELF-SERVICE (MYSAP ERP) • WORKING TIME • ATTENDANCE OVERVIEW • BADI: CONTROL PROCESSING OF LEAVE REQUESTS
IMG Activity	PCUI_ESS_PT_LRQ_080
BAdI Name	CL_PT_ARQ_REQ

6.2.3 Approve Working Time

The Cross-Application Time Sheet (CATS) is one of the best seller functionalities, allowing end users to enter their time entries for all SAP components. (Human Resources, Financial (FI), Controlling (CO), Plant Maintenance (PM), Service Management (SM), Material Management (MM), Sales and Distribution (SD), and Project System (PS). Because we are dealing with labor times, Product Planning is out of scope for the time sheet as it deals with machine times.)

IMG Access Path	BUSINESS PACKAGES/FUNCTIONAL PACKAGES • MANAGER SELF-SERVICE (MYSAP ERP) • WORKING TIME • APPROVE WORKING TIME

This time registration has many UIs, with the main interfaces being the SAP ERP backend (also known as CATS classic) UI and the web-based interface (also known as CATS regular).

Up to SAP ERP 5.0, SAP didn't have dedicated web screens for the approval process regarding working time. However, there was an alternative: web-enabling the standard SAP ERP Transaction CATS_APPR_LITE—Approve Working Times by creating a dedicated SAP NetWeaver Portal transaction iView, powered on the WebGUI. Although it works technically, this solution is still a workaround because the layout will probably trigger some consistency issues compared to standard functionalities using Web Dynpro.

The good news is that in SAP ERP 6.0, this functionality gap is now covered with new configuration options and the counterpart Web Dynpro screens for the approval of time entries.

This section covers the configuration of the MSS approval side.

The SAP NetWeaver Portal rendering for the approval of the working times is illustrated in Figure 6.2 for the selection VIEW of SAP APPROVAL BY LINE MANAGER, with the APPROVAL action APPROVE ALL.

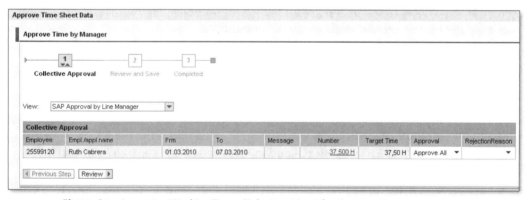

Figure 6.2 Approving Working Times (Selection View) for the Line Manager

Figure 6.3 illustrates the overview approval screen after data is selected. All screens are powered by Web Dynpros.

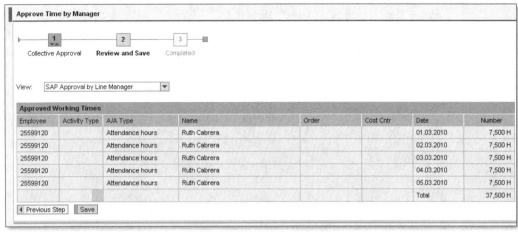

Figure 6.3 Approving Working Times (Overview Screen) for Line Manager

Define Approval Views

In this step, as illustrated in Figure 6.4, you configure the settings for the views to be provided. SAP provides two views:

▶ **SAP_LINE:** SAP Approval by Line Manager

▶ **SAP_PROJ:** SAP Approval by Project Lead

IMG Access Path	BUSINESS PACKAGES/FUNCTIONAL PACKAGES • MANAGER SELF-SERVICE (MYSAP ERP) • WORKING TIME • APPROVE WORKING TIME • DEFINE APPROVAL VIEWS
IMG Activity	PCUI_ESS_CATS_101
Transaction Code	S_AEN_10000289
Table Name	CATS_APPR_PERSPT

This configuration step enables the building up of the approval screen by setting the following information:

▶ PERIOD TYPE

▶ FIRST DAY

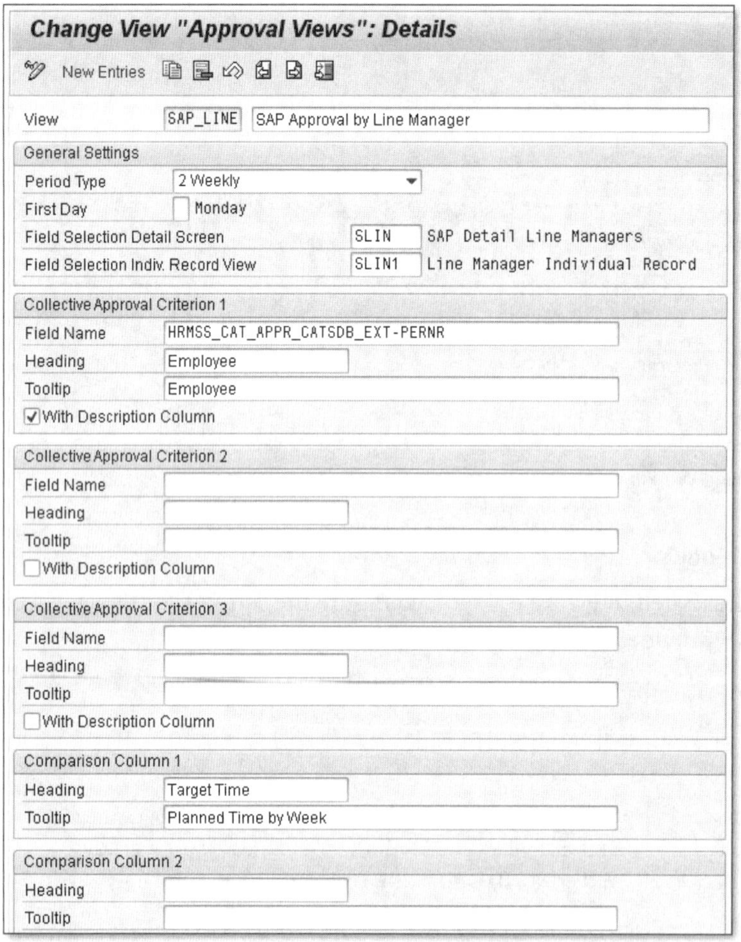

Figure 6.4 Define Approval View (Detailed Configuration View)

▶ FIELD SELECTION DETAIL SCREEN/FIELD SELECTION INDIV. RECORD VIEW: Choose from one of the following fields (functional/technical name) for approval of time sheet data:

 ▶ PERSONNEL NUMBER, PERNR (HRMSS_CAT_APPR_CATSDB_EXT)

 ▶ WORK BREAKDOWN SCHEDULE ELEMENT (WBS element), POSID (HRMSS_CAT_APPR_CATSDB_EXT)

 ▶ WBS ELEMENT TEXT, POSID_TEXT (HRMSS_CAT_APPR_TEXTS)

 ▶ ATTENDANCE OR ABSENCE TYPE, AWART (HRMSS_CAT_APPR_CATSDB_EXT)

- NAME OF ATTENDANCE OR ABSENCE TYPE, AWART_TEXT (HRMSS_CAT_APPR_TEXTS)
- PERSONNEL NUMBER, PERNR (HRMSS_CAT_APPR_CATSDB_EXT_DET)
- FORMATTED NAME OF EMPLOYEE OR APPLICANT, NAME (HRMSS_CAT_APPR_TEXTS)
- DATE, WORKDATE (HRMSS_CAT_APPR_CATSDB_EXT_DET)
- DATE CREATED, ERSDA (HRMSS_CAT_APPR_CATSDB_EXT_DET)
- TIME SHEET: NUMBER RELATED TO UNIT OF MEASURE, CATSQUANTITY (HRMSS_CAT_APPR_CATSDB_EXT_DET)
- UNIT OF MEASURE, UNIT (HRMSS_CAT_APPR_CATSDB_EXT_DET)
- START TIME, BEGUZ (HRMSS_CAT_APPR_CATSDB_EXT_DET)
- END TIME, ENDUZ (HRMSS_CAT_APPR_CATSDB_EXT_DET)
- CATS AMOUNT, CATSAMOUNT (HRMSS_CAT_APPR_CATSDB_EXT_DET)
- CURRENCY KEY, WAERS (HRMSS_CAT_APPR_CATSDB_EXT_DET)
- ATTENDANCE OR ABSENCE TYPE, AWART (HRMSS_CAT_APPR_CATSDB_EXT_DET)
- NAME OF ATTENDANCE OR ABSENCE TYPE, AWART_TEXT (HRMSS_CAT_APPR_TEXTS)
- WAGE TYPE, LGART (HRMSS_CAT_APPR_CATSDB_EXT_DET)
- LONG TEXT FOR WAGE TYPE, LGART_TEXT (HRMSS_CAT_APPR_TEXTS)
- SENDER COST CENTER, SKOSTL (HRMSS_CAT_APPR_CATSDB_EXT_DET)
- TEXT FOR SENDER COST CENTER, SKOSTL_TEXT (HRMSS_CAT_APPR_TEXTS)
- ACTIVITY TYPE, LSTAR (HRMSS_CAT_APPR_CATSDB_EXT_DET)
- TEXT FOR ACTIVITY TYPE, LSTAR_TEXT (HRMSS_CAT_APPR_TEXTS)
- RECEIVER COST CENTER, RKOSTL (HRMSS_CAT_APPR_CATSDB_EXT_DET)
- TEXT FOR RECEIVER COST CENTER, RKOSTL_TEXT (HRMSS_CAT_APPR_TEXTS)
- WORK BREAKDOWN SCHEDULE ELEMENT (WBS ELEMENT), POSID (HRMSS_CAT_APPR_CATSDB_EXT_DET)
- TEXT FOR WBS ELEMENT, POSID_TEXT (HRMSS_CAT_APPR_TEXTS)
- STATISTICAL KEY FIGURE, STATKEYFIG (HRMSS_CAT_APPR_CATSDB_EXT_DET)

You can use up to three criteria and set up one or two comparison columns.

Define Field Selection for Individual Approval View

Because the system has already been instructed to point to an individual record view, you can now configure the content of this view, as illustrated in Figure 6.5. You set up the different fields to be used for display and the relevant length to be displayed. The standard display, for example, for the eight digits of a personnel number, might not be useful because the customer is only using four digits.

IMG Access Path	BUSINESS PACKAGES/FUNCTIONAL PACKAGES • MANAGER SELF-SERVICE (MYSAP ERP) • WORKING TIME • APPROVE WORKING TIME • DEFINE FIELD SELECTION FOR INDIVIDUAL APPROVAL VIEW
IMG Activity	PCUI_ESS_CATS_102
Transaction Code	S_AEN_10000291
Table Names	V_PT_FIELD_SEL and V_PT_FIELD_SEL_C
View Area	CTS—CATS Approval: Individual Record

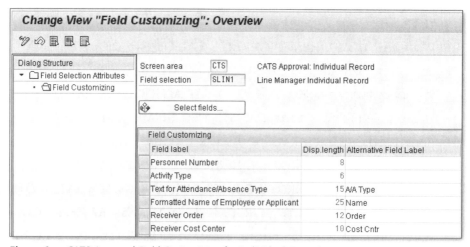

Figure 6.5 CATS Approval Field Customizing for Individual Record

Define Field Selection for Detail View

In this configuration step, as illustrated in Figure 6.6, because you have instructed the system to point to a detail screen view, you now configure the content of this view. This is the same table as the previous configuration step, with a different view area.

IMG Access Path	BUSINESS PACKAGES/FUNCTIONAL PACKAGES • MANAGER SELF-SERVICE (MYSAP ERP) • WORKING TIME • APPROVE WORKING TIME • DEFINE FIELD SELECTION FOR DETAIL VIEW
IMG Activity	PCUI_ESS_CATS_103
Transaction Code	S_AEN_10000292
Table Names	V_PT_FIELD_SEL and V_PT_FIELD_SEL_C
View Area	CTD—CATS Approval: Details

You set up the different fields to be used for display and the relevant length to be displayed.

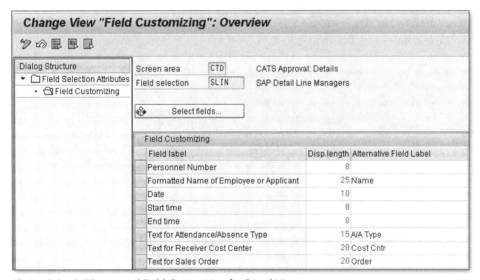

Figure 6.6 CATS Approval Field Customizing for Detail View

Define Profiles and Assign to Views

In this configuration step, illustrated in Figure 6.7, you define the approval profile(s) and make the assignment to the views created in previous configuration steps.

IMG Access Path	BUSINESS PACKAGES/FUNCTIONAL PACKAGES • MANAGER SELF-SERVICE (MYSAP ERP) • WORKING TIME • APPROVE WORKING TIME • DEFINE PROFILES AND ASSIGN TO VIEWS
IMG Activity	PCUI_ESS_CATS_104
Transaction Code	S_AEN_10000293
Table Name	V_CATS_APPR_CUST

You can also set the following options:

▶ TO HR: The data is immediately transferred to HR after it is approved. Tick this option box to enable it.

▶ REJECTION: The system will send a rejection notification to the end user, if the approval is rejected. Tick this box to enable it. This step uses the same configuration as used in Transaction CATC—Time Leveling. The text of the notification is maintained in the standard SAP program SAPLCAPP—Time Sheet: Approval in the text numbers 004 and 100-108.

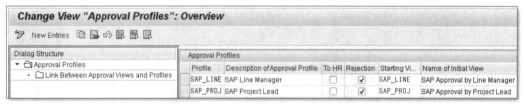

Figure 6.7 CATS Define Approval Profiles

Select Employees

In this step, you reuse the same table as you have maintained previously for the team calendar in ESS and MSS.

IMG Access Path	BUSINESS PACKAGES/FUNCTIONAL PACKAGES • MANAGER SELF-SERVICE (MYSAP ERP) • WORKING TIME • APPROVE WORKING TIME • SELECT EMPLOYEES

Create Rule Groups

As already mentioned, this grouping configuration step is the same as illustrated in the ESS team calendar configuration step. Create the relevant grouping for MSS.

IMG Access Path	BUSINESS PACKAGES/FUNCTIONAL PACKAGES • MANAGER SELF-SERVICE (MYSAP ERP) • WORKING TIME • APPROVE WORKING TIME • SELECT EMPLOYEES • CREATE RULE GROUPS
IMG Activity	PCUI_ESS_PT_LRQ_030
Transaction Code	S_FAD_62000011
Table Name	V_HRWEB_RULE_GRP

Adjust the feature WEBMO—Define Rule Group for Customizing Tables in Web Environment as needed.

Select Employees for Approval

As already mentioned, this configuration step, selecting employees, although bearing a different IMG activity for MSS, has a similar IMG activity PCUI_ESS_LRQ_085 in ESS. These two IMG activities are pointing to the same configuration table V_PTREQ_TEAM.

IMG Access Path	BUSINESS PACKAGES/FUNCTIONAL PACKAGES • MANAGER SELF-SERVICE (MYSAP ERP) • WORKING TIME • APPROVE WORKING TIME • SELECT EMPLOYEES • SELECT EMPLOYEES FOR APPROVAL
IMG Activity	PCUI_ESS_CATS_106
Transaction Code	S_AEN_10000295
Table Name	V_PTREQ_TEAM

As illustrated in Chapter 5, adjust the configuration, this time for the manager's approval entry.

BAdI: Refine Settings for Approval

As usual, SAP provides a BAdI for additional flexibility in the configuration. As needed, the BAdI HRCATS_APPR_CUST of enhancement spot APPR_CUST can be used.

IMG Access Path	Business Packages/Functional Packages • Manager Self-Service (mySAP ERP) • Working Time • Approve Working Time • BAdI: Refine Settings for Approval
IMG Activity	PCUI_ESS_CATS_105
Transaction Code	S_AEN_10000294

6.3 Employee Data

Employee data is made available, depending on authorization and legal requirements, to the managers and is integrated with all surrounding components. The main assumption is that the SAP Human Capital Management (HCM) components listed here have been deployed and maintained where needed.

▶ Personnel Administration (PA)

▶ Personnel Development (PD)

▶ Organizational Management (OM)

▶ Personnel Time Management (PT)

▶ Payroll (PY)

▶ SAP Learning Solution (LSO)

▶ Object Settings and Appraisals (PD-PM)

▶ Enterprise Compensation Management (ECM)

IMG Access Path	Business Packages/Functional Packages • Manager Self-Service (mySAP ERP) • Employee Data

6.3.1 Define Wage Types for Annual Salary

IMG Access Path	Business Packages/Functional Packages • Manager Self-Service (mySAP ERP) • Employee Data • Define Wage Types for Annual Salary
IMG Activity	PORT_MAN_EMPRO_003
Transaction Code	S_AX7_68000262

This configuration step is achieved in different milestones as described in the following subsections.

Check Wage Types Catalog

Before you dive into the wage types for annual salary configuration, you must assess whether or not the wage types catalog has already been maintained by the Payroll team. Check through configuration Transaction S_AHR_61011437—Create Wage Types Catalog to check that the wage type exists.

Figure 6.8 illustrates the completeness check, with test run, performed in the IMG for Germany (Molga 01), for example.

```
Completeness Check --- (Test)

📰 📰   Delete wage types

05.01.2011                      Copy wage type(s)

Country grouping:               01 Germany

You made the following choice:  Test run

The following wage types are not in T512W

S CWType   Wage type text              Short text
✓ 0001     Hourly wages                HrlyWage
✓ 0002     Pay-scale monthly wages     PSMoWage
✓ 0003     Pay-scale salary            PS salar
✓ 0004     Non-pay-scale bonus         NPS bon
✓ 0005     Hazardous work bonus        HazBonus
✓ 0006     Shift bonus                 ShiftPre
✓ 0007     Shift bonus
✓ 0008     Holiday bonus               Xmas bon
✓ 0009     Pension, own
✓ 0011     Wage/salary waiver          W/SWaivr
✓ 0013     Normal hours
✓ 0014     Vacation pay                Vac pay
✓ 0015     Vacation allowance          VacAllow
✓ 0019     Pension, widow(er)'s
✓ 0023     Shift bonus                 ShiftPre
✓ 0024     Shift bonus                 ShiftPre
✓ 0026     Sickness allowance          KrAllow
✓ 0029     Pension, orphan's           Pens.Orp
✓ 0035     Workers' council            WorkCoun
✓ 0036     Overtime 25% bonus          Overtime
✓ 0037     Overtime constant           Overtime
```

Figure 6.8 Wage Type Completeness Check

Define a Subapplication in Table V_596A_B

Figure 6.9 illustrates the definition of the subapplication. This value is important in the SAP NetWeaver Portal iView configuration.

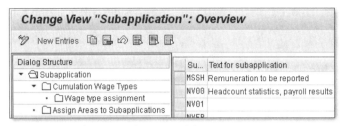

Figure 6.9 Define Subapplication (Table V_596A_B)

Define Cumulation Wage Types in Table V_596G_A

Figure 6.10 illustrates the definition of the different cumulation wage types.

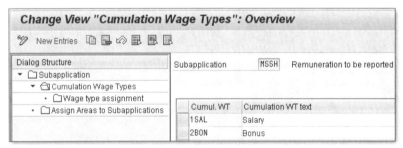

Figure 6.10 Define Cumulation Wage Types (Table V_596G_A)

Assign Wage Types in Table V_596I_A

Figure 6.11 illustrates the assignment of the wage type into the cumulation wage type configuration entry. Carefully maintain the start and end date. You set the amount value by ticking the field AMT.

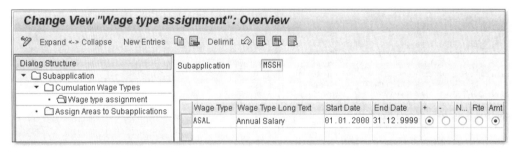

Figure 6.11 Wage Type Assignment (Table V_596I_A)

Maintain and Assign Portal Content Parameters

Now that the backend configuration is done, you must advise the SAP NetWeaver Portal iView to pick up the subapplication entry, which will retrieve all configuration attached to it. This is done in the iView Salary Development, which has the following technical name:

pcd:portal_content/com.sap.pct/line_manager/com.sap.pct.erp.mss.bp_folder/com.sap.pct. erp.mss.iviews/com.sap.pct.erp.mss.hcm/com.sap.pct.erp.mss.compensationprofiles_ salarydevelopment

In the section WAGE TYPE APPLICATION, you set up the value for the subapplication, in this case, MSSH.

Figure 6.12 illustrates this iView configuration.

Figure 6.12 Salary Development iView Configuration

6.3.2 Adjust Periods for Annual Salary

In this configuration step, you can use, if required, the user exit HRWPCEP1—SAP Enhancement for Employee. This user exit is powered by the function module EXIT_SAPLHRWPC_EXITS_001—Determine Salary Years for Employee Profile. This enhancement enables you to make specific changes to the periods used to determine the annual salary, based on customer-specific requirements, which translate into customer ABAP programming to be set up in this enhancement. (This step is optional.)

IMG Access Path	BUSINESS PACKAGES/FUNCTIONAL PACKAGES • MANAGER SELF-SERVICE (MYSAP ERP) • EMPLOYEE DATA • ADJUST PERIODS FOR ANNUAL SALARY
IMG Activity	PORT_MAN_EMPRO_004
Transaction Code	S_AX7_68000263

6.3.3 Filter Absence Records

In this configuration step, you can use, if required, the user exit HRWPCABS—SAP Enhancement for Employee. This user exit is powered by the function module EXIT_SAPLHRWPC_ABSENCES_001—Filtering Absence Records. This enhancement enables you to filter the absence records provided to managers in the UI, based on customer-specific requirements, which translate into customer ABAP programming to be set up in this enhancement. (This step is optional.)

IMG Access Path	BUSINESS PACKAGES/FUNCTIONAL PACKAGES • MANAGER SELF-SERVICE (MYSAP ERP) • EMPLOYEE DATA • FILTER ABSENCE RECORDS
IMG Activity	PORT_MAN_EMPRO_002
Transaction Code	S_AX7_68000144

6.4 Personnel Change Requests

As discussed in Chapter 3, the personnel change requests are powered by the Internal Service Request (ISR). The ISRs are detailed in this chapter.

This section illustrates the standard (light) configuration available for configuring the templates provided by SAP.

IMG Access Path	BUSINESS PACKAGES/FUNCTIONAL PACKAGES • MANAGER SELF-SERVICE (MYSAP ERP) • PERSONNEL CHANGE REQUESTS

In addition, you will detail the myriad BAdIs offered to get as close as possible to the business requirements.

Before starting the configuration, as already pointed out in Chapter 3, SAP recommends once more assessing the use of the current and next generation of change requests: the Human Resources Management (HCM) Processes and Forms.

6.4.1 SAP Recommendation

In regards to the forms processes in MSS processes, the SAP recommendation for implementing processes to change employee data is the following. With the (new) HR Administrative Services, personnel change requests and HCM Processes and Forms coexist in parallel. In SAP ERP 6.0, customers can use either of these functionalities.

Nevertheless, the next release will only support HCM Processes and Forms, not personnel change requests. This means that customers already using personnel change requests are likely to still use them, but perhaps, along with new customers, they will assess the possibility of setting up the HCM Processes and Forms to secure a long-term solution, supported by SAP.

> **Note**
>
> Read carefully, if you haven't already, SAP Note 952693—MSS: Interactive Forms and HCM Processes and Forms.

6.4.2 Define Employee Groupings

In this configuration step, you are defining the different employee groupings as illustrated in Figure 6.13. Some forms might only be relevant for certain employees, so you must create grouping to enable filtering. After the business blueprint is defined, you identify the different groups and set them up here.

IMG Access Path	BUSINESS PACKAGES/FUNCTIONAL PACKAGES • MANAGER SELF-SERVICE (MYSAP ERP) • PERSONNEL CHANGE REQUESTS • DEFINE EMPLOYEE GROUPINGS
IMG Activity	PORT_MAN_PCR_001
Transaction Code	S_AX8_68000156
Table Name	V_TWPC_PCR_EEGRP

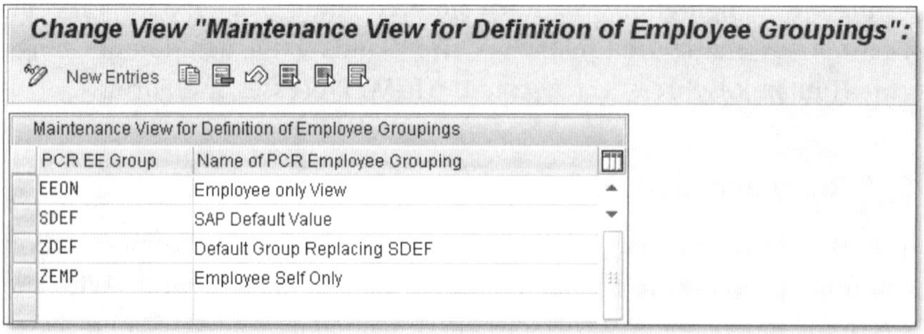

Change View "Maintenance View for Definition of Employee Groupings":

New Entries

Maintenance View for Definition of Employee Groupings

PCR EE Group	Name of PCR Employee Grouping
EEON	Employee only View
SDEF	SAP Default Value
ZDEF	Default Group Replacing SDEF
ZEMP	Employee Self Only

Figure 6.13 Define Personnel Change Request Employee Groupings

6.4.3 Define Change Request Types

In this step, as illustrated in Figure 6.14, you set the different request types. You list the different personnel change request names.

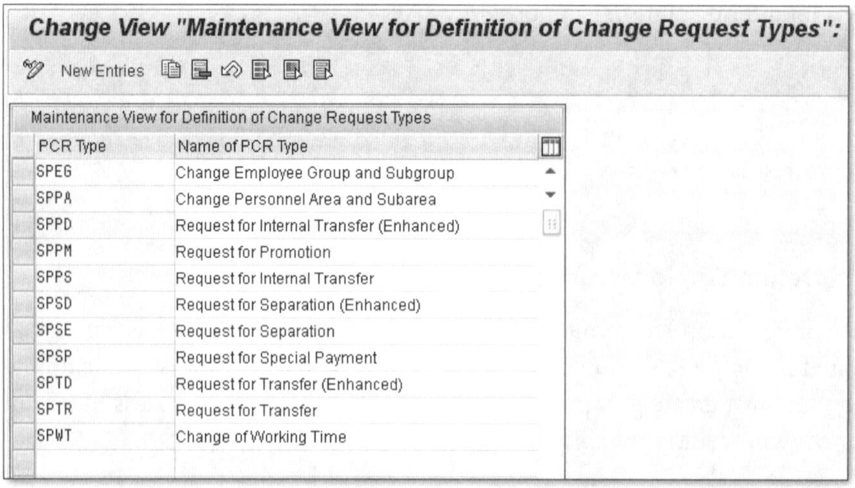

Change View "Maintenance View for Definition of Change Request Types":

New Entries

Maintenance View for Definition of Change Request Types

PCR Type	Name of PCR Type
SPEG	Change Employee Group and Subgroup
SPPA	Change Personnel Area and Subarea
SPPD	Request for Internal Transfer (Enhanced)
SPPM	Request for Promotion
SPPS	Request for Internal Transfer
SPSD	Request for Separation (Enhanced)
SPSE	Request for Separation
SPSP	Request for Special Payment
SPTD	Request for Transfer (Enhanced)
SPTR	Request for Transfer
SPWT	Change of Working Time

Figure 6.14 Define Change Request Types

IMG Access Path	BUSINESS PACKAGES/FUNCTIONAL PACKAGES • MANAGER SELF-SERVICE (MYSAP ERP) • PERSONNEL CHANGE REQUESTS • DEFINE CHANGE REQUEST TYPES
IMG Activity	PORT_MAN_PCR_002
Transaction Code	S_AX8_68000157
Table Name	V_TWPC_PCR_TYPES

6.4.4 Group Change Request Scenarios

In this step, you define, per change request scenario, the groupings for change requests. Set in this table a past end date to deactivate the display in the MSS selection screen.

IMG Access Path	BUSINESS PACKAGES/FUNCTIONAL PACKAGES • MANAGER SELF-SERVICE (MYSAP ERP) • PERSONNEL CHANGE REQUESTS • GROUP CHANGE REQUEST SCENARIOS
IMG Activity	PORT_MAN_PCR_004
Transaction Code	S_AX8_68000158
Table Name	V_WPC_PCR_GROUPS

Figure 6.15 illustrates configuration step for PCR TYPE SPSP — REQUEST FOR SPECIAL PAYMENT.

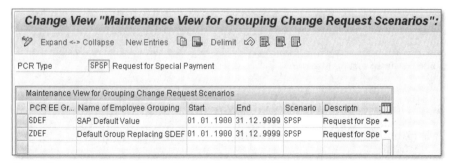

Figure 6.15 Grouping for Change Request Scenarios (SPSP—Request for Special Payment)

6.4.5 Define Scenario Attributes

In this configuration step, you define the scenario attributes. Besides setting up the start and end date, you can also assign the personnel development object in the column WORKFLOWFUNCT and, most important, the potential personnel administrator and the relevant personnel actions, if applicable.

IMG Access Path	BUSINESS PACKAGES/FUNCTIONAL PACKAGES • MANAGER SELF-SERVICE (MYSAP ERP) • PERSONNEL CHANGE REQUESTS • DEFINE SCENARIO ATTRIBUTES
IMG Activity	PORT_MAN_PCR_006
Transaction Code	S_AX8_68000159
Table Name	V_WPC_PCRGENERAL

Figure 6.16 illustrates the standard example entries for this configuration step.

Change View "Maintenance View General Settings for Change Requests": Overview

Expand <-> Collapse New Entries Delimit

Maintenance View General Settings for Change Requests

Scenario	ScenarioName	Start	End	Workflo...	Scenario	Pers. Administrator	Act.	Action Type
SPEG	Change Employee Grou...	01.01.1900	31.12.9999		SPEG	A Administrator for Administration Data	02	Change of Position
SPPA	Change Personnel Area ...	01.01.1900	31.12.9999		SPPA	A Administrator for Administration Data	02	Change of Position
SPPD	Request for Internal Tran...	01.01.1900	31.12.9999		SPPD	A Administrator for Administration Data	02	Change of Position
SPPM	Request for Promotion	01.01.1900	31.12.9999		SPPM	P Payroll Administrator		
SPPS	Request for Internal Tran...	01.01.1900	31.12.9999		SPPS	A Administrator for Administration Data	02	Change of Position
SPSD	Request for Separation (...	01.01.1900	31.12.9999		SPSD	A Administrator for Administration Data	10	Termination
SPSE	Request for Separation	01.01.1900	31.12.9999		SPSE	A Administrator for Administration Data	10	Termination
SPSP	Request for Special Pay...	01.01.1900	31.12.9999		SPSP	P Payroll Administrator		
SPTD	Request for Transfer (En...	01.01.1900	31.12.9999		SPTD	A Administrator for Administration Data	02	Change of Position
SPTR	Request for Transfer	01.01.1900	31.12.9999		SPTR	A Administrator for Administration Data	02	Change of Position
SPWT	Change of Working Time	01.01.1900	31.12.9999		SPWT	T Time Management Administrator		
ZPSE	Voluntary Separation	01.01.1900	31.12.9999		ZPSE	A Administrator for Administration Data	10	Termination

Figure 6.16 Define Scenario Attributes

6.4.6 Define Reasons for Special Payments

Figure 6.17 illustrates the definition of the reasons for special payments.

IMG Access Path	BUSINESS PACKAGES/FUNCTIONAL PACKAGES • MANAGER SELF-SERVICE (MYSAP ERP) • PERSONNEL CHANGE REQUESTS • DEFINE REASONS FOR SPECIAL PAYMENT
IMG Activity	PORT_MAN_PCR_003
Transaction Code	S_AX8_68000160
Table Name	V_TWPC_PCR_PAYM

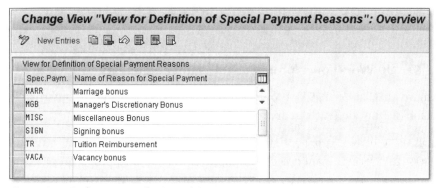

Figure 6.17 Define Reasons for Special Payment

6.4.7 Assign Wage Types to Special Payment Reasons

Figure 6.18 illustrates the assignment of the wage types to the special reasons. Carefully set a start and end date along with the wage type.

IMG Access Path	BUSINESS PACKAGES/FUNCTIONAL PACKAGES • MANAGER SELF-SERVICE (MYSAP ERP) • PERSONNEL CHANGE REQUESTS • ASSIGN WAGE TYPES TO SPECIAL PAYMENT REASONS
IMG Activity	PORT_MAN_PCR_005
Transaction Code	S_AX8_68000161
Table Name	V_WPC_PCR_PAYMWT

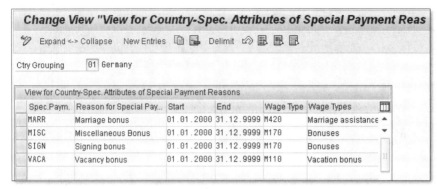

Figure 6.18 Assign Wage Types to Special Payment Reasons

6.4.8 Set Up Workflows for Personnel Change Requests

As illustrated in Chapter 3, SAP provides three templates for the personnel change requests, based on the levels of approval required:

▶ **ProcessPCR_0:** No approval step required is based on template task WS 50000042 — Process Change Request Employee Data (No Approval Step).

▶ **ProcessPCR_1:** One-step approval is based on template task WS50000041 — Process Change Request Employee Data (First Approval Step).

▶ **ProcessPCR_2:** Two-step approval is based on template task WS50000031 — Process Change Request Employee Data (Second Approval Step).

You can copy and configure these templates tasks under Transaction PFTC_CHG — Change Tasks.

IMG Access Path	BUSINESS PACKAGES/FUNCTIONAL PACKAGES • MANAGER SELF-SERVICE (MYSAP ERP) • PERSONNEL CHANGE REQUESTS • SET UP WORKFLOWS FOR PERSONNEL CHANGE REQUESTS
IMG Activity	PORT_MAN_PCR_WFL_001
Transaction Code	S_AX8_68000341 or PCRWF

Figure 6.19 illustrates template task WS50000031. Detailed information on this step can be found in Chapter 9.

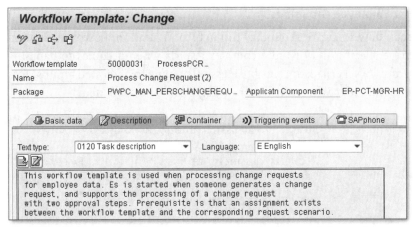

Figure 6.19 Template Workflow Tasks WS50000031 for Personnel Change Request

6.4.9 Business Add-Ins

As usual, SAP provides many BAdIs to enable flexible answers to business requirements. In regards to the personnel change requests, they are handy to use and should be part of the standard configuration. Many of them make sense when dealing with the business requirements.

IMG Access Path	BUSINESS PACKAGES/FUNCTIONAL PACKAGES • MANAGER SELF-SERVICE (MYSAP ERP) • PERSONNEL CHANGE REQUESTS • BUSINESS ADD-INS

In standard systems, these BAdIs are not maintained; it's up to the customer to decide to enable the BAdIs, which requires additional (reasonable) effort and ABAP programming.

BAdIs can be accessed and maintained under Transaction SE18 — Business Add-Ins: Definitions or Transaction SE19 — Business Add-Ins: Implementations, whereas class can be accessed and maintained under Transaction SE24 — Class Builder.

This section provides vital BAdI information, including the access path, IMG activity, transaction code, name, class interface name, and method name.

This information will be useful to the development team.

BAdI: Adjust Employee Groupings

You have seen how to create groupings through configuration; however, customers might have specific and/or more complex criteria when it comes to handling employee groupings. Perhaps specific business rules apply to dedicated groups. This BAdI is the placeholder where this business logic can be maintained.

IMG Access Path	BUSINESS PACKAGES/FUNCTIONAL PACKAGES • MANAGER SELF-SERVICE (MYSAP ERP) • PERSONNEL CHANGE REQUESTS • BUSINESS ADD-INS • BADI: ADJUST EMPLOYEE GROUPINGS
IMG Activity	HRWPC_PCR_EEGRP
Transaction Code	S_AX8_68000162
BAdI Name	HRWPC_PCR_EEGRP—Adjustment: Assignment Employees: Employee Grouping
Class Interface Name	IF_EX_HRWPC_PCR_EEGRP
Method	IF_EX_HRWPC_PCR_EEGRP~EVALUATE_EE_GROUPING

BAdI: Adjust Header Data in Request Forms

This BAdI enables customer to adjust the header data in request forms, if you need to abide by legal or customer requirements when designing and building forms.

IMG Access Path	BUSINESS PACKAGES/FUNCTIONAL PACKAGES • MANAGER SELF-SERVICE (MYSAP ERP) • PERSONNEL CHANGE REQUESTS • BUSINESS ADD-INS • BADI: ADJUST HEADER DATA IN REQUEST FORMS
IMG Activity	HRWPC_PCR_INIT
Transaction Code	S_AX8_68000163
BAdI Name	HRWPC_PCR_INIT—Adjusting Header Data in Change Request Forms
Class Interface name	CL_EX_HRWPC_PCR_INIT
Method	IF_EX_HRWPC_PCR_INIT~MANIPULATE_INIT_DATA

BAdI: Adjust Entry Help in Request Forms

Securing an intuitive UI is one thing, but providing context help and relevant values when dealing and filling in the forms is quite important. This BAdI supports customer requirements to enable additional help and values through the form filling-in process.

IMG Access Path	BUSINESS PACKAGES/FUNCTIONAL PACKAGES • MANAGER SELF-SERVICE (MYSAP ERP) • PERSONNEL CHANGE REQUESTS • BUSINESS ADD-INS • BADI: ADJUST ENTRY HELP IN REQUEST FORMS
IMG Activity	HRWPC_PCR_ADD_VALUES
Transaction Code	S_AX8_68000164
BAdI Name	HRWPC_PCR_ADD_VALUES—Adjusting Value Help for Change Request Forms
Class	CL_EX_HRWPC_PCR_ADD_VALUES
Method	IF_EX_HRWPC_PCR_ADD_VALUES~MANIPULATE_ADD_ VALUES

BAdI: Adjust Effective Date for Request Forms

Let's take an example from the performance management and compensation process Assume that the review outcome is more than positive for an employee, and he is granted a pay raise, but the effective date is in the next quarter. The customer must adjust the system handling of this effective date setup, and that's where the BAdI comes in. This BAdI enables the customer to make the necessary adjustment to the effective date in the request forms.

IMG Access Path	BUSINESS PACKAGES/FUNCTIONAL PACKAGES • MANAGER SELF-SERVICE (MYSAP ERP) • PERSONNEL CHANGE REQUESTS • BUSINESS ADD-INS • BADI: ADJUST EFFECTIVE DATE FOR REQUEST FORMS
IMG Activity	HRWPC_PCR_EFF_DATE
Transaction Code	S_AX8_68000141
BAdI Name	HRWPC_PCR_EFF_DATE—Adjust Effective Date for Request Forms

| Class | CL_EX_HRWPC_PCR_EFF_DATE |
| Method | IF_EX_HRWPC_PCR_EFF_DATE~MANIPULATE_EFF_DATE |

BAdI: Adjust Check for Effective Date

In addition to the previous BAdI, which sets up the effective date, this BAdI provides additional flexibility for executing more checks during the process.

IMG Access Path	BUSINESS PACKAGES/FUNCTIONAL PACKAGES • MANAGER SELF-SERVICE (mySAP ERP) • PERSONNEL CHANGE REQUESTS • BUSINESS ADD-INS • BADI: ADJUST CHECK FOR EFFECTIVE DATE
IMG Activity	HRWPC_PCR_CHECK_DATE
Transaction Code	S_AX8_68000346
BAdI Name	HRWPC_PCR_CHECK_DATE—Adjust Check for Effective Date
Class	CL_EX_HRWPC_PCR_CHECK_DATE
Method	IF_EX_HRWPC_PCR_CHECK_DATE~CHECK_EFFECTIVE_DATE

BAdI: Adjust Rule Resolution for Receiving Manager

You might consider implementing this business rule directly into the workflow tasks but assuming that you don't have SAP Workflow or that you want to maintain this into a piece of code, this BAdI enables you to adjust the rule(s) resolution for the receiving manager.

IMG Access Path	BUSINESS PACKAGES/FUNCTIONAL PACKAGES • MANAGER SELF-SERVICE (mySAP ERP) • PERSONNEL CHANGE REQUESTS • BUSINESS ADD-INS • BADI: ADJUST RULE RESOLUTION FOR RECEIVING MANAGER
IMG Activity	HRWPC_PCR_APPR_FORM
Transaction Code	S_AX8_68000344
BAdI Name	HRWPC_PCR_APPR_FORM—Adjust Rule Resolution for Receiving Manager

Class	CL_EX_HRWPC_PCR_APPR_FORM
Method	IF_EX_HRWPC_PCR_APPR_FORM~MANIPULATE_ACTOR_TAB

BAdI: Adjust Rule Resolution for Higher-Level Manager

Again, you might consider implementing this business rule directly into the workflow tasks but assuming that you don't have SAP Workflow or that you want to maintain this into a piece of code, this BAdI enables you to adjust the rule(s) resolution for determining the next higher level manager.

IMG Access Path	BUSINESS PACKAGES/FUNCTIONAL PACKAGES • MANAGER SELF-SERVICE (MYSAP ERP) • PERSONNEL CHANGE REQUESTS • BUSINESS ADD-INS • BADI: ADJUST RULE RESOLUTION FOR HIGHER-LEVEL MANAGER
IMG Activity	HRWPC_PCR_APPR_NEXT
Transaction Code	S_AX8_68000345
BAdI Name	HRWPC_PCR_APPR_NEXT—Adjust Rule Resolution for Higher-Level Manager
Class	CL_EX_HRWPC_PCR_APPR_NEXT
Method	IF_EX_HRWPC_PCR_APPR_NEXT~MANIPULATE_ACTOR_TAB

6.5   Recruitment

This section covers the basis configuration required to enable the e-recruitment component within SAP Human Capital Management (HCM).

6.5.1   Overview of Manager Involvement in SAP E-Recruiting

The integration with SAP E-Recruiting is introduced in the article *Integrating SAP E-Recruiting*, which is available for download on the web page dedicated to this book at *www.sap-press.com/H3154* or *www.sap-press.de/2430*.

IMG Access Path	BUSINESS PACKAGES/FUNCTIONAL PACKAGES • MANAGER SELF-SERVICE (mySAP ERP) • RECRUITMENT

We also recommend the book *E-Recruiting with SAP ERP HCM* (SAP PRESS 2010), which covers SAP E-Recruitment more in depth.

This section describes the configuration steps located under the MSS configuration.

6.5.2 Create an RFC Connection to the SAP E-Recruiting System

This configuration step is defined by the Basis team or the system administrator. It consists of defining the Remote Function Call (RFC), which enables communication between systems.

IMG Access Path	BUSINESS PACKAGES/FUNCTIONAL PACKAGES • MANAGER SELF-SERVICE (mySAP ERP) • RECRUITMENT • CREATE RFC CONNECTION TO E-RECRUITING SYSTEM
IMG Activity	PORT_MAN_EREC_RFC
Transaction Code	S_E34_98000020 or SM59

6.5.3 Assign SAP E-Recruiting System Names

In table V_T5UA0, you assign the RFC identified for the SAP E-Recruiting system.

IMG Access Path	BUSINESS PACKAGES/FUNCTIONAL PACKAGES • MANAGER SELF-SERVICE (mySAP ERP) • RECRUITMENT • ASSIGN E-RECRUITING SYSTEM NAME
IMG Activity	PORT_MAN_EREC_L_NAME
Transaction Code	S_PLN_62000410
Table Name	V_T5UA0

This is done under the group ERMSS and the RQ SEM.ABB (interface semantic abbreviation) LOGSY. The empty field must contain the customer system name for the LOGICAL NAME FOR RFC CONNECTION TO ERECRUITING SYS as illustrated in Figure 6.20.

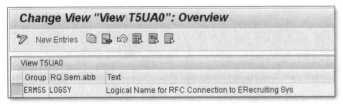

Figure 6.20 Logical Name for RFC Connection to ERecruiting Sys

6.6 Workforce Requirements

This configuration step is only necessary if organizational management and accounting are in two separate systems. It enables the Application Link Enabling (ALE) scenario for transferring quota planning results to the Accounting (AC) component.

IMG Access Path	BUSINESS PACKAGES/FUNCTIONAL PACKAGES • MANAGER SELF-SERVICE (MYSAP ERP) • WORKFORCE REQUIREMENTS

6.6.1 Table T77S0 Settings

Additional configuration is also necessary on the HR side in table T77S0. This well-known HR switches table contains the group SKFCO, which contains several semantic abbreviation as described here:

▸ **SKFCO/COPLS (plan source for CO data transfer)**
  For example, value HDCNT2SKF as provided by the Controlling team.

▸ **SKFCO/KFACNT (stat. key figures: number of positions [change])**
  For example, value 9090 as provided by the Controlling team.

▸ **SKFCO/KFBCNT (stat. key figures: number of positions [budget])**
  For example, value 9100 as provided by the Controlling team.

6.6.2 BAdI: Transfer Planning Results to Accounting

In addition to the standard configuring, SAP provides BAdI HRWPC00_HEAD-CNT2CO—Transferring Headcount to CO, which enables additional flexibility regarding the transfer of planning results into the Accounting component.

IMG Access Path	BUSINESS PACKAGES/FUNCTIONAL PACKAGES • MANAGER SELF-SERVICE (MYSAP ERP) • WORKFORCE REQUIREMENTS • BADI: TRANSFER PLANNING RESULTS TO ACCOUNTING
IMG Activity	HRWPC00_HEADCNT2CO
Transaction Code	S_AX7_68000142
BAdI Name	HRWPC00_HEADCNT2CO—BAdI: Transfer Planning Results to Accounting
Class	CL_EX_HRWPC00_HEADCNT2CO
Method	IF_EX_HRWPC00_HEADCNT2CO~GET_KEYFIGURE

6.7 Cost Center Monitor

This configuration step enables you to set up the cost center monitoring for MSS.

IMG Access Path	BUSINESS PACKAGES/FUNCTIONAL PACKAGES • MANAGER SELF-SERVICE (MYSAP ERP) • COST CENTER MONITOR

If you check a cost center in your system, you can use Transaction KS03—Display Cost Center.

6.7.1 Edit Administration Rules for Cost Center Variances

The configuration of the administration rules for cost center variance is provided by the Controlling team.

IMG Access Path	Business Packages/Functional Packages • Manager Self-Service (mySAP ERP) • Cost Center Monitor • Edit Administration Rules for Cost Center Variances
IMG Activity	FPB_MON_001
Transaction Code	S_ALN_01002591 or FCOM_RULE_CV

Figure 6.21 illustrates access to the configuration transaction.

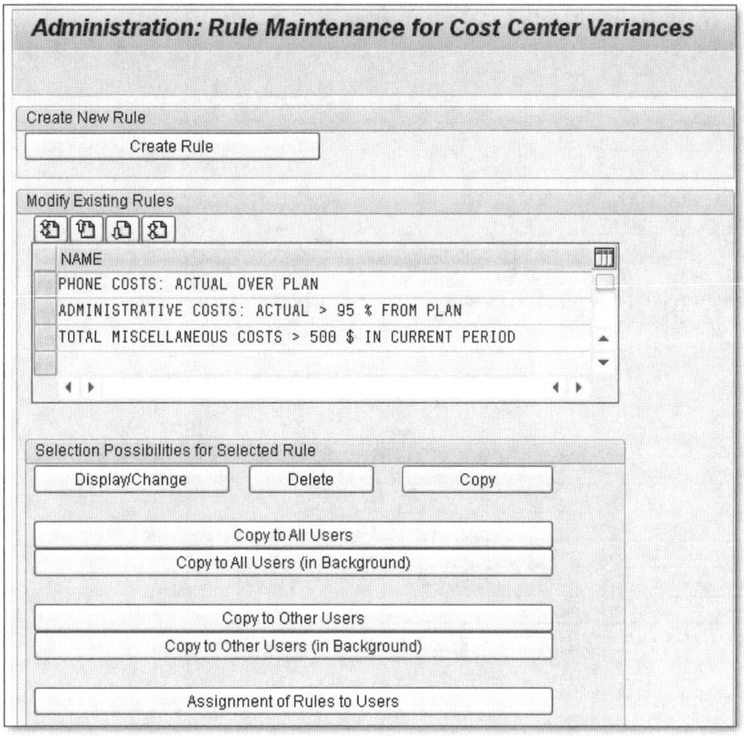

Figure 6.21 Edit Administration Rules for Cost Center Variances

6.7.2 Edit Administration Rules for Cost Center Line Items

The configuration of the administration rules for cost center line items is provided by the Controlling team.

IMG Access Path	BUSINESS PACKAGES/FUNCTIONAL PACKAGES • MANAGER SELF-SERVICE (MYSAP ERP) • COST CENTER MONITOR • EDIT ADMINISTRATION RULES FOR COST CENTER LINE ITEMS
IMG Activity	FPB_MON_002
Transaction Code	S_ALN_01002592 or FCOM_RULE_CL

Figure 6.22 illustrates access to the configuration transaction.

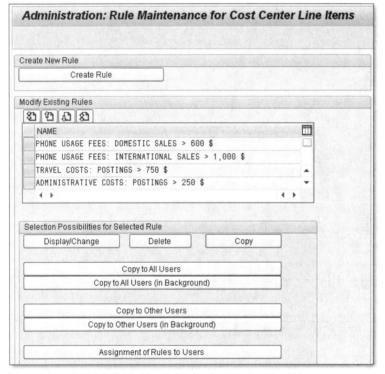

Figure 6.22   Edit Administration Rules for Cost Center Line Items

6.7.3   Execute Evaluations for Critical Cost Center Variances

In this configuration step, you set up the rules defined for the monitor and for posting the results to a database table. The monitor displays the data from this table, enabling faster access to the data than if the rules had to be evaluated again for each access.

IMG Access Path	BUSINESS PACKAGES/FUNCTIONAL PACKAGES • MANAGER SELF-SERVICE (MYSAP ERP) • COST CENTER MONITOR • EXECUTE EVALUATION FOR CRITICAL COST CENTER VARIANCES
IMG Activity	FPB_MON_003
Transaction Code	S_ALN_01002593 or FCOM_ALERT_CV
Program Name	FPB_MON_VAR_ALERT_GENERATE—Execute Rule Evaluation for Critical Variances

This program, illustrated in Figure 6.23, should be set as a background job and run on a daily basis with the rule type to be selected, for example, "C" (Cost Center Monitor).

Set LAST ACCESS AFTER and the DELETE: LAST ACCESS BEFORE per the business requirements. Run the program in test mode before running it in a productive environment.

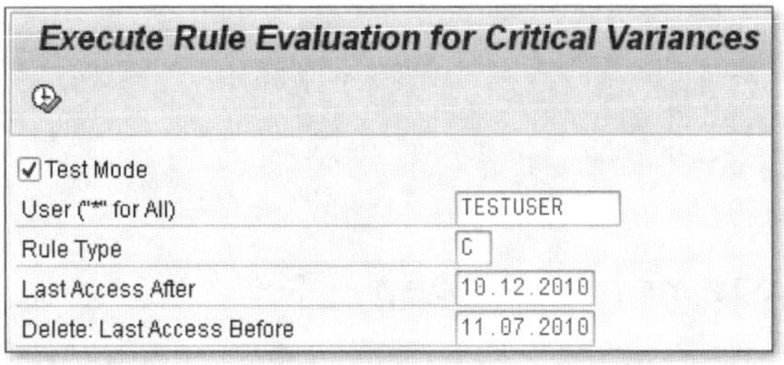

Execute Rule Evaluation for Critical Variances

☑ Test Mode	
User ("*" for All)	TESTUSER
Rule Type	C
Last Access After	10.12.2010
Delete: Last Access Before	11.07.2010

Figure 6.23 Execute Rule Evaluation for Critical Cost Center Variances

6.7.4   Execute Evaluation for Cost Center Line Items

In this configuration step, you set up the rules defined for monitoring and posting the results to a database table. The monitor displays the data from this table, enabling faster access to the data than if the rules had to be evaluated again for each access.

IMG Access Path	BUSINESS PACKAGES/FUNCTIONAL PACKAGES • MANAGER SELF-SERVICE (MYSAP ERP) • COST CENTER MONITOR • EXECUTE EVALUATION FOR COST CENTER LINE ITEMS
IMG Activity	FPB_MON_004

Transaction Code	S_ALN_01002594 or FCOM_ALERT_CL
Program Name	FPB_LINE_VAR_ALERT_GENERATE—Execute Rule Evaluation for Critical Line Items

This program, illustrated in Figure 6.24, should be set as a background job and run on a daily basis with the rule type to be selected, for example, "C" (Cost Center Monitor).

Set LAST ACCESS AFTER and the DELETE: LAST ACCESS BEFORE per the business requirements. Run the program in test mode before running it in a productive environment.

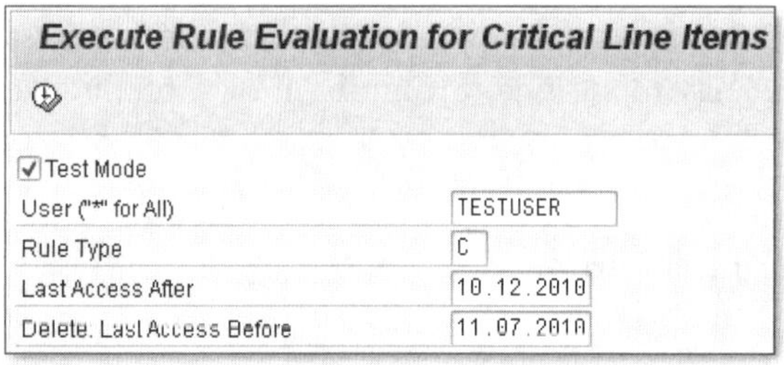

Figure 6.24 Execute Rule Evaluation for Cost Center Line Items

6.7.5   Delete Cost Center Line Items from the Display Set

When the end user confirms a posting in the monitoring process, the posting disappears from the monitoring and is written to a separate database table so that it does not reappear in the monitor after the data update.

To keep the table clean and up to date, in this configuration step, you can delete the entries from the table with the confirmed postings. All postings that were made before the current evaluation date of the rule are then deleted.

IMG Access Path	BUSINESS PACKAGES/FUNCTIONAL PACKAGES • MANAGER SELF-SERVICE (MYSAP ERP) • COST CENTER MONITOR • DELETE COST CENTER LINE ITEMS FROM DISPLAY SET
IMG Activity	FPB_MON_007
Transaction Code	S_ALN_01002597 or FCOM_LINE_SYNC_CL
Program Name	FPB_LINE_DELDATA_SYNC—Synchronization of Line Items

If the rule is reset later on to a new date, after deletion of this table, the postings reappear in the monitoring.

Figure 6.25 illustrates the synchronization of the line items for value "C" (Cost Center Monitor).

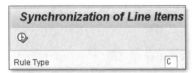

Figure 6.25   Delete Cost Center Line Items from the Display Set

This program should be set as a background job and run on a daily basis with the rule type to be selected, for example, "C" (Cost Center Monitor).

6.7.6   Display Rules for Cost Center Variances per User

This program enables you to identify the rules for end users.

IMG Access Path	BUSINESS PACKAGES/FUNCTIONAL PACKAGES • MANAGER SELF-SERVICE (MYSAP ERP) • COST CENTER MONITOR • DISPLAY RULES FOR COST CENTER VARIANCES PER USER
IMG Activity	FPB_MON_020
Transaction Code	S_PEN_05000148 or FCOM_RULE_USER_CV
Program Name	FPB_RULES_FOR_USER—Display Rules for a User

Figure 6.26 illustrates the program screen DISPLAY RULES FOR A USER, with MONITOR TYPE "V" (Variance Monitor) and MONITOR APPLICATION "C" (Cost Center Monitor).

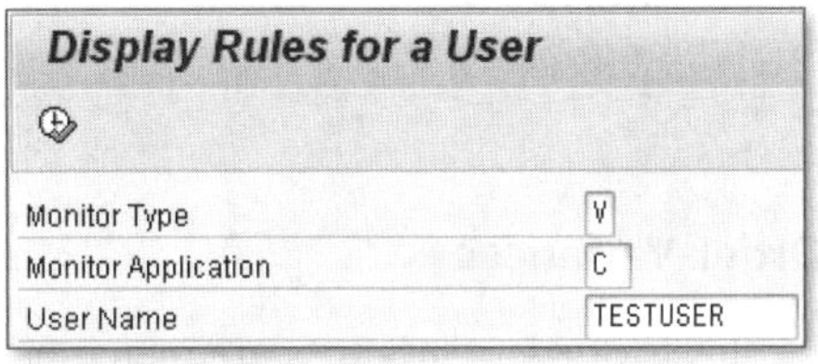

Figure 6.26   Display Rules for Cost Center Variances per User

6.7.7 Display Rules for Cost Center Line Items per User

This program enables you to identify the rules for end users.

IMG Access Path	BUSINESS PACKAGES/FUNCTIONAL PACKAGES • MANAGER SELF-SERVICE (mySAP ERP) • COST CENTER MONITOR • DISPLAY RULES FOR COST CENTER LINE ITEMS PER USER
IMG Activity	FPB_MON_021
Transaction Code	S_PEN_05000149 or FCOM_RULE_USER_CL
Program Name	FPB_RULES_FOR_USER—Display Rules for a User

Figure 6.27 illustrates the program screen DISPLAY RULES FOR A USER, with MONITOR TYPE "L" (Line Item Monitor) and MONITOR APPLICATION "C" (Cost Center Monitor).

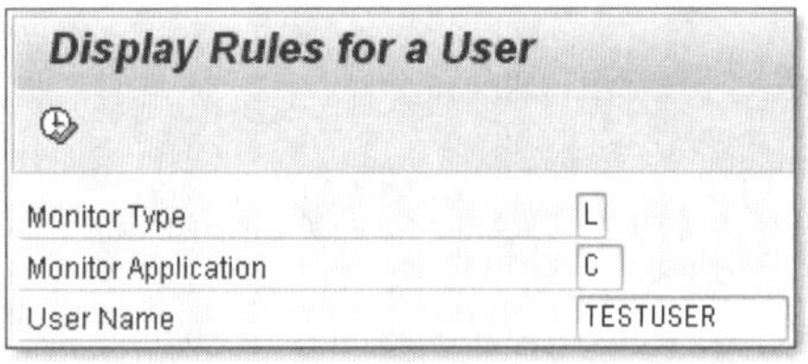

Figure 6.27 Display Rules for Cost Center Line Items per User

6.8 Internal Order Monitor

These configuration steps enable you to customize and adjust the monitoring of internal orders. If you want to display an internal order, you can use Transaction KO03—Display Internal Order.

IMG Access Path	BUSINESS PACKAGES/FUNCTIONAL PACKAGES • MANAGER SELF-SERVICE (mySAP ERP) • INTERNAL ORDER MONITOR

6.8.1 Edit Administration Rules for Order Variances

The configuration and administration of the rules for order variances are provided by the Controlling team.

IMG Access Path	BUSINESS PACKAGES/FUNCTIONAL PACKAGES • MANAGER SELF-SERVICE (mySAP ERP) • INTERNAL ORDER MONITOR • EDIT ADMINISTRATION RULES FOR ORDER VARIANCES
IMG Activity	FPB_MON_005
Transaction Code	S_ALN_01002595 or FCOM_RULE_OV

Figure 6.28 illustrates access to the configuration transaction for editing the administration rules for the order variances.

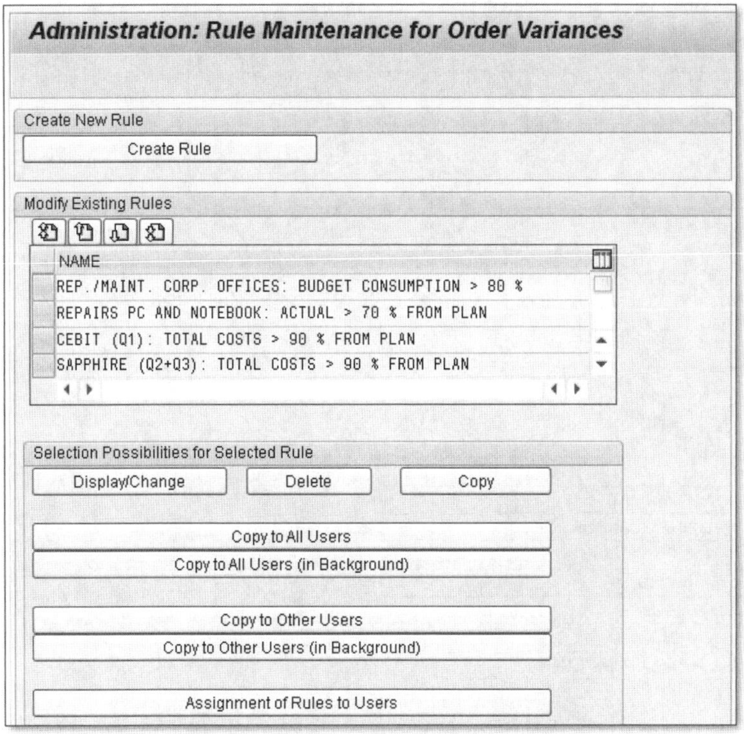

Administration: Rule Maintenance for Order Variances

Create New Rule

Create Rule

Modify Existing Rules

NAME

REP./MAINT. CORP. OFFICES: BUDGET CONSUMPTION > 80 %
REPAIRS PC AND NOTEBOOK: ACTUAL > 70 % FROM PLAN
CEBIT (Q1): TOTAL COSTS > 90 % FROM PLAN
SAPPHIRE (Q2+Q3): TOTAL COSTS > 90 % FROM PLAN

Selection Possibilities for Selected Rule

Display/Change   Delete   Copy

Copy to All Users
Copy to All Users (in Background)

Copy to Other Users
Copy to Other Users (in Background)

Assignment of Rules to Users

Figure 6.28 Edit Administration Rules for Order Variances

6.8.2 Edit Administration Rules for Order Line Items

The configuration and administration of the rules for order line items are provided by the Controlling team.

IMG Access Path	BUSINESS PACKAGES/FUNCTIONAL PACKAGES • MANAGER SELF-SERVICE (MYSAP ERP) • INTERNAL ORDER MONITOR • EDIT ADMINISTRATION RULES FOR ORDER LINE ITEMS
IMG Activity	FPB_MON_006
Transaction Code	S_ALN_01002596 or FCOM_RULE_OL

Figure 6.29 illustrates access to the configuration transaction.

Figure 6.29 Edit Administration Rules for Order Line Items

6.8.3 Execute Evaluation for Critical Order Variances

In this configuration step, you set up the rules defined for monitoring and posting the results to a database table. The monitor displays the data from this table, enabling faster access to the data than if the rules had to be evaluated again for each access.

IMG Access Path	BUSINESS PACKAGES/FUNCTIONAL PACKAGES • MANAGER SELF-SERVICE (MYSAP ERP) • INTERNAL ORDER MONITOR • EXECUTE EVALUATION FOR CRITICAL ORDER VARIANCES
IMG Activity	FPB_MON_008
Transaction Code	S_ALN_01002598 or FCOM_ALERT_OV
Program Name	FPB_MON_VAR_ALERT_GENERATE—Execute Rule Evaluation for Critical Variances

This program, illustrated in Figure 6.30, should be set as a background job and run on a daily basis with the rule type to be selected, for example, "O" (Internal Order Monitor).

Set LAST ACCESS AFTER and the DELETE: LAST ACCESS BEFORE per the business requirements. Run the program in test mode before running it in a productive environment.

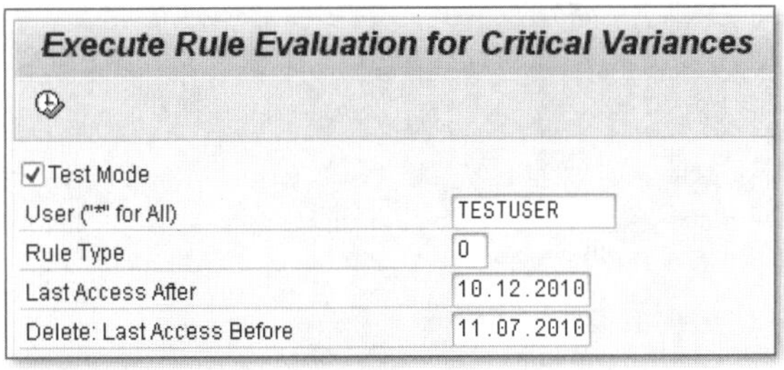

Figure 6.30 Execute Rule Evaluation for Critical Order Variances

6.8.4   Execute Evaluation for Order Line Items

In this configuration step, you set up the rules defined for monitoring and posting the results to a database table. The monitor displays the data from this table, enabling faster access to the data than if the rules had to be evaluated again for each access.

IMG Access Path	BUSINESS PACKAGES/FUNCTIONAL PACKAGES • MANAGER SELF-SERVICE (MYSAP ERP) • INTERNAL ORDER MONITOR • EXECUTE EVALUATION FOR ORDER LINE ITEMS
IMG Activity	FPB_MON_009
Transaction Code	S_ALN_01002599 or FCOM_ALERT_OL
Program Name	FPB_LINE_VAR_ALERT_GENERATE—Execute Rule Evaluation for Critical Line Items

This program, illustrated in Figure 6.31, should be set as a background job and run on a daily basis with the rule type to be selected, for example, "O" (Internal Order Monitor).

Set LAST ACCESS AFTER and the DELETE: LAST ACCESS BEFORE per the business requirements. Run the program in test mode before running it in a productive environment.

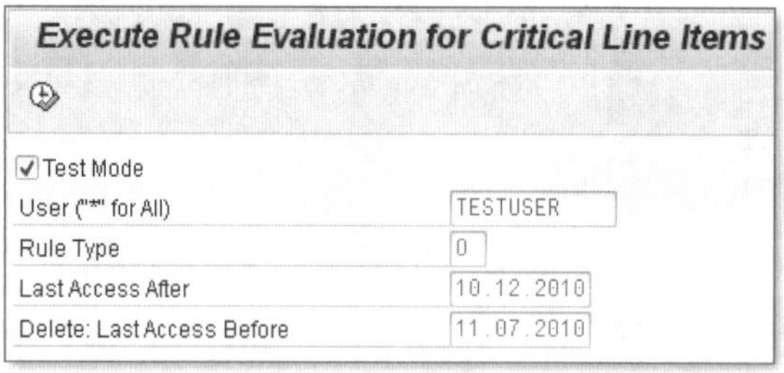

Execute Rule Evaluation for Critical Line Items

☑ Test Mode	
User ("*" for All)	TESTUSER
Rule Type	O
Last Access After	10.12.2010
Delete: Last Access Before	11.07.2010

Figure 6.31 Execute Rule Evaluation for Order Line Items

6.8.5 Delete Order Line Items from the Display Set

When the end user confirms a posting in the monitoring process, the posting disappears from the monitoring and is written to a separate database table so that it does not reappear in the monitor after the data update.

To keep the table clean and up to date, in this configuration step, you can delete the entries from the table with the confirmed postings. All postings that were made before the current evaluation date of the rule are then deleted.

IMG Access Path	BUSINESS PACKAGES/FUNCTIONAL PACKAGES • MANAGER SELF-SERVICE (MYSAP ERP) • INTERNAL ORDER MONITOR • DELETE ORDER LINE ITEMS FROM DISPLAY SET

IMG Activity	FPB_MON_010
Transaction Code	S_ALN_01002600 or FCOM_LINE_SYNC_OL
Program Name	FPB_LINE_DELDATA_SYNC—Synchronization of Line Items

If the rule is reset later on to a new date, after deletion of this table, the postings reappear in the monitoring.

Figure 6.32 illustrates the synchronization of the line items for value "O" (Internal Order Monitor).

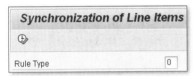

Figure 6.32   Delete Order Line Items from the Display Set

6.8.6   Display Rules for Order Variances per User

This program enables you to identify the rules for end users.

IMG Access Path	Business Packages/Functional Packages • Manager Self-Service (mySAP ERP) • Internal Order Monitor • Display Rules for Order Variances per User
IMG Activity	FPB_MON_018
Transaction Code	S_PEN_05000146 or FCOM_RULE_USER_O
Program Name	FPB_RULES_FOR_USER—Display Rules for a User

Figure 6.33 illustrates the program Display Rules for a User, with Monitor Type "V" (Variance Monitor) and Monitor Application "O" (Internal Order Monitor).

Display Rules for a User

Monitor Type	V
Monitor Application	O
User Name	TESTUSER

Figure 6.33   Display Rules for Order Variances per User

6.8.7   Display Rules for Order Line Items per User

This program enables you to identify the rules for end users.

IMG Access Path	BUSINESS PACKAGES/FUNCTIONAL PACKAGES • MANAGER SELF-SERVICE (MYSAP ERP) • INTERNAL ORDER MONITOR • DISPLAY RULES FOR ORDER LINE ITEMS PER USER
IMG Activity	FPB_MON_019
Transaction Code	S_PEN_05000147 or FCOM_RULE_USER_OL
Program Name	FPB_RULES_FOR_USER—Display Rules for a User

Figure 6.34 illustrates the program DISPLAY RULES FOR A USER, with MONITOR TYPE "L" (Line Item Monitor) and MONITOR APPLICATION "O" (Internal Order Monitor).

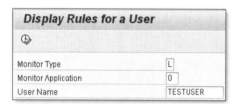

Figure 6.34   Display Rules for Order Line Items per User

6.9   Profit Center Monitor

These configuration steps enable you to customize and adjust the monitoring of the profit center. If you want to display a profit center, you can use Transaction KE53—Display Profit Center.

IMG Access Path	BUSINESS PACKAGES/FUNCTIONAL PACKAGES • MANAGER SELF-SERVICE (MYSAP ERP) • PROFIT CENTER MONITOR

6.9.1   Edit Administration Rules for Profit Center Variances

The configuration and administration of the rules for profit center variances for managers are provided by the Controlling team.

IMG Access Path	BUSINESS PACKAGES/FUNCTIONAL PACKAGES • MANAGER SELF-SERVICE (MYSAP ERP) • PROFIT CENTER MONITOR • EDIT ADMINISTRATION RULES FOR PROFIT CENTER VARIANCES
IMG Activity	FPB_MON_022
Transaction Code	S_PEN_05000158 or FCOM_RULE_PMV

Figure 6.35 illustrates access to the configuration transaction.

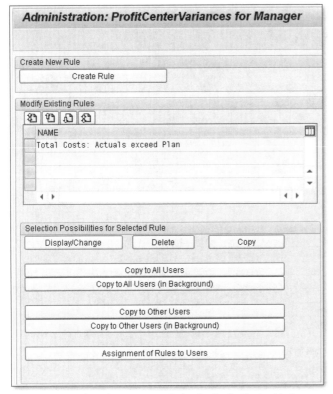

Figure 6.35 Edit Administration Rules for Profit Center Variances

6.9.2   Edit Administration Rules for Profit Center Line Items

The configuration and administration of the rules for profit center line items for managers are provided by the Controlling team.

IMG Access Path	BUSINESS PACKAGES/FUNCTIONAL PACKAGES • MANAGER SELF-SERVICE (mySAP ERP) • PROFIT CENTER MONITOR • EDIT ADMINISTRATION RULES FOR PROFIT CENTER LINE ITEMS
IMG Activity	FPB_MON_023
Transaction Code	S_PEN_05000159 or FCOM_RULE_PML

Figure 6.36 illustrates access to the configuration transaction.

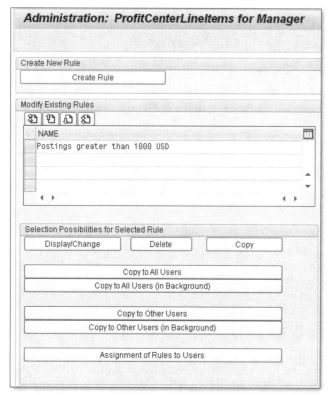

Figure 6.36 Edit Administration Rules for Profit Center Line Items

6.9.3 Execute Evaluation for Critical Profit Center Variances

In this configuration step, you set up the rules defined for monitoring and posting the results to a database table. The monitor displays the data from this table, enabling faster access to the data than if the rules had to be evaluated again for each access.

IMG Access Path	BUSINESS PACKAGES/FUNCTIONAL PACKAGES • MANAGER SELF-SERVICE (MYSAP ERP) • PROFIT CENTER MONITOR • EXECUTE EVALUATION FOR CRITICAL PROFIT CENTER VARIANCES
IMG Activity	FPB_MON_024
Transaction Code	S_PEN_05000160 or FCOM_ALERT_PMV
Program Name	FPB_MON_VAR_ALERT_GENERATE—Execute Rule Evaluation for Critical Variances

This program, illustrated in Figure 6.37, should be set as a background job and run on a daily basis with the rule type to be selected, for example, "PM" (Profit Center Manager).

Set LAST ACCESS AFTER and the DELETE: LAST ACCESS BEFORE per the business requirements. Run the program in test mode before running it in a productive environment.

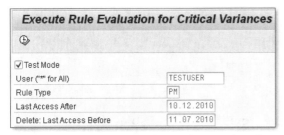

Figure 6.37 Execute Rule Evaluation for Critical Profit Center Variances

6.9.4   Execute Evaluation for Profit Center Line Items

In this configuration step, you set up the rules defined for monitoring and posting the results to a database table. The monitor displays the data from this table, enabling faster access to the data than if the rules had to be evaluated again for each access.

IMG Access Path	BUSINESS PACKAGES/FUNCTIONAL PACKAGES • MANAGER SELF-SERVICE (MYSAP ERP) • PROFIT CENTER MONITOR • EXECUTE EVALUATION FOR PROFIT CENTER LINE ITEMS
IMG Activity	FPB_MON_025
Transaction Code	S_PEN_05000161 or FCOM_ALERT_PML
Program Name	FPB_LINE_VAR_ALERT_GENERATE—Execute Rule Evaluation for Critical Line Items

This program, illustrated in Figure 6.38, should be set as a background job and run on a daily basis with the rule type to be selected, for example, "PM" (Profit Center Manager).

Set LAST ACCESS AFTER and the DELETE: LAST ACCESS BEFORE per the business requirements. Run the program in test mode before running it in a productive environment.

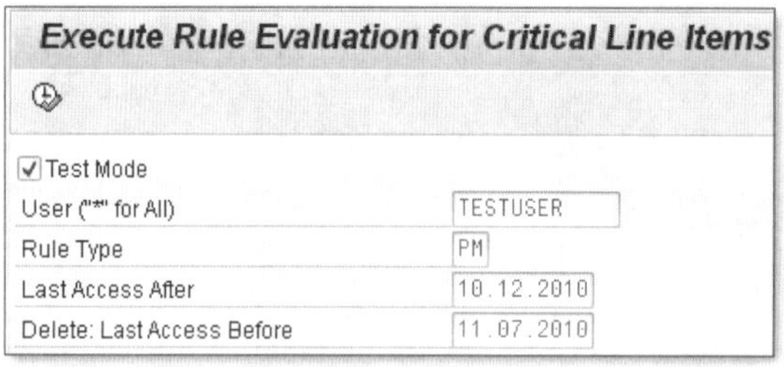

Figure 6.38 Execute Rule Evaluation for Profit Center Line Items

6.9.5 Delete Profit Center Line Items from the Display Set

When the end user confirms a posting in the monitoring process, the posting disappears from the monitoring and is written to a separate database table so that it does not reappear in the monitor after the data update.

To keep the table clean and up to date, in this configuration step, you can delete the entries from the table with the confirmed postings. All postings that were made before the current evaluation date of the rule are then deleted.

IMG Access Path	BUSINESS PACKAGES/FUNCTIONAL PACKAGES • MANAGER SELF-SERVICE (MYSAP ERP) • PROFIT CENTER MONITOR • DELETE PROFIT CENTER LINE ITEMS FROM DISPLAY SET
IMG Activity	FPB_MON_026
Transaction Code	S_PEN_05000162 or FCOM_LINE_SYNC_PML
Program Name	FPB_LINE_DELDATA_SYNC—Synchronization of Line Items

If the rule is reset later on to a new date, after deletion of this table, the postings reappear in the monitoring.

Figure 6.39 illustrates the synchronization of the line items for value "PM" (Profit Center Manager).

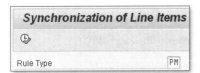

Figure 6.39 Delete Profit Center Line Items from the Display Set

6.9.6 Display Rules for Profit Center Variances per User

This program enables you to identify the rules for end users.

IMG Access Path	BUSINESS PACKAGES/FUNCTIONAL PACKAGES • MANAGER SELF-SERVICE (MYSAP ERP) • PROFIT CENTER MONITOR • DISPLAY RULES FOR PROFIT CENTER VARIANCES PER USER
IMG Activity	FPB_MON_027
Transaction Code	S_PEN_05000163 or FCOM_RULE_USER_PMV
Program Name	FPB_RULES_FOR_USER—Display Rules for a User

Figure 6.40 illustrates the program screen DISPLAY RULES FOR A USER, with MONITOR TYPE "V" (Variance Monitor) and MONITOR APPLICATION "PM" (Profit Center Manager).

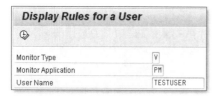

Figure 6.40 Display Rules for Profit Center Variances per User

6.9.7 Display Rules for Profit Center Line Items per User

This program enables you to identify the rules for end users.

IMG Access Path	BUSINESS PACKAGES/FUNCTIONAL PACKAGES • MANAGER SELF-SERVICE (MYSAP ERP) • PROFIT CENTER MONITOR • DISPLAY RULES FOR PROFIT CENTER LINE ITEMS PER USER
IMG Activity	FPB_MON_028
Transaction Code	S_PEN_05000164 or FCOM_RULE_USER_PML
Program Name	FPB_RULES_FOR_USER—Display Rules for a User

Figure 6.41 illustrates the program screen DISPLAY RULES FOR A USER, with MONITOR TYPE "L" (Line Item Monitor) and MONITOR APPLICATION "PM" (Profit Center for Manager).

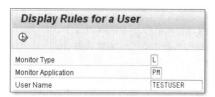

Figure 6.41 Display Rules for Profit Center Line Items per User

6.10 Equipment Monitor

This configuration step enables the display of equipment monitoring such as vehicles or personal laptops or computers.

IMG Access Path	BUSINESS PACKAGES/FUNCTIONAL PACKAGES • MANAGER SELF-SERVICE (MYSAP ERP) • EQUIPMENT MONITOR

6.10.1 Edit Views

Three views come standard:

▶ **Assignment view (ASSIGNMENT)**
Used in MSS and shows the employees which equipment on the manager's cost center is assigned.

▶ **Costs view (COST)**
Used in MSS and shows the costs incurred for the equipment on the manager's cost center.

▶ **Employee view (EMPLOYEE)**
Used in ESS and shows the equipment assigned to an employee.

IMG Access Path	BUSINESS PACKAGES/FUNCTIONAL PACKAGES • MANAGER SELF-SERVICE (MYSAP ERP) • EQUIPMENT MONITOR • EDIT VIEWS
IMG Activity	FPB_MAN_EQUIP_001
Transaction Code	S_ALN_01002601
Table Name	V_FCOM_EQMVIEW_C

As illustrated in Figure 6.42, Figure 6.43, and Figure 6.44, the configuration is done in three steps:

1. **Define the views**
In this step, as illustrated in Figure 6.42, you define the view(s), for example, "EMPLOYEE." In this view, you can define several entries. Regarding the self-services, you are defining the view Employee, which allows you to create a placeholder.

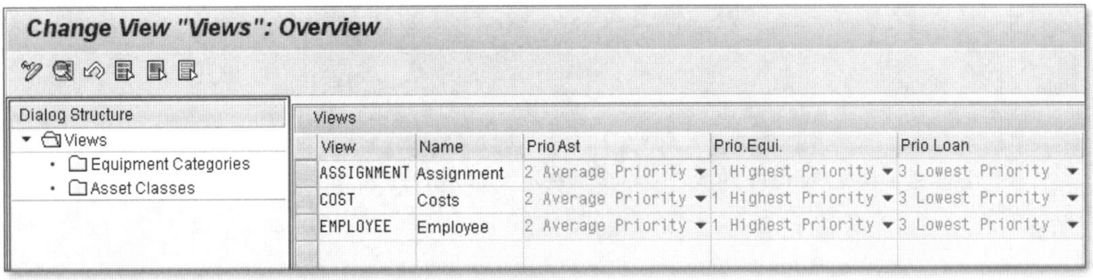

Figure 6.42 Maintain Views for Equipment Monitor

2. **Maintain equipment categories**

   In the next configuration step, you select the view, for example, "EMPLOYEE," and you maintain the equipment categories as illustrated in Figure 6.43.

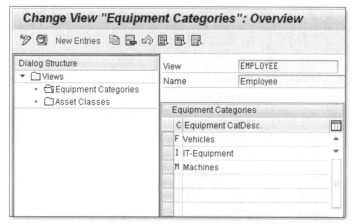

Figure 6.43 Maintain View Equipment Categories

3. **Assign asset classes**

   In the next configuration step, you assign the asset classes, as illustrated in Figure 6.44.

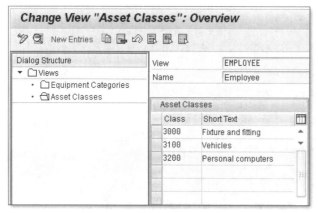

Figure 6.44 Maintain View Asset Classes for Equipment Monitor

6.10.2 Specify the RFC Connection to the HCM System

If you have the FI and the HR components in different systems, you must set up the RFC connection to retrieve additional data such as personal data. The FI system is the primary system to feed the MSS.

IMG Access Path	BUSINESS PACKAGES/FUNCTIONAL PACKAGES • MANAGER SELF-SERVICE (MYSAP ERP) • EQUIPMENT MONITOR • SPECIFY RFC CONNECTION TO HCM SYSTEM
IMG Activity	FPB_MAN_EQUIP_002
Transaction Code	S_ALN_01002616
Table Name	V_FCOM_EQMHCM_C

Figure 6.45 shows an example for the setup of the target system to reach and retrieve HR master data.

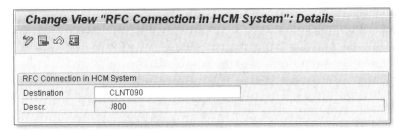

Figure 6.45 Specify the RFC Connection to the HCM System

6.10.3 Prepare Cost Determination

In this step, as a Controlling administrator, you set up the preparation of the cost determination in regards to the equipment.

IMG Access Path	BUSINESS PACKAGES/FUNCTIONAL PACKAGES • MANAGER SELF-SERVICE (MYSAP ERP) • EQUIPMENT MONITOR • PREPARE COST DETERMINATION
IMG Activity	FPB_MAN_EQUIP_003
Transaction Code	S_PLN_62000235 or FCOM_RULE_OA

Figure 6.46 illustrates the access to this standard program, which enables the preparation of the cost determination for all users or new users, as triggered by the Controlling team. All users will be selected when kicking off new projects; when new users come along, you select FOR NEW USERS.

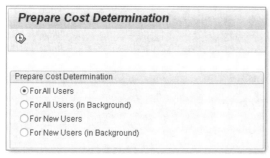

Figure 6.46 Prepare Cost Determination

6.10.4 Execute Cost Determination

In this step, as a Controlling administrator, you execute the cost determination in regards to the equipment thanks to the program FPB_MON_VAR_ALERT_GENER-ATE — Execute Rule Evaluation for Critical Variances.

IMG Access Path	BUSINESS PACKAGES/FUNCTIONAL PACKAGES • MANAGER SELF-SERVICE (MYSAP ERP) • EQUIPMENT MONITOR • EXECUTE COST DETERMINATION
IMG Activity	FPB_MAN_EQUIP_004
Transaction Code	S_PLN_62000248 or FCOM_EQM_COST
Program Name	FPB_MON_VAR_ALERT_GENERATE — Execute Rule Evaluation for Critical Variances.

We recommend running this program in test mode prior to any setup toward a productive environment.

Figure 6.47 illustrates the access to this standard program with RULE TYPE value "OA" (Equipment Cost Determination).

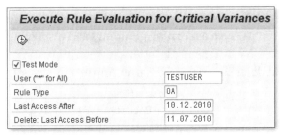

Figure 6.47 Execute Cost Determination

6.10.5 Business Add-Ins

As always, the journey continues with the enabling of more flexibility through the SAP BAdIs.

IMG Access Path	BUSINESS PACKAGES/FUNCTIONAL PACKAGES • MANAGER SELF-SERVICE (MYSAP ERP) • EQUIPMENT MONITOR • BUSINESS ADD-INS

BAdI: Change Equipment Monitor

This BAdI enables further enhancements, such as displaying additional cost center or warehouse identification data, in regards to the equipment screen rendering (screen layout) and its content.

IMG Access Path	BUSINESS PACKAGES/FUNCTIONAL PACKAGES • MANAGER SELF-SERVICE (MYSAP ERP) • EQUIPMENT MONITOR • BUSINESS ADD-INS • BADI: CHANGE EQUIPMENT MONITOR
IMG Activity	FCOM_EQM_CHANGE
Transaction Code	S_PLN_62000205
BAdI Name	FCOM_EQM_CHANGE—BAdI: Change Equipment Monitor
Class	CL_EX_FCOM_EQM_CHANGE
Methods	▶ IF_EX_FCOM_EQM_CHANGE~CHANGE_CONTENT ▶ IF_EX_FCOM_EQM_CHANGE~CHANGE_LAYOUT

BAdI: Assignment of Equipment to Users

This BAdI enables further enhancements, such as creating groupings and displaying equipment according to the business requirements, in both the determination of the equipment for the user and the determination of the user for the equipment.

IMG Access Path	BUSINESS PACKAGES/FUNCTIONAL PACKAGES • MANAGER SELF-SERVICE (MYSAP ERP) • EQUIPMENT MONITOR • BUSINESS ADD-INS • BADI: ASSIGNMENT OF EQUIPMENT TO USERS
IMG Activity	FCOM_EQM_EQUI_USER
Transaction Code	S_PLN_62000206
BAdI Name	FCOM_EQM_EQUI_USER—Equipment for User
Class	CL_IM_FCOM_EQM_EQUI_USER
Methods	IF_EX_FCOM_EQM_EQUI_USER~GET_EQUI_4_USER
	IF_EX_FCOM_EQM_EQUI_USER~GET_USER_4_EQUIS

BAdI: Equipment Monitor, Select Cost Determination

This BAdI enables further enhancements, such as meeting specific business requirements not met in the SAP standard when calculating and determining the costs for the equipment monitoring.

IMG Access Path	BUSINESS PACKAGES/FUNCTIONAL PACKAGES • MANAGER SELF-SERVICE (MYSAP ERP) • EQUIPMENT MONITOR • BUSINESS ADD-INS • BADI: EQUIPMENT MONITOR, SELECT COST DETERMINATION
IMG Activity	FCOM_EQM_COSTS
Transaction Code	S_PLN_62000207
BAdI Name	FCOM_EQM_COSTS—Equipment Monitor, Select Cost Determination
Class	CL_EX_FCOM_EQM_COSTS
Method	IF_EX_FCOM_EQM_COSTS~DETERMINE

6.11   Reporting

MSS is either powered by SAP ERP backend reporting (based on the manager desktop configuration) or with web-based queries (based on Business Intelligence (BI) such as SAP NetWeaver Business Warehouse (BW)).

IMG Access Path	BUSINESS PACKAGES/FUNCTIONAL PACKAGES • MANAGER SELF-SERVICE (MYSAP ERP) • REPORTING

A detailed walkthrough configuration is available in Chapter 7.

6.12   Internal Service Request (ISR)

The Internal Service Request (ISR) technology is empowering as you have seen with the personnel change requests (unless you are opting for the HCM Processes and Forms).

IMG Access Path	BUSINESS PACKAGES/FUNCTIONAL PACKAGES • MANAGER SELF-SERVICE (MYSAP ERP) • INTERNAL SERVICE REQUEST

The configuration steps for ISR were discussed in Chapter 3.

> **Note**
>
> A great starting point when working with the ISRs is to read the free standard SAP Cookbook provided in SAP Note 1049057—ISR documentation: "ISR Cookbook."

Internal Service Request: Overview

This node points to the standard documentation:

> *Internal Service Requests (ISRs) are integrated into various Web applications. Users can send a request in a Web application by clicking a pushbutton. For example, a Business Unit Analyst can request a change to master data.*

IMG Access Path	BUSINESS PACKAGES/FUNCTIONAL PACKAGES • MANAGER SELF-SERVICE (mySAP ERP) • INTERNAL SERVICE REQUEST: OVERVIEW

For more information on the ISR scenarios available in the applications of MSS or the Business Unit Analyst, refer to the SAP Library under CROSS-APPLICATION COMPONENTS • MANAGER SELF-SERVICE OR BUSINESS UNIT ANALYST, and to Chapter 3.

This documentation points to the customizing settings for ISRs located under CROSS-APPLICATION COMPONENTS • INTERNET/INTRANET SERVICES • INTERNAL SERVICE REQUEST.

6.13   Express Planning

Express Planning is also delivered as standard screens in the SAP NetWeaver Portal. The next three configuration steps support the enabling of this functionality.

IMG Access Path	BUSINESS PACKAGES/FUNCTIONAL PACKAGES • MANAGER SELF-SERVICE (mySAP ERP) • EXPRESS PLANNING

6.13.1   Define Planning Scenario

This configuration step leads to the configuration transaction where the Controlling team will enable the different planning scenarios.

IMG Access Path	BUSINESS PACKAGES/FUNCTIONAL PACKAGES • MANAGER SELF-SERVICE (mySAP ERP) • EXPRESS PLANNING • DEFINE PLANNING SCENARIO
IMG Activity	EXP_CUST
Transaction Code	S_PEN_05000016

Figure 6.48 illustrates this customizing access point for defining the planning scenario.

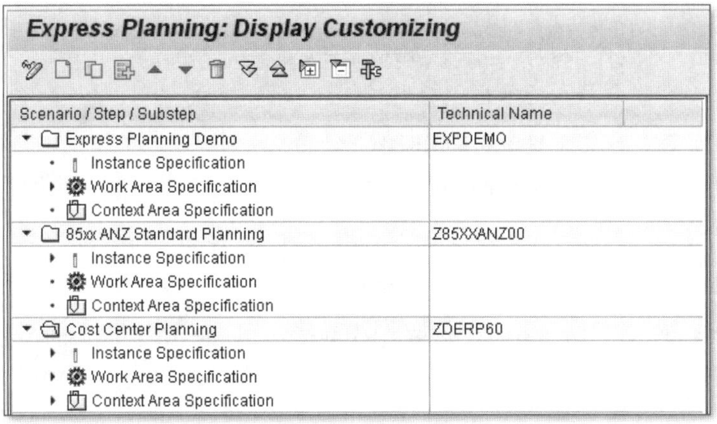

Figure 6.48 Define Planning Scenario

6.13.2 Define Key Figure Prices

This step leads to the configuration and the definition of the key figure prices, as provided by the Controlling department. The key figure can be checked in Transaction KAK3—Display Statistical Key Figures.

IMG Access Path	BUSINESS PACKAGES/FUNCTIONAL PACKAGES • MANAGER SELF-SERVICE (MYSAP ERP) • EXPRESS PLANNING • DEFINE KEY FIGURE PRICES
IMG Activity	EXP_V_FCOM_KFPRICE
Transaction Code	S_PEN_05000177

6.13.3 BAdI: Change Room Parameters

This BAdI is used in the role Business Unit Analyst (BUA) 2.0. In this role, you can create planning rounds for Express Planning. In the SAP NetWeaver Portal, a room is created for every planning round in which you can send Express Planning tasks to the manager and then enable follow up on the status of these planning tasks.

This BAdI enables more flexibility in regards to defining the person responsible, adjusting and changing the role names, adjusting and changing the room parameters, and adjusting or changing the application parameters.

IMG Access Path	Business Packages/Functional Packages • Manager Self-Service (mySAP ERP) • Express Planning • BAdI: Change Room Parameters
IMG Activity	FCOM_PLR_ROOMPARAMS
Transaction Code	S_PEN_05000401
BAdI Name	FCOM_PLR_ROOMPARAMS—Change Room Parameters
Class	CL_EX_FCOM_PLR_ROOMPARAMS
Methods	▶ IF_EX_FCOM_PLR_ROOMPARAMS~CHANGE_OWNER
	▶ IF_EX_FCOM_PLR_ROOMPARAMS~CHANGE_ROLENAMES
	▶ IF_EX_FCOM_PLR_ROOMPARAMS~CHANGE_PARAMS
	▶ IF_EX_FCOM_PLR_ROOMPARAMS~CHANGE_APPL_PARAMS

6.14 Employee Self-Services in Manager Self-Services

Managers can execute ESS on behalf of their employees. Manager can launch ESS for their team members from the iView General Information.

Enabling ESS for MSS reuses the standard ESS and is powered by the configuration of the Homepage Framework (HPFM), which is explained in Chapter 3.

The HPFM configuration table V_T7XSSSERRES—Define Resources (Add Entries) contains dedicated entries for MSS, bearing the naming convention MSS_HCM_SERV_RELACTIVITY_ESS_XXXX_YY where XXXX stands for the ESS functionality and YY for the country.

For example, German ESS for address maintenance for MSS is MSS_HCM_SERV_RELACTIVITY_ESS_ADDR_DE—ESS in MSS PersInfo: German Address.

Figure 6.49 illustrates an excerpt of the configuration for the related employee activities for MSS in table V_T7XSSSERRES. This table describes, for example, the Maintain Address service, which can be called through MSS, on behalf of the employee.

Resource Object Key	Directory Path	Object Name	Description
MSS_HCM_SERV_RELACTIVITY_ESS_ADDR_AR	sap.com/ess~ar~addr	Per_Address_AR	ESSinMSS PersInfo: Argentina Address
MSS_HCM_SERV_RELACTIVITY_ESS_ADDR_AT	sap.com/ess~at~addr	Per_Address_AT	ESSinMSS PersInfo: Austria Address
MSS_HCM_SERV_RELACTIVITY_ESS_ADDR_AU	sap.com/ess~au~addr	Per_Address_AU	ESSinMSS PersInfo: Australia Address
MSS_HCM_SERV_RELACTIVITY_ESS_ADDR_BE	sap.com/ess~be~addr	Per_Address_BE	ESSinMSS PersInfo: Belgium Address
MSS_HCM_SERV_RELACTIVITY_ESS_ADDR_BR	sap.com/ess~br~addr	Per_Address_BR	ESSinMSS PersInfo: Brazil Address
MSS_HCM_SERV_RELACTIVITY_ESS_ADDR_CA	sap.com/ess~ca~addr	Per_Address_CA	ESSinMSS PersInfo: Canada Address
MSS_HCM_SERV_RELACTIVITY_ESS_ADDR_CH	sap.com/ess~ch~addr	Per_Address_CH	ESSinMSS PersInfo: Switzerland Address
MSS_HCM_SERV_RELACTIVITY_ESS_ADDR_CN	sap.com/ess~cn~addr	Per_Address_CN	ESSinMSS PersInfo: China Address
MSS_HCM_SERV_RELACTIVITY_ESS_ADDR_DE	sap.com/ess~de~addr	Per_Address_DE	ESSinMSS PersInfo: German Address
MSS_HCM_SERV_RELACTIVITY_ESS_ADDR_DK	sap.com/ess~dk~addr	Per_Address_DK	ESSinMSS PersInfo: Denmark Address
MSS_HCM_SERV_RELACTIVITY_ESS_ADDR_ES	sap.com/ess~es~addr	Per_Address_ES	ESSinMSS PersInfo: Spain Address
MSS_HCM_SERV_RELACTIVITY_ESS_ADDR_FR	sap.com/ess~fr~addr	Per_Address_FR	ESSinMSS PersInfo: France Address
MSS_HCM_SERV_RELACTIVITY_ESS_ADDR_GB	sap.com/ess~gb~addr	Per_Address_GB	ESSinMSS PersInfo: Great Britain Address
MSS_HCM_SERV_RELACTIVITY_ESS_ADDR_HK	sap.com/ess~hk~addr	Per_Address_HK	ESSinMSS PersInfo: Hong Kong Address
MSS_HCM_SERV_RELACTIVITY_ESS_ADDR_ID	sap.com/ess~id~addr	Per_Address_ID	ESSinMSS PersInfo: Indonesia Address
MSS_HCM_SERV_RELACTIVITY_ESS_ADDR_IT	sap.com/ess~it~addr	Per_Address_IT	ESSinMSS PersInfo: Italy Address
MSS_HCM_SERV_RELACTIVITY_ESS_ADDR_JP	sap.com/ess~jp~addr	Per_Address_JP	ESSinMSS PersInfo: Japan Address
MSS_HCM_SERV_RELACTIVITY_ESS_ADDR_KR	sap.com/ess~kr~addr	Per_Address_KR	ESSinMSS PersInfo: South Korea Address
MSS_HCM_SERV_RELACTIVITY_ESS_ADDR_MX	sap.com/ess~mx~addr	Per_Address_MX	ESSinMSS PersInfo: Mexico Address
MSS_HCM_SERV_RELACTIVITY_ESS_ADDR_MY	sap.com/ess~my~addr	Per_Address_MY	ESSinMSS PersInfo: Malaysia Address
MSS_HCM_SERV_RELACTIVITY_ESS_ADDR_NL	sap.com/ess~nl~addr	Per_Address_NL	ESSinMSS PersInfo: Netherland Address
MSS_HCM_SERV_RELACTIVITY_ESS_ADDR_NO	sap.com/ess~no~addr	Per_Address_NO	ESSinMSS PersInfo: Norway Address
MSS_HCM_SERV_RELACTIVITY_ESS_ADDR_NZ	sap.com/ess~nz~addr	Per_Address_NZ	ESSinMSS PersInfo: New Zealand Address
MSS_HCM_SERV_RELACTIVITY_ESS_ADDR_PH	sap.com/ess~ph~addr	Per_Address_PH	ESSinMSS PersInfo: Philippines Address
MSS_HCM_SERV_RELACTIVITY_ESS_ADDR_PT	sap.com/ess~pt~addr	Per_Address_PT	ESSinMSS PersInfo: Portugal Address
MSS_HCM_SERV_RELACTIVITY_ESS_ADDR_SE	sap.com/ess~se~addr	Per_Address_SE	ESSinMSS PersInfo: Sweden Address
MSS_HCM_SERV_RELACTIVITY_ESS_ADDR_SG	sap.com/ess~sg~addr	Per_Address_SG	ESSinMSS PersInfo: Singapore Address
MSS_HCM_SERV_RELACTIVITY_ESS_ADDR_TH	sap.com/ess~th~addr	Per_Address_TH	ESSinMSS PersInfo: Thailand Address
MSS_HCM_SERV_RELACTIVITY_ESS_ADDR_TW	sap.com/ess~tw~addr	Per_Address_TW	ESSinMSS PersInfo: Taiwan Address

Figure 6.49 Excerpt of Table V_T7XSSSERRES Configuration ESS in MSS

It goes without saying that to enable managers to handle ESS for their team members, proper authorization must also be set. The primary authorization object to enable managers to maintain personnel numbers other than their own is the authorization object P_PERNR—HR: Master Data—Personnel Number Check, which belongs to the class HR—Human Resources.

6.15 Performance Management: Objective Setting and Appraisal

The configuration of the performance management functionality and Objective Setting and Appraisals doesn't come directly under MSS; however, this functionality must be integrated most of the time because it is a common HR process.

> **Note**
>
> This broad topic has its own book, *SAP ERP HCM Performance Management* (SAP PRESS 2008), which covers the functionalities in more detail.

However, in this self-services configuration book, it is important to point out the two options you currently have to enable Objective Setting and Appraisals.

6.15.1 Objective Setting and Appraisals without Enhancement Package 4

The standard Objective Setting and Appraisals, prior to SAP ERP 6.0 and EhP 4, is powered by a Business Server Page (BSP).

BSPs are handy because they can be launched without an SAP NetWeaver Portal and allow you more configuration and technical adjustments as it is programmed with HTML and HTMLB (HTML for Business).

The standard BSP for the Objective Setting and Appraisals is HAP_DOCUMENT. This BSP contains several pages as illustrated in Figure 6.50.

Figure 6.50 Pages for the BSP HAP_DOCUMENT

The BSP can be maintained and tested through Transaction SE80—Object Navigator. The BSP must also be duly activated to enable its use. Failing to activate the BSP triggers an error message "service cannot be reached," which returns an error code "403."

BSPs do require additional or other "technical" BSPs. Carefully read SAP Note 517484—Inactive Services in the Internet Communication Framework, which points out the objects and services, for example:

▶ */sap/bc/bsp/sap/system*

▶ */sap/bc/bsp/sap/public/bc*

▶ */sap/public/bsp/sap/public/bc*

▶ */sap/public/bsp/sap/system*

▶ */sap/public/bsp/sap/htmlb*

▶ */sap/public/bc*

▶ */sap/public/bc/ur*

Tip

Alternatively, you can also use Transaction SICF—HTTP Service Hierarchy Maintenance, which maintains the services and activates the selected BSPs among other services.

To launch the BSP HAP_DOCUMENT, call Transaction PHAP_START_BSP—Generate Internet Addresses.

The HAP_DOCUMENT BSP contains different pages to handle all the Objective Setting and Appraisals processes, for example, the page To DOS, which is illustrated in Figure 6.51.

The BSP HAP_DOCUMENT can be easily integrated in the SAP NetWeaver Portal by using a SAP NetWeaver Portal iView template, as described in Chapter 2. This template points to the BSP HAP_DOCUMENT and the relevant page.

Within the standard SAP NetWeaver Portal objects, SAP also provides standard Web Dynpro iViews to give appraisal overviews:

▶ The iView name is *com.sap.pct.erp.mss.personneldev_appraisals,* which is located under the PCD:

*pcd:portal_content/com.sap.pct/line_manager/com.sap.pct.erp.mss.bp_folder/com.
sap.pct.erp.mss.iviews/com.sap.pct.erp.mss.hcm/com.sap.pct.erp.mss.personneldev_
appraisals*

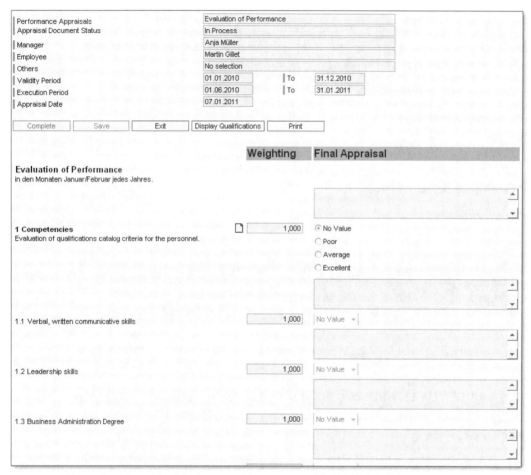

Figure 6.51 Example of Performance Management with BSP HAP_DOCUMENT

▶ The iView name is *com.sap.pct.erp.mss.performance_management*, illustrated in Figure 6.52, which is located under the PCD:

*pcd:portal_content/com.sap.pct/line_manager/com.sap.pct.erp.mss.bp_folder/com.sap.
pct.erp.mss.manager_self_service/com.sap.pct.erp.mss.manager/overview/com.sap.pct.
erp.mss.team/performance_management/com.sap.pct.erp.mss.performance_manage-
ment/com.sap.pct.erp.mss.performance_management*

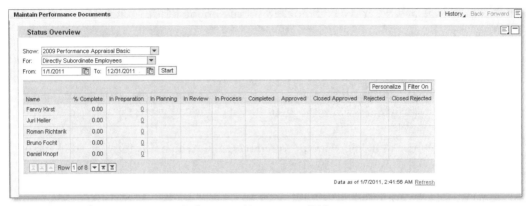

Figure 6.52 Web Dynpro Maintain Performance Management (PM)

Appraisals can also be linked to Enterprise Compensation iView if you enable the hyperlink from columns maintained through the Object and Data Provider (OADP). This step was introduced in Chapter 3.

6.15.2 Objective Setting and Appraisals with Enhancement Package 4

As of EhP 4, available since May 2009 for SAP ERP 6.0, which in this case bears the name EA-HR 604, SAP has enhanced the Performance Management functionalities and, most importantly, migrated the BSPs into Web Dynpros.

To benefit from these new functionalities, activate the business function as already seen previously, in Transaction SFW5—Switch Framework Customizing. The business function for Performance Management is HCM_OSA_CI_1—HCM: Performance Management 01, which enables the switch HRHAP_SFWS_UI_ENH_01.

> **Note**
>
> SAP Note 1239426—Business Function HCM_OSA_CI_1 describes Performance Management for EhP 4 and points to other useful notes for documentation.

6.16 Enterprise Compensation Management (ECM)

The Enterprise Compensation Management (ECM) configuration doesn't come directly under the MSS; however, this functionality must be integrated most of the time because it is a common HR process, right after the Objective Setting and Appraisals.

Note

This broad topic has its own book, *Enterprise Compensation Management with SAP ERP HCM* (SAP PRESS 2009), which covers the functionalities in more detail.

The columns of the ECM are powered by OADP, which was introduced in Chapter 3.

The following InfoTypes are useful in the compensation process of ECM:

- **InfoType 1271 Salary Survey**
  When performing the compensation process, you might want to have reference information collected by third-party providers. These firms sell you salary survey data, which you store in InfoType 1271 Salary Survey. This data helps compensation specialists assess and verify the company or customer salary bands versus the market.

- **InfoType 0758 Compensation Program**
  This InfoType is critical because it contains the pointers to the configuration done in the IMG for the compensation process. The configuration entries are the following:

  - Compensation Area
  - 1st Program Grouping
  - 2nd Program Grouping

- **InfoType 0759 Compensation Process**
  This InfoType is also quite important because it contains the information regarding the compensation process and the salary adjustment/bonus payment data.

  The configuration entries for the compensation process are the following:

  - Comp. Review Item
  - Effective Date
  - Status of Process
  - Compensation Area

  The configuration entries for salary adjustment/bonus payment data are the following:

- ▸ Compensation Amount

- ▸ Compensation Percent

- ▸ Calculation Base

- ▸ Currency

▸ **InfoType 0760 Compensation Eligibility Override**
This InfoType enables the eligibility and the eligibility override for taking part in ECM.

▸ **InfoType 0761 Long Term Incentives Granting**
If the customer also includes Long Term Incentives (LTI) in the compensation process, this InfoType contains the required information after they are granted.

▸ **InfoType 0762 Long Term Incentives Exercising**
This InfoType contains the required information and the amount of LTI that the employees want to exercise.

▸ **InfoType 0763 Long Term Incentives Participant Data**
This InfoType gathers the LTI participant data.

6.17   Additional Configuration

For your convenience, this section includes some handy additional configuration that enables you to reuse standard templates and web-enable data display for managers.

6.17.1   Generic iView for Lists

Because customer will have specific requirements not supported in standard SAP functionalities, a generic iView has been provided. This generic iView (screen) enables customers to create their own iViews, based on a query powered by an InfoSet. This generic iView will display the data as a table or a flat list.

The Floor Plan Manager (FPM), which guides the end user step by step through the process, can also be used for this customer iView.

The standard iView template provided by SAP is *com.sap.pct.erp.mss.genericiview_teamviewer* and, for example, *com.sap.pct.erp.mss.genericiview_communication* as illustrated in Figure 6.53 and Figure 6.54.

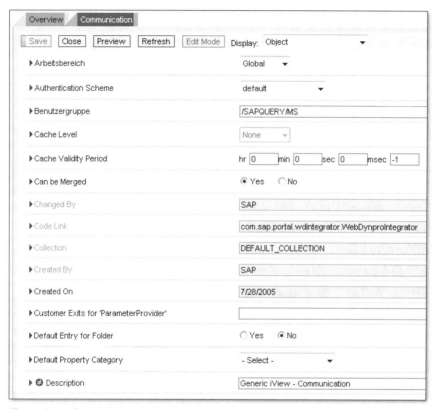

Figure 6.53 Generic iView Communication with Query Parameters (User Group: /SAPQUERY/MS—Query Area: Global)

Figure 6.54 Generic iView Communication with Query Parameters (Query Name)

The iViews are integrated in test page *com.sap.pct.erp.mss.genericiviewtestpage in the standard system*.

The system retrieves data from the SAP ERP backend system, through a SAP query created by the customer. This SAP query is built on an InfoSet.

You will need the following parameters when creating a customer generic iView:

- Query work area

- Query user group

- Query name

- iView name

- Number of columns displayed in iView

- Sort sequence

- Selection period in the past

- Selection period in the future

Optional parameters can also be added to the generic iView:

- Groupings

- Titles of first, second, third, and fourth groups

6.17.2 Internet Graphical Server (IGS)

When dealing with SAP NetWeaver Portal screens, you can sometimes come across graphic error rendering, as illustrated in Figure 6.55. This is most of the time due to missing Internet Graphical Server (IGS) deployment on the SAP NetWeaver Portal or faulty configuration.

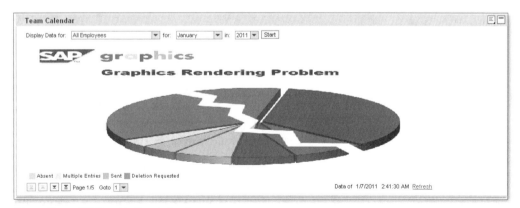

Figure 6.55 IGS Graphic Rendering Issue

To avoid these error messages, read the (nonexhaustive) list of SAP Notes provided here with the Basis team:

- ▶ 454042 — IGS: Installing and Configuring the IGS

- ▶ 946153 — Parameters of the IGS Configuration File igs.xml

- ▶ 896400 — Upgrade Your Integrated IGS 7.x Installation

- ▶ 844669 — Profile Parameter of IGS as of Version 7.x

- ▶ 718267 — Upgrade Your Integrated IGS 6.40 Installation

- ▶ 514841 — Troubleshooting When a Problem Occurs with the IGS

6.17.3 Active Component Framework (ACF)

When dealing with processes and forms and personnel change requests, if not already deployed on the SAP NetWeaver Portal, the system will also render an error message when triggering a form or a change request. The most common error is an empty screen with an "X" in the upper-left side of the screen.

To avoid these error messages, read the (nonexhaustive) list of SAP Notes provided here with the Basis team:

- ▶ 1488874 — ACF: Automatic Download or Installation

- ▶ 766191 — Active Component Framework Installation

- ▶ 1150277 — Prerequisites for Using ACF

- ▶ 1036205 — ACF Support for Adobe Reader 8.1 in SAP Interactive

6.18 Conclusion

Through this chapter, you have seen that SAP delivers several functionalities for MSS. Most of these functionalities can be deployed quickly and enable quick wins for both the company and the employees, assuming that all prerequisites are met, such as master data and technical business functions activation.

Despite the fact that the standard functionalities are easy to set up, they do challenge you in many ways per the manager expectations or just the business requirements. This chapter illustrated the standard configuration steps as well as the additional configuration. We also discussed the integration with E-Recruitment, Objective Setting and Appraisals, and Enterprise Compensation Management (ECM).

Now that you have walked through the Manager Self-Services, let's move to the introduction of the Project Self-Services, which empowers project managers.

You'll find that there is never too much data or too much information, just poor data and information filters. In this chapter, we discuss enabling all types of reports in a consolidated main placeholder to allow the creation and the feeding of key performance indicators (KPIs).

7   Reporting

Today, reporting plays a crucial role in every step we make throughout the day, whether you are a team lead or a manager. Reporting ranges from making assumptions to real-time business decisions. One of the key benefits of having Manager Self-Services (MSS) is that you can enable online reporting, which most managers need to fulfill their responsibilities, and provide and review the well-known key performance indicators (KPIs).

SAP offers a wide range of reporting tools, from the standard reports that you can run in the backend system, to the SAP Queries and ad hoc queries customers can create, up to the Business Intelligence (BI).

SAP does not fail its reputation when it comes to business analytics as reporting has always been further enhanced to provide more capabilities, faster data access, and more options for sorting out the information for the end users.

Today, you can also take advantage of different options or new technologies introduced and supported by SAP, such as SAP NetWeaver Business Warehouse (BW), SAP BusinessObjects (BO), Crystal Reports, Xcelsius, and High-Performance Analytic Appliance (HANA), which was introduced in 2010. These reporting channels provide online access to the functionalities and the reports that can be easily embedded into SAP NetWeaver Portal.

You can summarize and identify the reporting areas listed in Figure 7.1.

In this chapter, we will focus on the main areas:

▶ Standard reports

▶ ABAP queries

▶ Ad hoc queries

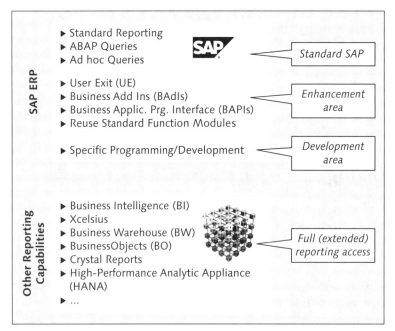

Figure 7.1 Reporting Areas Overview

This chapter covers the configuration settings available in the Implementation Guide (IMG) for the Human Capital Management (HCM) analytics to web-enable them through MSS. This configuration is based on the Manager's Desktop (MDT) configuration, as well as the Homepage Framework (HPFW) configuration. We will also discuss integration with Business Intelligence (BI).

We will also cover the alternative direct configuration of a service map iView in SAP NetWeaver Portal. This configuration unchains customers from backend configuration and customizing.

Because reporting is also based on different options, we also introduce payroll InfoTypes, InfoSets HR switches, and self-services integration points.

Finally, because authorization and data tracking for data changes or updates is also part of reporting, we cover the different options in SAP standard for creating HR logs.

To complete this chapter, we provide some additional reports that are useful when deploying the HR self-services.

7.1   Prerequisites

To run reports, you need the relevant authorizations, and reports are made available throughout the menus or the end user roles. You also must assess whether the relevant master data is available for the report to display; there is nothing more frustrating than reports showing empty columns or fields.

You should also check that the report selection variants are made available to the end users to either make their life easier or to default the selection variant for the report to be run automatically without a selection screen. Also check the display variants provided to the end users. Even if end users want to create their own display variants in the reports, it makes sense to deliver at least a few standard templates to avoid delivering report results that are not sorted or organized when running the report for the first time.

Finally, because we deal mainly with MSS reporting, do not forget, as we have already reminded you several times, that the manager does need to be identified in the organizational structure thanks to the chief position. The chief position is displayed with the icon of a person's head and a hat; technically speaking, it is the personnel development relationship A/B 012 Manages/Is Managed By, as you can see in the transparent table T777E—Allowed Relationships.

Also bear in mind that structural authorizations most likely come on top of regular Basis authorizations because managers can have team members spread out across the organizational structure.

7.2   Report Types

As illustrated previously in Figure 7.1, when it comes to SAP backend reporting, with the exclusion of customer developer programs, you have roughly three kinds of reporting:

▶ Standard reporting as provided by SAP.

▶ ABAP queries, which allow users, key users, and super users to make their own reports without knowing any ABAP language or programming. This is made available to all SAP components, from Finance to HR and Logistics.

▶ Ad hoc queries, which allow HR users, key users, and super users to make their own reports without knowing any ABAP language or programming. This is made available exclusively for the HR component only.

It provides the added value to have a consolidated view when creating the ad hoc query, unlike the SAP query where you have to go through several screens to finally deliver a query. Furthermore, the ad hoc query provides real-time access to master data, enabling preview directly on the configuration screen. The ad hoc query also provides the option SET OF OPERATIONS, which enables users to set a group of data "A" and a second group of data "B." You can then execute the operations A−B, A + B, B−A, or just identify the intersections. These operations narrow down the personnel numbers selection, for example, when looking for colleagues with active status or five years or more of service in the Bay area.

7.3 Identifying the Technical Name of the Reports

Identifying the name of reports is important not only for documentation purposes or authorization access clearance but also for configuration. Also, remember that SAP, faithful to its reputation, does not leave anything to chance when it comes to naming conventions.

7.3.1 HCM Reports Standard Naming Convention

Every report has a clear naming convention, identifying the group of reports to which it belongs:

▸ RP: Belongs to Personnel Administration (PA)

▸ RH: Belongs to Organizational Management (OM) and Personnel Development (PD)

▸ RPT: Belongs to Personnel Time Management (PT)

▸ RPC: Belongs to Payroll (PY)

▸ RPL: Belongs to Listings

▸ RPB: Belongs to Statements

> **Tip**
>
> A quick way to identify a report name and its technical name is using Transaction SARP— Reporting (Tree Structure): EXECUTE.

7.3.2   A Quick Glance at the Standard HCM Reporting Offering

Even though you have to work with the user menu from the authorization roles (Transaction PFCG) or from the area menus (Transaction SE43N), you can still use the best of the so-called "old" transactions codes. SAP provided reporting tree menus prior to introducing the nice left-handed user menus as of release 4.6. At the time, you could call up the reporting trees from any SAP components. Although the list of reports is not exhaustive, it provides a fair list of programs for newcomers or SAP rookies.

The technical name can also be displayed next to the program, which is handy when writing system specifications or business blueprints. Figure 7.2 illustrates Transaction SARP, with report tree HR00 and the activation of TECHNICAL NAMES ON/OFF.

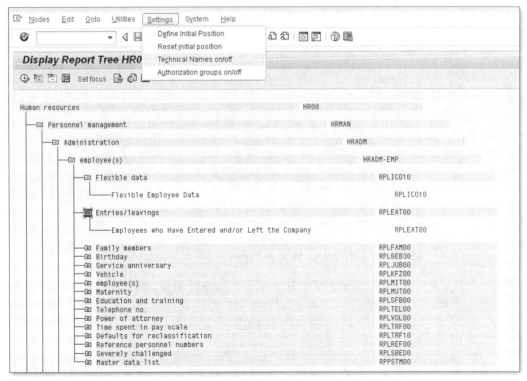

Figure 7.2   Reporting Tree HR00 via Transaction SARP

7.4   Payroll InfoTypes

Another fact you must deal with when deploying reporting for MSS is the lack of options when you need access to payroll results. In most companies, only a happy few users have access clearance to the payroll cluster, for example, the cluster RT — Results Table, because these employees deal with payroll-sensitive data.

This data can be accessed through the program RPCLSTRD — Display Cluster RD (although this program is theoretically meant for the German payroll results). This leaves most end users, including managers, on the bench and frustrated because they cannot add these figures in their reporting or, even worse, have to wait for that "super user" to download the data into Excel or Access software to get access to the figures.

As of SAP 4.6B, SAP introduced the Payroll InfoTypes. Even though the solution provided does not cover all business needs, it is already a step forward for providing real net payroll results. It can be easily added through the Payroll InfoTypes and then added into a query.

This customizing feature can be accessed under IMG access path SAP CUSTOMIZING IMPLEMENTATION GUIDE • PERSONNEL MANAGEMENT • HUMAN RESOURCES INFORMATION SYSTEM • PAYROLL RESULTS.

The five configuration settings illustrated here are done through a cross-client table, which can set your customizing settings at risk. Carefully check any side effects on other project or team configurations. Furthermore, this table is Molga driven (in SAP speak, Molga refers to the country code). For example, Molga "01" is the country key for Germany.

7.4.1   Define Evaluation Wage Types

As illustrated in Figure 7.3, in this step, you have to define your evaluation wage type, decide if there is a cumulation (such as monthly, quarterly, etc.), and decided whether to pick the amount or the number.

IMG Access Path	SAP CUSTOMIZING IMPLEMENTATION GUIDE • PERSONNEL MANAGEMENT • HUMAN RESOURCES INFORMATION SYSTEM • PAYROLL RESULTS • DEFINE EVALUATION WAGE TYPES

IMG Activity	OHIXP0402_02
Transaction Code	S_AHR_61010413
Table Name	V_T52IC

The last two rows of the table in Figure 7.3 shows evaluation wage type Z777—
TOTAL GROSS AMOUNT and the same wage type Z777 along with a monthly (M)
cumulation.

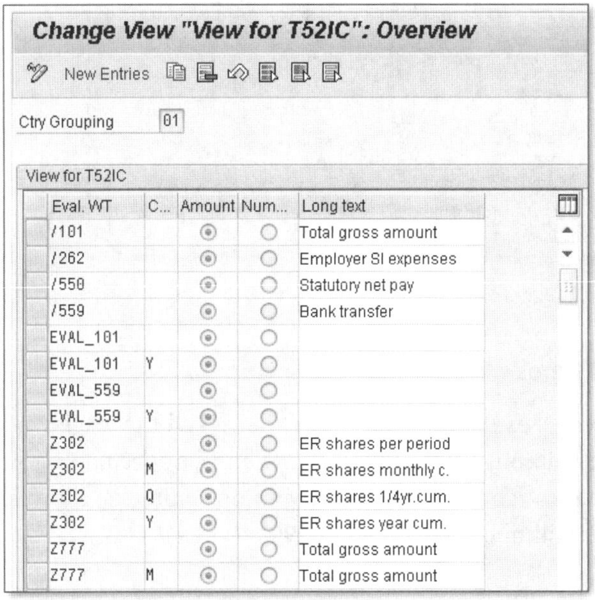

Change View "View for T52IC": Overview

New Entries

Ctry Grouping 01

View for T52IC

Eval. WT	C...	Amount	Num...	Long text
/101		⊙	○	Total gross amount
/262		⊙	○	Employer SI expenses
/550		⊙	○	Statutory net pay
/559		⊙	○	Bank transfer
EVAL_101		⊙	○	
EVAL_101	Y	⊙	○	
EVAL_559		⊙	○	
EVAL_559	Y	⊙	○	
Z302		⊙	○	ER shares per period
Z302	M	⊙	○	ER shares monthly c.
Z302	Q	⊙	○	ER shares 1/4yr.cum.
Z302	Y	⊙	○	ER shares year cum.
Z777		⊙	○	Total gross amount
Z777	M	⊙	○	Total gross amount

Figure 7.3 Define Evaluation Wage Types

7.4.2 Assign Wage Types

As illustrated in Figure 7.4, in this configuration step, you map the evaluation wage
type created (Z777) in the previous step against the wage types used in payroll,
for example, wage type /101—TOTAL GROSS AMOUNT as illustrated in Figure 7.4.
This ensures that you are retrieving the right payroll data. Leave the option NEG.
inactivated because you do not want the amount of the chosen wage type to be a
negative value when calculating the evaluation wage type.

IMG Access Path	SAP Customizing Implementation Guide • Personnel Management • Human Resources Information System • Payroll Results • Assign Wage Types
IMG Activity	OHIXP0402_03
Transaction Code	S_AHR_61010418
Table Name	V_T52IE

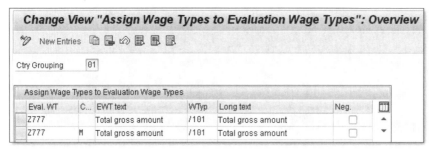

Figure 7.4 Assign Wage Types

7.4.3 Set Up Payroll InfoTypes

Now that you have decided which evaluation wage type to use and the wage type assignment, you can generate, without any technical knowledge, a specific Payroll InfoType such as 94XX. You must pick up the naming convention among the allowed InfoType customer include (CI) number range 9000–9999.

IMG Access Path	SAP Customizing Implementation Guide • Personnel Management • Human Resources Information System • Payroll Results • Set Up Payroll InfoTypes
IMG Activity	OHIXP0402_01
Transaction Code	S_AHR_61010423
Table Name	T582S

As illustrated in Figure 7.5, you set the following values:

▶ INFOTYPE 9975

Number chosen by the customer within the SAP customer include range 9000–9999.

▶ COUNTRY GROUPING

Determine the parameter MOL, in this case, "01" for Germany.

▶ TYPE OF PAYROLL INFOTYPE

Currently only relevant for the United States, so leave it blank to have the default value International Payroll InfoType.

▶ CUMULATION TYPE

Choose the relevant entry per the business requirements, for example, M for monthly cumulation type.

▶ IT TEXT

Set the name for the customer InfoType, for example, "SAP PRESS PY InfoType."

▶ PAYROLL INFOTYPE ACTIVE

Flag this tick box to make the InfoType active.

▶ PAYROLL INFOTYPE GENERATED

This field is populated by the system to indicate that you have generated the InfoType.

Figure 7.5 Set Up Payroll InfoType 9975 for SAP PRESS PY InfoType

Now you select the InfoType entry 9975, and from the left hand side, select ASSIGN EVALUATION WTs. Click on NEW ENTRY, and enter the value as illustrated in Figure 7.6, which points to the previous configuration entries done in customizing.

Tip

In the standard system, you have the following InfoType examples, which have exactly the same structure. The main differences between the InfoTypes are the predefined wage types.

▸ 0402 Payroll results: periodic values

▸ 0403 Payroll results: periodic values

▸ 0458 Monthly cumulations

▸ 0459 Quarterly cumulations

▸ 0460 Annual cumulations

▸ 0446–0457 Various tax cumulations for the United States

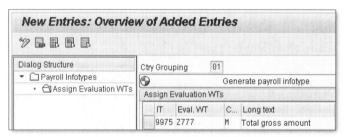

Figure 7.6 Set Up Payroll InfoTypes: Assigning Evaluation Wage Types and Generating InfoTypes

Save your data and generate the InfoType using the icon GENERATE PAYROLL INFOTYPE. The system triggers a message (message technical ID: RP673) "Payroll InfoType 9975 generated successfully" at the bottom of the screen.

During the generation, carefully check the automatic addition to the InfoSets that the system performs. Not all InfoSets may require you to add this Payroll InfoType.

You just created and generated a customer InfoType (with its relevant table, structure, and fields, as illustrated in Figure 7.7) without needing any technical skills or awareness of Transaction PM01—Enhance InfoTypes or Transaction PPCI—Copy InfoType.

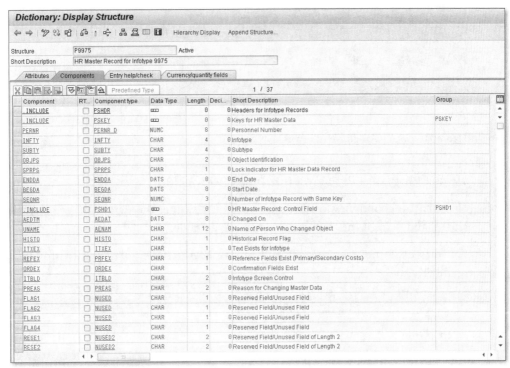

Figure 7.7 Customer InfoType 9975 Structure as Seen Through Transaction SE11—ABAP Dictionary Maintenance

7.4.4 Set Up Assignment to Payroll

The last remaining action is to confirm the activation of this Payroll InfoType you just created, as illustrated in Figure 7.8.

Simply create a new entry, add the customer Payroll InfoType, and press ⌨Enter. The box ACTIVE is now flagged by the system. Save your entries, and exit the configuration step.

IMG Access Path	SAP CUSTOMIZING IMPLEMENTATION GUIDE • PERSONNEL MANAGEMENT • HUMAN RESOURCES INFORMATION SYSTEM • PAYROLL RESULTS • SET UP ASSIGNMENT TO PAYROLL
IMG Activity	OHIXP0402_04
Transaction Code	S_AHR_61010427
Table Name	V_T52IF

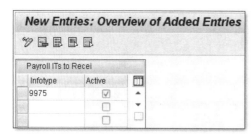

Figure 7.8 Set Up Assignment to Payroll

7.4.5 Program Fill Payroll InfoTypes (RPABRI00)

Now that the configuration is done, you must extract the data from the payroll cluster and place it into the customer InfoType table.

For this example, you trigger the report RPABRI00—Fill Payroll InfoTypes manually.

Report name	RPABRI00
Report title	Fill Payroll InfoTypes
Transaction Code	(none)
Authorization Group	(none)
Package	PCAL—SAP HR Payroll Application Development

In normal SAP implementations, as illustrated in Figure 7.9, you schedule the report RPABRI00—Fill Payroll InfoTypes to run right after your payroll program (RPCALCX0, X being your country; for example, Belgium uses RPCALCB0). This ensures that payroll data is made available after payroll has run.

Through Transaction SA38—ABAP Reporting, execute the report RPABRI00 as no direct transaction is assigned to this report.

Select the relevant personnel area or personnel numbers (or other options) for whom the system must garnish the customer InfoType, choose the time frame, and set the payroll customer InfoType you just created: 9975. Set the system to retrieve data for FOR-VIEW PAYROLL PERIODS.

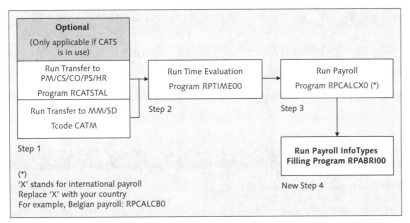

Figure 7.9 Report RPABRI00 Steps in a Typical Time-Payroll Process

Fill Payroll infotypes

Further selections	⇨	Search helps

Period

- ○ Today
- ◉ Up to today
- ○ Other period
- ○ Current month
- ○ From today
- ○ Current year

Period		To	
Payroll period			

Selection

Personnel Number	1000	⇨
Payroll area		⇨
Pers.area/subarea/cost cente		⇨
Employee group/subgroup		⇨

Other Parameters

| Infotype(s) | 9975 | to | | ⇨ |

- ◉ For-view payroll periods
- ○ In-view payroll periods
- ○ Only Original Results
- ☑ Display Statistics

Figure 7.10 Log (Successful Completion) Fill Payroll InfoType Report RPABRI00

The example illustrated in Figure 7.10 shows the time frame option UP TO TODAY selected and (for response time issues) only one PERSONNEL NUMBER "1000" that you can find in your SAP IDES sandbox system. The option DISPLAY STATISTICS is also selected.

Execute the report. The system issues the requested statistics as illustrated in Figure 7.11.

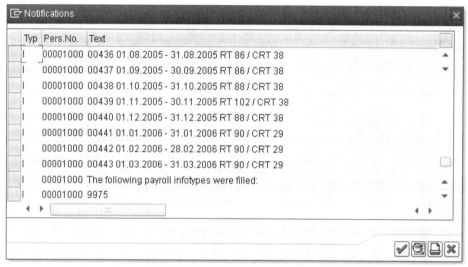

Figure 7.11 Fill Payroll InfoType Report RPABRI00

7.4.6 Access to Customer Payroll InfoType

After the configuration is done, as illustrated in the previous steps, and after the Fill Payroll InfoType has run, the InfoType becomes available for display only in the Personnel Administration (PA) transactions such as Transaction PA20—Display HR Master Data or Transaction PA30—Maintain HR Master Data.

This InfoType, as illustrated in Figure 7.12, now provides real data access to the payroll clusters without requesting access to the cluster itself, which is a relief for the authorization team. The access clearance to the whole payroll clusters data is kept to a minimum because the data is sensitive.

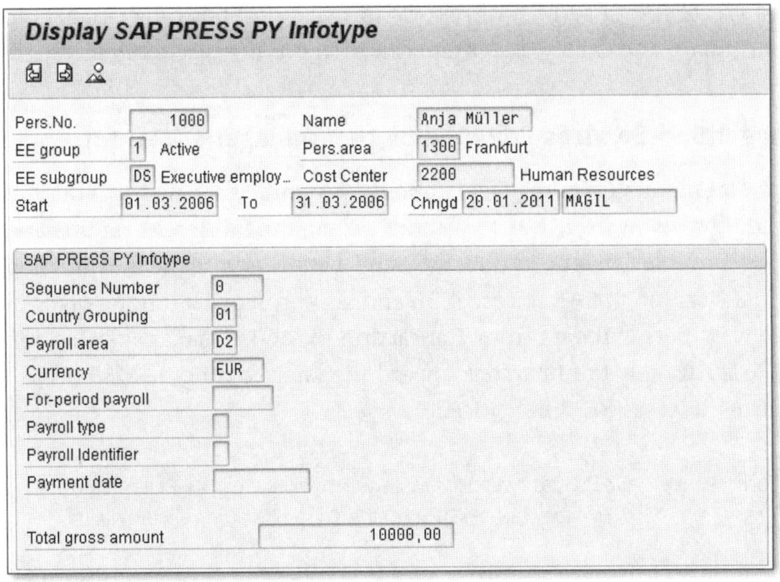

Figure 7.12 Displaying Customer Payroll InfoType through Transaction PA20

7.4.7 Adding the Payroll InfoType into the Customer InfoSet

Now that you have a customer InfoType, the values and the information contained in this customer InfoType can be easily integrated into SAP queries by creating or updating the InfoSet on which the SAP query is based.

From Transaction SQ02 — SAP Query: Maintain InfoSet, add this customer InfoType into the customer InfoSet. Regenerate the whole InfoSet.

Tip

If the InfoSet is already in use among SAP queries, execute an adjustment so that all technical bridges between the updated InfoSet and the existing SAP queries are also updated.

7.5 Manager Self-Services Configuration for Reporting

Now that you have identified the reports, the queries, and their technical names, let's web-enable these reports on MSS. You first need to create a placeholder for all the reports, create the categories of reports to make it easier for managers to browse and sort them, and finally assign the categories to the placeholder.

7.5.1 Manager Self-Services Powered by the Manager's Desktop

In response to complaints from managers about how difficult it was to find and run reports and how awkward it was to wander through the different reports and transactions, SAP provided all reports directly to the managers with the introduction of the Manager's Desktop in SAP release 4.5B and also provided a unique place of entry with the view personal data from Transaction PPMDT—Manager's Desktop (see Figure 7.13). This was the first step toward the later coming of MSS in SAP release 4.70 also known as R/3 Enterprise.

IMG Access Path   SAP CUSTOMIZING IMPLEMENTATION GUIDE • PERSONNEL MANAGEMENT • MANAGER'S DESKTOP

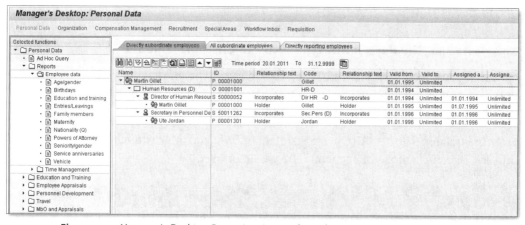

Figure 7.13   Manager's Desktop Reporting Access through Transaction PPMDT

A wizard is available for beginners, but the UI is a little awkward and also, from time to time, it does not save the customizing entries. Because of this, we'll go through the configuration step by step.

Regarding configuration naming conventions, we are strictly using the rules provided and defined by SAP in table TRESC—Reserved Names for Customizing Tables/

Objects, which means that customer customizing entries will start with a "Z" to clearly identify entries belonging to the customer and not to SAP.

7.5.2   Define Scenario-Specific Settings: Define Application Scenarios

In this step, you create the placeholder, which is actually the scenario that will contain all the MSS configuration.

IMG Access Path	SAP CUSTOMIZING IMPLEMENTATION GUIDE • PERSONNEL MANAGEMENT • MANAGER'S DESKTOP • CUSTOMER ADJUSTMENT • DEFINE SCENARIO-SPECIFIC SETTINGS • DEFINE APPLICATION SCENARIOS
IMG Activity	SIMG_MACMWBS
Transaction Code	S_AHR_61019104
Table Name	T77MWBS (Maintenance Dialog) Caution, this table is cross client. Technical Transparent Table T77MWBT

Carefully notice, as illustrated in Figure 7.14, the standard default entries used with the standard solution from SAP:

▶ SCENARIO MSS: MANAGER SELF-SERVICE

▶ SCENARIO RPT0: MANAGER SELF-SERVICE

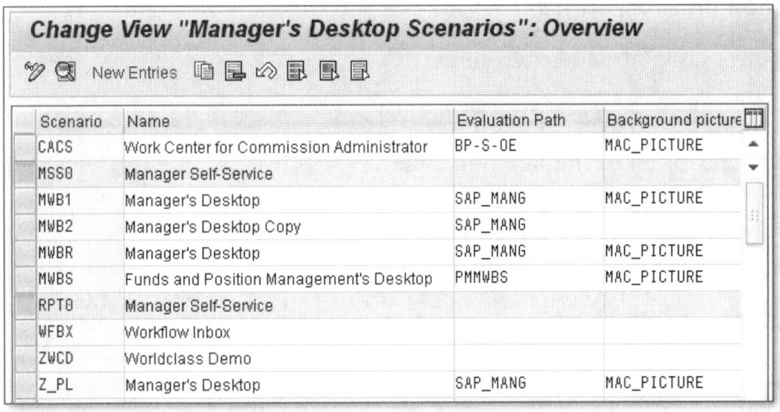

Scenario	Name	Evaluation Path	Background picture
CACS	Work Center for Commission Administrator	BP-S-OE	MAC_PICTURE
MSS0	Manager Self-Service		
MWB1	Manager's Desktop	SAP_MANG	MAC_PICTURE
MWB2	Manager's Desktop Copy	SAP_MANG	
MWBR	Manager's Desktop	SAP_MANG	MAC_PICTURE
MWBS	Funds and Position Management's Desktop	PMMWBS	MAC_PICTURE
RPT0	Manager Self-Service		
WFBX	Workflow Inbox		
ZWCD	Worldclass Demo		
Z_PL	Manager's Desktop	SAP_MANG	MAC_PICTURE

Figure 7.14   Standard Manager's Desktop Scenarios with Focus on MSS0 and RPT0 for Manager Self-Services

As instructed by SAP in table TRESC—Reserved Names for Customizing Tables/ Objects, you will use customer name convention Z* or Y* for the standard table T77MWBT.

As an example, you will now create the scenario "ZMSS" for the company SAP PRESS, as illustrated in the Figure 7.15.

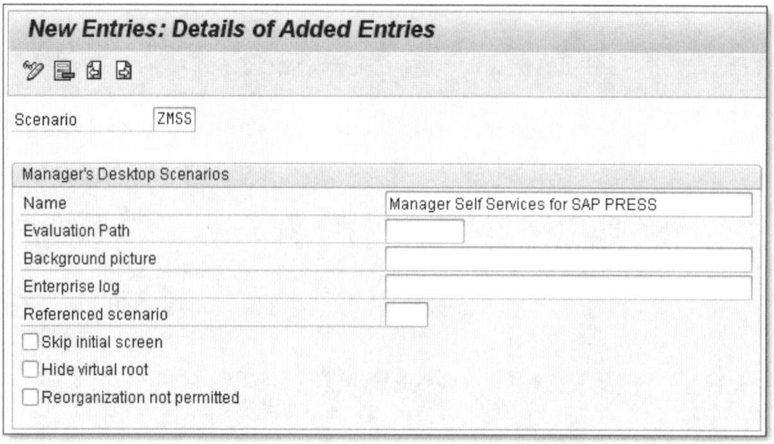

New Entries: Details of Added Entries

Scenario   ZMSS

Manager's Desktop Scenarios

Name	Manager Self Services for SAP PRESS
Evaluation Path	
Background picture	
Enterprise log	
Referenced scenario	
☐ Skip initial screen	
☐ Hide virtual root	
☐ Reorganization not permitted	

Figure 7.15   Customer Manager Self-Services Scenario ZMSS

Assign the configuration to the relevant workbench transport order, and move to the next step.

7.5.3   Define Function Codes

This configuration table provides two steps:

1. Define the function codes for Manager's Desktop.
2. Change the description of the function codes.

IMG Access Path	SAP CUSTOMIZING IMPLEMENTATION GUIDE • PERSONNEL MANAGEMENT • MANAGER'S DESKTOP • ENHANCEMENT OF FUNCTION CODES • DEFINE FUNCTION CODES: ACTIVITY DEFINE FUNCTION CODES FOR MANAGER'S DESKTOP
IMG Activity	SIMG_MACBFCD

Transaction Code	S_AHR_61000481
Table Name	T77MWBFCT Caution, this table is cross client.

A function code as defined by SAP is actually the program, either the standard program for SAP or an ad hoc query. This configuration step illustrates the addition of a SAP report and a SAP query.

As instructed by SAP in table TRESC—Reserved Names for Customizing Tables/ Objects, you will use customer name convention Z* or Y* for the standard table T77MWBFCD.

These three functions codes will be set to type "NODE" (non-executable node).

In this step, you will create the following entries:

▶ As illustrated in Figure 7.16, you create a root node MSS Home linked to our scenario ZMSS, which will be the overall placeholder of all function codes to be created.

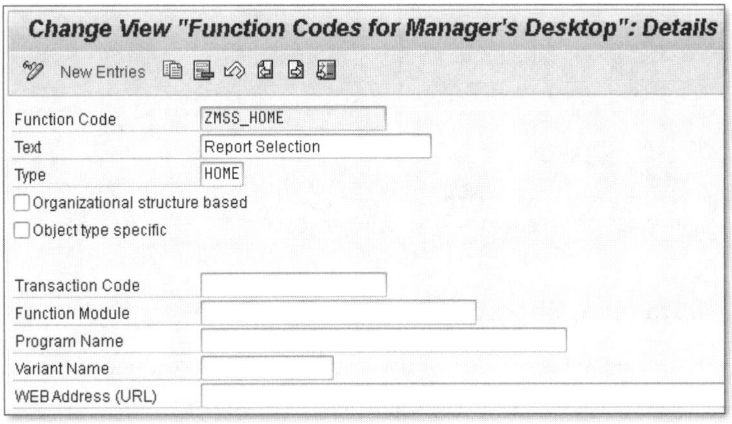

Figure 7.16 Function code ZMSS_Home Node

▶ As illustrated in Figure 7.17 and Figure 7.18, you create two categories: "Personnel Administration" (Z_MSS_PA) and "Personnel Time Management" (Z_MSS_PT), which help you organize the list of function codes. If you have a list of 50+ reports, for example, it would be difficult for end user to find the relevant report. Instead, you create categories, which are like drawers within the placeholder.

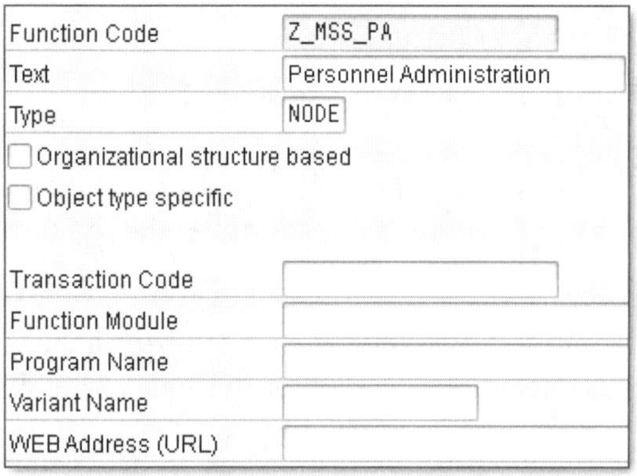

Function Code	Z_MSS_PA
Text	Personnel Administration
Type	NODE
☐ Organizational structure based	
☐ Object type specific	
Transaction Code	
Function Module	
Program Name	
Variant Name	
WEB Address (URL)	

Figure 7.17 Function Code ZMSS_PA—Personnel Administration

Function Code	Z_MSS_PT
Text	Personnel Time Management
Type	NODE
☐ Organizational structure based	
☐ Object type specific	
Transaction Code	
Function Module	
Program Name	
Variant Name	
WEB Address (URL)	

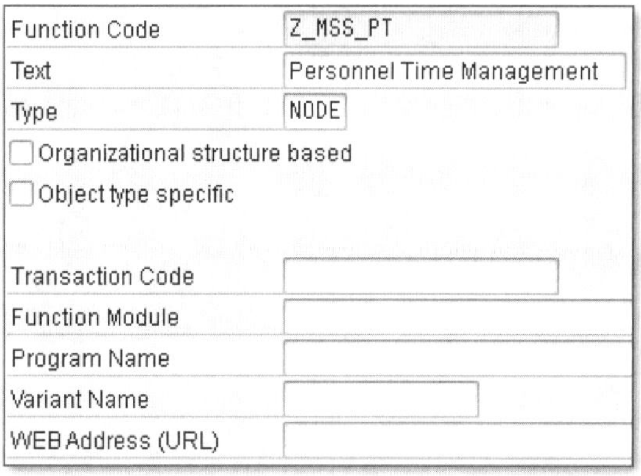

Figure 7.18 Function Code ZMSS_PT—Personnel Time Management

7.5.4   Defining a Standard Report with a Function Code

In this section, we will use two reports to show you how to add a function code. These function codes are Employee List (program RPLMIT00) in function code ZHR_RPLMIT00, illustrated in Figure 7.19, and Personal Work Schedule (program RPTPSH10) in function code ZHR_RPTPSH10, illustrated in Figure 7.20.

Both reports are set to report type "REPO" (reports) so you add their respective names in the field PROGRAM NAME.

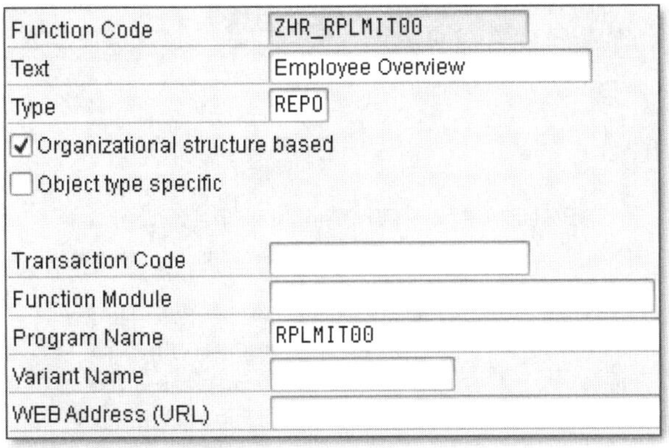

Function Code	ZHR_RPLMIT00
Text	Employee Overview
Type	REPO
☑ Organizational structure based	
☐ Object type specific	
Transaction Code	
Function Module	
Program Name	RPLMIT00
Variant Name	
WEB Address (URL)	

Figure 7.19 Function Code ZHR_RPLMIT00

Function Code	ZHR_RPTPSH10
Text	Personal Work Schedule
Type	REPO
☑ Organizational structure based	
☐ Object type specific	
Transaction Code	
Function Module	
Program Name	RPTPSH10
Variant Name	
WEB Address (URL)	

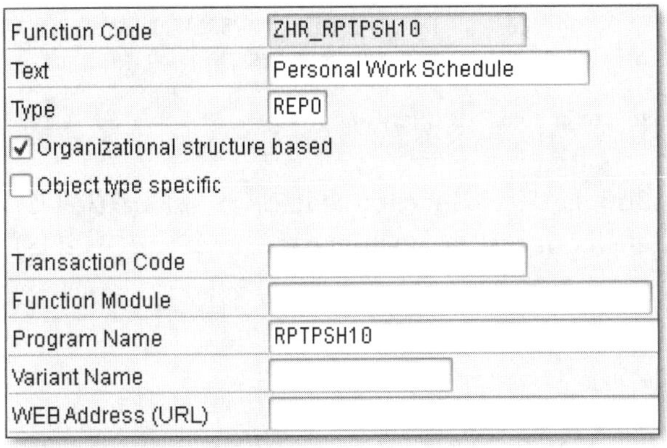

Figure 7.20 Function Code ZHR_RPTPSH10

These reports are also based the Organizational Structure for the employees selection screen. This will enable the manager to selected employees or staff members along his organizational structure or his area of responsibility.

7.5.5 Defining a SAP Query into a Function Code

Adding SAP queries requires the same procedure as for standard reports, except that you must add a few more parameters as illustrated in Table 7.1.

The configuration is easy as long as you abide by the instructions provided by SAP (in the SAP AG Configuration Guide for the Reporting Workset 60.1).

Field Name	Description	Value	Comment
TYPE	Type of Function code	REPO	
PROGRAM NAME		*SAPQUERY*	This enables the system to identify that it is a SAP query.
WEB ADDRESS (URL)		\<Work Area>*\<User Group>*\<Query Name>	A query is identified using these three parameters. If you want to use the query PHONE_LIST from the user group /SAPQUERY/H2, which belongs to the global work area (X), you should enter the value X*/SAPQUERY/H2/ PHONE_LIST in the URL field.

Table 7.1 Manager's Desktop Parameters to Enable SAP Query Reporting

You are adding two SAP queries: Birthday List in function code ZMSS_BIRTHDAYLIST, illustrated in Figure 7.21, and Telephone List in function code ZMSS_PHONELIST, illustrated in Figure 7.22.

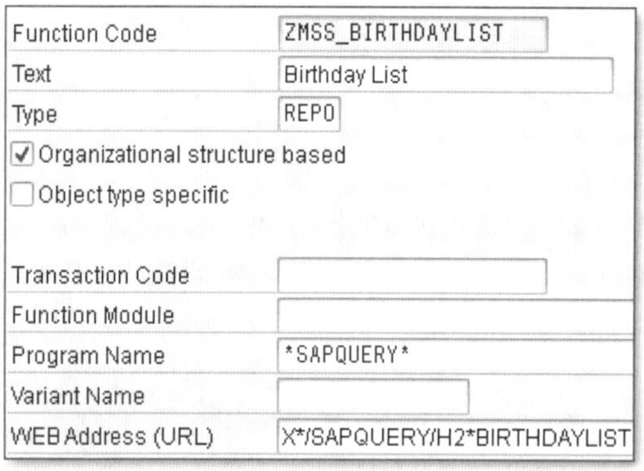

Figure 7.21 Function Code ZMSS_BIRTHDAYLIST

Add the information illustrated in the figures into the configuration. Make sure to set the value in the right sequence in the WEB ADDRESS URL text box.

Assign the configuration to the relevant workbench transport order, and move to the next step.

Function Code	ZMSS_PHONELIST
Text	Telephone List
Type	REPO
☑ Organizational structure based	
☐ Object type specific	
Transaction Code	
Function Module	
Program Name	*SAPQUERY*
Variant Name	
WEB Address (URL)	X*/SAPQUERY/H2*PHONE_LIST

Figure 7.22 Function Code ZMSS_PHONELIST

7.5.6 Change the Description of Function Codes

If needed, translate the report names, depending on the languages used for the self-services project, as illustrated in Figure 7.23.

Lang.	Function Code	Text
DE	ZNF01	Übersicht Nachfolgeplanun
DE	ZQUALSRCH	Suche n. Qualifikationen
EN	ZCOMP_1	Job Pricing
EN	ZCOMP_2	Compa-Ratios
EN	ZCOMP_3	Salary actual : planned
EN	ZNF01	Succession Overview
EN	Z_NACHFOLGE	Succession Overview
FR	ZCOMP_1	Evaluation monétaire
FR	ZCOMP_2	Ratios
FR	ZCOMP_3	Salaire réel : théorique
FR	ZHR_RPLMIT00	Liste de salariés
FR	ZNF01	Succession Overview
FR	Z_CH_PK	Caisse de pensions
JA	ZCOMP_1	ジョブプライシング
JA	ZCOMP_2	コンパレシオ
JA	ZCOMP_3	給与 実際: 予定
JA	ZNF01	後任者概要
TR	ZNF01	Yedekleme plnl.gnl.bakış
TR	ZQUALSRCH	Nitelikler araması
Z1	ZCOMP_1	Job Pricing
Z1	ZCOMP_2	Compa-Ratios
Z1	ZCOMP_3	Salary actual : planned
Z1	ZNF01	Succession Overview
Z1	Z_NACHFOLGE	Succession Overview

Figure 7.23 Change the Description of Function Codes

373

| IMG Access Path | SAP CUSTOMIZING IMPLEMENTATION GUIDE • PERSONNEL MANAGEMENT • MANAGER'S DESKTOP • ENHANCEMENT OF FUNCTION CODES • DEFINE FUNCTION CODES: ACTIVITY CHANGE DESCRIPTION OF FUNCTION CODES |

For example, we have maintained the text in French (FR) for the function code ZHR_RPLMIT00 (report RPLMIT00): Employee List, which is *Liste des salariés* in French.

7.5.7   Define the Structure of Function Codes

In this configuration step, you create the hierarchy, so all configuration entries and categories come together. You set the reports into the report categories, which then are linked to the home node, which is then assigned to the customer Manager's Desktop scenario ZMSS. In this step, you may not be aware of it, but you are organizing the UI rendering for the end user.

IMG Access Path	SAP CUSTOMIZING IMPLEMENTATION GUIDE • PERSONNEL MANAGEMENT • MANAGER'S DESKTOP • ENHANCEMENT OF FUNCTION CODES • DEFINE STRUCTURE OF FUNCTION CODES: ACTIVITY DEFINE FUNCTION CODE HIERARCHIES
IMG Activity	SIMG_MACFCH
Transaction Code	S_AHR_61000473
Table Name	T77MWBFCH. Caution, this table is cross client.

Figure 7.24 illustrates the new customizing entries for mapping all the relevant entries.

Scenario	Higher-level Fcode	N.	Function Code	Function Module
ZMSS		1	ZMSS_HOME	
ZMSS	ZMSS_HOME	1	Z_MSS_PA	
ZMSS	ZMSS_HOME	2	Z_MSS_PT	
ZMSS	Z_MSS_PA	1	ZHR_RPLMIT00	
ZMSS	Z_MSS_PA	2	ZMSS_BIRTHDAYLIST	
ZMSS	Z_MSS_PA	3	ZMSS_PHONELIST	
ZMSS	Z_MSS_PT	2	ZHR_RPTPSH10	

Figure 7.24   Define Function Code Hierarchies

You attach first the categories Z_MSS_PA and Z_MSS_PT to the Z_MSS_HOME node, which is mapped to the root function code ZMSS_HOME.

Within each category, you set the function code with a sequence number, for example, in category Z_MSS_PA, you will find the Employee List (RPLMIT00) in the first position and the Birthday List in the second position.

> **Note**
>
> For these customizing entries, in table TRESC—Reserved Names for Customizing Tables/Objects, SAP instructs us to use naming convention Z* or Y*. To keep a relevant traceability, however, we decided to keep the Z* naming convention for these steps and therefore not use customer name convention Z* or Y* for the standard table T77MWBFCT because the risk is nonexistent.

Assign the configuration to the relevant workbench transport order, and move to the next step.

Repeat all steps to provide more reports categories and/or report assignments.

7.5.8   Homepage Framework Configuration

Now that you have defined the placeholder with all the reports to be provided to managers, you still have to give instructions to the system to pick up the ZMSS scenario you created.

You may wonder how the system actually knows how to retrieve data from the Manager's Desktop scenario ZMSS? The answer is far from a fancy SAP NetWeaver Portal configuration.

IMG Access Path	SAP CUSTOMIZING IMPLEMENTATION GUIDE • CROSS-APPLICATION COMPONENTS • HOMEPAGE FRAMEWORK • RESOURCES • DEFINE RESOURCES • DEFINE RESOURCES (ADD ENTRIES)
IMG Activity	PCUI_HPF_065
Transaction Code	S_FAD_62000051
Table Name	V_T7XSSSERRES (Customer view V_T7XSSSERRESC)

This scenario is actually passed over, as a URL parameter allocated in the Homepage Framework standard resource MSS_HCM_SERV_REPORTING_REPSELECTION, as illustrated in Figure 7.25.

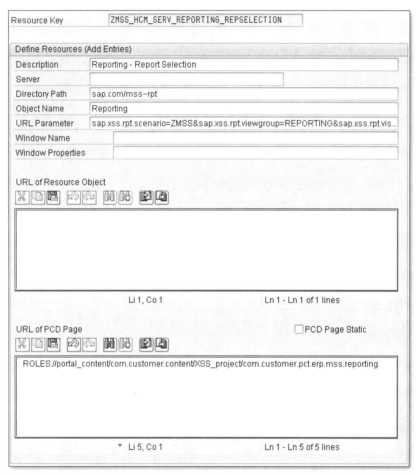

Figure 7.25 Resource ZMSS_HCM_SERV_REPORTING_REPSELECTION

You now copy the standard resources entry from MSS_HCM_SERV_REPORTING_REPSELECTION into ZMSS_HCM_SERV_REPORTING_REPSELECTION.

Within this new copied entry, you set the URL parameter to the configured scenario ZMSS:

sap.xss.rpt.scenario=ZMSS&sap.xss.rpt.viewgroup=REPORTING&sap.xss.rpt.
visiblerowcount=0

Replace the value "ZMSS" with your customer MSS (Manager's Desktop) reporting scenario.

You also make the resource point to the XSS Project folder in the PCD:

ROLES://portal_content/com.customer.content/XSS_project/com.customer.pct.erp.mss.
reporting

Copy the address from the portal object iView.

> **Open Question**
>
> There is an ongoing discussion concerning whether or not you can create a customer entry in the standard SAP table V_T7XSSSERRES because the customer standard configuration table V_T7XSSSERRESC is provided. We did run into some minor issues when using the customer configuration table. When requesting permission as customer, ensuring that we use the authorized naming convention, we have always configured our entries in the standard SAP table V_T7XSSSERRES.
>
> As always, the SAP standard should not be touched in any way; we will create a copy of the customizing entry in a reserved naming convention for the customer.
>
> Therefore, as instructed by SAP in table TRESC—Reserved Names for Customizing Tables/Objects, we will use customer name convention Z* or Y* for the standard table V_T7XSSSERRES.
>
> For more information regarding the HPFW, refer to Chapter 3, Section 3.1.

7.5.9 Adjusting iView Reporting Parameter Scenarios with Value ZMSS

Now that the connection is made from SAP ERP to the SAP NetWeaver Portal thanks to the values contained in the resource ZMSS_HCM_SERV_REPORTING_REPSE-LECTION, you can make the connection from the SAP NetWeaver Portal to the R/3 system.

To achieve that, you must also adjust the setting of the iView *com.customer.pct.erp.* *mss.reporting* by editing the iView with the value ZMSS, as illustrated in Figure 7.26, to make sure that the SAP NetWeaver Portal iView will pick up the MSS scenario and all inherent configuration content, which includes the report categories and all types of reports configured.

Figure 7.26 Adjusting the Parameter Scenario with Value ZMSS

7.5.10 Manager Self-Service Reporting Role

From the SAP NetWeaver Portal role, the manager triggers the iView reporting and reaches the backend reports made available through the configuration steps.

Reporting Categories

Once logged on to the SAP NetWeaver Portal, you can find the two report categories you configured previously, as illustrated in Figure 7.27.

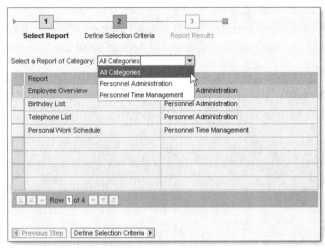

Figure 7.27 Manager Self-Services Report Categories

The end user can select from each report category. Once selected, the report category only shows the reports that have been allocated to that specific category.

Executing Standard Reports

End user can also access standard reports and queries, as configured previously and illustrated in Figure 7.28. You can now select the report and execute it.

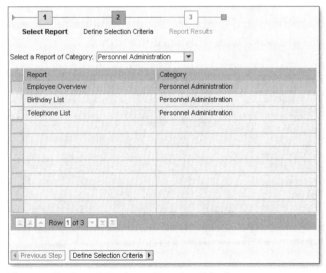

Figure 7.28 Report Employee Overview Selection

You now select the EMPLOYEE list and click on the icon DEFINE SELECTION CRITERIA. The system then prompts for staff selection, as configured earlier, based on the organizational structure. The end user selects all relevant persons, and then moves on to the report results.

Figure 7.29 illustrates the selection list of employees, which is based on the organizational structure per your configuration entries.

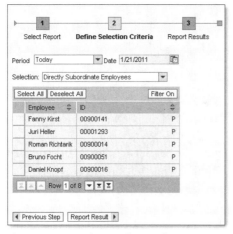

Figure 7.29 Employee Selection for Report Employee Overview

Report Results

Assuming that you have master data and the relevant authorizations, the system provides the results in a separate window, as illustrated in Figure 7.30.

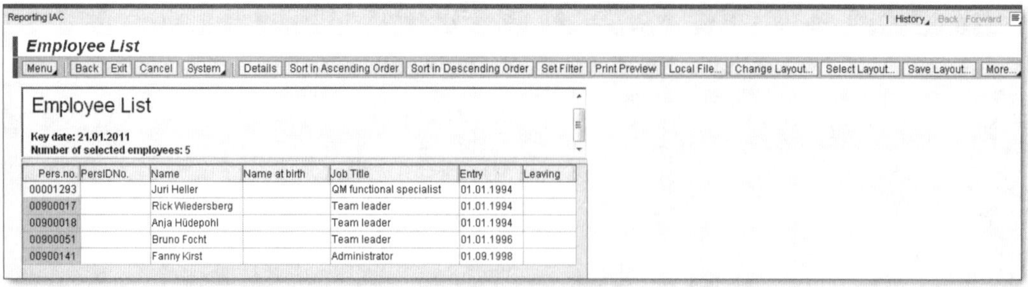

Pers.no	PersIDNo.	Name	Name at birth	Job Title	Entry	Leaving
00001293		Juri Heller		QM functional specialist	01.01.1994	
00900017		Rick Wiedersberg		Team leader	01.01.1994	
00900018		Anja Hüdepohl		Team leader	01.01.1994	
00900051		Bruno Focht		Team leader	01.01.1996	
00900141		Fanny Kirst		Administrator	01.09.1998	

Figure 7.30 Report Rendering in WebGUI Mode

The results are provided in a WebGUI window; local download is also possible, depending on the type of report previously selected.

7.5.11 SAP NetWeaver Portal Alternative Configuration: Service Map iView

You have seen that enabling all report types is easily done through the configuration of the Manager's Desktop to enable reporting in MSS. This is a good approach because you have more control of the backend configuration when it comes to configuration options, entries consistency checks, versioning, and the transport request process.

However, if you find this backend configuration too complex or just want to stay away from backend configuration, you do have a configuration alternative.

SAP NetWeaver Portal Access	CONTENT ADMINISTRATION • CONTENT PROVIDED BY SAP • LINE MANAGER • MANAGER SELF SERVICE

By using the SAP NetWeaver Portal objects, you can create a service map iView, which consolidates all reports the end user should have access to. Configuration is straightforward as described in this section.

Simply copy the template Service iView, which is located in the PCD under the following address: PORTAL CONTENT • TEMPLATES • IVIEW TEMPLATES • SERVICE MAP IVIEW.

As described in Chapter 2, create the relevant iViews, pointing to reports via their transaction, and then add these iViews into their respective worksets.

Add the worksets along with the service iView to the MSS roles as illustrated in Figure 7.31.

Figure 7.31 Service Map iView in Role

Now the system does not read any configuration from the backend system; it just compiles directly from the SAP NetWeaver Portal the information into the Service iView, as illustrated in Figure 7.32.

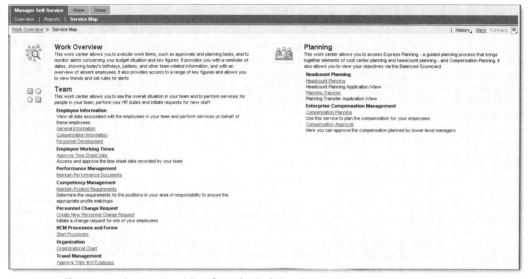

Figure 7.32 Service Map iView from the End User Perspective

7.6 Integration Points

Throughout this book, we have also illustrated several integration points that use report to support access to personnel HR data. As a reminder, this section reviews these integration points and provides references to their respective chapters and sections.

7.6.1 Integration with SAP NetWeaver Business Warehouse

The reporting capabilities have been illustrated through the standard reporting, which includes ABAP and ad hoc queries. However, in today's modern UI era, which is now powered, for example, with Adobe Reader, the standard offering is falling a bit short. Although technically easy to set up, most users are having a hard time dealing with the report results, mainly for the following reasons:

- Screen rendering is done with the WebGUI interface used, which is a bit out of date.

- Printing is based on the Internet browser functionality, which is everything but user friendly. Would you dare submit this printout to your manager?

- Download capability is available to the local file, Rich Text Format, and others, but in today's world, users expect a PDF local copy.

Also, from time to time, authorization administrators have reported that these web-enabled transactions can lead to security breaches. Even if the SAP NetWeaver Portal user is not a dialog user, if reachable, the user could directly launch a transaction from the command area through the WebGUI interface.

SAP is well aware of these facts and did not wait to provide a tailored solution. Thanks to SAP NetWeaver Business Warehouse (BW) and the latest reporting capabilities, the user will not only benefit from an intuitive and user-friendly interface but also from all the current offerings such as integration with Excel and PDF.

Background Information through SAP Notes

As background information, carefully review the following SAP Notes, which deal with SAP integration into Manager's Desktop. Although they are not relevant in the current release, these notes can help you comprehend the standard configuration:

- 1090084: Add a Way to Include Parameters to MSS Reporting for BW
- 307413: MDT: Start BW Reports from Manager's Desktop

Business Warehouse Direct Integration through the Manager's Desktop

As you have seen, the Manager's Desktop is a powerful tool to enable backend reporting. You can, however, add a pointer to a BW query on top of standard reports and queries. This can either be done directly from the portal, if you integrate web reporting directly into SAP NetWeaver Portal, or by making the relevant entries as discussed in Section 7.5.4, but this time for a BW entry.

Repeat the configuration steps as illustrated earlier in Chapter 3, Section 3.1.4 for the Manager's Desktop function codes.

Figure 7.33 illustrates a Manager's Desktop function code for a BW query.

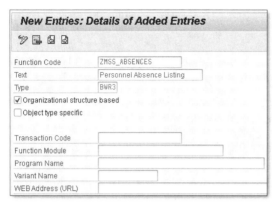

Figure 7.33 Function Code ZMSS_ABSENCES

Table T77MWBBWS BW System Data for Manager's Desktop

In addition to the Manager's Desktop configuration, you must also maintain table T77MWBBWS—BW System Data for Manager's Desktop.

Unfortunately, no IMG activity maintenance exists for this table, so you must maintain it using Transaction SM31—Call View Maintenance.

Ask the BW team to set the parameters such as the BW query template to be used and the logical system.

As for the other function codes, you base the report on the OBJECT TYPE "O" for the organizational unit.

Figure 7.34 illustrates the configuration entry for ZMSS_ABSENCES.

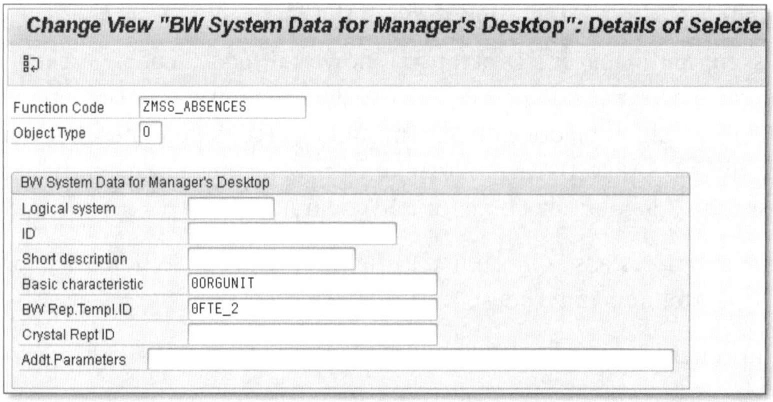

Figure 7.34 Table T77MWBBWS for Business Warehouse through Manager's Desktop

Direct integration from the SAP NetWeaver Portal Role

The configuration done through the direct integration into the Manager's Desktop is not mandatory when it comes to BI. You can also consolidate the end user SAP NetWeaver Portal role with a workset dedicated to BW queries, as illustrated in Figure 7.35.

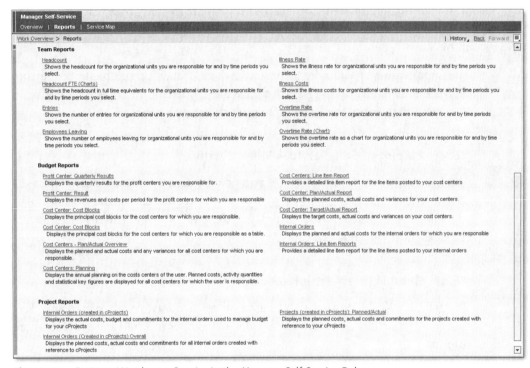

Figure 7.35 Business Warehouse Queries in the Manager Self-Service Role

7.6.2 Convert MDT Data to MSS Reporting Launch Pad

If needed, SAP also enables you to convert Manager's Desktop and MSS into a Reporting Launch Pad. This launch pad might be more user friendly depending on the business user.

IMG Access Path	SAP Customizing Implementation Guide • Personnel Management • Manager's Desktop • Customer Adjustment • Convert MDT Data to MSS Reporting Launch Pad

IMG Activity	MDT_LPA_CONV
Transaction Code	S_PCO_36000434 or PWPC_CONV_MDT_TO_LPA
Report Name	PWPC_CONVERT_MDT_TO_LPA—Convert MDT Table Entries to LPA Table Entries

In this configuration step, you execute the report to convert Manager's Desktop (MDT) table entries to Report Launch Pad (LPA) table entries, which will be used in MSS.

This report must be run whenever you make a change or an update to the configuration table. Customizing entries must already exist for Manager's Desktop as illustrated with the previous configuration steps.

7.6.3 Employee Self-Services Who's Who

The ESS Who's Who is powered by a standard InfoSet. Customers can adjust the Who's Who service by copying the standard InfoSet or by creating a new one. Refer to Chapter 5, Section 5.1.1, "Selection and Output," which illustrates this step and provides more information.

7.6.4 Generic iView Template

The generic iView template is also based on a SAP query; refer to Chapter 6, Section 6.17.1, "Generic iView for Lists," which illustrates this step and provides more information.

7.6.5 InfoSets and Respective Switches

InfoSets are generated easily, but users complain about side effects in their reporting, ranging from duplicate lines showing up to not being able to process locked records, and so on. Figure 7.36 illustrates a scenario with duplicate lines retrieved from the master data.

Existing Records on Database:

PersNr.	Last Name	First Name	City	Street	Lock
10001000	Smith	Philipp	Chicago	Wilshire Blvd.	
10001000	Smith	Philipp	Boston	Lake Avenue	X
20002000	Gillet	Helene	New York	12th. Street	
20002000	Gillet	Helene	San Francisco	Bay Street	

Basic List with Switch Active:

PersNr.	Last Name	First Name	City
10001000	Smith	Philipp	Chicago
10001000	Smith	Philipp	Boston
20002000	Camino	Helena	New York
20002000	Camino	Helena	San Francisco

Basic List with Switch Not Active (Standard):

PersNr.	Last Name	First Name	City
10001000	Smith	Philipp	Chicago
20002000	Camino	Helena	New York
20002000	Camino	Helena	San Francisco

Figure 7.36 Master Data with Duplicate Lines in the Reporting List

To solve this problem, SAP provides reporting switches (as of release 4.70) that can be easily added in the InfoSet, as illustrated in Figure 7.37. The following illustrates the switch BL_ALLOW_DUPL_LINES switched on (with the return value 'X') in the InfoSet:

```
*$HR$* [COMMON]
*$HR$* REPORT_CLASS = 'PNPCE'

*$HR$* [COMMON]
*$HR$* BL_ALLOW_DUP_LINES = 'X'
```

In SAP Note 305118—Eliminating Various Query Problems in HR, SAP provides a PDF guide (in English and German) regarding the HR_QUERY_GENERATOR_SWITCHES.PDF with detailed documentation and information on other switches you can activate.

These switches are only permitted for the HR logical database.

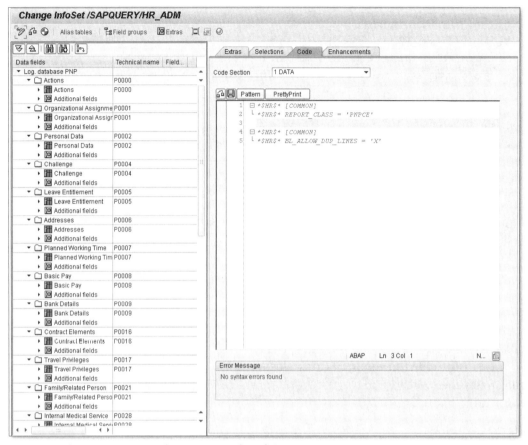

Figure 7.37 HR Switch Activation in the InfoSet

7.7 Authorization Consideration

Authorizations are covered in Chapter 11; however, this section focuses on the authorization objects that you must maintain for reporting.

In addition to the standard reporting objects, you must also maintain the authorization object for the Manager's Desktop because you will enable the Manager's Desktop configuration for MSS reporting.

7.7.1 Authorization Objects

The authorization objects are the following:

▶ **Object P_ABAP**

This object belongs to the class HR: Reporting, and it contains the following authorization fields:

- ▶ REPID (ABAP Program Name)

- ▶ COARS (Degree of Simplification for Authorization Check)

▶ **Object S_PROGRAM**

This object belongs to the class BC_C: ABAP—Program Flow Checks, and it contains the following authorization fields:

- ▶ P_GROUP (Authorization Group ABAP/4 Program)

- ▶ P_ACTION (User Action ABAP/4 Program)

▶ **Object S_MWB_FCOD**

This object belongs to the class HR and bears the name BC-BMT-OM: Allowed Function Codes for Manager's Desktop. It contains the authorization field:

- ▶ MWBFCODE (Function Code).

These authorization objects can be viewed using Transaction SU03—Maintain Authorizations in their respective authorization classes. These objects will be further described in Chapter 11.

Furthermore, when it comes to authorization, you must also abide by some global risk and compliance (GRC) rules and requirements. For example, as you deal with personnel HR data, you must provide audit tools to monitor data access, data updates, and any misuse or fraud. SAP provides different alternatives that are listed and illustrated in this section.

7.7.2 Audit Reports

Audit reports are critical and significant in most processes but they are even more imperative in HR where you deal with sensitive data such as payroll and employee performance information.

If you do not want to use the new functionality data tracking of self-services, you do have alternatives as described following this section. They also can be used and meet all customer requirements. Because most of you are likely already using the existing functionalities, know the configuration options, and understand the system behavior, you should probably stick with the current functionalities such as the standard reports or if needed the customer event linkage table.

7.7.3 Log Report Starts

This customizing step enables you to protect and log report starts for sensitive reports such as payroll and time evaluation. Figure 7.38 illustrates this customizing step in table V_T599R.

IMG Access Path	SAP CUSTOMIZING IMPLEMENTATION GUIDE • PERSONNEL MANAGEMENT • PERSONNEL ADMINISTRATION • TOOLS • REVISION • LOG REPORT STARTS
IMG Activity	OHIX0018
Transaction Code	S_AHR_61011176
Table Name	V_T599R

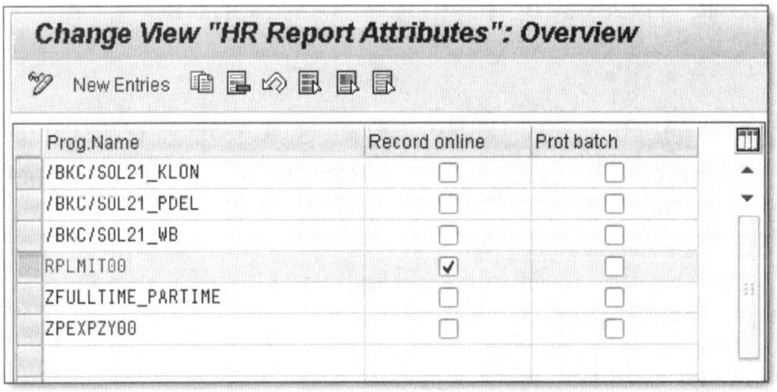

Figure 7.38 Log Report Starts for RPLMIT00—Employee List

For all HR using the logical database PNP, the system can create a log when the report is started, which can be handy for reports such as payroll, time, leave request, and time sheet approval.

You must set and activate the relevant report in this configuration table. The system then creates a record in the database each time a user starts a report listed in the configuration table. In this configuration step, you can also specify whether this record should be created only for online or background reports, or for both.

The log contains the following data:

▸ Report

▸ Report title

▶ User

▶ Date on which the report was started

▶ Time at which the report was started

▶ Report parameters and select options

The log entries created can be viewed using the standard report RPUPROTD—Log of Report Starts, as illustrated in Figure 7.39.

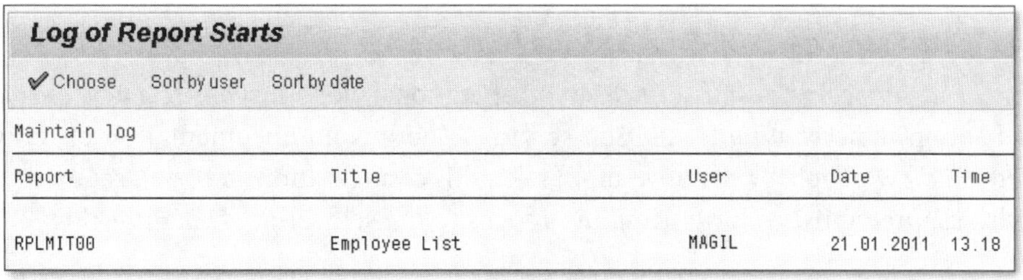

Log of Report Starts

✔ Choose	Sort by user	Sort by date

Maintain log

Report	Title	User	Date	Time
RPLMIT00	Employee List	MAGIL	21.01.2011	13.18

Figure 7.39 Log Results After the Program RPLMIT00 Has Been Used Online

Three standard transactions are pointing to this report:

▶ S_AHR_61015506: Log of Report Starts

▶ S_AHR_61016381: Log of Report Starts

▶ S_ALR_87014082: Log of Report Starts

From time to time, to clean up the database and free up some space, log entries should be removed if permitted using the report RPUPROTU—Maintain Log. The Transaction S_PH0_48000151—Maintain Log can also be called to reach this report. You might want to investigate this log maintenance with your Basis team.

7.7.4 Data Tracking for Self-Services

This functionality, which is the latest tool provided by SAP, was introduced with EhP 3 and is the standard approach for tracking data creation and changes in the field of services.

Data tracking can be used for the following self-services activities:

▶ ESS that employees trigger or perform

▶ ESS that are performed in the Employee Interaction Center (EIC)

- MSS that the managers trigger or perform on behalf of the employee in the ESS in MSS scenario

- Self-services of the HR administrator portal role (HRASR)

Configuring the data tracking for self-services requires different steps, which are described next. Carefully review the different alternatives before using this standard (new) functionality to better understand what it provides versus the user requirements and to recognize the potential pitfalls.

Configure Case Type H_XSS for XSS (Self-Services)

For the data tracking of self-services to be operational, you must create a new entry and set up the case type H_XSS self-services. There is no documentation on this step, and few people even know about it. In this configuration step, you set up the technical prerequisites for putting in services to the self-services data tracking.

IMG Access Path	CASE MANAGEMENT • DEFINE CASE TYPES • DEFINE CASE TYPES
IMG Activity	SCMG_CASETYPE
Transaction Code	S_EKW_85000002 or SCASE_CUSTOMIZING
Table Name	SCMGV_CASETYPE

Case Type Maintenance

In this configuration step, you create a new entry, as illustrated with Figure 7.40, with the following values:

- CASE TYPE: "H_SS"

- NAME: "Self Services"

- RMS ID (Record Management System ID): "SSC_SERV"

- ELEMENT TYPE ID (CASE): "SSC_SERV_SPS_CASE"

- ATTRIB.PROFILE: "SSC_SERV Self-Services"

- FUNCT. PROFILE: "SSC_SERV Self-Services"

- INT.NO.RANGE: "01"

Leave the other fields empty because they are either not relevant or not required for the self-services maintenance of case type H_XSS.

IMG Access Path	CASE MANAGEMENT • DEFINE CASE TYPES • DEFINE CASE TYPES • CASE TYPE MAINTENANCE
Table Name	SCMGV_CASETYPE

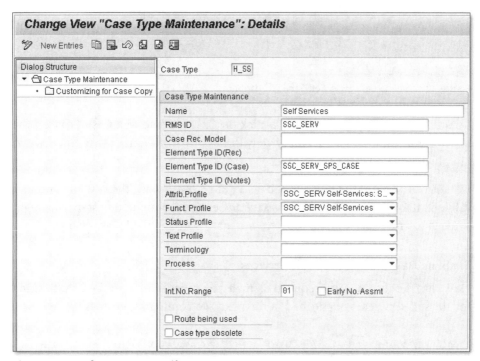

Figure 7.40 Define Case H_SS Self-Services

Save your entries, and move on to the next configuration step.

Customizing for Case Copy

Now that you have configured the case type H_XSS, you create the attributes with the technical value COPY as illustrated in Figure 7.41.

IMG Access Path	CASE MANAGEMENT • DEFINE CASE TYPES • DEFINE CASE TYPES • CASE TYPE MAINTENANCE • CUSTOMIZING FOR CASE COPY
Table Name	SCMGV_COPYCASE

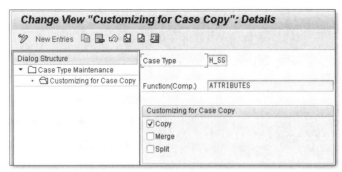

Figure 7.41 Define Case H_SS Self-Services Attributes

Select the entry H_XSS, and double-click on Customizing for Case Copy on the left side of the screen. In the empty view that appears, click on Create New Entry. Simply tick the box Copy, and save.

Do not worry about the name in the field Function(Comp.), the system automatically sets it to ATTRIBUTES after you save and exit the configuration step. You might want to re-enter the configuration step to make sure the field was renamed.

Enabling Data Tracking for Self-Services

Now that the technical prerequisite is met, you must switch on the data tracking for the self-services, as described in the next two configuration steps.

IMG Access Path	SAP Customizing Implementation Guide • Personnel Management • Data Tracking for Self-Services

Activate Data Tracking for All Self-Services

In this configuration table, activate data tracking for self-services by flagging the tick box, as illustrated in Figure 7.42.

IMG Access Path	SAP Customizing Implementation Guide • Personnel Management • Data Tracking for Self-Services • Activate Data Tracking for All Self-Services
IMG Activity	XSS_ANALYTICS_002
Transaction Code	S_P8K_45000015
Table Name	V_T5SSCSWITCHON

Figure 7.42 Activate Data Tracking for All Services

When tracking is no longer required, use the same configuration step to deactivate the data tracking for self-services by unflagging this tick box.

Set Data Tracking for Individual Self-Services
In this configuration step, as illustrated in Figure 7.43, add the self-services you need to activate data tracking for, and then flag the tick box next to the service name to activate the data tracking.

Self-Service	Name	Tracking
ESS_START_MEMBERFEES_XX_WDABAP		✓
ESS_START_TERMINATION_DE	Termination (DE)	✓
ESS_START_TERMINATION_DE_WDABAP	Termination (DE)	✓
ESS_START_TERMINATION_US	Termination (US)	✓
ESS_START_TERMINATION_US_WDABAP	Termination (US)	✓
MSS_ATO	Attendance Overview	✓
MSS_CAT_APPROVAL_MANAGER	Manager Approves Working Times	✓
MSS_CAT_APPROVAL_PROJECT	Project Leader Approves Working Times	✓
MSS_ECM_APPROVAL	Approve Compensation Planning	✓
MSS_ECM_PLANNING	Compensation Planning	✓
MSS_EEPRO_COMPENSATIONINFORMATION	Employee Information (Compensation Information)	✓
MSS_EEPRO_COMPENSATIONPROFILES	Employee Information (for Compensation Planning)	✓
MSS_EEPRO_GENERALDATA	Employee Information (General Data)	✓
MSS_EEPRO_GENERALINFORMATION	Employee Information (General Information)	✓
MSS_EEPRO_MONITORINGOFTASKS	Employee Information (Monitoring of Tasks)	✓
MSS_EEPRO_ORGANIZATIONALASSIGNMENTS	Employee Information (Organizational Assignment)	✓
MSS_EEPRO_PERSONNELDEVELOPMENT	Employee Information (Personnel Development)	✓
MSS_EEPRO_TRAININGEVENTDETAILS	Detail for an Event	✓
MSS_ISRSTATUSOVERVIEW	Status Overview of Change Requests	✓
MSS_LEA_TEAMCALENDER	Team Calendar	✓
MSS_LPA	Report Launchpad	✓
MSS_MBO	Performance Management Overview	✓
MSS_OCI	Display Organizational Chart	✓
MSS_OPRO	Organizational Unit Profile	✓
MSS_OPRP_QUALIFICATIONDETAIL	Organizational Unit Profile (Qualification Details)	✓
MSS_PCR	Create New Change Request	✓
MSS_PCR_DIRECTLAUNCH	Create New Change Request (from Employee Profile)	✓
MSS_PPRO	Position Profile	✓
MSS_PPRO_POSITIONHOLDERS	Position Profile: Holders	✓
MSS_PRQ	Maintain Position Requirements	✓
MSS_QTP	Workforce Requirements Planning	✓

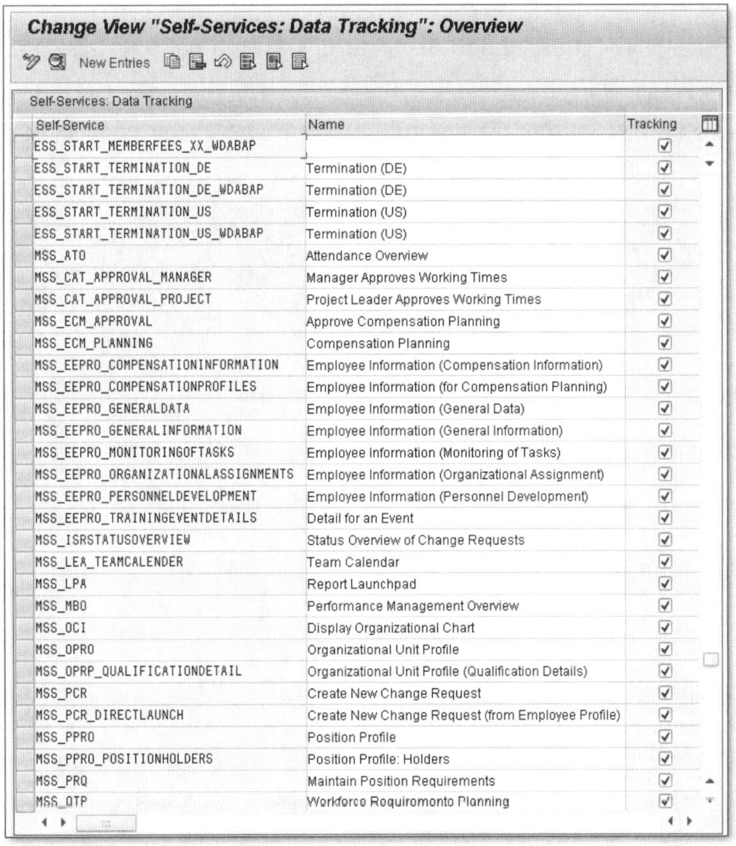

Figure 7.43 Activate the Self-Services to Be Tracked

IMG Access Path	SAP CUSTOMIZING IMPLEMENTATION GUIDE • PERSONNEL MANAGEMENT • DATA TRACKING FOR SELF-SERVICES • SET DATA TRACKING FOR INDIVIDUAL SELF-SERVICES
IMG Activity	XSS_ANALYTICS_003
Transaction Code	S_P8K_45000016
Table Name	V_T5SSCTRACKXSS

As illustrated in Figure 7.44, you do have additional options for each service added in this table. The additional configuration options are the following:

▶ APPL. TYPE: Set the application type.

▶ APPL. NAMESPACE: Set the application namespace.

▶ APPLICATION NAME: Set the application name.

▶ TRACKING ID: Perhaps the most important feature, set a unique tracking ID to make audit reporting easier.

▶ DEFAULT INITIATOR ROLE: Set the initiator role, for example, the employee, that will trigger the data tracking.

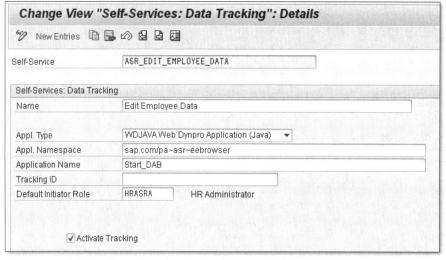

Figure 7.44 Additional Configuration Options for Data Tracking

You have the following standard roles:

- HRASRA: HR administrator

- HRASRB: Manager

- HRASRC: XI inbound

- HRASRD: Employee

- HREICA: Employee Interaction Center (EIC) agent

Activity Logged in Table T5SSCXSSSERVICES

Now that the data tracking is active, you might be wondering where you actually see the logged activities.

Once activated, data tracking then stores a log of change activities in the standard table T5SSCXSSSERVICES — XSS Self-Service Instances. Depending on your SAP release, you can view the content of this table through Transaction SE16N — General Table Display or Transaction SE16 — Data Browser.

Note

Transaction SE16 is widely known as the core basis of SAP R/3. Originally, it was only configured for three languages: German, English, and Japanese. With Release 4.6C, SAP offers the new Transaction SE16N, which is more user friendly. Transaction SE16N is fully translated in SAP ERP 6.0. For more information, refer to SAP Note 853603 — CO-OM tools: Translation in All Languages.

Important Information!

When dealing with changes in the ESS, nothing is logged in the standard tables! After much investigation, this appears to be a bug. A fix was provided in November 2010, thanks to the SAP Note 1531162 — ESS HCM P & F Process Not Tracked.

Nevertheless, this bug only applies for ESS being tracked; it does not apply for MSS, which works as designed or rather as configured.

The system now logs all changes activities for self-services and provides the following information in the log table T5SSCXSSSERVICES — XSS Self-Service Instances, as illustrated in Figure 7.45.

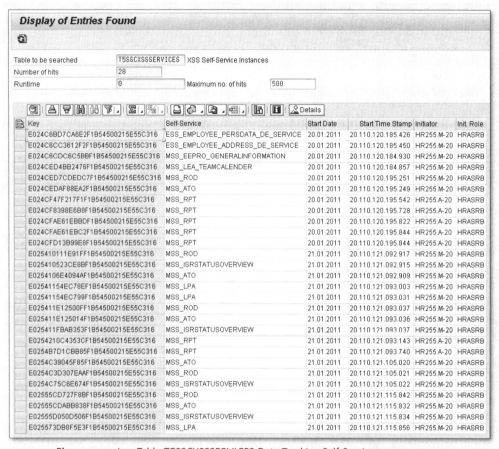

Figure 7.45 Log Table T5SSCXSSSERVICES Data Tracking Self-Services

You can read the record as follows:

▶ KEY: E024C6CC3612F2F1B54500215E55C316 is the system key.

▶ SELF-SERVICE: ESS_EMPLOYEE_ADDRESS_DE_SERVICE is the service logged.

▶ START DATE: 20.01.2011 is the date of the logged activity.

▶ START TIME STAMP: 20.110.120.185.450 is the time stamp with the date of logged activity.

▶ INITIATOR: HR255-M-20 is the SAP UserID as defined in Transaction SU01 by the system administrator. In this case, HR255-M-20 refers to training user for manager.

▶ INIT. ROLE: HRASRB is the role that initiated the logging. In this case, HRASRB refers to the manager.

7.7.5 Logged Changes in InfoType Data for Personnel Administration Data

From the beginning of SAP, in the field of HR, the program RPUAUD00—Logged Changes in InfoType Data was provided to log all InfoType changes in the Personnel Administration (PA) area. This report can be accessed directly using the following transactions, which execute the same report:

▶ PC00_M16_UAUD: Payroll Audit Trail

▶ S_AHR_61015505: Logged Changes in InfoType Data

▶ S_AHR_61016380: Logged Changes in InfoType Data

▶ S_ALR_87014081: Logged Changes in InfoType Data

To tell the system which fields to log, you must make very little configuration.

Set Up a Change Document

To enable the setup of the personnel change document, you must tell the system which InfoTypes to log, which fields to use, and in which document type they belong (short-term or long-term storage).

IMG Access Path	SAP CUSTOMIZING IMPLEMENTATION GUIDE • PERSONNEL MANAGEMENT • PERSONNEL ADMINISTRATION • TOOLS • REVISION • SET UP CHANGE DOCUMENT
IMG Activity	OHIX0017
Transaction Code	S_AHR_61011175

To achieve that, in this configuration step, you have three steps:

1. Add the HR Documents: InfoTypes to be logged, as illustrated in Figure 7.46.

Table Name	V_T585A

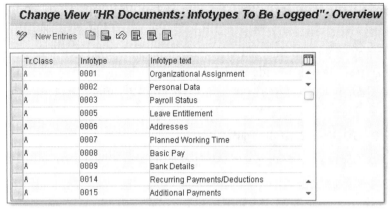

Figure 7.46 Table V_T585A

2. For each InfoType, select the fields to be logged because all of them might not apply for the logging procedure. Organize the different fields to be logged into a field group, for example, "01," as illustrated in Figure 7.47.

Table Name V_T585B

Change View "HR Documents: Field Group Definition": Overview

New Entries

Infotype	Infotype text	Field grp	Field Name	A/L
0006	Addresses	01	*	
0007	Planned Working Time	01	*	
0008	Basic Pay	01	*	
0009	Bank Details	01	BANKL	
0009	Bank Details	01	BANKN	
0009	Bank Details	01	BANKS	
0009	Bank Details	01	BKONT	
0009	Bank Details	01	EMFSL	
0009	Bank Details	01	ZLSCH	
0014	Recurring Payments/Deductions	01	*	
0015	Additional Payments	01	*	

Figure 7.47 Table V_T585B

3. Add the DocFieldGr, for example, "01," against the document type (Doc.type) "L" (long term) or "S" (short term), as shown in Figure 7.48. This step is the

technical setting to instruct the system in regards to the logs retention period. Short term is not used often; the long term (L) value in set up this screen.

Table Name	V_T585C

Change View "HR Documents: Field Group Characteristics": Overview

New Entries

Tr.Class	Infotype	Infotype text	DocFieldGr	Doc.type	SupFldGr.
A	0001	Organizational Assignment	01	L	
A	0002	Personal Data	01	L	
A	0003	Payroll Status	01	L	
A	0005	Leave Entitlement	01	L	
A	0006	Addresses	01	L	
A	0007	Planned Working Time	01	L	
A	0008	Basic Pay	01	L	
A	0009	Bank Details	01	S	
A	0014	Recurring Payments/Deductions	01	L	
A	0015	Additional Payments	01	L	

Figure 7.48 Table V_T585C

Although this standard program provides a log of all changes, including the previous value, which is useful when user or incoming data interfaces overwrite the data, this reports triggers a massive amount of data. This workload often seems overwhelming for system administrators because it requires data storage on the SAP servers.

On the other hand, end users also are tempted to challenge the standard rendering because the UI is not the slickest. These two reasons combined, often make customers choose the last remaining course of action, which is the customer event linkage. The customer event linkage is described later in this chapter.

7.7.6 Display Change Documents for Personnel Development Data

In addition to the PA being logged, another standard program is provided for monitoring the Personnel Development (PD) object creation and changes. The program is RHCDOC_DISPLAY—Display Change Documents, which has no direct transaction assigned.

When dealing with PD, such as the nonexhaustive list provided here, HR officials and security officers also want to monitor changes. This standard program logs all change documents.

This program is useful when dealing with self-services with PD objects in the following processes (objects are provided in parentheses):

▸ Transfer within the organizational structure that impacts the object position (S), perhaps also the cost center (K), and the organizational unit (O)

▸ New requisition request for a position or a job that impacts the object position (S), job (C), cost center (K), organizational unit (O), requisition (NB), candidate (NA), and perhaps tasks (T)

▸ Training management, including follow up on course attendance and related training activities that impact object course (E), curriculum (EC), course program (EK), and e-learning (object ET)

▸ Personal Development Plans (PDPs) assigned to the employees that impact the development plan (B) and the development plan group (BL)

▸ The handling of the applicants (AP) in the recruitment process

▸ When dealing with the qualification catalog that impacts the qualification group (QK), qualification (Q), and qualification block (QB)

▸ When undergoing the appraisal process that impacts the appraisal model (BS) and appraisal (BA)

> **Tip**
>
> All the standard objects you are dealing with can be accessed and viewed with the expert Transaction PP02—Maintain Plan Data (Open).

7.7.7 Event Linkage for Customer (Table T779X)

The last remaining course of action regarding data tracking and audit in the field of HR is table HR-CA: Event Linkage for Customer (table T779X), which is part of the cross-application daily HR activities. This table provides an overview of configured entries. (Caution, this table is cross client.)

The table HR Cross Application: Event Linkage for Customer needs to be activated in the HR switch table, also referred to as table T77S0.

With the GROUP WORKF, SWITCH: WORKFLOW ACTIVE IN UPDATE TASK, set the VALUE ABBR. to "X" to set it as active, as illustrated in Figure 7.49.

IMG Access Path	SAP CUSTOMIZING IMPLEMENTATION GUIDE • PERSONNEL MANAGEMENT • PERSONNEL ADMINISTRATION • TOOLS • BUSINESS WORKFLOW EVENTS • ACTIVATE EVENT LINKAGE
IMG Activity	OHIXWFAC
Transaction Code	S_AHR_61011177
Table Name	T77S0; the first column is labeled as GROUP with the value "WORKF," and the second column labeled with the semantic abbreviation with the value "ACTIV." The switch description is: WORKFLOW ACTIVE IN UPDATE TASK. The return value is either left empty, which means inactive, or an "X," which means activated.

Figure 7.49 Switch Workflow Active in Update Task

Gathering the Object Data via the Function Module

Differing from the standard programs provided in PA and PD, this table provides a technically closer answer for logging requests and requirements. Instead of logging all data changes and updates like the standard programs do (even if "narrowed" due to configuration), this table allows customer to select each object and in which action (such as Insert mode—INS, copy mode—COP, etc.) they want the data to be logged.

IMG Access Path	SAP CUSTOMIZING IMPLEMENTATION GUIDE • PERSONNEL MANAGEMENT • PERSONNEL ADMINISTRATION • TOOLS • BUSINESS WORKFLOW EVENTS • DEFINE EVENTS FOR CUSTOMER-SPECIFIC BUSINESS OBJECTS
IMG Activity	OHIX0036

Transaction Code	S_AHR_61011178
Table Name	V_T779X_1; Caution, this table is cross client.

This logging process is powered mainly by function modules that are holding the business rules and requirements. Obviously, the help of a developer is required. In addition to table T779X, you need to create a basic table that collects the results of the tracking and logging.

For you to fetch the data changes, a function module must be created. To make creating the function module a bit easier, SAP provides two samples:

▶ **Personnel Administration**
  HR_EVENT_RULES_PAXXXX (where XXX stands for the InfoType number, for example, HR_EVENT_RULES_PA0001)

▶ **Personnel Development**
  HR_EVENT_OT_NNNN_UUUU_TEMPLATE

An example of a standard entry for InfoType 0036—Social Insurance Switzerland is illustrated in Figure 7.50.

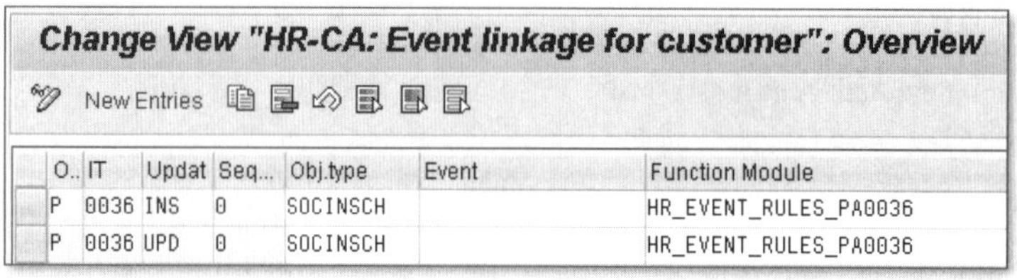

Figure 7.50 Sample Example InfoType 0036 in Table V_T779X_1

Additional Readings

In regards to table T779X, you should read the following SAP Notes, which will come in handy during projects:

▶ 508405: Workflow: Event Connection PA/PD Update Task

▶ 500569: Event Linkage: Events Are Triggered Twice

▶ 385357: FAQ: Development Plans

▶ 748247: No Event Triggering When Organizational Unit Is Deleted

- ▸ 202371: No New Entry in V_T779X_1 Possible
- ▸ 334843: HR: Workflow Is Started Too Often

7.8 Additional Useful Reports

Although not perhaps used by the managers in the self-services area, this section consolidates a list of useful reports when handling self-services deployment.

Most reports listed here have direct transaction access. However, when no transaction is assigned, either use Transaction SA38—ABAP Reporting, which is meant for functional super users or key users, and/or Transaction SE38—ABAP Editor, which is normally reserved for developers and not allowed in a productive SAP environment in most cases.

When no authorization group is maintained, just use the standard authorization object S_PROGRAM—ABAP: Program Flow Checks, which is also called when running Transaction SA38—ABAP Reporting. Transaction SE38—ABAP Editor calls authorization object S_DEVELOP—ABAP Workbench when in use.

7.8.1 Repairing Data Sharing Inconsistencies (RPUFIXDS)

Since the introduction of concurrent employment in SAP R/3 4.7, also known as R/3 Enterprise, and/or the introduction of the new InfoType framework later, you might encounter a typical error message as illustrated in Figure 7.51.

This message is not due to misconfiguration but rather to some data inconsistencies triggered mainly by the central person object (CP).

This issue exists in SAP Releases ERP 5.0 and ERP 6.0.

To support customers, SAP released the following SAP Notes:

- ▸ 783499: Incorrect Framework Synchronization
- ▸ 845592: Incorrect Framework Synchronization—Retroactive Accounting

Review these notes carefully to check any collateral damages or side effects on your HR data, although SAP states there should be no ill effects.

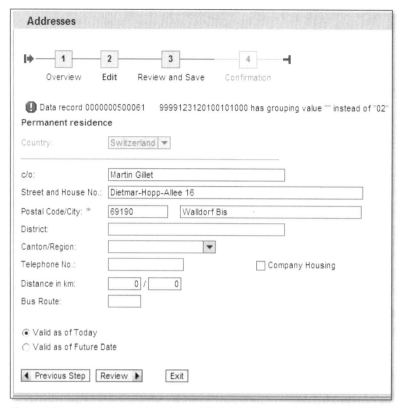

Figure 7.51 SAP NetWeaver Portal Issue When Dealing with Self-Services: Grouping value " " instead of "XX"

This table illustrates the properties a developer would find through Transaction SE38. It highlights some of the program attributes.

Report Name	RPUFIXDS
Report Title	Repairing Data Sharing Inconsistencies
Transaction Code	(none)
Authorization Group	(note)
Package	PBAS_SERVICE—HR Master Data: Service Functions

This program can also be reached through the IMG, which is illustrated in the next table. This is how consultants and analysts will access this program.

IMG Access Path	SAP CUSTOMIZING IMPLEMENTATION GUIDE • PERSONNEL MANAGEMENT • PERSONNEL ADMINISTRATION • BASIC SETTINGS • BASIC SETTINGS FOR CONCURRENT EMPLOYMENT • EDITOR FOR PERSONNEL ASSIGNMENT GROUPINGS • CONSISTENCY CHECK AND REPAIRS FOR GROUPINGS • REPAIRING DATA SHARING INCONSISTENCIES
IMG Activity	CCE_00_GP_011
Transaction Code	S_L6B_69000049

You should run this report in a test mode first to assess the number of inconsistencies in the system. An important reason to do this is As explained in the standard documentation, which states that the report may delete data from personnel numbers linked to each other depending on the customer settings in data sharing (refer to tables T582A—InfoTypes: Customer-Specific Settings and T582G—InfoType: Grouping Reason) or any additional settings, for example, done through a BAdI such as HRPA_SHARING_REPOR—Data Sharing—Repair Sequence.

This is usually a one-shot report just before the go live to correct all data inconsistencies. So although it is rarely used, it is wise to be aware that such a standard report exists to fix inconsistencies.

Figure 7.52 illustrates the selection screen of report RPUFIXDS—Repairing Data Sharing Inconsistencies.

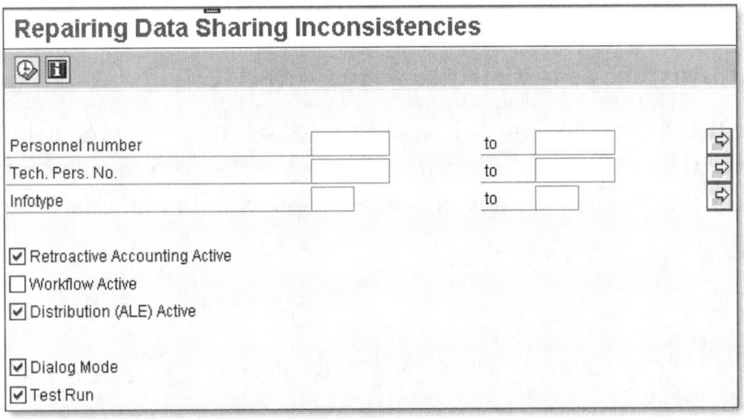

Figure 7.52 Selecting Personnel Numbers in Report Repairing Data Sharing Inconsistencies

Figure 7.53 shows the inconsistencies the report has identified.

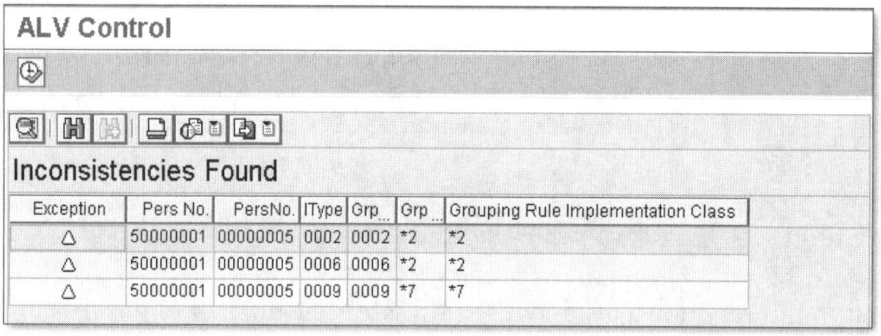

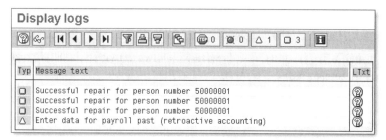

Figure 7.53 Inconsistencies Found

Figure 7.54 illustrates the successful repair of the inconsistent data, if you have not executed the report in test mode.

Figure 7.54 Successful Repairs for Personnel Numbers

7.8.2   Find Inconsistencies in Time Constraints (RPUSCNTC)

When dealing with HR data, you might face some inconsistencies or errors with the InfoType records and their respective time constraints. This standard report will help you find the potential inconsistencies or support the troubleshooting team members.

Report Name	RPUSCNTC
Report Title	Find Inconsistencies in Time Constraints
Transaction Code	(none)

Authorization Group	(note)
Package	PBAS_SERVICE—HR Master Data: Service Functions

You should read the standard documentation in addition to the following SAP Notes:

- 1302067—RPUSCNTC: Correction of Inconsistencies in Time Constraints
- 1052552—ITy. Delimitable Despite Time Constraint 1 & Data Sharing
- 1303276—ITy. Delimitable Despite Time Constraint 1 & Data Sharing II

7.8.3   Reconcile User Master with HR Master (ESS_USERCOMPARE)

You have seen in previous chapters that each SAP UserID must be mapped to a valid personnel number. This is achieved through the InfoType 0105—Communication, subtype 0001—System User Name (SY-UNAME).

The question is how to identify who is mapped to which SAP UserID, besides looking at each InfoType 0105—Communication Record?

Report Name	ESS_USERCOMPARE
Report Title	Reconcile User Master with HR Master
Transaction Code	(none)
Authorization Group	(none)
Package	PWWW—HR: Internet Services and BAPIs

You can use Transaction HRUSER—Set Up and Maintain ESS Users, and in the PREPARATION area, choose ASSIGNMENT OF EMPLOYEES TO EXISTING USERS. But this transaction is often reserved for system and portal administrators. The easy solution is to request the addition of the program ESS_USERCOMPARE to your user menu so that you can directly access it without the authorization for Transaction HRUSER.

Figure 7.55 illustrates the SAP user mapping against the personnel number for standard SAP training class HR255—Employee and Manager Self Services in a Training System.

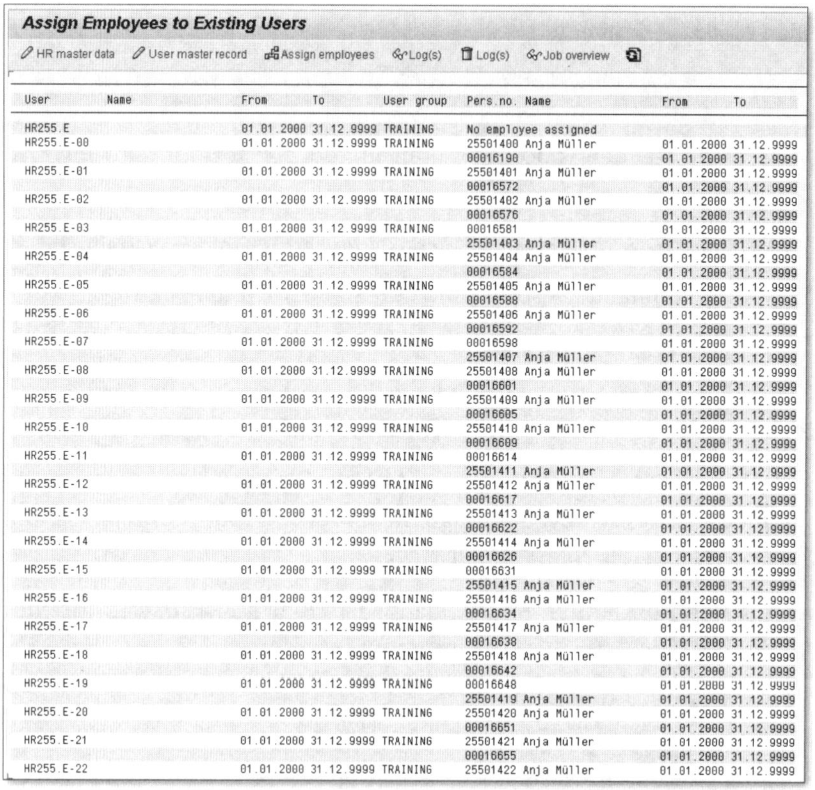

User	Name	From	To	User group	Pers.no.	Name	From	To
HR255.E		01.01.2000	31.12.9999	TRAINING	No employee assigned			
HR255.E-00		01.01.2000	31.12.9999	TRAINING	25501400	Anja Müller	01.01.2000	31.12.9999
					00016190		01.01.2000	31.12.9999
HR255.E-01		01.01.2000	31.12.9999	TRAINING	25501401	Anja Müller	01.01.2000	31.12.9999
					00016572		01.01.2000	31.12.9999
HR255.E-02		01.01.2000	31.12.9999	TRAINING	25501402	Anja Müller	01.01.2000	31.12.9999
					00016576		01.01.2000	31.12.9999
HR255.E-03		01.01.2000	31.12.9999	TRAINING	00016581		01.01.2000	31.12.9999
					25501403	Anja Müller	01.01.2000	31.12.9999
HR255.E-04		01.01.2000	31.12.9999	TRAINING	25501404	Anja Müller	01.01.2000	31.12.9999
					00016584		01.01.2000	31.12.9999
HR255.E-05		01.01.2000	31.12.9999	TRAINING	25501405	Anja Müller	01.01.2000	31.12.9999
					00016588		01.01.2000	31.12.9999
HR255.E-06		01.01.2000	31.12.9999	TRAINING	25501406	Anja Müller	01.01.2000	31.12.9999
					00016592		01.01.2000	31.12.9999
HR255.E-07		01.01.2000	31.12.9999	TRAINING	00016598		01.01.2000	31.12.9999
					25501407	Anja Müller	01.01.2000	31.12.9999
HR255.E-08		01.01.2000	31.12.9999	TRAINING	25501408	Anja Müller	01.01.2000	31.12.9999
					00016601		01.01.2000	31.12.9999
HR255.E-09		01.01.2000	31.12.9999	TRAINING	25501409	Anja Müller	01.01.2000	31.12.9999
					00016605		01.01.2000	31.12.9999
HR255.E-10		01.01.2000	31.12.9999	TRAINING	25501410	Anja Müller	01.01.2000	31.12.9999
					00016609		01.01.2000	31.12.9999
HR255.E-11		01.01.2000	31.12.9999	TRAINING	00016614		01.01.2000	31.12.9999
					25501411	Anja Müller	01.01.2000	31.12.9999
HR255.E-12		01.01.2000	31.12.9999	TRAINING	25501412	Anja Müller	01.01.2000	31.12.9999
					00016617		01.01.2000	31.12.9999
HR255.E-13		01.01.2000	31.12.9999	TRAINING	25501413	Anja Müller	01.01.2000	31.12.9999
					00016622		01.01.2000	31.12.9999
HR255.E-14		01.01.2000	31.12.9999	TRAINING	25501414	Anja Müller	01.01.2000	31.12.9999
					00016626		01.01.2000	31.12.9999
HR255.E-15		01.01.2000	31.12.9999	TRAINING	00016631		01.01.2000	31.12.9999
					25501415	Anja Müller	01.01.2000	31.12.9999
HR255.E-16		01.01.2000	31.12.9999	TRAINING	25501416	Anja Müller	01.01.2000	31.12.9999
					00016634		01.01.2000	31.12.9999
HR255.E-17		01.01.2000	31.12.9999	TRAINING	25501417	Anja Müller	01.01.2000	31.12.9999
					00016638		01.01.2000	31.12.9999
HR255.E-18		01.01.2000	31.12.9999	TRAINING	25501418	Anja Müller	01.01.2000	31.12.9999
					00016642		01.01.2000	31.12.9999
HR255.E-19		01.01.2000	31.12.9999	TRAINING	00016648		01.01.2000	31.12.9999
					25501419	Anja Müller	01.01.2000	31.12.9999
HR255.E-20		01.01.2000	31.12.9999	TRAINING	25501420	Anja Müller	01.01.2000	31.12.9999
					00016651		01.01.2000	31.12.9999
HR255.E-21		01.01.2000	31.12.9999	TRAINING	25501421	Anja Müller	01.01.2000	31.12.9999
					00016655		01.01.2000	31.12.9999
HR255.E-22		01.01.2000	31.12.9999	TRAINING	25501422	Anja Müller	01.01.2000	31.12.9999

Figure 7.55 Personnel Number Mapping Against SAP UserIDs

7.8.4 Determine Approver (RPTREQAPPRCHK)

When dealing with functionalities such as Time Management approval processes in the field and time registration of leave requests, or just when using the line manager as the workflow agent for approval, you need a report that enables a quick tracing of the actual approver for a person.

Report Name	RPTREQAPPRCHK
Report Title	Determine Approver
Transaction Code	(none)
Authorization Group	(none)
Package	PAOC_TIM_REQUEST_COMP—Database of Requests: Functions for All Request Types

Without a report, you would have to go to InfoType 0001 — Organizational Assignment, identify the position of the person, go to the organizational structure, and then identify the chief position to which the employee reports. To most of us, using two transactions to achieve that is a bit too fastidious.

The good news is that thanks to the leave request environment in Transaction PTARQ, you have a standard report that can point to the line manager (person assigned to the chief position) directly for a personnel number. You simply authorize direct use of the program RPTREQAPPRCHK.

You use the application ID ESS_LR — Employee Leave Request Application.

Figure 7.56 illustrates the line manager for personnel number 1000, directly identified through the program RPTREQAPPRCHK; the supervisor (line manager) is Nicolas Gillet.

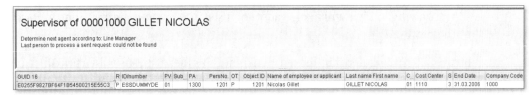

Figure 7.56 Determining the Approver

7.8.5 Personnel Numbers That Have to be Unlocked for Payroll Runs (HFIUCPL0)

When working with a personnel number, you lock the personnel number for others. In most cases, no other side update by another person is possible. Often the business team is requesting to have a look at the HR lock entries via Transaction SM12 — Display and Delete Locks. As this is a system transaction, which can also enable lock entries deletion and create a mess, you can understand why the Basis team denies access to this transaction.

Report name	HFIUCPL0
Report title	Personnel Numbers That Have to Be Unlocked for Payroll Runs
Transaction Code	PC00_M44_UCPL

Authorization Group	(none)
Package	PB44—HR Master Data: Finland

Too often, the business team is unaware of the SAP standard report that allows you to see who is locking a personnel number: program HFIUCPL0. From this program, you can do the following:

▶ Get an overview on the locked personnel numbers and who is locking them

▶ Send an unlocking request through a system message that the user will receive on screen, which is then stored in the SAP Business Workplace (Transaction SBWP).

▶ Delete the lock entry. Avoid deleting the lock entries without first checking with the person who is currently locking the personnel number. Otherwise, the person gets a system message notifying him that he's out but without a reason why, which will likely cause the user to retry to maintain (thus to lock) the personnel number.

Figure 7.57 illustrated the locked personnel number 5 by user Martin Gillet in the system.

Figure 7.57 Report HFIUCPL0 Locked Personnel Number

7.8.6 Employee List (RPLMIT00)

Businesses often need a quick way to pull a list of staff members or personnel associates, which can be accomplished with standard report RPLMIT00. This report can also be accessed through Transaction PAR2.

Report Name	RPLMIT00
Report Title	Employee List
Transaction Code	PAR2

Authorization Group	(none)
Package	PBAS—SAP HR Master Data Application Development

Figure 7.58 illustrates a typical listing provided by report RPLMIT00. The data obtained can also be downloaded to Office applications such as Word or Excel with the download icon.

Employee List

Key date: 21.01.2011
Number of selected employees: 342

Pers.no.	Name	Job Title	Entry Date	Leaving	Cost Ctr	CoCd	PA
00001027	Dr. Martin Jost	Head of department	01.01.1994		3200	1000	1000
00001099	Judy Miller	Administrator	01.01.2000		2200	1000	1000
00001100	Dieter Martens	Team leader	01.01.2000			1000	1000
00001110	Norbert Kernen	Skilled worker	01.01.2000			1000	1000
00001120	Jürgen Jeckel	Skilled worker	01.01.2000			1000	1000
00001204	Thomas von Falkenberg	Sales employee	01.01.1994		3150	1000	1000
00001206	Sebastian Schulz	Head of department	01.01.1994		1110	1000	1000
00001207	Werner Lachemann	Head of department	01.01.1994		1110	1000	1000
00001208	Michael Hintz	Team leader	01.01.1994		4220	1000	1000
00001209	Wilfried Schmitdke	Robotics specialist	01.01.1994		4220	1000	1000
00001210	Peter Bauer	Assembly worker	01.01.1994		4230	1000	1000
00001211	Fritz Stürmer	Assembly worker	01.01.1994		4230	1000	1000
00001212	Dieter Heck	Assembly worker	01.01.1994		4230	1000	1000
00001213	Hildegard Dörffler	Assembly worker	01.01.1994		4220	1000	1000
00001214	Stefan Huber	Team leader	01.01.1994		4277	1000	1000
00001215	Heidi Drechsel	Team leader	01.01.1994		4278	1000	1000
00001216	Franz Riegel	Assembly worker	01.01.1994		4278	1000	1000
00001217	Herbert Öding	Assembly worker	01.01.1994		4277	1000	1000
00001218	Max Schmidt	Assembly worker	01.01.1994		4220	1000	1000
00001219	Otto Degen	Assembly worker	01.01.1994		4220	1000	1000
00001220	Georg Spitz	Team leader	01.01.1994		4250	1000	1000
00001221	Harald Stürmer	Administrator	01.01.1994		4250	1000	1000
00001266	Manfred Effenberg	Team leader	01.01.1994		4230	1000	1000
00001267	Achmed Scholl	Assembly worker	01.01.1994		4230	1000	1000
00001268	Karl Babbel	Assembly worker	01.01.1994		4230	1000	1000
00001269	Egon Basler	Robotics specialist	01.01.1994		4220	1000	1000
00001270	Bernd Kraus	QM functional specialist	01.01.1994		4280	1000	1000
00001271	Heiner Lauterbach	Team leader	01.01.1994		4200	1000	1000
00001272	Boris Becker	Skilled worker	01.01.1994		4200	1000	1000
00001273	Hugo Boss	Skilled worker	01.01.1994		4200	1000	1000

Figure 7.58 Employee List

413

7.8.7   InfoType Overview for Employee (RPLINFC0)

This standard program is like Transaction PA10—Personnel File, which consolidates all InfoTypes maintained for a personnel number. This program is even better because it provides an overview of all InfoType records for the personnel numbers at a glance.

Report Name	RPLINFC0
Report Title	InfoType Overview for Employee
Transaction Code	PC00_M02_LINF0 or S_AHR_61015785
Authorization Group	(none)
Package	PK02—HR: Pension Fund International Parts

Figure 7.59 illustrates the results with the display of InfoType records for personnel number 1000: Anja Mueller.

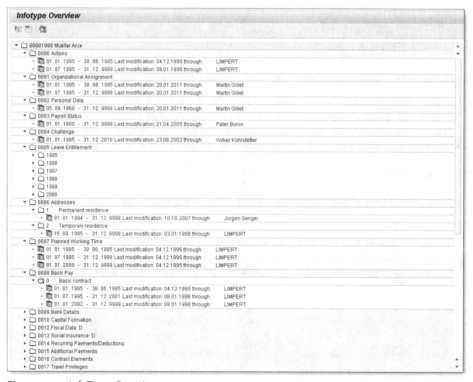

Figure 7.59   InfoTypes Overview

7.8.8 Converting SAPscript (OTF) or ABAP List Spool Jobs to PDF (RSTXPDFT4)

This neat program allows you to transform a spool request into a PDF. You can also provide this program to the developers when in the self-services form development process to get inspiration from the ABAP code.

Report Name	RSTXPDFT4
Report Title	Converting SAPscript (OTF) or ABAP List Spool Jobs to PDF
Transaction Code	(none)
Authorization Group	(none)
Package	STXD—SAPscript

7.8.9 Test Process (RPASR_TEST_PROCESS_EXECUTION) for HR Forms

Rather than testing from the SAP NetWeaver Portal directly, for test purposes and thus not productive use, you can perform tests here in regards to the HR forms. This allows you to trigger the forms and check whether you have technical issues or data to show. You can also provide this program to the development and configuration team to test directly in R/3.

Report Name	RPASR_TEST_PROCESS_EXECUTION
Report Title	Test Process
Transaction Code	HRASR_TEST_PROCESS
Authorization Group	(none)
Package	PAOC_ASR_PROCESS_MODELLING—Modeling Processes

7.8.10 Test Program: Version Information (for Analysis Only) (FP_PDF_TEST_00)

This program provides the version information for the Adobe Document Server (ADS), which comes in handy when checking technical prerequisites and version numbers, or just troubleshooting the application.

Report Name	FP_PDF_TEST_00
Report Title	Test Program: Version Information (for Analysis Only)
Transaction Code	(none)
Authorization Group	(none)
Package	SAFP—SAP Forms Processing

Figure 7.60 illustrates the version that you currently have on your system for ADS.

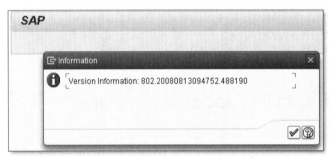

Figure 7.60 Version Information

7.9 Recommended Readings

Although the reporting definition is out of scope for this book, you should read *HR Reporting with SAP* (SAP PRESS 2008) to become familiar with SAP's reporting capabilities.

You may also want to take a look at my blog entry on the SAP Community Network (SCN): "Everything You Ever Wanted to Know about SAP HCM Reporting" (including a courtesy article provided by ERPTips):

www.sdn.sap.com/irj/scn/weblogs?blog=/pub/wlg/20726

7.10 Conclusion

You have seen that the SAP standard reporting offering, including the ABAP queries, can easily be integrated into SAP NetWeaver Portal and the MSS reporting area.

Reports can easily be adjusted per object selection, but you usually use the typical "P" person object. The reports are mostly based on the organizational structure to make it easier for the manager in the selection process.

However, despite enabling the standard reports through SAP NetWeaver Portal, you must not lose sight that there are a few pitfalls as explained earlier. The most important pitfalls concern the end user regarding the UI rendering and the ability to save under a *.* format.

If you use the latest reporting functionalities, you should select one of the additional tools provided by SAP in BI. Not only do these tools provides advanced sorting and data handling configuration, but they also provide the latest and hippest user-friendly UI. This is not mandatory, but it is important to know the reporting options and what can be provided to the end users.

We have focused enough on the reporting side. Now we will look into another SAP NetWeaver Portal dimension, known as the SAP NetWeaver Portal Administrator Role. The next chapter will unveil the additional functionalities we can enable for another end-user population.

The Human Resources administrator is a bridge between Employee Self-Services (ESS) and Manager Self-Services (MSS), which empower HR business partners and HR professionals to handle common administrative tasks through a web interface.

8   Human Resources Administrator Role

From the early beginning of ESS back in 1998 up to the introduction of MSS in 2004, there was a gap for end users. SAP provided and took care of the employee and manager processes, but except enabling transactions in the SAP NetWeaver Portal, no dedicated functionalities existed for HR administrators.

The HR administrator is also identified among customers as the HR business partner or team lead. In fact, the HR administrator covers the functionalities for the employees that are not managers but do have more responsibilities than a regular end user. For most firms or companies, this HR administrator is a role that fulfills administrative tasks. At the SAP level, the administrator role is a dedicated role, a placeholder to provide and cover these business functionalities.

Faithful to its motto of "innovation without disruption," SAP covered this gap for end users with the enhancement packages suite starting with EhP 1.

The HR administrator role also enables integration with the Digital Personnel File (DPF), which summarizes all the employee information at once. This file enables a smoother process for archiving employee-related information and combining it with all customer or legal documents such as the work contract.

8.1   Prerequisites

Assuming that all master data and authorizations have been maintained, you still must assess the technical prerequisites for enabling the HR administrator role. After checking the recommended support package level, you must review the enhancement packages to be activated as well as the authorizations to be maintained.

8.1.1   Enabling the Business Function

The HR administrator role started with EhP 1. It was then further enhanced throughout the following enhancement packages.

To benefit from the HR administrator role, the business function must be activated in Transaction SWF5—Switch Framework Customizing.

The business functions to be activated are the following:

▶ HCM_ASR_CI_1: HCM, Administrative Services 01
▶ HCM_ASR_CI_2: HCM, Administrative Services 02

8.1.2   Authorization Objects for the HR Administrator Role

In regards to authorizations, the administrator role requires authorization clearance in addition to the standard Personnel Administration (PA) of P_ORGIN: HR—Master Data; PLOG: Personnel Planning; and others.

Processes in HR Administrative Services represent business transactions in PA. The processes access application-specific data (in PA, this is InfoType data) that is entered using forms. Thus, the authorization object P_ASRCONT: HR Authorization for Process Content should also be maintained.

8.1.3   Human Capital Management Processes and Forms Assigned to the Administrator Role

The HR administrator role is mainly powered by HCM Processes and Forms. It renders an intuitive end-user document that is either web-based or in a PDF.

The personnel change requests and the HCM Processes and Forms are introduced in Chapter 3.

8.2   User Interface

The user interface (UI) is important because it secures the end user buy in. In addition, you need to know which technology is used so you can assess which technology you need to master for potential enhancements or developments.

Quoting SAP Note 1024326—Corrected UI for Role HR Administrator Available:

> *As of SAP ERP Enhancement Package 2005.1 (EhP1), the user interfaces used in the function "HCM Processes and Forms" and the portal role "HR administrator" were migrated from the Web Dynpro technology for Java to the Web Dynpro technology for ABAP.*
>
> *In future, we will only support the Web Dynpro for ABAP technology for the role "HR administrator."*

Web Dynpro for ABAP is thus the technology supported. The UI differences with Web Dynpro Java are minimal; however, it does change quite a few things when dealing with enhancements and developments.

We prefer ABAP because it is the SAP programming language, and most customers have internal skilled personnel that can "read" ABAP opposed to Java programming language.

8.2.1 Logon

The HR administrator role logon is available through SAP NetWeaver Portal. Log on as an end user, and locate the portal role HR ADMINISTRATOR as illustrated in Figure 8.1.

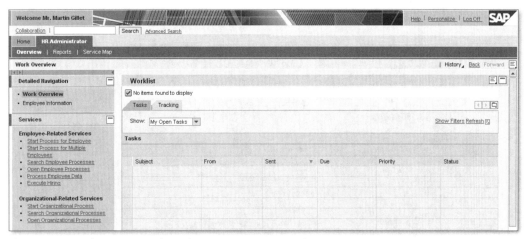

Figure 8.1 HR Administrator Role in the SAP NetWeaver Portal

Alternatively, the end user can choose the SERVICE MAP, which also consolidates all the functionalities made available, illustrated in Figure 8.2.

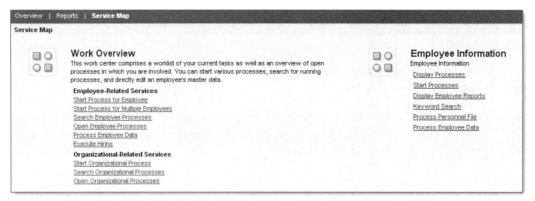

Figure 8.2   Service Map for the HR Administrator Role in SAP NetWeaver Portal

8.2.2   Employee Search

The Employee Search functionality is located under EMPLOYEE INFORMATION, which allows access to personnel master data (assuming that the end user has all relevant authorizations).

The selection screen is similar to a standard report selection screen, allowing selection through multiple values, as illustrated in Figure 8.3.

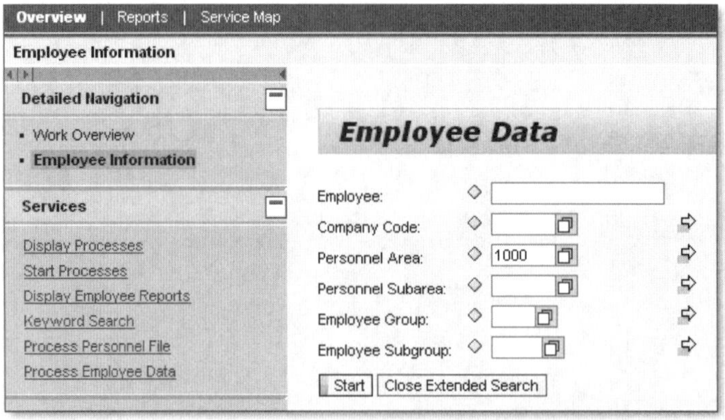

Figure 8.3   HR Administrator Selection Screen for Employee Data

The results provide a short list of employees found by the system. The system returns all the default information for the employee, such as Personnel Administration and Time Management information (see Figure 8.4).

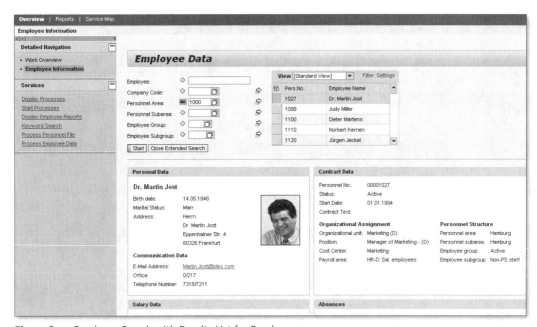

Figure 8.4 Employee Search with Results List for Employees

8.2.3 InfoType Maintenance

The HR component's master data is built on the InfoTypes. These InfoTypes are divided into main categories also known as ranges:

▶ 0000 up to 0999: Personnel Administration (PA) InfoTypes

▶ 1000 up to 1999: Personnel Development (PD) InfoTypes

▶ 2000 up to 2999: Time Management (TM) InfoTypes

▶ 4000 up to 4999: Recruitment InfoTypes

▶ 9000 up to 9999: Customer Include (CI) InfoTypes

Normally, the maintenance of these InfoTypes is done through the backend system by using, for example, Transactions PA30—Maintain HR Master Data, PA61—Maintain Time Data, or PB30—Maintain Applicant Master Data.

Thanks to the HR administrator role, this maintenance can now be done through the SAP NetWeaver Portal as illustrated in Figure 8.5.

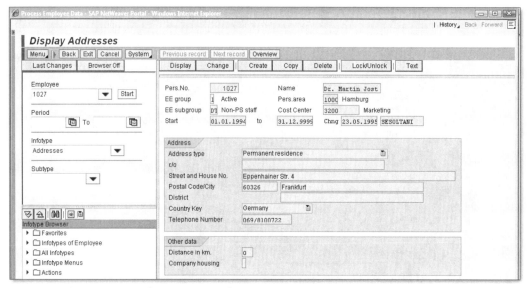

Figure 8.5 HR Administrator: Employee Data Maintenance

8.2.4 Reports

The HR administrative services for the HR administrator wouldn't be complete if not enriched with all the standard reports. Standard reports include the employee master data sheet, the employee time statement or pay slip, and the monitoring of dates.

From the portal menu, select EMPLOYEE REPORTS. A popup window appears, letting you choose from many reports as illustrated in Figure 8.6.

You can also use the launch pad to select reports. This launch pad is configurable in the Implementation Guide (IMG).

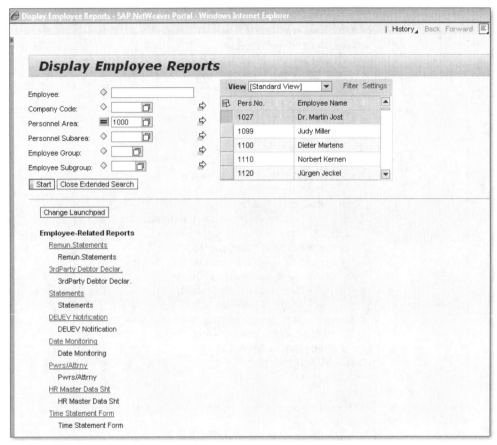

Figure 8.6   HR Administrator Report Selection

8.3   Access to the Administrator Role

Access to the administrator role is available via the IMG or via SAP NetWeaver Portal.

8.3.1   Implementation Guide (IMG) Access

After the business functions have been duly activated thanks to the enhancement package, SAP IMG unveils the functionalities to be configured.

The configuration of the HR administrator can be found under the IMG: PERSONNEL MANAGEMENT • HR ADMINISTRATIVE SERVICES as illustrated in Figure 8.7.

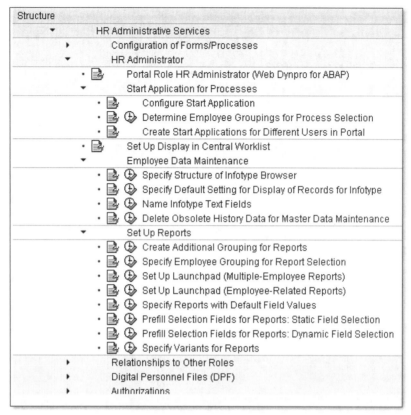

Figure 8.7 HR Administrator Role IMG Access

8.3.2   Portal Content Directory (PCD) Access

After the business functions have been activated with the enhancement package, SAP NetWeaver Portal makes them appear in the portal objects to be configured, through the Portal Content Directory (PCD, illustrated in Figure 8.8).

The folder for the HR administrator role contains all the relevant standard portal objects, which are listed here, to enable the functionalities:

▸ HR administrator iViews

▸ HR administrator pages

▶ HR administrator worksets

▶ HR administrator roles

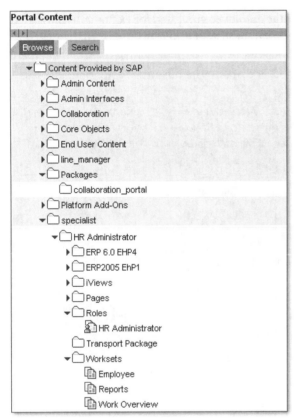

Figure 8.8   Portal Content Directory for the HR Administrator Role

As you have seen and as was illustrated in Chapter 2, each object contain properties or attributes that can be adjusted based on the business requirements.

8.4   Configuration of the Administrator Role

Let's now take a closer look into the configuration steps for the HR administrator role.

8.4.1 Start Application for Processes and Determine Employee Groupings for Process Selection

In this configuration step, you set up the employee grouping for process selection, which can be based on country or the employee grouping, for example, as illustrated in Figure 8.9. You identify the different groups of individuals you will have to deal with in the HR processes. First, review the SAP standard entries, and then amend their configuration table as needed or listed in the business requirements.

IMG Access Path	PERSONNEL MANAGEMENT • HR ADMINISTRATIVE SERVICES • HR ADMINISTRATOR • START APPLICATION FOR PROCESSES • DETERMINE EMPLOYEE GROUPINGS FOR PROCESS SELECTION
IMG Activity	HRAS_FT_PASRG
Feature Name	PASRG—Determining of Employee Grouping for Process Selection

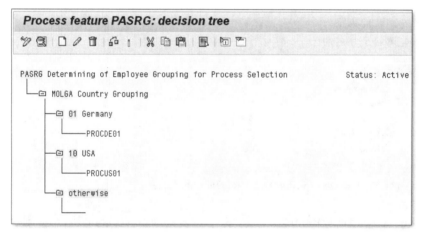

Figure 8.9 Feature (Decision Tree) PASRG

8.4.2 Employee Data Maintenance

In this section, we must configure the information for employee data maintenance as it should be provided to the administrator role.

Specify the Structure of the InfoType Browser

In this configuration step, you set up the sequence of functionalities that will be displayed in the end user browser. The configuration also provides the option to hide these functionalities. This is illustrated in Figure 8.10. You build up the UI by organizing the display sequence of the functionalities. Use the standard approach: Select FAVORITES, then INFOTYPES OF EMPLOYEE, then INFOTYPES MENUS, then ALL INFOTYPES, and, finally, ACTIONS. However, based on the feedback from the business team or from the listed business requirements, you can adjust this sequence as needed.

IMG Access Path	PERSONNEL MANAGEMENT • HR ADMINISTRATIVE SERVICES • HR ADMINISTRATOR • EMPLOYEE DATA MAINTENANCE • SPECIFY STRUCTURE OF INFOTYPE BROWSER
IMG Activity	HRAS_T5ASRFOLDERSEQ
Transaction Code	S_AEN_10000110
Table Name	T5ASRDABFOLDERS

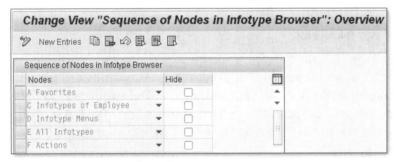

Figure 8.10 Sequence Node Configuration

Specify the Default Setting for the Display of Records for the InfoType

In this configuration step, you set up for each InfoType whether the single screen or list screen is called, as illustrated in Figure 8.11.

IMG Access Path	PERSONNEL MANAGEMENT • HR ADMINISTRATIVE SERVICES • HR ADMINISTRATOR • EMPLOYEE DATA MAINTENANCE • SPECIFY DEFAULT SETTING FOR DISPLAY OF RECORDS FOR INFOTYPE

IMG Activity	HRAS_T5ASRDABDEF
Transaction Code	S_AEN_10000111
Table Name	T582S

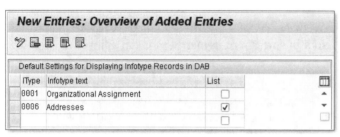

Figure 8.11 Maintaining New Entries for the Display of Data Records

Be aware that this setting is valid only if you start an InfoType from the data selection area using START or ENTER, rather than using the InfoType browser. When you select an InfoType using the InfoType browser, the single screen is called, regardless of this setting.

Name the InfoType Text Fields

As illustrated in Figure 8.12, this configuration step allows you to enable the storage of comments, for example, for InfoType 0019—Monitoring of Tasks. For each screen (called module pool in SAP), you assign the relevant text field to be used. For example, for InfoType 0019, we used MODULE POOL "MP001900" and assigned the FIELD NAME "RP50M-TEXT1" as the first sequence in the SCREEN "2000" provided by SAP.

IMG Access Path	PERSONNEL MANAGEMENT • HR ADMINISTRATIVE SERVICES • HR ADMINISTRATOR • EMPLOYEE DATA MAINTENANCE • NAME INFOTYPE TEXT FIELDS
IMG Activity	HRAS_T582ITTXTFIELDS
Transaction Code	S_PEN_05000030
Table Name	T582ITTXTFIELDS

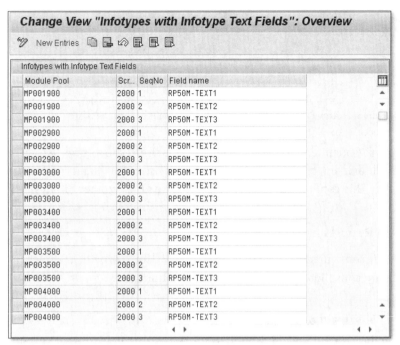

Figure 8.12 Maintaining the InfoType with InfoType Text

Delete Obsolete History Data for Master Data Maintenance

To avoid an overly large historical trace, this report allows you to delete the obsolete history data maintenance for all HR administrator maintenance activities performed through the SAP NetWeaver Portal, as illustrated in Figure 8.13.

IMG Access Path	PERSONNEL MANAGEMENT • HR ADMINISTRATIVE SERVICES • HR ADMINISTRATOR • EMPLOYEE DATA MAINTENANCE • DELETE OBSOLETE HISTORY DATA FOR MASTER DATA MAINTENANCE
IMG Activity	HRAS_DAB_HISTORY
Transaction Code	S_AEN_10000999
Program Name	RPASR_DAB_HISTORY

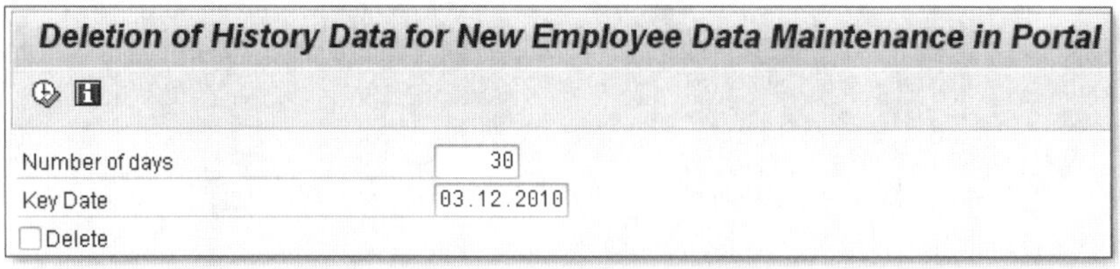

Figure 8.13 Deletion of History Data for New Employee Data Maintenance in Portal

In the employee data maintenance, you can view the last InfoType records that were changed (created, deleted, copied, or locked) for each user. The default period for this is 30 days. In this configuration step, you can adjust the number of days.

8.4.3 Set Up Reports

Now that we have configured the data to be provided, we must provide the relevant reports, which are consolidated through different groupings.

Create Additional Grouping for Reports

In this configuration step, illustrated in Figure 8.14, you create additional groupings to narrow down the different functionalities end users can have access to. This avoids overwhelming users with information by just showing what is required. We recommend grouping the reports into functional categories, for example, based on the job description or the business role attached to the position description in Organizational Management (OM). Avoid creating a grouping for fewer than 5 to 10 reports; a group of too few reports is frustrating for the end user.

IMG Access Path	PERSONNEL MANAGEMENT • HR ADMINISTRATIVE SERVICES • HR ADMINISTRATOR • SET UP REPORTS • CREATE ADDITIONAL GROUPING FOR REPORTS
IMG Activity	HRAS_T5ASRADDCRIT
Transaction Code	S_AEN_10000967
Table Name	V_T5ASRADDCRIT

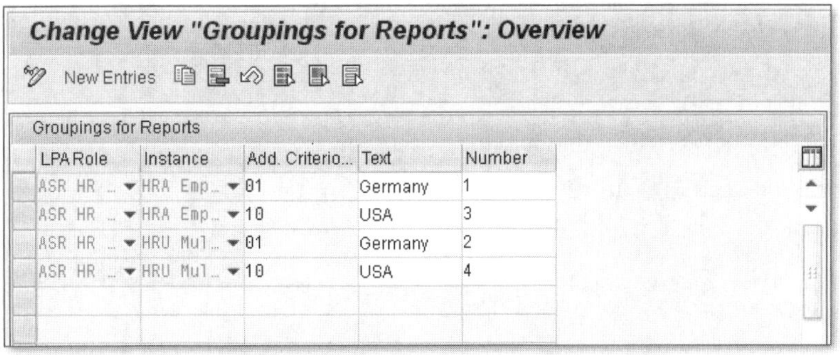

Change View "Groupings for Reports": Overview

New Entries

Groupings for Reports

LPA Role	Instance	Add. Criterio...	Text	Number
ASR HR ...	HRA Emp...	01	Germany	1
ASR HR ...	HRA Emp...	10	USA	3
ASR HR ...	HRU Mul...	01	Germany	2
ASR HR ...	HRU Mul...	10	USA	4

Figure 8.14 Maintaining Grouping for Reports

For the HR administrator role, a differentiation is made between two different instances of report lists for which you can enter groupings for the display of report lists:

- Employee-related reports, such as remuneration statements
- Multiple-employee reports, such as employee lists

Specify Employee Grouping for Report Selection

In this configuration step, you set up the employee grouping for report selection. This decision tree uses the country or employee grouping to identify the grouping for report. For example, if you work in the United States, which has country code (Molga, in SAP terminology) "10," you will get report grouping "10" as configured in the IMG (see Figure 8.15).

IMG Access Path	Personnel Management • HR Administrative Services • HR administrator • Set Up Reports • Specify Employee Grouping for Report Selection
IMG Activity	HRASR_DPASRR
Transaction Code	S_AEN_10001026
Feature Name	PASRR—Determination of Employee Grouping for Report Selection

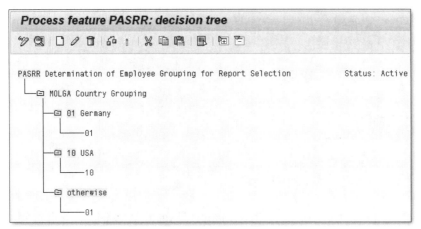

Figure 8.15 Feature (Decision Tree) PASRR

Set Up Launch Pad (Multiple-Employee Reports)

In this configuration step, as illustrated in Figure 8.16, you build up the reporting launch pad for multiple employee reports.

IMG Access Path	PERSONNEL MANAGEMENT • HR ADMINISTRATIVE SERVICES • HR ADMINISTRATOR • SET UP REPORTS • SET UP LAUNCH PAD (MULTIPLE-EMPLOYEE REPORTS)
IMG Activity	HRAS_LPD_CUST_HRU
Transaction Code	S_P8K_45000118

You first create the different folders as placeholders to allocate the reports to be provided to the end users. If relevant, use the country and then the different department to create a "clean" structure that will avoid confusion for the end user.

Into each folder, you then allocate the reports by clicking the NEW APPLICATION button. From this new application, you select the application category, for example, their transaction codes or a SAP NetWeaver Business Warehouse (BW) query.

You can also insert a separator in between that makes the screen "breathe" and avoids a crammed display for the end user.

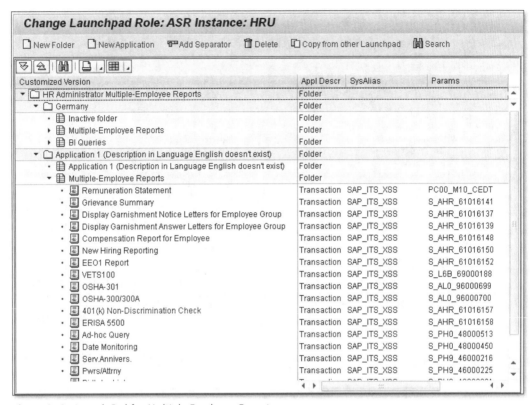

Figure 8.16 Launch Pad for Multiple Employee Reports

Set Up the Launch Pad (Employee-Related Reports)

In this configuration step, as illustrated in Figure 8.17, you build up the Reporting Launch Pad for employee-related reports. You repeat the same configuration steps as explained in the previous section, but this configuration entry is for the employee-related reports.

IMG Access Path	PERSONNEL MANAGEMENT • HR ADMINISTRATIVE SERVICES • HR ADMINISTRATOR • SET UP REPORTS • SET UP LAUNCH PAD (EMPLOYEE-RELATED REPORTS)
IMG Activity	HRAS_LPD_CUST_HRA
Transaction Code	S_P8K_45000119

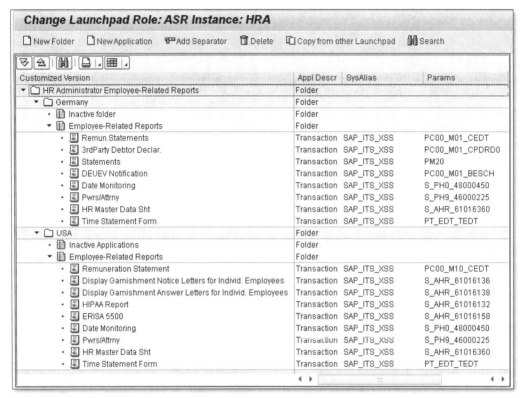

Figure 8.17 Launch Pad for Employee-Related Reports

Specify Reports with Default Field Values

In this configuration step, you specify which reports you want to start directly without having to enter any data in the mandatory fields of the selection screens, as illustrated in Figure 8.18. In this table, you identify the reports previously added in the launch pad that will need default values. You list the reports in this configuration step for the Administrative Service Request (ASR), which is the technical name for the HR administrator, by adding the report ID.

IMG Access Path	PERSONNEL MANAGEMENT • HR ADMINISTRATIVE SERVICES • HR ADMINISTRATOR • SET UP REPORTS • SPECIFY REPORTS WITH DEFAULT FIELD VALUES
IMG Activity	HRAS_T5ASRSELFLDID

Transaction Code	S_PEN_05000295
Table Name	V_T5ASRSELFLDID

To achieve this, it is mandatory that the selection fields are prefilled with default values of fields assigned to the report ID. These fields will be configured in the next IMG step.

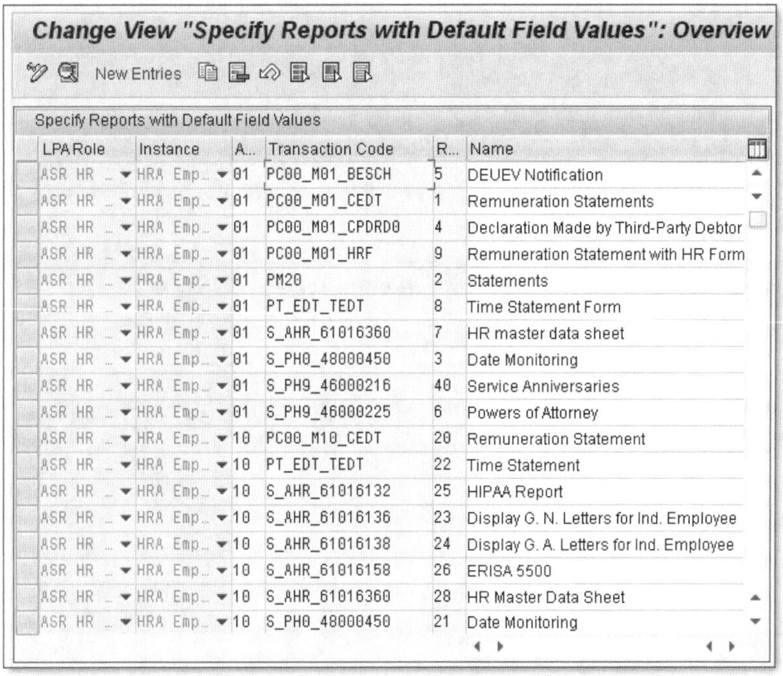
Change View "Specify Reports with Default Field Values": Overview

New Entries

Specify Reports with Default Field Values

LPA Role	Instance	A...	Transaction Code	R...	Name
ASR HR ...	HRA Emp...	01	PC00_M01_BESCH	5	DEUEV Notification
ASR HR ...	HRA Emp...	01	PC00_M01_CEDT	1	Remuneration Statements
ASR HR ...	HRA Emp...	01	PC00_M01_CPDRD0	4	Declaration Made by Third-Party Debtor
ASR HR ...	HRA Emp...	01	PC00_M01_HRF	9	Remuneration Statement with HR Form
ASR HR ...	HRA Emp...	01	PM20	2	Statements
ASR HR ...	HRA Emp...	01	PT_EDT_TEDT	8	Time Statement Form
ASR HR ...	HRA Emp...	01	S_AHR_61016360	7	HR master data sheet
ASR HR ...	HRA Emp...	01	S_PH0_48000450	3	Date Monitoring
ASR HR ...	HRA Emp...	01	S_PH9_46000216	40	Service Anniversaries
ASR HR ...	HRA Emp...	01	S_PH9_46000225	6	Powers of Attorney
ASR HR ...	HRA Emp...	10	PC00_M10_CEDT	20	Remuneration Statement
ASR HR ...	HRA Emp...	10	PT_EDT_TEDT	22	Time Statement
ASR HR ...	HRA Emp...	10	S_AHR_61016132	25	HIPAA Report
ASR HR ...	HRA Emp...	10	S_AHR_61016136	23	Display G. N. Letters for Ind. Employee
ASR HR ...	HRA Emp...	10	S_AHR_61016138	24	Display G. A. Letters for Ind. Employee
ASR HR ...	HRA Emp...	10	S_AHR_61016158	26	ERISA 5500
ASR HR ...	HRA Emp...	10	S_AHR_61016360	28	HR Master Data Sheet
ASR HR ...	HRA Emp...	10	S_PH0_48000450	21	Date Monitoring

Figure 8.18 Configuring Reports with Default Field Values

Prefill Selection Fields for Reports: Static Field Selection

In this step, you configure, as illustrated in Figure 8.19, the static default values to be used when launching reports in the HR administrator role. Common default values include the fields PNPWERKS: Personnel Area, PNPBTRTL: Personnel Subarea, or PNPKOSTL—Cost Center. All these fields can be easily identified in the standard InfoTypes screen by calling the help for each field and then the technical information. Because we deal mainly with PA, we are using the logical database PNP. The logical database is a consolidated database with all InfoTypes for a particular grouping such as PA. Depending on the fields used in this configuration step, the logical database name can be added in front of the technical name of the field. For example, the personnel area field "WERKS" becomes "PNPWERKS."

This is probably no concern for most of us who already use this concept when creating SAP queries.

IMG Access Path	PERSONNEL MANAGEMENT • HR ADMINISTRATIVE SERVICES • HR ADMINISTRATOR • SET UP REPORTS • PREFILL SELECTION FIELDS FOR REPORTS: STATIC FIELD SELECTION
IMG Activity	HRAS_T5ASRSELFLDSF
Transaction Code	S_PEN_05000296
Table Name	V_T5ASRSELFLDSF

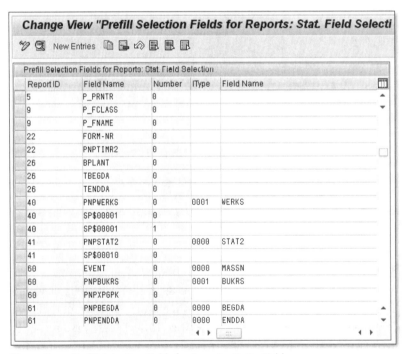

Figure 8.19 Prefill Selection Fields for Reports: Static Fields

Prefill Selection Fields for Reports: Dynamic Field Selection

In this step, you configure the dynamic default values to be used when launching reports in the HR administrator role, as illustrated in Figure 8.20.

For each report ID previously defined, you add the logical database field name, for example, PNPABKRS. PNP is the logical database for PA, and ABKRS is the field for the personnel area. You are mapping the logical database field against the InfoType number and its field. For example, the InfoType 0001 — Organizational Assignment is mapped to field ABKRS — Payroll Area.

IMG Access Path	PERSONNEL MANAGEMENT • HR ADMINISTRATIVE SERVICES • HR ADMINISTRATOR • SET UP REPORTS • PREFILL SELECTION FIELDS FOR REPORTS: DYNAMIC FIELD SELECTION
IMG Activity	HRAS_T5ASRSELFLDDF
Transaction Code	S_PEN_05000297
Table Name	V_T5ASRSELFLDDF

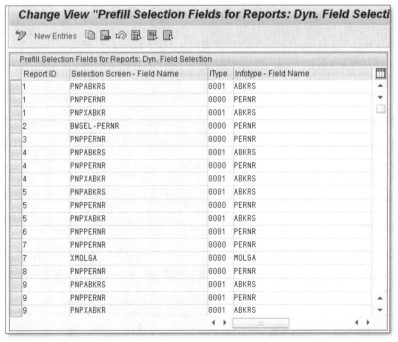

Change View "Prefill Selection Fields for Reports: Dyn. Field Selecti

New Entries

Prefill Selection Fields for Reports: Dyn. Field Selection

Report ID	Selection Screen - Field Name	IType	Infotype - Field Name
1	PNPABKRS	0001	ABKRS
1	PNPPERNR	0000	PERNR
1	PNPXABKR	0001	ABKRS
2	BWSEL-PERNR	0000	PERNR
3	PNPPERNR	0000	PERNR
4	PNPABKRS	0001	ABKRS
4	PNPPERNR	0000	PERNR
4	PNPXABKR	0001	ABKRS
5	PNPABKRS	0001	ABKRS
5	PNPPERNR	0000	PERNR
5	PNPXABKR	0001	ABKRS
6	PNPPERNR	0001	PERNR
7	PNPPERNR	0000	PERNR
7	XMOLGA	0000	MOLGA
8	PNPPERNR	0000	PERNR
9	PNPABKRS	0001	ABKRS
9	PNPPERNR	0001	PERNR
9	PNPXABKR	0001	ABKRS

Figure 8.20 Prefill Selection Fields for Reports: Dynamic Fields

Specify Variants for Reports

Because you run most reports in SAP with a selection variant, in this configuration step, you assign the selection variant to be used when running the report through the HR administrator role, as illustrated in Figure 8.21.

IMG Access Path	PERSONNEL MANAGEMENT • HR ADMINISTRATIVE SERVICES • HR ADMINISTRATOR • SET UP REPORTS • SPECIFY VARIANTS FOR REPORTS
IMG Activity	HRAS_T5ASRSELFLDVAR
Transaction Code	S_PEN_05000298
Table Name	V_T5ASRSELFLDVAR

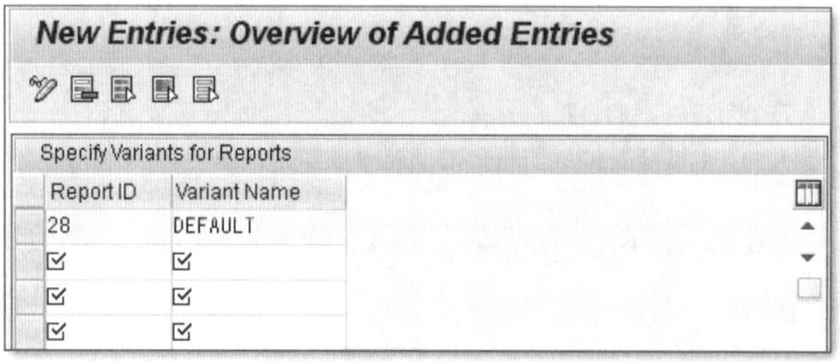

Figure 8.21 Select Variant for HR Administrator Reports

For example, REPORT ID "28" master data sheet will start with the "DEFAULT" selection variant. Maintain this table as needed per the business requirements.

8.4.4 Delete Logs from the Application Log

When working with the HR administrator role, error messages created when the HCM Processes and Forms functions are executed are saved in the application log, under the HRAS object.

This storage can lead to heavy content in the database. By using Transaction SLG2 — Application Log: Delete Logs, as illustrated in Figure 8.22, you can delete the logs that are no longer required in the application log.

IMG Access Path	PERSONNEL MANAGEMENT • HR ADMINISTRATIVE SERVICES • HR ADMINISTRATOR • TOOLS • DELETE LOGS FROM APPLICATION LOG
IMG Activity	HRAS_APPLICATIONLOG
Transaction Code	S_PEN_05000029 or SLG2
Program Name:	SBAL_DELETE

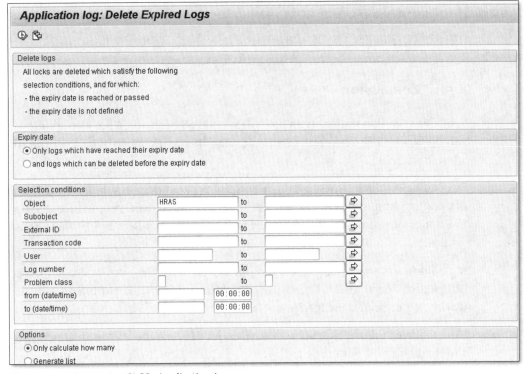

Figure 8.22 Transaction SLG2: Application Log

8.4.5 Message Mapping

If the standard messages are too technical or not suitable for end users, SAP provides additional configuration that allows the customer to personalize the system messages provided to the end users. The customer can adjust, where appropriate, the messages triggered by the system. An example, Time Management process errors when dealing with the leave request or the clock in or out entries, is provided in Chapter 5 for ESS because you use the same approach.

Figure 8.23 illustrates the different configuration options.

```
Message Mapping
SAP: Define Context for Message Mapping
Customer: Define Message Mapping for Message Type
Customer: Define Message Mapping for Error Category
SAP: Define Message Mapping for Message Type
SAP: Define Message Mapping for Error Category
Determine Alternate Messages
```

Figure 8.23   Configuring Message Mappings for the HR Administrator Role

8.5   Conclusion

You have seen that not only can ESS, MSS, and PSS be enabled but also additional add-on functionalities (from the enhancement packages) are provided for the HR administrator.

Depending on the business requirements, these functionalities provide a detailed answer to administrative services. These services empower the productivity and SAP integration coherence because every process is handled in SAP through an intuitive UI.

In addition to these self-services, additional functionalities such as the Employee Interaction Center (EIC), the Learning Solution (LSO), E-Recruitment, and the workflow can be also enabled.

Now that we have covered the self-services, let's review these additional function-alities and kick off with the Employee Interaction Center (EIC).

SAP Business Workflow provides state-of-the art workflow templates and standard tasks that enable real-time information to be dispatched to the stakeholders via notifications and email.

9   Workflow

Workflows are useful because they allow flexible and automatic communication throughout the different stakeholders involved in business processes. Setting up and configuring a SAP standard workflow is not complicated. This chapter uses an example to review the prerequisites for setting up a workflow, explain the SAP Business Workflow configuration, and cover the required customizing.

The chapter also describes helpful reports that provide options to monitor and troubleshoot workflow processes.

This chapter is not meant to replace the great book *Practical Workflow for SAP* (SAP PRESS, 2nd ed. 2009). Instead, this book covers the basis for enabling standard out-of-the-box workflow scenario templates as provided by SAP.

9.1   Introduction

A *standard workflow* is the process delivered within the SAP ERP 6.0 backend. It consists of different steps and an agent rule determination, as illustrated in Figure 9.1, which enables the dispatch of notification, for example, the time sheet approval.

Enabling the standard workflow is a quick win that can either answer a basic requirement or extend flexibility into the HCM processes. By using the workflow, you are making sure that your processes are optimized and automatically sent to the right approval manager or the stakeholder involved in the process.

SAP provides myriad workflow templates and tasks, but for this example, we'll use the Cross-Application Time Sheet (CATS). With this example, we will walk through the different steps of the configuration process using the standard tasks. Obviously, on a customer project, you would copy this standard task into a customer task and then make the configuration in the customer task.

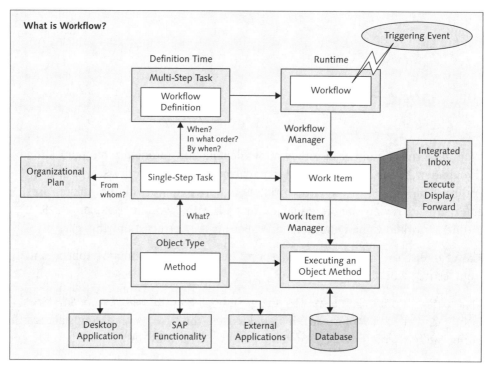

Figure 9.1 Overview of a Workflow Process

To copy the standard tasks, use Transaction PFTC_COP—Copy Tasks. The prerequisite is that the Basis team maintains the workflow prefix numbers for standard object types.

Prefix numbers for standard object types are maintained as follows:

IMG Access	SAP CUSTOMIZING IMPLEMENTATION GUIDE • SAP NETWEAVER • BUSINESS MANAGEMENT • BASIC SETTINGS • MAINTAIN PREFIX NUMBERS
IMG Activity	SIMG_WF1500W4
Transaction Code	S_BCE_68000595
Table	T78NR/Q78NR

As illustrated in Figure 9.2, you allocate a prefix number, usually 900 for customer prefix for each system client, for example, 979 in client 800.

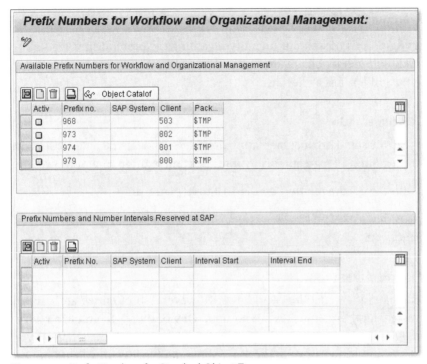

Figure 9.2 Prefix Numbers for Standard Object Types

The approval by a superior, based on the chief position (relationship A/B012) in the organizational structure, is identified in the standard by task TS20000460 (up to SAP ERP 5.0) and task TS 31000007 (as of SAP ERP 6.0).

> **Note**
>
> For more information, read SAP Note 951708: CATS Agent Determination with CATS Workflow Tasks.

9.2   Basic Configuration

These steps show the configuration of a standard workflow so you can set up a workflow without being an expert in this field. This chapter covers the prerequisites (make sure to check with your Basis team), configuration, customizing, and testing.

9.2.1 Prerequisites for Setting Up Workflow Processes

First things first—let's refresh our memory regarding the prerequisites for setting up the workflow. Even if you are familiar with workflow configuration, don't skip this section; consider it as a checklist.

Standard Documentation

Be sure to read the standard documentation provided online if you haven't already. It is the starting point of a great journey into the configuration of workflow!

You can get to the documentation on the SAP Help platform:

http://help.sap.com/erp2005_ehp_04/helpdata/DE/92/bc26a6ec2b11d2b4b5006094b 9ea0d/frameset.htm

Technical Prerequisites

Nothing is greater than enabling workflows. However, too often we are trapped because the technical prerequisites are not met. Obviously, in due time, a review assessment with the Basis team of the prerequisites is needed. For example, if you want—to push notifications to the user's mailbox, the functionality SAP Connect must be enabled in the system. To access the SAPconnect functionality, you can either use Transaction SCOT or Transaction SCON—SAPconnect—Administration.

Additionally, SAP Note 455140—Configuration of E-mail, Fax, Paging, or SMS Using SMTP, will shed additional light on setting up communication using SMTP in the standard SAP system.

You can also check the automatic workflow customizing status by calling Transaction SWU3—Automatic Workflow Customizing.

Organizational Management

Although SAP Business Workflow could work without HR Organizational Management (OM), the workflow does run better with it. Not only is OM useful for configuration, reporting, and structural authorizations, but it also provides a flexible way to dispatch the information across the organizational structure. A typical organizational structure is depicted in Figure 9.3.

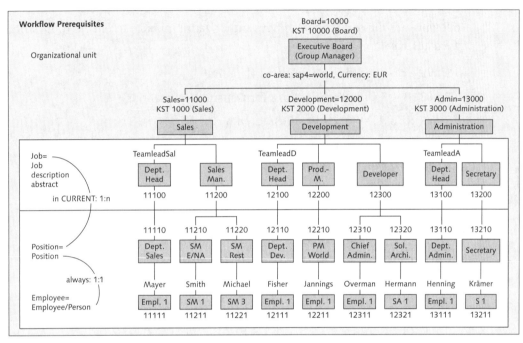

Figure 9.3 A Company Organizational Structure

From the employee assignment to a position, up to the chief position that identifies the person in charge (also known as the line manager or project manager), the organizational structure describes the company's personnel structure. Do not be misled by the legal or logistics structure, although similarities could exist.

OM also allows the maintenance of substitutes, which empowers the delegation process to team leads, secretaries, and so on.

OM can be accessed through standard Transaction PPOME—Change Organization and Staffing, which has been available since release 4.6, or the simple (but not obsolete) interface through Transaction PPOM_OLD—Maintain Organizational Plan.

To best comprehend the setup of OM, consider attending the standard SAP Training HR505—Organizational Management, and/or read *Mastering SAP ERP HCM Organizational Management* (SAP PRESS 2008).

Workflow Authorizations

To trigger and operate a workflow, you need to check with the authorization team to get the required authorizations objects.

Following are the standard workflow authorization objects to enable (this is not an exhaustive list):

► S_WF_WI—Workflow: Work Item Handling

► B_NOTIF—Follow-Up Functions for General Notifications

► S_WF_SUBST—Workflow: Substitute Rule

► I_QMEL—PM/QM: Notification Types

► I_VORG_MEL—PM/QM: Business Operation for Notifications

Authorizations will be covered in Chapter 11 in more detail.

SAP UserID Mapping Against Personnel Number and Email Address

To run properly, the system requires a valid mapping (check the start and end dates) between a SAP UserID and a personnel number. This is done, as you will see in more detail in Chapter 11, Section 11.4.7, in InfoType 0105—Communication, subtype 0001—System User Name (SY-UNAME).

The same applies for a valid email address, if you push the workflow notification and tasks to the receiver's mailbox. The 0010—Email subtype of InfoType 0105—Communication serves that purpose.

9.2.2 Configuring a Standard Workflow in a Human Capital Management Process

SAP offers multiple templates when it comes to workflows. Like any other configuration or customizing step, standard entries should not be changed. You should instead make a copy into an authorized SAP (and customer) name space.

In this section, the configuration is done directly to the standard task, but in a real-life system, you should always make a copy of the standard task.

Maintain Task

After you identify the standard task to be copied and maintained, access Transaction PFTC_CHG—Change Tasks.

Remember, the task illustrated in this example is TS31000007—CATS Approval by Supervisor, as illustrated in Figure 9.4. In this case, the "supervisor" is the manager.

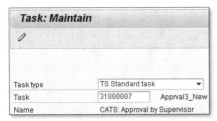

Figure 9.4 Standard Task CATS Approval by Supervisor

Basic Data Tab

In the first tab to be maintained for the task, BASIC DATA (illustrated in Figure 9.5), switch the RELEASE STATUS from NOT DEFINED to R RELEASED in the dropdown list.

Standard Task: Change

Standard task	31000007 Apprval3_New	
Name	CATS: Approval by Supervisor	
Package	CATS	Applicatn Component CA-TS

Basic data | Description | Container | » Triggering events | » Terminating events | Default rules | SAPphone

Name

Abbr.	Apprval3_New
Name	CATS: Approval by Supervisor
Release status	R Released

Work Item Text

Work item text	Approval of Working Times

Object method

Object Category	BO BOR Object Type
Object Type	CATS CATS
Method	APPROVE Approval request

☐ Synchronous object method
☑ Object method with dialog

Execution

☐ Background processing   ☐ Executable with SAPforms

Figure 9.5 Basic Data Tab for the Workflow Task

Description Tab

The second tab, DESCRIPTION (illustrated in Figure 9.6), although optional, will gather the description and/or the documentation required by the customer or the company rules. You can set the Change Request (CR) ID here, which speeds up the browsing of the documentation later when troubleshooting or reviewing the documentation during an upgrade.

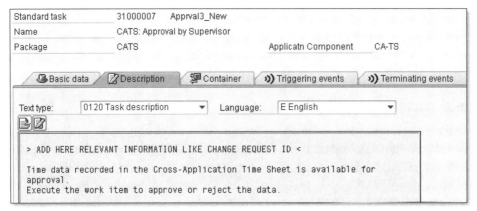

Figure 9.6 Description Tab for the Workflow Task

Container Tab

The third tab, CONTAINER (illustrated in Figure 9.7), holds all technical information required to run the workflow task. As nothing particular is required here, you can leave this tab as provided by SAP.

Triggering Events Tab

The fourth tab, TRIGGERING EVENTS (illustrated in Figure 9.8), is the most important because it tells the workflow task what the triggering event is. For this example, you set the value BO BOR OBJECT TYPE in the column OBJECT CATEGORY, set the value CATS in the column OBJECT TYPE, and set the value CREATED in the column EVENT. Press ⌈Enter⌋ and watch all the technical relations the system is performing as shown on the bottom of the screen.

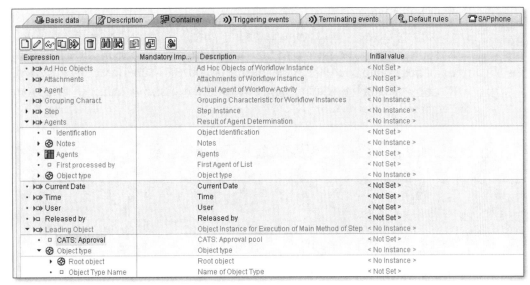

Figure 9.7 Container Tab for the Workflow Tab

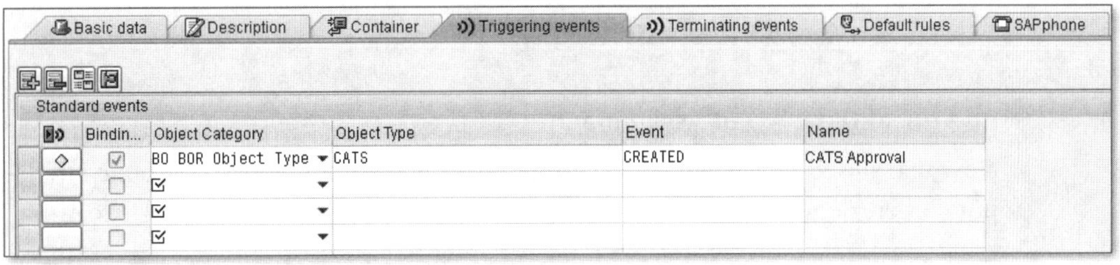

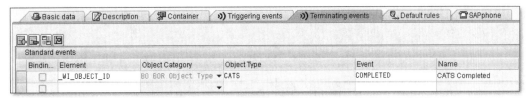

Figure 9.8 Triggering Event for the Workflow Task

Terminating Events Tab

The fifth tab, TERMINATING EVENTS (illustrated in Figure 9.9), is automatically filled, after the tab TRIGGERING EVENTS is maintained, in this case. Review the EVENT column carefully where the value "COMPLETED" should have been added by the system.

Bindin...	Element	Object Category	Object Type	Event	Name
☐	WI_OBJECT_ID	BO BOR Object Type ▼ CATS		COMPLETED	CATS Completed
☐		▼			

Figure 9.9 Terminating Event for the Workflow Task

Default Rules Tab

The sixth tab, DEFAULT RULES (illustrated in Figure 9.10), is the technical value you must set to instruct the system to find and identify the superior (the chief position). In this example, use the standard rule 00000157—Superior (Chief Position), which is retrieving the relationship A/B012—Manages.../ Is Managed By... from the organizational structure.

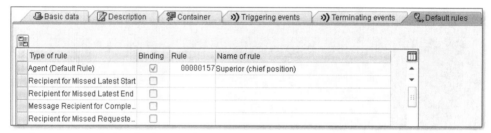

Figure 9.10 Default Rules for Workflow Task

SAPphone Tab

This tab is not relevant for this discussion.

Additional Data: Agent Assignment

Now that all six steps have been maintained, save your work on a workbench transport order (depending on the system client settings set up by your Basis team).

From the menu, go to ADDITIONAL DATA • AGENT ASSIGNMENT • MAINTAIN. This step ensures that the task is set as a GENERAL TASK (illustrated in Figure 9.11) and that the index is generated.

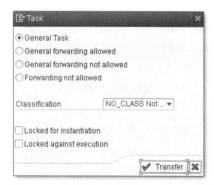

Figure 9.11 Setting the Task as General Task

Also refresh the index by clicking on the ⟳ icon, as illustrated in Figure 9.12.

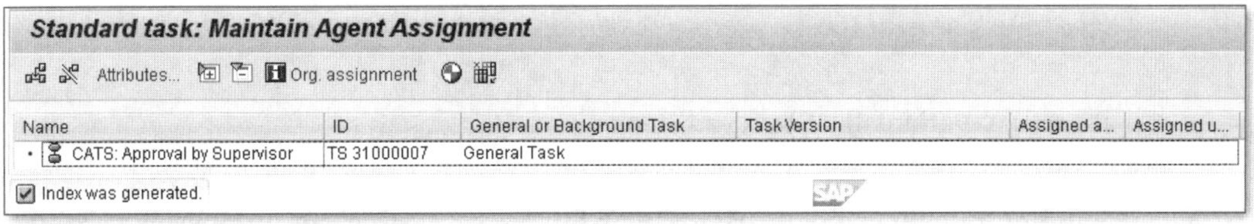

Standard task: Maintain Agent Assignment

Attributes... Org. assignment

Name	ID	General or Background Task	Task Version	Assigned a...	Assigned u...
• CATS: Approval by Supervisor	TS 31000007	General Task			

☑ Index was generated.

SAP

Figure 9.12 Refreshing the Index

9.2.3 Adjusting the Customizing Configuration

Now that the workflow task is appropriately configured, activated, and saved under a transport order, you must assign this task to the relevant customizing step for the CATS functionality. This is achieved directly in the IMG. This is the case for most workflow configuration. Carefully review the standard documentation and, where relevant, the next configuration that must take place.

Cross-Application Time Sheet (CATS) Data Entry Profile for Workflow

From Transaction CAC1—Time Sheet: Maintain Profiles (illustrated in Figure 9.13), in the CATS Data Entry Profiles screen, enable the option WITH APPROVAL PROCEDURE. In the section WORKFLOW, flag the tick box WITH SAP BUSINESS WORKFLOW, which enables and unleashes the use of SAP Business Workflow, along with the tick box WITH AUTO. DETERMINATION OF RECIPIENT, which automatically points to the chief position thanks to the organizational structure provided in HR.

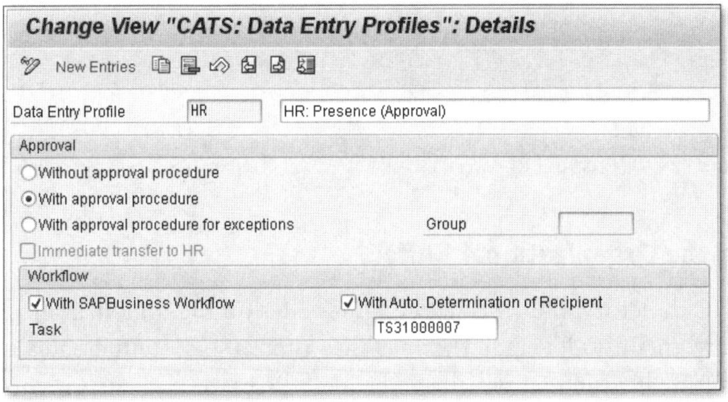

Change View "CATS: Data Entry Profiles": Details

New Entries

| Data Entry Profile | HR | HR: Presence (Approval) |

Approval
○ Without approval procedure
◉ With approval procedure
○ With approval procedure for exceptions   Group
☐ Immediate transfer to HR

Workflow
☑ With SAP Business Workflow   ☑ With Auto. Determination of Recipient
Task   TS31000007

Figure 9.13 Adjusting the Workflow Configuration for the Cross-Application Time Sheet

453

Under this tick box, set the workflow tasks ID that you have previously copied from the standard naming range to customer naming range.

Save your configuration.

Workflow Variant for Standard Reports

In this example, and in many other workflow processes, you might have a program that requires a workflow variant. Visually check that this variant does exist. If it is missing, create the variant in all relevant systems across your landscape.

In this example, program RCATSB01—Time Sheet: Approve Times requires the VARIANT NAME WORKFLOW (see Figure 9.14), which is a placeholder for the configuration. If this variant is missing, it will lead to a non-triggering workflow event.

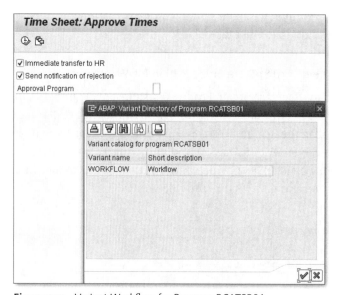

Figure 9.14 Variant Workflow for Program RCATSB01

9.2.4 Refreshing the Organizational Buffer

It's a fact that to get its directory, the workflow engine relies on the organizational structure. However, to (mainly) leverage the response time, the system creates a buffer of the organizational structure, which can be a bit disorienting at first if you don't know it's happening.

The system refreshes this buffer at least overnight, depending on the program's job properties. To trigger the buffer manually, for example, during test scenarios when you have updated the organizational structure and want the changes to be taken into account by the workflow, run Transaction SWU_OBUF—Runtime Buffer PD Org, illustrated in Figure 9.15.

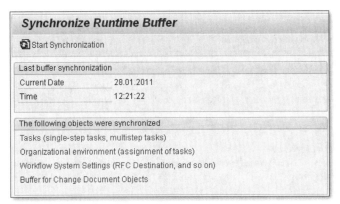

Figure 9.15 Refreshing the Organizational Structure Buffer

> **Note**
>
> To find out more about the transactions and programs, download the free appendices at *www.workflowbook.com/TransactionIndex.pdf*.

9.2.5 Receiving the Workflow Notification

After the workflow has been triggered, it is sent out to the professional inbox. You have two options to reach the notifications and the messages: use the Business Workplace (BWP) or use the SAP NetWeaver Portal Universal Worklist (UWL).

Business Workplace (BWP)

Depending on the type of SAP UserID, if the user has access to SAP ERP, Business Workplace can be reached through Transaction SBWP—SAP Business Workplace.

Transaction SBWP is fairly complete and provides different folders such as INBOX, RESUBMISSIONS, OUTBOX, and so on to sort out the different notifications and messages types. Figure 9.16 illustrates the time sheet approval request received in the inbox.

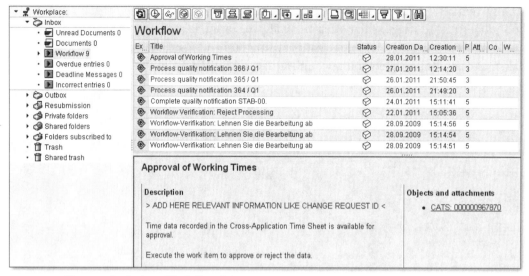

Figure 9.16 Business Work Place Inbox

In BWP, select the item to be processed from the inbox, and open the notification. Double-click on the notification to get to the functionality, in this case, the manager time sheet approval request.

Universal Worklist (UWL)

In this book, we deal with online self-services reached through SAP NetWeaver Portal, so it makes sense to provide online access to these notifications and messages as well. Most of the time, SAP NetWeaver Portal users do not have access to the SAP ERP backend system. Furthermore, the layout of the backend and frontend systems is quite different. Users will certainly notice this layout difference and be disappointed.

In SAP NetWeaver Portal, the Universal Worklist (UWL) can be deployed as a main point of entry to reach the different notifications and messages types (see Figure 9.17).

In the UWL, select the item to be processed from the inbox, and open the notification. Double-click on the notification to get to the functionality, in this case, the manager time sheet approval request.

Be careful, in this example, the web-enabled approval screens for CATS are only available as of SAP ERP 6.0 (standard, no enhancement package required).

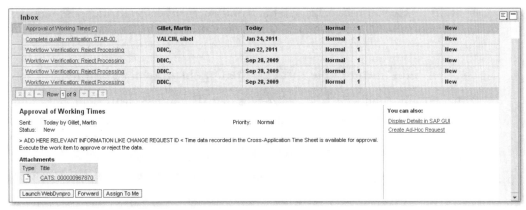

Figure 9.17 Receiving Task UWL

From SAP ERP 5.0 downward, the TIME SHEET APPROVAL screens could be web-enabled but would be powered by WebGUI. WebGUI is, in fact, an SAP backend transaction web-enabled into SAP NetWeaver Portal. Although it technically works, integrating these technologies is challenging because they different significantly from the Web Dynpro provided by SAP. From experience, it can be difficult to convince the portal communication team to include these in the user menus.

9.3 Configuring a Substitution Rule

Of course, the chief position must offer the possibility to set a substitute in his line of duties, for practical reasons. Management often requires that a substitute is set on a periodic basis, such as holidays, or a permanent basis, such as delegation to team lead.

The following sections provide a few leads where you can set a substitute in the workflow process.

9.3.1 Substitution Rule through Workflow Agent Determination

The first option that can be independent from the organizational structure is to set the substitution rule directly in the workflow agent determination rule. It's straightforward, but the issue is that it might be as easy to maintain for the end user, if the substitute changes often. Furthermore, because it is directly set in the agent determination, it might not be (totally) reusable among other workflows.

Setting up the substitution rule in the workflow agent determination also requires you to add the relevant authorization to the substitute.

9.3.2 Substitution Rule through the Organizational Assignment

The second option, which is preferred, is to maintain the substitute in the organizational structure by maintaining the relationship A/B 010 — Substitute/Substitute, as illustrated in Figure 9.18 for the position Director Human Resources with the substitute Dipl.Kfm. Ulrike Zaucker. This standard relationship can then be reused not only by other workflows but also in other processes, reporting, and structural authorizations.

```
─□ 0  00001001 Is line supervisor of    Human Resources (D)                    01.01.1994 - 31.12.9999
          Anja Müller                                                          01.07.1995 - 31.12.9999

    ─□ S  50000052  Incorporates           Director of Human Resources - (D)      01.01.1994 - 31.12.9999

        ─P  00001000 Holder                     Anja Müller                       01.07.1995 - 31.12.9999
        ─P  00001002 Substitute                 Dipl.Kfm. Ulrike Zaucker          01.01.2011 - 31.12.9999

    ─□ S  50011262 Incorporates            Secretary in Personnel Dept (Germany)  01.01.1996 - 31.12.9999
    ─□ 0  50000147 Is line supervisor of   Personnel Administration (D)           01.01.1994 - 31.12.9999
          Alexander Rickes                                                        01.01.1994 - 31.12.9999
    ─□ 0  50000148 Is line supervisor of   Personnel Development & Controlling (D) 01.01.1994 - 31.12.9999
          Maria Rauenberger                                                       01.01.1994 - 31.12.9999
    ─□ 0  50000149 Is line supervisor of   Social and legal (D)                   01.01.1994 - 31.12.9999
          Martin Beck                                                             01.01.1994 - 31.12.9999
    ─□ 0  50014178 Is line supervisor of   Personnel Training (D)                 01.01.1998 - 31.12.9999
          Dr. Henriette Kuhl-Mayer                                                01.01.1999 - 31.12.9999
```

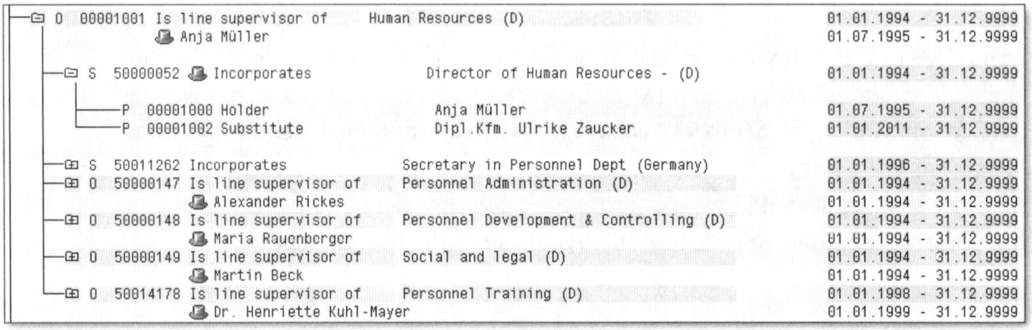

Figure 9.18 *Maintaining Relationships*

Setting up the substitution rule in the organizational structure also requires you to add the relevant authorization to the substitute, which is easier due to the structural authorizations.

The hardest part is to convince the HR department because this maintenance might cause additional work.

9.3.3 Substitution Rule through the Business Workplace

A third option is to set the substitution rule directly from the BWP. The advantage is that the end user remains totally in control of who his substitute is. On the other hand, from a central control point of view, this could quickly turn into a nightmare.

As illustrated in Figure 9.19, this substitution can be set from the BWP with Transaction SBWP. From the menu, choose SETTINGS • OFFICE SETTINGS. When the popup appears, choose the SUBSTIT. tab. Maintain the substitute.

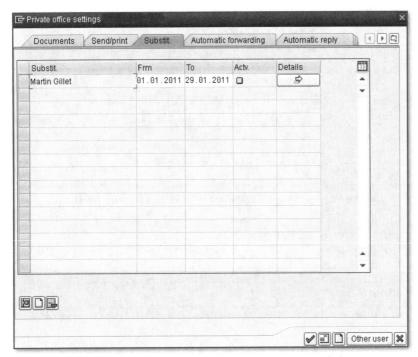

Figure 9.19 Maintaining the Substitution Rule in the Business Workplace

Setting up the substitution rule in BWP also requires you to add the relevant authorization to the substitute.

9.3.4 Substitution Rule through the Universal Worklist

Just like in the BWP, this functionality is also available directly from the Universal Worklist (UWL).

In the main screen, next to the HIDE PREVIEW functionality (illustrated in Figure 9.20), select MANAGE SUBSTITUTION RULES from the dropdown list.

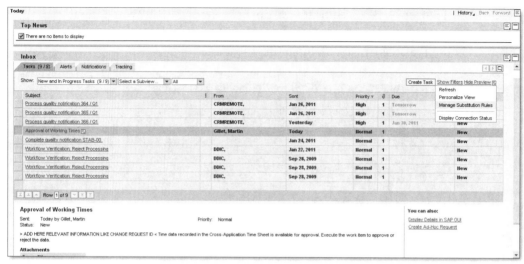

Figure 9.20 Accessing the Management of Substitution Rules in the Universal Worklist

A popup appears, as illustrated in Figure 9.21.

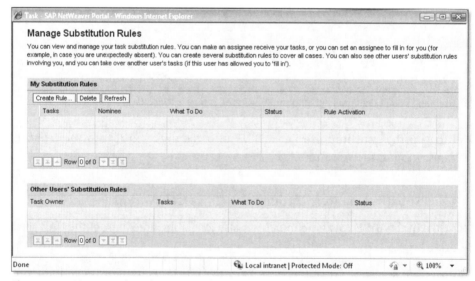

Figure 9.21 Managing the Substitution Rule in the Universal Worklist

Create the substitution rule, and save your entry, as illustrated in Figure 9.22.

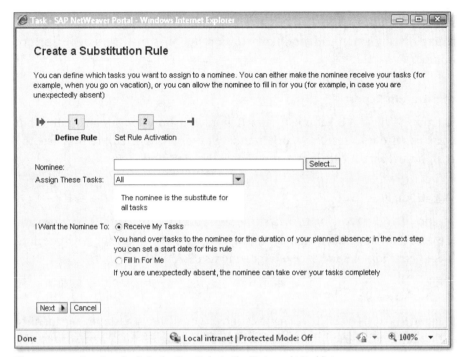

Figure 9.22 Creating the Substitution Rule in the Universal Worklist

Setting up the substitution rule in UWL also requires you to add the relevant authorization to the substitute.

9.4 Troubleshooting

So what do you do if workflow doesn't get triggered, doesn't work, or stop working? The following subsections provide a cheat sheet that includes a list of standard reports and a list of to-dos when troubleshooting issues with workflows. This cheat sheet depicts different scenarios that often lead to solving the issue.

9.4.1 Standard Reports for Troubleshooting

This section introduces a few standard reports that can help when troubleshooting workflows.

Selection Report for Workflows

Transaction SWI1—Selection Report for Workflows allows you to select workflows by setting a status or a task ID for a given period, for example. This is handy for searching quickly among all workflows to find the ones that are stopped or not working.

Administration Report

Transaction SWIA—WI Administration Report is mainly for administrators but you can also use it to search a work item (a workflow triggered), re-initialize the process, or just act on behalf of and relaunch the workflow.

Workload Analysis

Transaction SWI5—Workload Analysis allows you to monitor the workload for each workflow, which can be handy during the stress tests phase or when dealing with the definition of Service Level Agreements (SLA).

Workload Diagnosis

Transaction SWUD—Workflow Diagnosis allows you to verify customizing, identify tasks that have not started, identify workflows hanging in the system, or test the system.

Restart Workflow after Error

Transaction SWPR—WFM: Restart Workflow enables you to restart faulty workflows after you have identified and solved the issue.

Set Up and Maintain Employee Self-Services (ESS) Users

Transaction HRUSER—Set Up and Maintain ESS Users enables you to easily monitor and maintain in mass the assignment of personnel numbers to SAP UserIDs. This is quite handy compared to going manually into every InfoType 0105—Communication.

From the selection screen, select the functionality ASSIGNMENT OF EMPLOYEES TO EXISTING USERS in the PREPARATION box. Alternatively, you can use program ESS_ USERCOMPARE—Reconcile User Master with HR Master directly from Transaction

SA38—ABAP: Program Execution. Unfortunately this program is not assigned to a standard transaction, so you must add it in a user menu.

Test Environment for the Leave Request

Transaction PTARQ—Test Environment for Leave Request is theoretically out of scope when dealing with the workflow processes. However, in the SET UP box, this transaction provides report that avoids having to browse through personnel data and the organizational structure to identify an employee's superior (the line manager).

This report, RPTREQAPPRCHK—Determine Approver, illustrated in Figure 9.23, can also be called directly from Transaction SA38—ABAP: Program Execution. Unfortunately, this program is not assigned to a standard transaction, so you must add it in a user menu.

Figure 9.23 Determining the Approver from the Test Environment Transaction

9.4.2 Some Tips for Troubleshooting (Cheat Sheet)

This short list of activities is helpful when deploying, testing, and troubleshooting workflows. It depicts different leads to possible solutions to give you a starting point in the system.

Workflow Doesn't Start

If the workflow fails to start, assess the following:

▶ Is the Workflow task released?

▶ Is the configuration for this process updated in the IMG?

▶ Is the right task assigned in the IMG?

▶ Have you upgraded or patched the system lately? For example, when upgrading to SAP ERP 6.0, some workflow IDs might change and thus not work anymore.

▶ What does the log tell you when you check authorizations by running Transaction SU53—Evaluate Authorization Check?

Workflow Is Not Working

Most of the time, it's easy to blame the system, but it is most likely the configuration. Carefully review all configuration steps one by one, and review the process documentation. Check that relevant master data exist in the system.

Workflow Is Not Sent to the Line Manager

In this case, among other things, assess the following in the organizational structure:

▶ Have you worked in the active plan version?

▶ Are the start and end dates for the chief position correct?

▶ Are the start and end dates for the employee assignment (relationship) to the chief position relationships correct?

▶ Are the workflow agent attributes set to GENERAL TASK?

▶ Has the organizational structure buffer been refreshed? Run Transaction SWU_OBUF—Runtime Buffer PD Org.

▶ What does the log tell you when you check authorizations by running Transaction SU53—Evaluate Authorization Check?

Changes from the Organizational Structures Are Not Taken into Account When Running Workflow

In this case, check the organizational structure, and assess the following:

- Have you worked in the active plan version?

- Are the start and end dates for the objects correct?

- Are the start and end dates for the relationships correct?

- Has the organizational structure buffer been refreshed? Run Transaction SWU_ OBUF—Runtime Buffer PD Org.

- What does the log tell you when you check authorizations by running Transaction SU53—Evaluate Authorization Check?

No Email Notification Is Dispatched to the Employee

In this case, check InfoType 0105—Communication along with subtypes 0001—System User Name (SY-UNAME) and 0010—Email.

Assess the following:

- Does the record exist?

- Are the start and end dates correct?

- Is the personnel number still active?

- Is the SAP UserID still valid?

- Have the SAPconnect and technical prerequisites been met?

- What does the log tell you when you check authorizations by running Transaction SU53—Evaluate Authorization Check?

9.5 Conclusion

This SAP Business Workflow introduction chapter covered the basic steps to enable standard workflow templates, allowing you some flexibility by not having to request a workflow expert.

You should now know that the statement "Workflows are complex" is a myth. As you have seen through this basic example, a first release of standard workflows can be a quick win for the customer or the company you work for. You should leave the complex workflow for a second release.

Although the workflow is easy on paper, it can get rapidly complex. Rely on the checklists in the chapter take advantage of the recommended readings to further extend your workflow knowledge to prepare for these complexities.

Now that we understand more about workflow, an important related element is also the person and/or the SAP UserID that will receive the notifications or workflow items. In the next chapter, we will introduce and cover the User Management aspects when dealing with self-services.

User management provides the credentials information and attributes to enable users to connect and benefit from all the functionalities introduced. This chapter provides the required strategy for administrators to maintain user IDs.

10 User Management

This chapter provides a basic overview of all the surrounding aspects and tasks involved with user management when deploying SAP self-services. We will discuss the different user management maintenance strategies, using SAP UserIDs, attributes, and parameters; and using portal UserIDs. Finally, we'll cover using Single Sign-On (SSO) to get a powerful quick win when dealing with multiple systems.

10.1 User Management Engine (UME)

The following is the standard definition of the User Management Engine (UME) by SAP:

The UME is a separate software component that manages user data and group data stored in the User Persistence Store. Individual portal applications are not assigned to their own user management, and administrators can manage user data centrally, using the UME.

The UME is the central reconciliation point, gathering all user information and attributes, to ease end user maintenance and enable the potential use of Single Sign-On (SSO), for example.

Because you can have different sources providing UserID data and attributes, the UME enables other data sources to be selected as the user persistence store for the users. For example, the users of a specific SAP ERP client can be read directly.

The configuration of UME can be found in the SAP Help Portal:

http://help.sap.com/erp2005_ehp_04/helpdata/EN/e5/618a3eacd49076e10000000a11 4084/content.htm

The configuration of the UME can be done in the SAP NetWeaver Portal under the following access path: SYSTEM ADMINISTRATION • SYSTEM CONFIGURATION • UME CONFIGURATION, as illustrated in Figure 10.1.

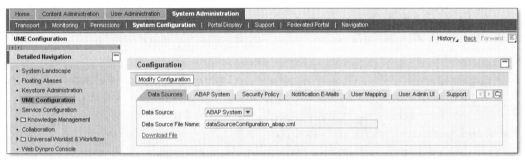

Figure 10.1 SAP NetWeaver Portal Access to UME Configuration

10.2 Lightweight Directory Access Protocol (LDAP)

The Lightweight Directory Access Protocol (LDAP) is usually already in use within the company or the customer landscape. It consists of a database storing all relevant credentials for each user with that user's pertinent attributes. Every system can then go centrally to this database to grant access clearance. This quick win is a must-have feature because it enables users to work across multiple systems and platforms with only one user ID and password if you've also enabled SSO.

The Lightweight Directory Access Protocol (LDAP) is defined as a central placeholder for consolidating UserIDs and their respective attributes such as organization details, address, and phone details. The LDAP is used to simplify access through different platforms and systems. You can think of it as a centralized "mini database" that we can consult with for all access-clearance related matters. The LDAP is often used in combination with the Single Sign-On (SSO) feature, which is introduced in more detailed later in this chapter.

You should also read SAP Note 861461—Activating LDAP Registration Manually, which provides more detailed information for manual activation of the LDAP.

10.3   SAP UserIDs

To get access to the system, you must receive all SAP UserIDs. Each UserID must include valid start/end dates, user attributes, and perhaps some useful parameters.

SAP UserIDs can be maintained through Transaction SU01—User Maintenance. Mass creation is enabled through Transaction SU10—User Mass Maintenance.

Although it is unlikely you will have access to these transactions because they are the responsibility of the authorization and/or the Basis team, it is useful to request access to Transaction SU01D—User Display. This transaction provides read-only access to the SAP UserID, which is handy when dealing with UserID attributes and parameters because you have a flexible option rather than being forced to bother the system administrator or authorization administrator to obtain this information.

10.3.1   SAP UserID Definition

SAP UserIDs, due to customer naming conventions, must abide by many rules. They must first be unique. They must also comply with all internal and external authorizations such as the global risk and compliance (GRC).

10.3.2   SAP UserID Attributes

SAP UserIDs contain, for example, the following information, as illustrated in Figure 10.2:

- General data such as First Name, Last Name, and Title
- Authorization group the user belongs to
- Validity start and end dates for the user
- Default values for the language, the printer (output device), and the decimal format
- Roles, which help the end user if working in the backend (not relevant for portal users)
- Profiles, which contain the authorization access clearance as illustrated in Chapter 11

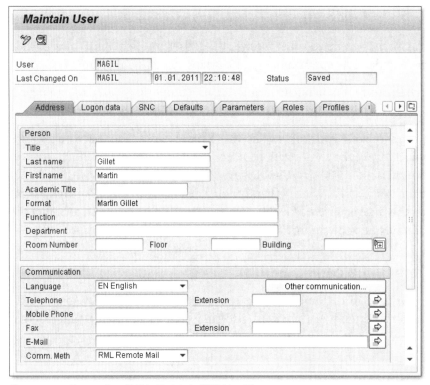

Figure 10.2 Transaction SU01: Maintain SAP UserID

10.3.3 SAP UserID Parameters

Besides the imperative step of creating the SAP UserID, you must also allocate all relevant user parameters to the SAP UserID. These parameters are used by the system to determine default values or actions to be performed in certain functionalities.

For example, the parameter CVR—CATS: Variant for Time Recording, which is used to default the Cross-Application Time Sheet (CATS) data entry profile, is used to determine which profile to use when accessing the time registration self-service. If the system does not find this parameter, it will look for the default value ESS in the customizing.

Table 10.1 and Table 10.2 provide a non-exhaustive list of the user parameters you might need to allocate, if required or relevant.

Parameter	Meaning
HR_DISP_INFTY_NUM	Displays InfoType number in functional transactions
NAT	HR: Nationality
SPR	Language
LND	Country key
UGR	User group (HR master data)
BU	Company code usually used by the user
GSB	Business area regularly used by the user
PBR	Personnel area (default value)
PBS	Personnel subarea (default value)
PKR	Employee subgroup (HR master data; default value)
AQQ	ABAP/4 query: query
AQB	ABAP/4 query: user group
AQW	ABAP/4 query: work area
AQS	InfoSet or functional area in ABAP/4 query
MASSG	Action reason
MRK	HR feature; proposal for processing in PE03
CATSXT_PERNR	Personnel number for Time Sheet (CATSXT)
FWS	Default value of currency for job advertisements
APG	Applicant group
APR	Applicant range

Table 10.1 Parameters for Personnel Administration

Parameter	Meaning
HRPDV_OTYPE	Specifies the standard object type for Personnel Development (PD)

Table 10.2 Parameters for Personnel Development

Parameter	Meaning
HRPDV_SEARCH_OTYPES	Specifies standard object for the search of qualifications and requirements; two-character entry without separator For example, USP AP: User, person, applicant
HRPDV_BEGDA_EVAL	Evaluation period: start date System sets the parameter via user-specific settings
PEM	Include essential requirements
PES	Include alternative qualifications
PEH	Disregard depreciation meter
PEV	Career planning: Display vacant positions only
APPRAISEE_OTYPE	Object type: Appraisee
APPRAISER_OTYPE	Object type: Appraiser
APPSCHEME_ID	Object ID of appraisal model
FWS	Currency unit
MOL	Personnel country grouping
POK X	PD: Views (key, short text, validity, etc.)
POP	Plan version (PD)
SCL	Uppercase and lowercase in source code: 'X' = lowercase; '' = uppercase
UGR	User group (HR master data)

Table 10.2   Parameters for Personnel Development (Cont.)

Tip: Function Module for Retrieving User Parameters

In reports and programs, the function module RH_USER_VIEW_PARAMETER—View Parameters According to User Input (With Possible Change), as illustrated in Figure 10.3, can be used when either enhancing or developing SAP HR Self-Services.

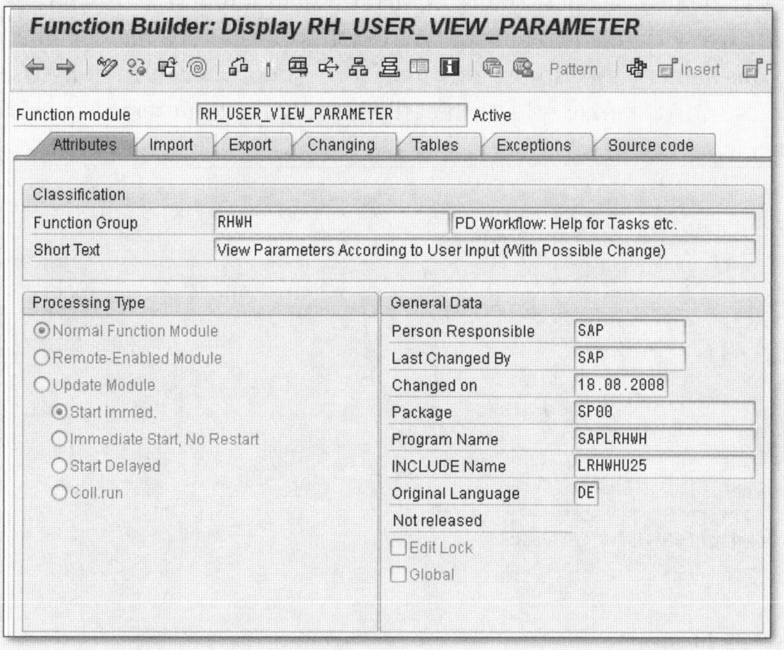

Figure 10.3 Function Module RH_USER_VIEW_PARAMETER

10.3.4 SAP UserID Mapping with Personnel Numbers

As discussed earlier in this book several times, do not forget to map or link all self-services SAP UserIDs against a valid personnel number. Failing to proceed with this step, although all SAP and portal UserIDs exist, will lead to a system error message "No users exist in this period."

A personnel number can only be assigned to one SAP UserID at a time. For functional reasons, only one personnel number is mapped to a SAP UserID. It makes sense that one employee (generic term for all personnel and staff) can only have one personnel number because each person is unique in the system.

Carefully check the start and end dates in InfoType 0105—Communication, subtype 0001—System User Name (SY-UNAME). Sometimes a wrong end date, perhaps changed by an incoming interface, for example, in the past will lead to an error message in SAP NetWeaver Portal.

As you have already seen, the program ESS_USERCOMPARE—Reconcile User Master with HR Master (see Figure 10.4) can help you monitor in mass a larger number of employee assignments all at once. This is useful for system administrators who need a quick tool to overview the mapping of SAP UserIDs versus personnel numbers. Functional consultants may also use this tool, for example, when running User Acceptance Tests (UAT) because they can easily identify the test users assigned to the personnel numbers.

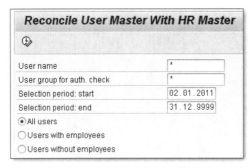

Figure 10.4 Program ESS_USERCOMPARE

10.4 Portal UserIDs

Now that you have identified the SAP R/3 UserIDs, you must also create the counterpart SAP NetWeaver Portal UserIDs, which will be receiving the relevant portal roles and permissions according to the business requirements.

10.4.1 Portal UserID Attributes

Just like the SAP UserIDs, the Portal UserIDs must also contain attributes such as the following:

▶ Last name, first name, prefix

▶ User group the user belongs to

▶ Portal role allocated to the user (if not already assigned to a user group)

Figure 10.5 illustrates the overview of all users available in the SAP NetWeaver Portal, which, in this case, is the SAP standard training environment with portal user HR255 for the self-services course.

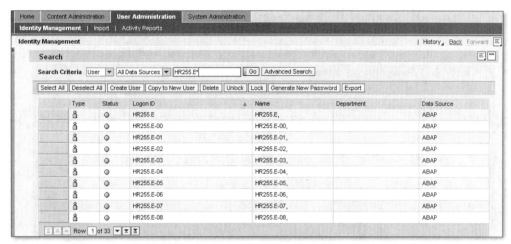

Figure 10.5 SAP NetWeaver Portal Identity Management

Figure 10.6 illustrates the creation of a SAP NetWeaver Portal user, just like you would do in the Transaction SU01—User Maintenance.

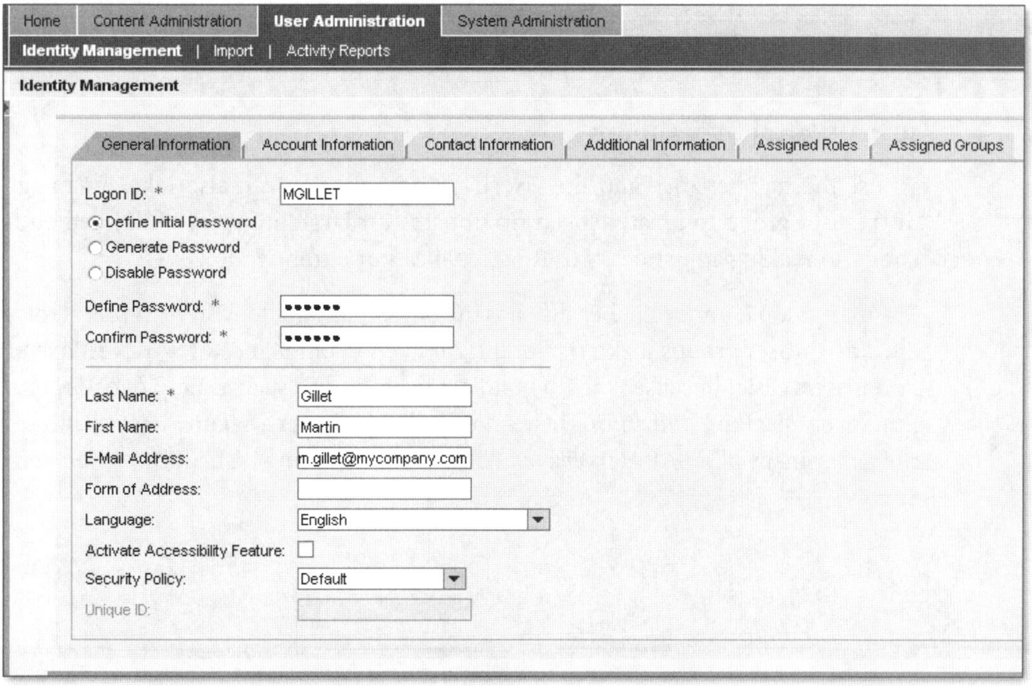

Figure 10.6 Creation of a SAP NetWeaver Portal User

Figure 10.7 illustrates the assignment of roles to the SAP NetWeaver Portal user. Roles have already been created in the Portal Content Directory (PCD). In this case, the term *role* is indeed a role but can also be a bit misleading because this is the SAP NetWeaver Portal menu that will be provided to the end user.

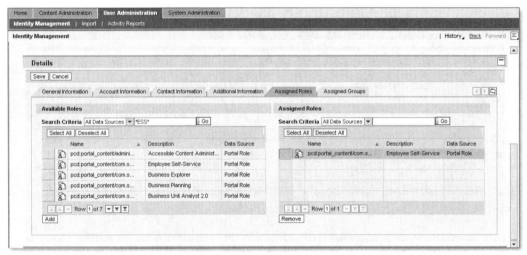

Figure 10.7 Portal User: Assigned Roles

10.4.2 Portal User Groups

To use the maintenance and the UserID allocation, you can also take advantage of the user group to greatly speed up updates for large numbers of user when it comes to making adjustments to functionalities or authorizations.

The user group is important because it is the buffer placeholder where all portal roles are stored. User groups make the long-term mass maintenance of SAP NetWeaver Portal users easier because you can maintain users groups such as Employee-France, Employee-Belgium, and so on, instead of individual users. Figure 10.8 illustrates the assignment of a SAP NetWeaver Portal to a user group called Employee Self-Services.

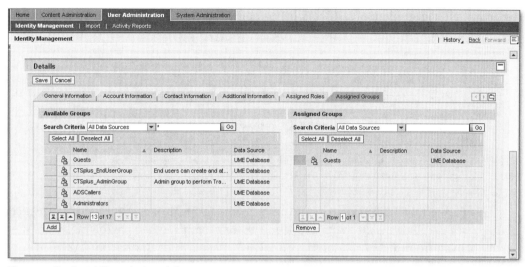

Figure 10.8 Portal User: Assigned Groups

You can, for example, create user groupings per country, with a subgrouping per employee group, such as user group Belgium+Employees, Belgium+Workers, or Belgium+Managers.

10.4.3 Lock Entries

If the end user does not disconnect properly or kills the session inadequately, the data called previously in the functionality might still be locked.

We strongly recommend not touching the information displayed in the lock entries list because it will jeopardize the system data consistency. Instead, wait for the system to purge the lock entries, which it does on a frequent basis with a minimum of once a day, usually overnight. Alternatively, system administrators can schedule this unlocking program to run as much or as little as they deem necessary.

The lock entries transactions are provided to monitor/corroborate with the end user. Manual deletion is a high risk activity and must be done by authorized personnel only.

Backend User Locked Entries

In the backend system, Transaction SM12 — Display and Delete Locks (Figure 10.9) allows you to see the locked entries. For example, if an end user is performing time registration in CATS and his computer crashes, his personnel number is still locked.

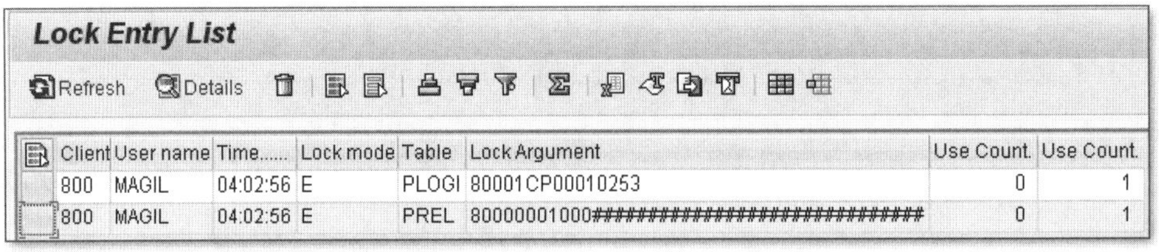

	Client	User name	Time......	Lock mode	Table	Lock Argument	Use Count.	Use Count.
	800	MAGIL	04:02:56	E	PLOGI	80001CP00010253	0	1
	800	MAGIL	04:02:56	E	PREL	80000001000############################	0	1

Lock Entry List — Refresh, Details

Figure 10.9 Transaction SM12: Locked Entries

Furthermore, if you want to find out who is blocking the personnel numbers (which technically translates with a lock entry); for example, when payroll must run, stay away from technical Transaction SM04—User List or Transaction AL08—Users Logged On for user monitoring because they are Basis transactions that are usually not provided to end users.

Instead, use the standard program HFIUCPL0—Personnel Numbers That Have to be Unlocked for Payroll Run, which provides an overview of the person locking the personnel number and can even notify the person(s) currently blocking the personnel number(s) with a system message.

From the selection screen illustrated in Figure 10.10, choose the relevant selection criteria, such as the personnel area or payroll area.

Choose one of the three options:

▶ SHOW LOCKING USERS ONLY: This option only displays a list of the personnel numbers currently locked.

▶ SEND MAIL TO LOCKING USERS: This option sends a direct reminder mail via a popup on the end user screen. This message is stored in the Business Workplace (Transaction SBWP).

▶ DELETE LOCKING USERS' SESSIONS: This option kicks out the end user from the transaction he is working in. This option is unlikely to be used because the end user will not understand why he is kicked out. The system displays a system administrator message but gives no reason why.

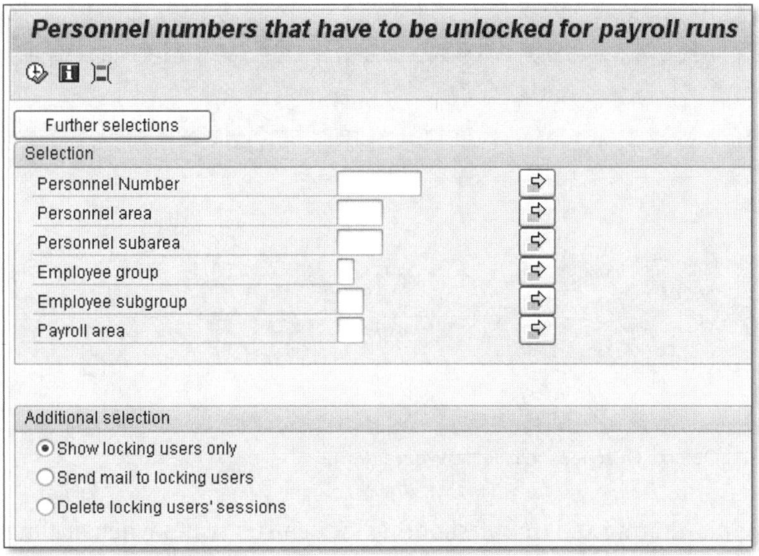

Personnel numbers that have to be unlocked for payroll runs

Further selections

Selection

Personnel Number		⇨
Personnel area		⇨
Personnel subarea		⇨
Employee group		⇨
Employee subgroup		⇨
Payroll area		⇨

Additional selection

◉ Show locking users only
○ Send mail to locking users
○ Delete locking users' sessions

Figure 10.10 Program HFIUCPL0

Figure 10.11 illustrates that SAP UserID MAGIL (Martin Gillet) is currently locking personnel number 1000. Now you can advise that user by phone, email or text message to exit the transaction because he is locking the personnel number.

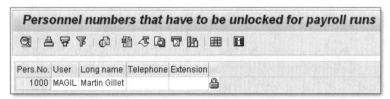

Personnel numbers that have to be unlocked for payroll runs

Pers.No.	User	Long name	Telephone	Extension
1000	MAGIL	Martin Gillet		🔒

Figure 10.11 Report HFIUCPL0: Result List of Locked Personnel Number(s) with Locking User

Portal User Locked Entries

The same functionality exists for SAP NetWeaver Portal under SYSTEM ADMINISTRATION • MONITORING • OBJECT LOCKING, as illustrated in Figure 10.12.

Figure 10.12 Locked Objects Overview in SAP NetWeaver Portal

This is handy for monitoring and troubleshooting lock entries issues when dealing with configuration or daily use with end user connections.

10.5 Single Sign-On (SSO)

SSO is a nice-to-have feature that is quickly becoming essential when deploying IT systems. SSO allows end user to use a unique UserID and password to access all systems related to professional activities. In most cases, SSO requests information from LDAP to grant positive access clearance.

Single Sign-On is defined as a powerful tool enabling the connection between a myriad of systems, assuming that these systems "trust" each other, most of the time by issuing and accepting security certificates. You could compare this to the security certificate you could use on the internet, when for example connecting to your bank account online.

SSO is more than a quick win, as it only requires one logon from the end user, which then opens all relevant doors where needed, in all required systems.

For example, the Basis team sets up the relevant security certificate in each system so they can trust each other and allow connections between them. In SAP R/3, you can access Transaction STRUSTSSO2—Trust Manager for Logon Ticket, as illustrated in Figure 10.13.

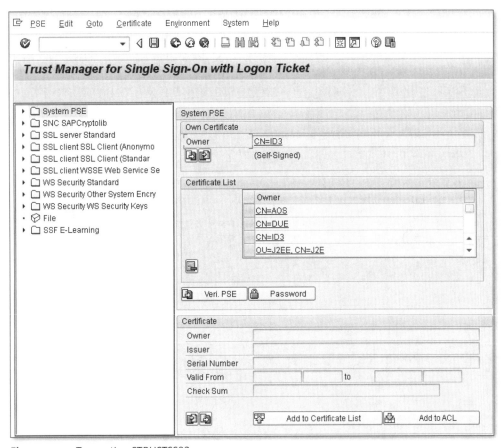

Figure 10.13 Transaction STRUSTSSO2

10.6 Conclusion

Throughout this chapter, we have depicted the different user management options, either through UME or LDAP. We have covered the SAP UserIDs, their attributes, and their parameters; introduced the SAP NetWeaver Portal SAP UserIDs; and described the concept of SSO.

This user management is a matter for the authorization team and/or the Basis team. However, because it involves the business requirements, master data, and your input for attributes, it is a topic that you must closely monitor and keep under control.

It also makes sense to perform this user management (along with the authorization management) at the very early stage of the project. Too often, these topics are underestimated and quickly jeopardize the project go live when not dealt with properly. Furthermore, because you are dealing with sensitive HR master data, you must verify which personal information is passed on to other applications such as the LDAP or SSO processes.

You can find more information on these topics in the SAP Community Network at the following address: *www.sdn.sap.com/irj/sdn/security*.

Now that we've covered the user management concept, let's take a closer look at the next decisive setup: the management of authorizations.

Authorization management is the gatekeeper of the functional processes, making sure you have access to what you need and abiding by all the governance, risk, and compliance rules. This is a critical subject, which should not be delayed or underestimated in SAP implementations.

11   Authorizations

Now that you have seen how to enable self-services for the employees, the managers, and the surrounding functionalities, you must secure the access to the data.

Because you are dealing with HR master data, which includes sensitive information, it is compulsory to define the access parameter regarding the authorizations.

This chapter introduces the configuration settings for authorization management through the profile configurator, including a walkthrough of the technical authorization objects.

We will also cover the SAP NetWeaver Portal permissions for the self-services, just in case it has not already been done. We will also discuss how to provide detailed documentation and troubleshoot the system.

11.1   Prerequisites

Before moving on, let's consider the authorization and legal compliance that is likely to be enforced during the setup phase of a self-services project.

11.1.1   Authorization Compliance

Most of the time, the setup of authorizations are coming into a bigger process, which is meant to abide by the global risk and compliance (GRC) rules, for example. Other well-known compliances rules might also be enforced, such as the Sarbanes-Oxley Act (SOX) or the Food and Drugs Administration (FDA).

11.1.2 Legal Compliance

Also, depending on the location where the data will be stored, legal matters might be enforced. For example, when a U.S. firm deploys self-services for the European staff, proper legal authorities must be advised as required by the European Union. In most projects, you should involve a member from the legal team to verify these requirements. Such requirements might be the authorized information that you can display in self-services, such as gender, age, and address. Legal local requirements do apply most of the time. Legal requirements are also involved when dealing with Equal Employment Opportunity (EEO) in self-services and recruitment. Legal team members also define the disclaimer to be set for the self-services through the SAP NetWeaver Portal and—if applicable—an appendix to the employees' work contract.

Table 11.1 lists the main websites for legal master data handling information.

Country	Link
Australia (EN)	*www.privacy.gov.au*
Austria (DE, EN)	*www.bka.gv.at/datenschutz*
Belgium (FR, NL, EN)	*www.privacycommission.be*
Canada (FR, EN)	*www.priv.gc.ca*
Denmark (DK, EN)	*www.datatilsynet.dk*
Finland (FI, EN)	*www.tietosuoja.fi*
France (FR, EN, ES)	*www.cnil.fr*
Germany (DE, EN, FR)	*www.bfd.bund.de/*
U.K. (EN, FR, ES)	*www.ico.gov.uk*
Greece (GR, EN)	*www.dpa.gr*
Honk Kong (EN)	*www.pco.org.hk*
Ireland	*www.dataprivacy.ie*

Table 11.1 Sources for Legal Requirements in ESS Projects

Country	Link
Italy (IT, EN)	*www.garanteprivacy.it/garante/navig/jsp/index.jsp*
The Netherlands (NL, EN)	*www.registratiekamer.nl*
New Zealand (EN)	*www.privacy.org.nz*
Norway (NO, EN)	*www.datatilsynet.no*
Portugal (PT, EN, FR)	*www.cnpd.pt*
Sweden (SE, EN)	*www.datainspektionen.se*
Switzerland (EN, FR, IT, DE)	*www.edsb.ch*
USA (Safe Harbor) (EN)	*www.export.gov/safeharbor*

Table 11.1 Sources for Legal Requirements in ESS Projects (Cont.)

11.2 System Landscape Overview

All standard authorizations are created as close as possible to the master data because the master data is stored in a unique place (unless other requirements apply) in SAP ERP. Authorizations are thus created, maintained, and assigned to the user in the backend system.

Because SAP wants to avoid redundancy, authorizations must not be duplicated. However, because you are providing access to self-services, the current authorization role(s) and profile(s) must be adjusted. Portal authorization is in fact the definition of the Portal menu, which provides access to the different portal objects, normally structured as roles that contain one or more worksets that contain one or more pages that contain one or more iViews. The iView is actually the placeholder for the functionality to be accessed and ran by the user.

So, when the user connects to the portal through the Portal menu, the system uses a Remote Function Call (RFC) to request the authorization checks for providing the master data and information to the end user; as illustrated in Figure 11.1.

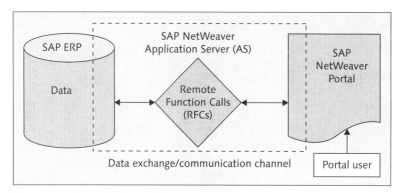

Figure 11.1 System Landscape Overview

11.3 SAP Notes

For background information, carefully review the SAP Notes dealing with SAP Authorizations in Table 11.2.

SAP Note	Description	Release Applicability
785345	Copying Authorization Default Values for Services	6.20, 6.40, 7.00
798967	MSS: Authorizations and Roles for WD Services in SAP ERP 2004	5.0
857431	ESS: Authorizations and Roles for WD Services in SAP ERP 2005	6.0
844639	MSS: Authorizations and Roles for WD Services in SAP ERP 2005	6.0
1261193	Composite SAP Note: HCM Authorizations Documentation	Release independent

Table 11.2 SAP Notes Dealing with SAP Authorizations

All SAP Notes can be accessed from the Marketplace: *http://service.sap.com/notes* (user name and password required).

11.4   Backend Roles and Profiles

Each user is assigned in the backend system to an authorization profile, as illustrated in Figure 11.2. Each profile contains a selection of authorization objects, which contain fields for maintaining the values, to grant or deny access to the information.

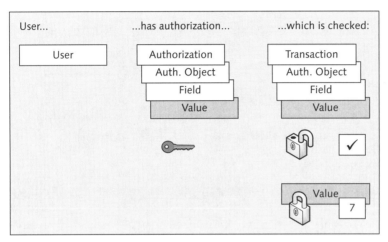

Figure 11.2   Authorization Overview

11.4.1   Authorization Profile for Employee Self-Services (ESS)

The authorization profile can be defined as the technical authorization assignment, whereas the authorization role is business driven, defined with the business team members to provide a clear menu and access to the content. Based on the authorization role, the system can also suggest and/or derive the authorization profile. In this chapter, we are focusing on the authorization profiles, which highlight all technical requirements for ESS and MSS.

When dealing with self-services, the system is fitted throughout SAP programs with a technical statement known as the authority check, which triggers the authorization mechanism and verification. Figure 11.3 describes the standard authority check function module properties, as provided by SAP.

Although technically designed on the same grounds and using one of the authority checks, you can distinguish two authorization checks:

▶ One for checking the access clearance to a functionality, for example, can the user run self-services Maintain Address?

▶ One for checking the access to the master data, for example, can the user access in EDIT or DISPLAY mode?

Figure 11.3 Authority Check

Tip

Before starting the configuration, you can get inspiration from the standard authorization profile template provided by SAP. Table 11.3 illustrates the two standard roles provided.

Role	Description
SAP_ESSUSER_ERP	Single role that comprises all functions that are not country specific.
SAP_EMPLOYEE_ERP_xx_ERP	Single role comprising country-specific functions. A separate role exists for each country version (xx = country ID). The corresponding composite role is SAP_EMPLOYEE_ERP.

Table 11.3 Standard Roles Provided Since SAP ERP 5.0

Templates Provided by SAP

Since SAP ERP 5.0, SAP provides a template role for authorizations that are and are not country specific:

▶ SAP_ESSUSER: Employee Self-Service (HR)

▶ SAP_ESSUSER_ERP: Employee Self-Service (HR)

As of SAP ERP 6.0, SAP provides a third updated role: SAP_ESSUSER_ERP05: Single Role with All Non-Country-Specific Functions.

> **Caution**
>
> Because these are templates, they cannot be used as they are. Standard templates must be copied into customer naming conventions and adjusted where necessary. They are only provided as a starting point for authorization administrators.

Figure 11.4 illustrates the standard content of template ESS role SAP_ESSUSER_ERP05.

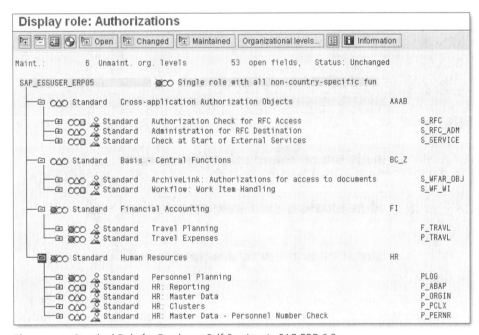

Figure 11.4 Standard Role for Employee Self-Services in SAP ERP 6.0

The assumption is that the following authorization objects have already been maintained regarding the access clearance and handling of master data:

▸ PLOG—Personnel Planning

▸ P_ORGIN—HR: Master Data

▶ P_PERNR—HR: Master Data—Personnel Number Check

▶ P_ABAP—HR: Reporting

▶ P_TCODE—HR: Transaction Codes

▶ P_HAP_DOC—Appraisal Systems: Appraisal

▶ P_PCLX—Clusters (e.g., displaying pay slip or attendance report)

Object S_SERVICE

On top of these standard authorization objects, the authorization object S_SERVICE checks the start of external services. Figure 11.5 highlights the properties of the authorization object S_SERVICE.

Object	S_SERVICE	
Text	Check at Start of External Services	
Class	AAAB	Cross-application Authorization Objects
Author	SAP	
Authorization fields		
Field name	Heading	
SRV_NAME	Program, transaction or function module name	
SRV_TYPE	Type of Check Flag and Authorization Default Values	

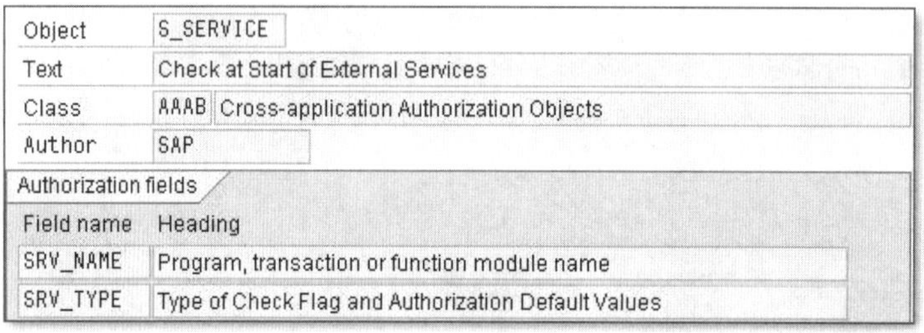

Figure 11.5 Close-up on Object S_SERVICE

To grant access to the self-services, you need to maintain these fields:

▶ **SRV_TYPE**
Type of the external service that must be set to value "HS" External Service.

▶ **SRV_NAME**
Hash value of the external service, from which, thanks to the table entries, you select the relevant self-service functionality. ESS functionalities start with the standard naming convention: *sap.com/ess**.

> **Caution**
>
> Because self-services are driven by the country (Molga, in SAP terminology) of the person, self-service per country should also be enforced, where applicable.
>
> Figure 11.6 illustrates the standard value SRV_NAME for the authorization object S_SER-VICE, as shown in SAP ERP 6.0.

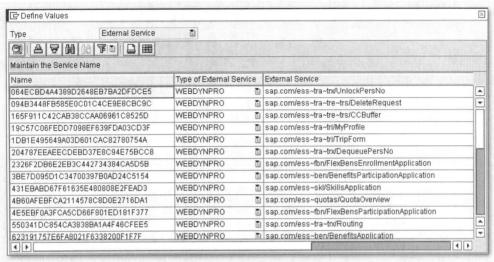

Figure 11.6 Values of Objects S_SERVICE

Caution

In SAP ERP 5.0, you might find empty tables. To populate the entries in an empty table, you can run, for every country, the functionalities directly in SAP NetWeaver Portal. This leads to an authorization error message, but it updates the table entries in the backend system for SRV_NAME.

User Parameters

Although often forgotten, the user parameters are part of the SAP user attributes. They must be stored to make the end user journey in the system earlier or just to be available to run the functionality. Carefully review which parameters to use with the business department and the technical team.

For example, to use the standard time registration through the ESS time sheet (CATS), the system requires the parameter PER to identify the personnel number and the parameter CVR to identify the default time data entry profile.

Table 11.4 contains an excerpt of frequently used parameters.

Parameter	Description
MOL	Specifies the personnel country grouping
ABK	Payroll area
NAT	Nationality
SPR	Language
UGR	User group
PBR	Personnel area (default value)
PBS	Personnel subarea (default value)
POK	PD: Views
PON	Specified ID to be processed in various interfaces
BEG	Start date (PD)
END	End date (PD)
POP	Plan version: default variant in various transactions of Organizational Management (OM)
PEM	Include essentials requirements
PES	Include alternative qualifications
PEH	Disregard the depreciation meter
PER	Default personnel number
CVR	Default CATS data entry profile

Table 11.4 Frequently Used User Parameters

All these parameters can be viewed using Transaction SU01D to display the user parameters of a SAP UserID.

Tip

If you adjust standard reports and programs, or create your own, the function module RH_USER_VIEW_PARAMETER—View Parameters According to User Input (with Possible Change) can be used.

11.4.2 Authorization Profile for Manager Self-Services (MSS)

Although SAP provides a template for ESS, none is provided for MSS.

As shown in the previous section, authorization object S_SERVICE must be maintained. On top of this standard authorization object, additional authorization objects must also be maintained. MSS functionalities start with the standard naming convention: *sap.com/mss*.

In addition to this authorization object, the following authorization objects must be added.

Appraisal Systems

To have access to all standard reporting provided in MSS, authorization object P_HAP_DOC—Appraisal Systems: Appraisal must also be maintained when using Business Server Pages (BSP).

Figure 11.7 illustrates the standard fields available in the authorization object P_HAP_DOC.

Field Text	Field name	Maint.From	MaintainTo	ActiveFrom	Active To
Class: HR Text: Human Resources Object: P_HAP_DOC Text: Appraisal Systems: Appraisal Authorization: &_SAP_ALL Text: Generated authorization for profile SAP_ALL					
▽ ☐ Activity	ACTVT				
▤				*	
▽ ☐ Appraisal Category ID	HAP_CAT				
▤				*	
▽ ☐ Appraisal Category Group ID	HAP_CAT_G				
▤				*	
▽ ☐ Appraisal Template	HAP_TEMPL				
▤				*	
▽ ☐ Plan Version	PLVAR				
▤				*	
▽ ☐ Authorization Profile	PROFL				
▤				*	

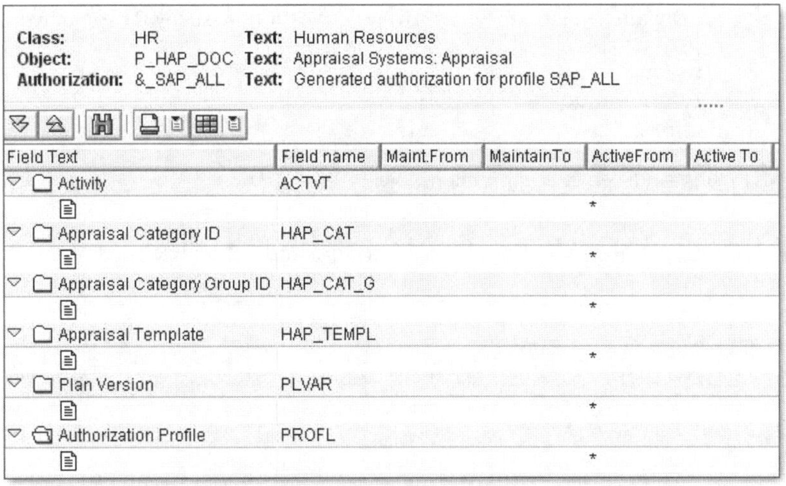

Figure 11.7 P_HAP_DOC Authorization Object

Table 11.5 describes the different fields checked.

Field	Description
ACTVT	Activity (display, change, delete).
HAP_CAT	Appraisal category ID (determines the appraisal categories a user can access). The customer-specific appraisal categories are created in Transaction PHAP_CATALOG_PA and are stored in table T77HAP_C. (You can view the numbering of the categories in Transaction OOHAP_CATEGORY.)
HAP_CAT_G	Appraisal category group ID (determines the appraisal category groups that a user can access). These appraisal category groups are stored in table T77HAP_C_GRP (maintenance in Transaction OOHAP_CAT_GROUP). The category group for personnel appraisals is 00000001 (also refer to SAP Note 497773).
HAP_TEMPL	Appraisal template ID. A customer-specific appraisal template is created in Transaction PHAP_CATALOG_PA. It is an object of type VA. In this field, enter the eight-digit object ID from table HRP1000 of object type VA. This dictates the appraisal templates a user can access.
PLVAR	Plan Version (default taken from table T77S0 PLOGI PLOGI: Integration Plan Version/Active Plan Version). Usually 01 for active Plan Version.
PROFL	Authorization profile (only relevant if structural authorizations are in place).

Table 11.5 Fields to Be Maintained in Authorization Object P_HAP_DOC

Authorization configuration is also achieved through dedicated HR InfoTypes as described in Table 11.6.

Infotpe	Description
5023	Column access
5024	Roles
5025	Processing

Table 11.6 HR InfoTypes for Authorization Configuration

InfoType 5023 — Column Access

The Column Access InfoType allows you to make the settings regarding the access to columns within the (part) appraisal process. You specify the display and change authorizations for elements in the appraisal template by making the following settings:

▸ Specify the column owner of each separate column group.

▸ Alternatively, you can use BAdI HRHAPP00_COL_OWNER, which defines the column access for a particular end user or group of users.

▸ Specify who is authorized to perform which activities in each phase of the appraisal process and which columns are to be shown in the appraisal template.

InfoType 5024 — Role

The roles to be used in the appraisal process must be selected at the category and appraisal-template level.

The Role InfoType defines which roles in the appraisal templates are to be used for part appraisals. You can use roles to define the relationship between the part appraiser and appraisee in the appraisal process. You can store roles explicitly in the SAP system.

Alternatively, you can also use BAdI HRHAP00_SELECTION, which determines the roles from the company's organizational structure.

You can use roles to restrict or control part appraisal authorizations at the level of individual elements. You make the relevant settings for individual elements in the customizing settings for the Role InfoType. If you do not use the colleague role for a particular element in the appraisal template, this element cannot be appraised by the appraisee's colleague, for example. Only the element name is displayed, and all values entered by other users are hidden.

This allows you to differentiate between the manager's part appraisal authorizations and the employee's part appraisal authorizations in relation to part appraisal columns in the same appraisal template.

InfoType 5025 — Processing

The Processing InfoType contains two settings:

▶ SELF-APPRAISAL NOT PERMITTED

If this setting is activated, a user (i.e., the user who is logged on) cannot simultaneously perform the role of appraiser and appraisee.

▶ NO AUTHORIZATION CHECK FOR APPRAISER

If this setting is activated, an authorization check is not performed for the appraiser. This means that even if a user does not have authorization for the appraiser's person, he can nevertheless display and edit all appraisal documents that include this appraiser.

Extended Authorization Checks

SAP also provides a BAdI to meet the business requirements not fully covered by the standard delivery. BAdI HRHAP00_AUTHORITY is delivered as an extended authorization check.

Reporting

To have access to all standard reporting provided in MSS, the S_MWB_FCOD BC-BMT-OM authorization object—Allowed Function Codes for Manager's Desktop must also be maintained. This might seem odd at first because it deals with the Manager's Desktop, but as you saw in Chapter 7, MSS reporting is based on the configuration of the Manager's Desktop.

Figure 11.8 illustrates the standard fields available in the authorization object S_MWB_FCOD.

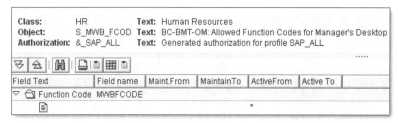

Figure 11.8 S_MWB_FCOD Authorization Object

Flag all the relevant function codes for which you would like to enable authorizations, as illustrated in Figure 11.9. You can select an entry per entry or set a generic entry such as MSS*, which enables access to all function codes starting with "MSS."

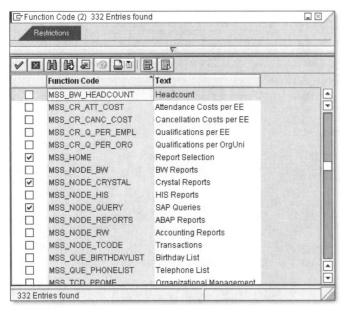

Figure 11.9 Function Codes for Reporting

In addition, the standard reporting objects should also be maintained, if applicable:

▸ **P_ABAP—HR Reporting**
Set all relevant HR reporting names the user should be granted access to.

▸ **S_PROGRAM—ABAP Program Flow Checks**
Set all relevant additional reporting names the user should be granted access to.

Substitution Concept

Also bear in mind that most managers need a delegation and/or substitution functionality. Some managers just provide their UserID and password to their secretaries, but this is not only risky but also either illegal or against company rules!

In SAP standard systems, you have two possibilities:

▸ Maintain the substitution relationship (A/B010) in the organizational structure.

▸ Allow managers to set a substitute through their Business Workplace (BWP) or the Universal Worklist (UWL).

11.4.3   Authorizations Objects Involved

Having a cheat sheet of all authorization objects used in the maintenance of self-services is always handy. The following lists the objects you are most likely to use in your authorization processes:

- PLOG—Personnel Planning
- P_ORGIN—HR: Master Data
- P_PERNR—HR: Master Data—Personnel Number Check
- P_ABAP—HR: Reporting
- P_TCODE—HR: Transaction Codes
- P_HAP_DOC—Appraisal Systems: Appraisal
- S_MWB_FCOD—BC-BMT-OM: Allowed Function Codes for Manager's Desktop
- S_SERVICE—Check at Start of External Services
- K_CCA—CO-CCA: General Authorization Object for Cost Center Accounting
- K_CSKS—CO-CCA: Cost Center Master
- S_TCODE—Transaction Code Check at Transaction Start
- S_PROGRAM—ABAP: Program Flow Checks
- S_RFC—Authorization Check for RFC Access
- S_DATASET—Authorization for File Access
- S_TABU_DIS—Table Maintenance (via standard tools such as Transaction SM30)
- S_BDS_DS—BC-SRV-KPR-BDS: Authorizations for Document Set
- S_WF_WI—Workflow: Work Item Handling
- B_NOTIF—Follow-Up Functions for General Notifications
- S_WF_SUBST—Workflow: Substitute Rule
- I_QMEL—PM/QM: Notification Types
- I_VORG_MEL—PM/QM: Business Operation for Notifications

Although not exhaustive, this list provides a focus on authorization objects used in the field of HR master data, financial master data, reporting, personnel number checks, technical accesses, and workflow.

11.4.4 Role for Technical Users

When dealing with the ongoing connection between the backend system and SAP NetWeaver Portal, technical users must be maintained.

Technical users must be set up in due time to allow the system to either be fully operational regarding SAP standard functionalities or to allow the system to "talk" to another system.

Because they are technical users, not dialog users, these users cannot connect to the system using the standard UI. These users are meant for technical purposes only.

Regarding self-services, you can distinguish mainly two technical users:

▶ **J2EE**
This technical user is used in the technical linking between the SAP ERP system and SAP NetWeaver Portal. You can consider this user as a "messenger."

▶ **WF-BATCH**
This technical user is used when dealing with SAP Business Workflow.

Because these technical users cannot connect as dialog users, they have rather large authorizations.

These users are created by system administrators.

11.4.5 Roles for Regular Users

Before requesting functional roles, every regular user should get a default standard role and profile automatically. It's easy to provide a default role that points to a welcome portal role, avoiding the bad press of a typical authorization failure when trying to log in for the first time. The role might be a pointer to the company intranet. Users then see that currently this is the only role available, without having any unfriendly "No portal role or backend assigned" messages.

Along with some authorizations based on business requirements, it's useful to have typical authorizations by default, such as the following:

- ▸ Access to the display of my authorization data (Transaction SU53)
- ▸ Access to own spool request (Transaction SP01)
- ▸ Access to own user parameters (Transaction SU3)

11.4.6 Central User Administration (CUA)

From the beginning, we have assumed that the authorizations were maintained in a dedicated system, for example, a development system; then transported into a test system; and then sent on to the production system.

Although not mandatory, it is recommended to use the Central User Administration (CUA) when deploying the SAP NetWeaver Portal self-services. CUA decreases the maintenance efforts in complex system landscapes.

Figure 11.10 illustrates the master central reference system mapped with receiving systems.

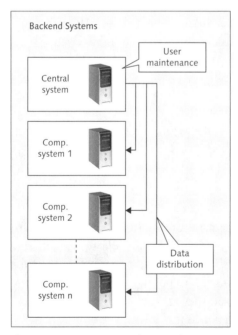

Figure 11.10 Master Central User Administration

CUA consists of maintaining all user profiles and roles in one dedicated system, identified as a master central reference system. Depending on the systems onto which you will distribute the authorization profiles and roles, you define transport attributes. For example, when sending the information from the master system to the receiving system, you adjust the password settings:

▶ From the reference system to the test system, the password is "initpass."

▶ From the reference system to the production system, the password is a customer predefined algorithm.

The following information can be distributed:

▶ **User master records**
This information includes addresses, logon data, user fixed values, and parameters.

▶ **Roles and profiles**
The corresponding single and composite roles and profiles are assigned to users for all component systems.

▶ **Initial password**
An initial password is sent to the component systems when a new user is created. The user can change this password in the usual manner.

▶ **Lock status**
This status is in addition to the known reasons for locking (failed attempt to logon or lock by an administrator).

The distribution of the attributes is powered by the Application Link Enabling (ALE), which allows the interconnection between the systems. Figure 11.11 illustrates the field distribution in CUA.

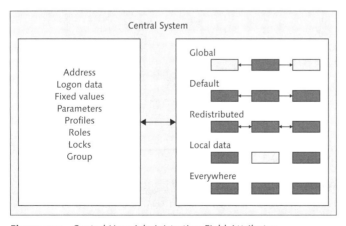

Figure 11.11 Central User Administration Field Attributes

Depending on your configuration, local authorization maintenance can also be allowed, which provides extended flexibility to local authorization administrators.

The CUA configuration access path is illustrated in Figure 11.12.

Direct Menu Access	From Transaction SALE, choose MODELLING AND IMPLEMENTING BUSINESS PROCESSES • CONFIGURE PREDEFINED ALE BUSINESS PROCESSES • CROSS-APPLICATION BUSINESS PROCESSES • CENTRAL USER ADMINISTRATION • SET DISTRIBUTION PARAMETERS FOR FIELDS
Transaction Code	SCUM

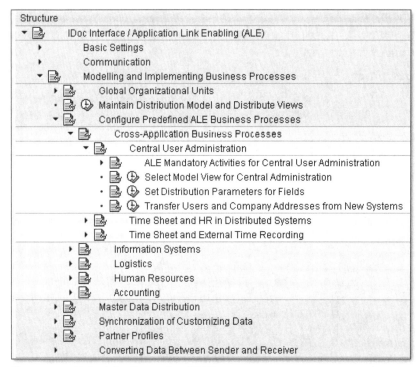

Figure 11.12 Maintaining Transaction SCUM

11.4.7 InfoType Communication

The InfoType 0105—Communication contains crucial information used across most processes in SAP HCM. Although we have the InfoType 0032—Internal Data, which gathers additional information, InfoType Communication is a placeholder for storing system and functional information.

InfoType 0105 — Communication fits in the InfoType number range 0000–0999 which confirms that it belongs to the Personnel Administration (PA) InfoTypes.

The access to this InfoType is managed through the authorization object P_ORGIN, which controls access clearance to the InfoTypes. InfoType 0105 — Communication is accessible through the standard HCM Transaction PA30 — Maintain Personnel Data or Transaction PA20 — Display Personnel Data, for example.

Like many other InfoTypes, InfoType 0105 — Communication is divided into several subtypes. Among the shortlist of subtypes, we will focus on the major subtype: 0001 — System User Name.

Technical Information

The unique field provided in InfoType Communication, which stores the content, has a potential of 30 characters. This technical field is known as USRID — Communication ID/Number. It is the default field used in InfoType Communication.

If you are involved in the writing of business blueprints or technical specifications, note that developers can use the standard function module HR_GET_EMPLOY-EES_FROM_USER to fetch the personnel number from the SAP UserID. A function module is a kind of SAP program that can be reused in any SAP program. Function modules can be accessed through Transaction SM37. This information is useful if you need to develop or enhance your own SAP NetWeaver Portal self-services (e.g., for employees or managers).

InfoType Communication — Subtype 0001 SAP UserID

The primary subtype of InfoType 0105 — Communication is the subtype 0001 — System User Name, which has the technical name SY-NAME. As illustrated in Figure 11.13, this subtype binds the personnel number to a SAP UserID. Whenever you connect to the system, this is how the system can determine that you are Mr. or Ms. XZY, as the information is retrieved through the personnel number assigned to your SAP UserID.

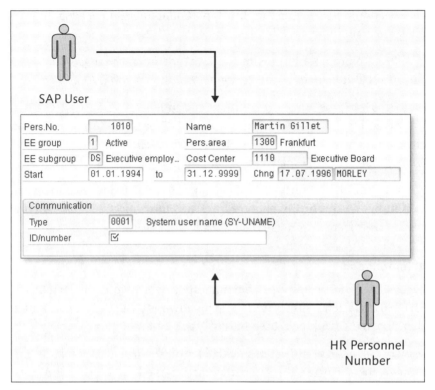

Figure 11.13 InfoType 0105—Communication with Subtype 0001

Although it should, the system does not check whether or not the SAP UserID exists. You must verify whether the UserID exists within a valid time frame by using Transaction SU01D.

The system only checks if the SAP UserID is already assigned elsewhere to another personnel number. SAP's philosophy, for technical and licensing reasons mainly, is that one personnel number is assigned to one SAP UserID.

This user mapping is critical because the system is required to identify your personnel number when you log into the system using the SAP UserID.

InfoType 0105—Communication, subtype 0001, is also used to ensure that employees have exclusive access only to their own data, for example, when booking time entries through CATS. This security characteristic is maintained through the authorization object P_PERNR—HR: Master Data—Personnel Number Check, as illustrated in Figure 11.14.

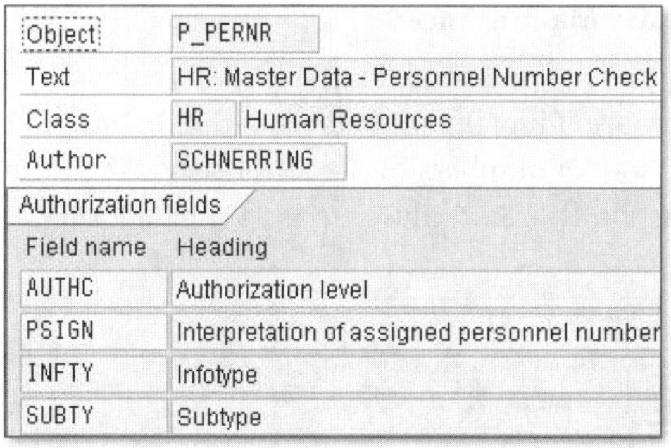

Object	P_PERNR	
Text	HR: Master Data - Personnel Number Check	
Class	HR	Human Resources
Author	SCHNERRING	
Authorization fields		
Field name	Heading	
AUTHC	Authorization level	
PSIGN	Interpretation of assigned personnel number	
INFTY	Infotype	
SUBTY	Subtype	

Figure 11.14 Authorization Object P_PERNR

This authorization object will only work successfully if a valid SAP UserID is mapped to the personnel number.

If no personnel number is mapped to the SAP UserID, a typical error message, for example, as shown in Figure 11.15 for ESS, will be displayed.

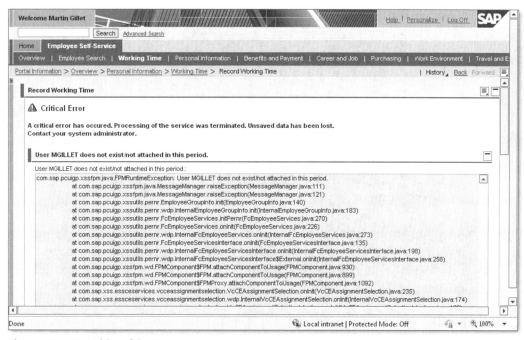

Figure 11.15 Typical Portal Error

InfoType 0105 Communication—Mass Maintenance

Because most customers have thousands of personnel numbers, SAP removes the burden of checking each InfoType by providing the program ESS_USERCOMPARE to check the assignments of the personnel numbers to the SAP UserIDs. You can access this program through Transaction HRUSER, illustrated in Figure 11.16.

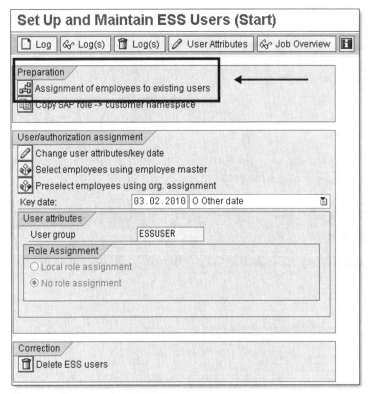

Figure 11.16 Transaction HRUSER

After you have selected ASSIGNMENT OF EMPLOYEE TO EXISTING USERS, the system leads you to the screen shown in Figure 11.17. Enter the USER NAME or leave the field blank, select ALL USERS, and verify the start date of the selection. Run the program.

Reconcile User Master With HR Master
User name
INSERT ID
User group for auth. check
*
Selection period: start
03.02.2010
Selection period: end
31.12.9999
All users
Users with employees
Users without employees

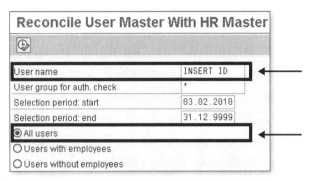

Figure 11.17 Transaction HRUSER Selection Screen

The program then returns a list of mapped personnel numbers against a SAP UserID (Figure 11.18).

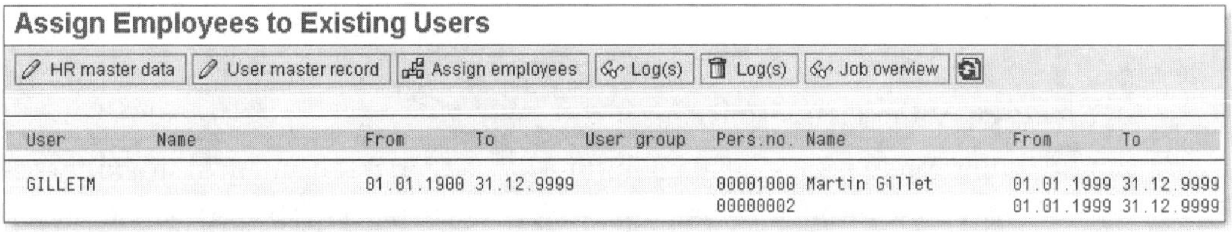

Assign Employees to Existing Users
HR master data
User master record
Assign employees
Log(s)
Log(s)
Job overview
User Name From To User group Pers.no. Name From To
GILLETM 01.01.1900 31.12.9999 00001000 Martin Gillet 01.01.1999 31.12.9999
00000002 01.01.1999 31.12.9999

Figure 11.18 List of Employees Mapped

If no personnel number is assigned, the message "No employee assigned" appears (see Figure 11.19). This tool is handy for personnel and system administrators, so you should add either program ESS_USERCOMPARE or Transaction HRUSER in their authorization profile.

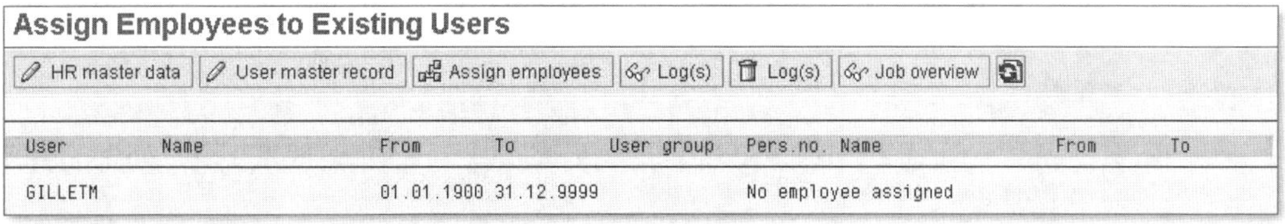

Assign Employees to Existing Users
HR master data
User master record
Assign employees
Log(s)
Log(s)
Job overview
User Name From To User group Pers.no. Name From To
GILLETM 01.01.1900 31.12.9999 No employee assigned

Figure 11.19 List of Employees Not Mapped

More information on the InfoType 0105—Communication is available in the HR Expert articles:

► "Quick Tip: Monitor SAP User Assignments with the HRUSER Transaction Code" by Martin Gillet (*www.hrexpertonline.com/article.cfm?id=3483*)

► "Having Trouble Storing Legacy Alphanumeric Personnel Numbers? Try This" by Martin Gillet (*www.hrexpertonline.com/article.cfm?id=4085*)

11.4.8 Troubleshooting Authorizations

You can use authorizations troubleshooting to not only provide an extended detailed documentation (handy for authorization audits) but also a quick way to solve basic issues.

There are several ways to troubleshoot authorizations. As you probably know, the easiest way to check the authorization failure for a user is to check Transaction SU53 — Display Authorization Log for User. However, because we are dealing with SAP NetWeaver Portal, this does not work all the time, and most of the time, it is inefficient. Therefore, the preferred approach is to create an authorization trace.

Create an Authorization Trace

The authorization trace is a fair compromise between the standard basic authorization check done through Transaction SU53 and the (technical) approach of setting up a breakpoint in the SAP program.

The trace consists of recording all authorizations calls for a dedicated user, not the whole staff. After the trace stops, you can easily check which objects and values were called and what is missing or failing in the end user profile.

The authorization trace is achieved in five steps:

1. Access Transaction ST01. Figure 11.20 illustrates the standard transaction for authorization trace. Switch on the trace by clicking on ACTIVATE CHANGE TRACE (🔲).

   Only the AUTHORIZATION CHECK trace is activated because currently the other options are not relevant.

2. Activate the authorization for a test user (deactivate after use). From the menu, choose EDIT • FILTER • SHARES • TRACE FOR USER ONLY so you can run the trace only for one test user and not the whole staff. Figure 11.21 shows the popup in which you set the name of the test SAP UserID.

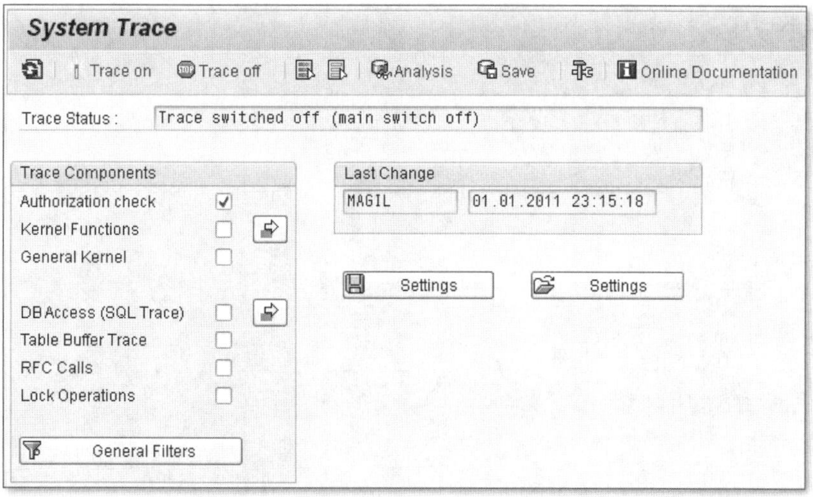

Figure 11.20 Activating the Trace

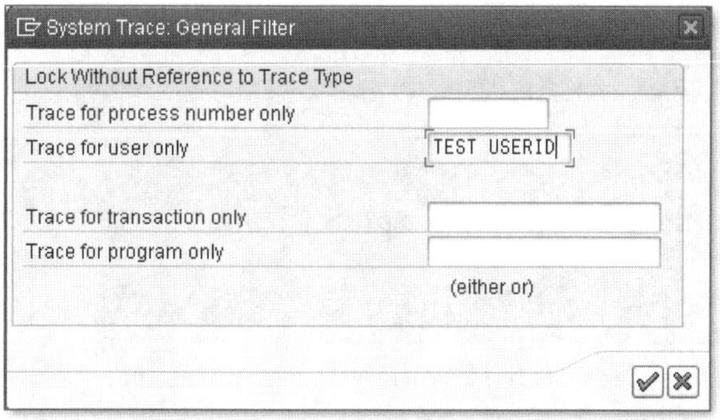

Figure 11.21 System Trace: General Filter

3. Now that the trace is activated, log on with your test user and perform the business tasks as usual in the system (note the start time). Exit the system after all tasks are performed (note the end time).

4. Now that the trace is completed, switch off the trace (click the TRACE OFF icon). Failing to do so creates a growing log in the tracing logging database, which you want to avoid to keep from running out of disk space.

5. The system has now created a log entry with all authorization checks for our users. In the selection screen, only activate TRACE RECORDS—AUTHORIZATION CHECK, set the test user UserID, and then set the date and start time, as illustrated in Figure 11.22.

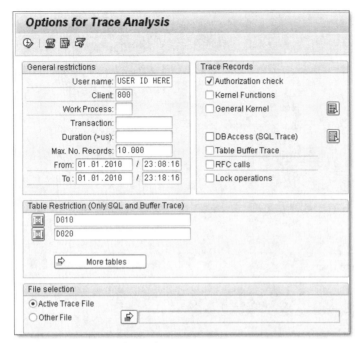

Figure 11.22 Trace Analysis Selection Screen

Run the program by clicking on the EXECUTE icon (or press F8).

Caution

Depending on where the SAP servers are located, the start and end time may differ according to your time zone.

The system delivers a detailed log entry for your test user, as illustrated in Figure 11.23.

This log provides the authorization object, the fields, and the values. To see a detailed view, double-click on the line for more details.

As you can see, the system is returning a return code (RC), which can have different statuses:

▶ **RC = 0 (Green)**
No authorizations errors or failures have been found.

▶ **RC = 4 = (Error!)**

No authorizations to run or access this functionality have been maintained.

▶ **RC = 12 = (Warning)**

The authorization ran successfully but with warnings. Warnings can be just fine. For example, when dealing with the authorization object PLOG for Personnel Development (PD), you don't provide authorization clearance for all PD objects. The user has, for example, only access clearance for position (object S) and tasks (object T); all other objects issue a warning because no authorization has been granted.

You might want to download this trace for your record and/or the configuration documentation appendices.

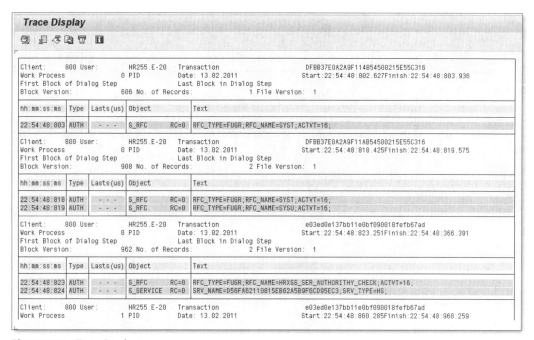

Figure 11.23 Trace Display Log

Set a Breakpoint in the SAP Program

If the previous options do not lead to any hints or solutions, you might want to investigate with your development team the feasibility to set a breakpoint (a STOP) in the SAP program itself, when the system is performing the `authority-check` statement and checking the end user authorizations.

11.4.9 Standard Authorization Reporting

SAP enables you to report and assess authorization objects as well as monitor users.

The standard reporting tree AUTH—Authority provides many handy reporting programs.

Transaction Code	SUIM (User Information System)

Figure 11.24 provides the overview of all reporting accessible through the user information system.

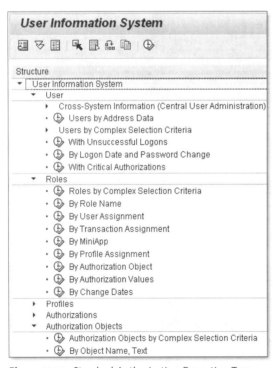

Figure 11.24 Standard Authorization Reporting Tree

One transaction you should always request is the display of the SAP user attributes.

For obvious security reasons, most of the time, access to the standard Transaction SU01 – Maintain SAP UserID is disabled in a productive environment because it belongs to the system administration and/or authorization team. The display variant (Transaction SUO1D) is enough for you to identify the roles and profiles that are assigned, as well as the user parameters.

Transaction Code	SUO1D (Display SAP User Maintenance)

11.4.10 Portal Permissions

You should be convinced by now that 95 percent of the authorizations are maintained in the SAP ERP system close to the data. However, because you run basic transaction in the SAP ERP system, checking with the authorization objects S_TCODE and/ or P_TCODE concerning whether or not the user can actually run the transaction, SAP NetWeaver Portal must also have permissions.

These settings are normally already maintained, but the system might issue an error message, "no permission to run service ...." You should therefore know where these permissions are maintained in SAP NetWeaver Portal.

Portal Access	Maintain Portal Permissions
Access Path	(Role Administrator) From SYSTEM ADMINISTRATION, go to PERMISSIONS, select the portal object (e.g., iView), and right-click on OPEN PERMISSIONS.

Figure 11.25 illustrates the permissions for the Web Dynpro iView Addresses.

The figure highlights that all user have read access to the functionality ESS Addresses, which is the equivalent of granting the access to the transaction in the SAP ERP system (via authorization object S_TCODE). Notice as well that the functionality is flagged as END USER.

It is unlikely that you will maintain these permissions, but you should know where to start in case the system issues an authorization permission failure on your portal screen.

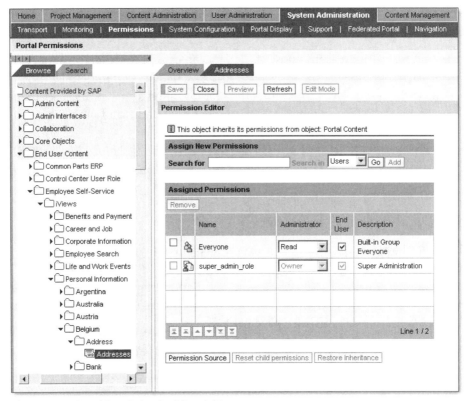

Figure 11.25 Portal Permission for iView Address

More information regarding the configuration of the portal permission (including the guide *How to Configure Permission for Initial Content in SAP NetWeaver Portal (NW7.0)*, 22 pages) can be viewed (free) on the SAP Community Network (SCN, user name and password required):

www.sdn.sap.com/irj/sdn/go/portal/prtroot/docs/library/uuid/00bfbf7c-7aa1-2910-6b9e-94f4b1d320e1#rating

Portal Role Definition and Configuration

Now that you have secured the authorizations from the SAP ERP system and checked the portal permissions on SAP NetWeaver Portal, it is time to define and configure the portal role.

Although it is called a portal role, in this case, the role is rather a functional menu, providing access to functionalities rather than an authorization role.

Figure 11.26 shows both the typical setup of a portal role and other possible setups.

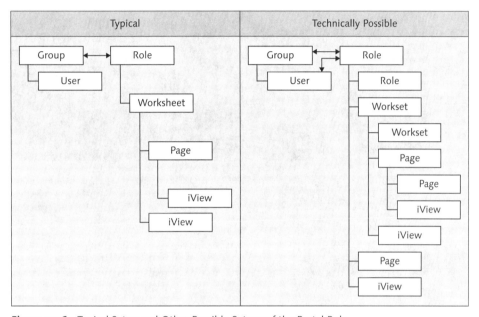

Figure 11.26 Typical Setup and Other Possible Setups of the Portal Role

The standard approach is to create a portal role as a placeholder. This placeholder contains the worksets (tabs) created for the end users. The worksets then point to the pages, and the pages point to the iViews.

Portal Access	PCD
Access Path	From the content administration role, choose PORTAL CONTENT, and then your XSS PROJECT folder. Select ROLES placeholder, and right-click on NEW • ROLE (see Figure 11.27).

Figure 11.27 Portal Role Creation

Figure 11.28 illustrates the first step of the wizard to create a role.

To create a role, follow these steps:

1. Define the different information in STEP 1 of the ROLE WIZARD screen.

   ▸ ROLE NAME: Enter the name of the role mandatory field.

   ▸ ROLE ID: Enter the ID of the role mandatory field.

   ▸ ROLE ID PREFIX: Set the prefix com.yourcompanyname to clearly mark this entry as a customer entry and not an SAP entry.

   ▸ MASTER LANGUAGE: Choose the language to use.

   ▸ DESCRIPTION: Link the project or change request ID here to improve the documentation traceability (optional field).

2. Move to the next step by clicking on NEXT.

3. Review the summary, and click FINISH.

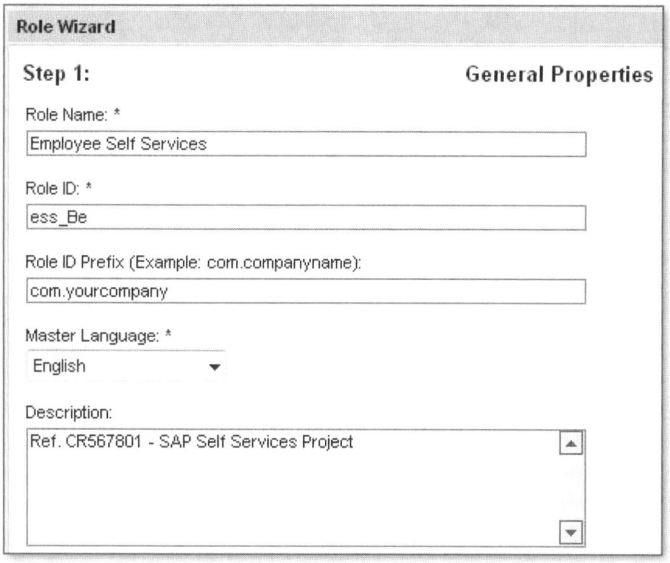

Figure 11.28 Portal Role Creation Wizard

Portal Role Attributes

Now that you have created a portal role, choose Open the object for editing to get to the next step in the wizard. We will now edit some of the portal role attributes.

> **Note**
>
> Make sure you have defined a clear naming convention with your team. Clear naming conventions support a better search when assigning the roles to the users, as well as a more structured content in the PCD.

Figure 11.29 shows the portal attributes on the right hand side of the screen.

Maintain the settings as required, and set the role as an entry point; otherwise, it will fail to show up in the portal after it is assigned to the end user. This is done by reaching out to the portal role attribute Entry Point and clicking the Yes radio button to activate it as an entry point.

Figure 11.29 Portal Role Attributes

Save the portal role by clicking on the SAVE icon, and the system issues the message "Action completed successfully." Close the wizard by clicking on the CLOSE icon.

Worksets Assignment to the Portal Role

Now that the portal role is created, you need to add the worksets (the tabs) that the end user will see from the user menu.

Portal Access	PCD
Access Path	From the content administration role, choose PORTAL CONTENT, and then choose your XSS PCD folder. Select role EMPLOYEE SELF SERVICES, right-click, and choose OPEN • OBJECT.

The system now opens the portal role, which is currently empty.

Now, as shown previously in Chapter 2, select the workset to be assigned to the portal role.

Portal Access	PCD
Access Path	From the content administration role, choose PORTAL CONTENT, and then choose your XSS PCD folder. Select WORKSET, right-click, and then choose ADD WORKSET TO ROLE • DELTA LINK (Figure 11.30).

The workset is now allocated to the portal role. The delta link is used because a simple copy would have cut the relationship with the object. A delta link makes sure that a change in the workset is reflected in the portal role.

Repeat the assignment of worksets as needed. Adjust their position sequence, using the icon UP and DOWN buttons provided in the portal role. Close your role by clicking on the CLOSE icon; it was automatically saved by the system.

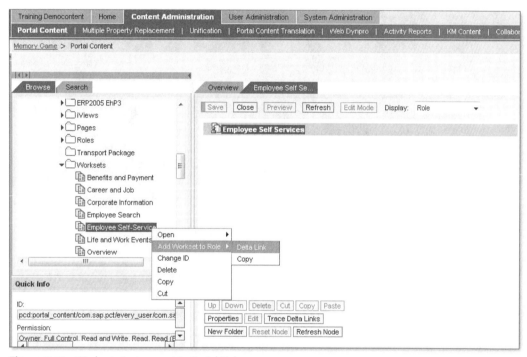

Figure 11.30 Worksets Assignment to Portal Role

Portal Assignment to User Group

Now that the role is created, you can assign it to a user. However, to be efficient, a portal role should be assigned to a group of users, as illustrated in Figure 11.31. You should avoid creating a single user.

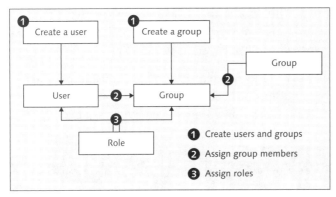

Figure 11.31 Adding a Portal Role to a Portal User Group

Tip

As illustrated in Chapter 3, in the Homepage Framework (HPFW) configuration, you can use a proxy class with a decision tree to tell the system which worksets, pages, or iViews should be displayed to end users. This proxy class feature becomes quite handy because it keeps system administrators from having to create multiple portal roles just because there is one functionality that differs, for example, per country or user group.

11.5   Conclusion

As you have seen in this chapter, self-services authorizations do require attention, even if the basic and functional authorizations have already been maintained. It's also critical to check with the legal department when it comes to abiding by legal requirements concerning master data access clearance in most countries.

You have seen how to adjust ESS and MSS, and we provided a cheat sheet of the most common authorization objects used. We described the additional role for the regular user as well as the added value of the Central User Administration (CUA). The key InfoType 0105—Communication with its subtype 0001 SAP UserID is also a major authorization feature for self-services.

Even if no problems are reported, you now know the different means for troubleshooting the authorizations (or just extending the configuration documentation with a detailed walkthrough).

Finally, we provided an overview of the portal permissions and the portal role configuration.

If you want to continue toward authorizations, we recommend the following readings:

- *Authorizations in SAP ERP HCM* (SAP PRESS 2008)
- *Authorizations in SAP Software: Design and Configuration* (SAP PRESS 2010)
- *R/3 Authorization Made Easy 4.6A/B* (SAP Labs 2000)

Table 11.7 lists standard SAP classes that can also provide further insight.

SAP Course	Course Description	Duration
ADM940	Authorization Concept AS ABAP	3 days
HR940	Authorizations in HCM	3 days

Table 11.7 SAP Classes

12   Conclusion

Well, this is as good as it gets! I'm very pleased you have made it to the end of this book, and I thank you for even taking the time to read the conclusion. I hope you enjoyed this book and found it useful in many ways.

Together, we completed a lot of configuration steps as we explored the self-services functionalities. While I did tour your system and take you down to the configuration level in great detail, I hope my enthusiasm and eagerness to "entertain" you showed throughout the different chapters.

I trust the strength of this book does not only rely on my theoretical knowledge and expertise, but also to the fact that detailed technical information—IMG access paths, table names, IMG activity names, direct transaction accesses—was provided for all configuration steps, which makes the knowledge hand-over much easier for you. I have also pointed out useful SAP notes where applicable, which could either save you time when working with the functionality and/or strengthen your knowledge of self-services.

I have directed your attention to critical configuration nodes, and pointed out known pitfalls or workarounds as I (we) encountered them during implementations. I have also aimed at providing a helicopter view of the core Employee and Manager Self-Services, along with surrounding functionalities that could be enabled, providing quick wins and empowering our management to attain a better grasp on the system's Total Cost of Ownership (TCO), and most importantly, boosting the Return on Investment (ROI), whereas I would also focus on the end user's satisfaction.

Last but not least, as you might probably need time to digest all of the information provided throughout the different chapters and sections, I provided handy "cheat sheets," consolidating the most commonly used tables, transactions, and programs, not to mention a great starting checklist to have by your side for troubleshooting or testing.

Please note that only trained professionals and stuntmen are used in the testing of productive live systems; all the information provided here has to be configured and tested in a test or quality environment. Quality configuration does matter to secure business continuity and satisfaction.

Quoting our famous Belgian national, Jean-Claude Van Damme, "you have to be aware." So don't loose sight that your need to feed your awareness, and look out for forthcoming technologies and functionalities. Keep your eyes and ears wide open for the so-called technology watch. Look for new SAP products announcements, and stay tuned through different channels such as SAP online platforms, communities, and social media. You can even go the extra mile and attend a relevant conference, depending on your area of expertise.

I have taken great care when writing this book, making sure to go deep enough into the technical details and provide you inside information to understand and optimize your learning curve.

I'm pretty far from being perfect, but trust that all parties involved have succeeded in producing a great book on how to configure Human Resources Self-Services. We value your feedback, and would appreciate a small part of your time to report your experience with this configuration book (likes, dislikes, information you think could be missing, comments, or just your satisfaction).

If you want to share your feedback on this book, feel free to contact the publisher at *florian.zimniak@galileo-press.com*.

Now that you have learned the foundations of self-services, explored the prerequisites and enhancement package concepts, and walked through the configuration steps, we wish you all the best in your next self-services implementation. Perhaps consider sharing the love, and recommend this book to your colleagues or teammate.

This is certainly not a goodbye, but rather a farewell into the SAP Human Resources world, which is no doubt a small village. I am certain our roads will cross again some day. I look forward to catching up with you online, perhaps in the social media channels!

Thank you for your time and interest.

Yours faithfully,
Martin Gillet
SAP HCM Consultant, SAP Mentor, and SAP Trainer

A   Appendices

Through this book, we have depicted the configuration of the SAP Human Resources self-services. These appendices consolidate the SAP Notes you have seen, most transactions and tables, and authorizations.

The appendix also lists the standard courses provided by SAP, as well as some recommended readings to further extend your knowledge and understanding of SAP functionalities.

You will also learn about the opportunities to join the social media tools and channels, along with the SAP communities you can use in your daily professional life while dealing and working with SAP. This includes online sessions and webcasts, which illustrate some of the functionalities discussed in the book.

Finally, this appendix lists some useful events that you might consider attending to gain the latest information on SAP products and functionalities as well as a chance to network with your peers.

This information should come in handy, and using these cheat sheets should speed up the knowledge transfer of the SAP HR self-services functionalities.

A.1   Acronyms

This list consolidates the acronyms used through the book. This list will be most useful for those of you just starting with the self-services configuration.

ABAP	Advance Business Application Programming
ACF	Active Component Framework
ADS	Adobe Document Services
BAdI	Business Add-Ins
BAPI	Business Application Program Interface
BI	Business Intelligence
BSP	Business Server Page

BW	Business Warehouse
CATS	Cross-Application Time Sheet
CSS	Cascading Style Sheet
CUA	Central User Administration
EhP	Enhancement Package
EIC	Employee Interaction Center
EP	SAP Enterprise Portal
E-Rec	E-Recruitment
ERP	Enterprise Resources Planning
ESS	Employee Self-Services
FAQ	Frequently Asked Questions
HCM	Human Capital Management
HPFM	Homepage Framework
HR	Human Resources
HRBP	Human Resources Business Partner
HTML	Hypertext Market Language
HTMLB	HTML-Business for Java
HTTP	Hypertext Transfer Protocol
HTTPS	Hypertext Transfer Protocol (Secured)
IDES	International Demonstration and Education System
IGS	Internet Graphical Server
IMG	Implementation Guide
INFTY	InfoType (contraction of information-type)
ISR	Internal Service Request
ITS	Internet Transaction Server
JCo	Java Connector
JSP	Java Server Page

KPI	Key Performance Indicator
LDAP	Lightweight Directory Access Protocol
LMS	Learning Management System
LSO	Learning Solution
MDT	Manager's Desktop
MSS	Manager Self-Services
NW	SAP NetWeaver
NWDI	SAP NetWeaver Development Infrastructure
NWDS	SAP NetWeaver Development Studio
OADP	Object and Data Provider
OSS	Online Service System
PA	Personnel Administration
PAM	Product Availability Matrix
PCD	Portal Content Directory
PD	Personnel Development
PERNR	Personnel Number
PFCG	Profile Configurator
PSS	Project Self-Services
PT	Personnel Time Management
PY	Payroll
RFC	Remote Function Call
SAPGUI	SAP Graphical User Interface
BWP	Business Workplace (Inbox)
SDN	SAP Developer Network (SAP Communities)
SLA	Service Level Agreement
SSC	Share Services Center
SSO	Single Sign-On

SWOT	Strength, Weaknesses, Opportunities, and Threads analysis
TEM	Training & Events Management
UE	User Exits
UI	User Interface
UME	User Management Engine
USRID	SAP UserID
UWL	Universal Worklist (Inbox)
WebGUI	SAP GUI in the Web Environment
XSS	Self-Services (generic term covering all services)

A.2   SAP Notes

Throughout the different chapters, SAP Notes were provided where relevant or required. The following lists consolidate these useful SAP Notes, including notes found useful during project implementations, documentation investigation, or troubleshooting. These are must-reads prior to any self-services implementation. Feel free to email me to add the SAP notes you found useful.

All these SAP Notes can be accessed in the Service Marketplace at *http://service.sap. com/notes* (user name and password required).

Check the SAP Note relevancy according to the SAP release and the technical pre-requisites, based on your SAP environment.

A.2.1   Consolidated SAP Notes

1245560	Composite SAP Note: XSS Documentation
1246420	Composite SAP Note: Cross-Application Time Sheet (CATS)
1258649	Composite SAP Note: HCM Forms Documentation
1261193	Composite SAP Note: HCM Authorizations Documentation

A.2.2   SAP NetWeaver Portal

1154828	Cross-site Scripting (XSS) Attack Using Control Sequences
1093267	Remote Connection for XSS
1013521	Configuration of Supported Languages within the Portal
982023	Import a Web Dynpro Patch for Support Package 09
947081	Locales, Languages, Date and Time Formats in Web Dynpro
946153	Parameters of the IGS Configuration File igs.xml
896400	Upgrade your Integrated IGS 7.x Installation
855498	Installation Prerequisite Checker
853878	HTTP WhiteList Check (Security)
850886	Enable Remote Connection for NetWeaver Usage EP
844669	Profile Parameter of IGS as of Version 7.x
784677	Web Dynpro Entity Names Must Be Globally Unique
766191	Active Component Framework Installation
742674	Required Information for Web Dynpro Problem Reporting
734861	WorkProtect Mode—Global Settings
718267	Upgrade Your Integrated IGS 6.40 Installation
709038	SAP Integrated ITS
669669	Updating the SAP Component Repository in the SLD
624929	How to Limit the Entries Displayed in the Language List
514841	Troubleshooting When a Problem Occurs with the IGS
458731	Internet Graphics Service: Main Note
454042	IGS: Installing and Configuring the IGS
197746	Maint. Strategy: Internet Transaction Server (ITS)

A.2.3 Backend Configuration

1290158	Delayed Response Time in ESS Homepage Framework
1127087	SAP ERP 6.0: ECM OADP Set Only Returns Direct Reports
1106196	Configuration of Search in Object and Data Provider
1098009	Limitations for Web Dynpro ABAP
956399	XSS: Newline in Area/AreaGroup/Service Description Texts
953254	Transfer of ERP Processes (HCM) into New Functions
897623	User Exits and BAdIs in the PT Area
533888	Example for Language Import and Error Specification
517484	Inactive Services in the Internet Communication Framework

A.2.4 Employee Self-Services

1303362	ESS/MSS and Enhancement Packages
1253136	Fix for ESS Foreign Address Country Dropdown Field
1232473	Limitations on Usage of ForcedRequestLanguage in WD iView
1149620	Migration of ESS Scenarios to Web Dynpro Using Java
1146860	ESS LEA: Incorrect Display of Non-Transferred Quotas
1145068	Migration of ESS Scenarios to Web Dynpro
1142601	GS: Migration ESS Scenarios to Web Dynpro—Phase 2
1134874	ESS LEA: Index: 0, Size: 0 Exception in Team Calendar
1124917	ESS LEA:Customer Fields Not Populated for Certain Scenario
1091083	ESS: Screen Control—Table T588M_ESS
1089912	Error Handling in Change Own Data scenario
1087158	Record Locking in Guided Procedure Business Process
1064182	Radio Buttons Not Refreshed Properly
1055469	Migration of ESS Scenarios to Web Dynpro
1049110	ESS Emergency Contact

1021261	ESS: Blank Dropdown List Boxes of Nationality Field
1012708	PA40: Message "Person Is Already Being Processed by User"
1007341	SAP ERP 2004/2005—Supported ESS/MSS System Landscapes
1004528	SAP Self-Services: Business Packages and Components
978773	Information: BP ESS/MSS ERP2004 on EP6.0 against XSS 600/E
988053	Additional Fields and Subtypes in US Family/Dependants
987549	ESS PersInfo Address Scenario: Country Field
965324	Multiple Data Record and Date Handling Enhancements
947172	ESS PersInfo: Retroactive Data Maintenance
941229	ESS InfoType 21—Incorrect Values in Nationality Field
932311	Workaround to Utilize BSP-iViews in ESS/ERP2005 until NW-SP7
929447	Adopting Life and Work Events for Countries Other Than US
925129	ERP2005: Profile Matchup Course Details Link Activated
924829	Change Own Data Changes Related to Return Error Messages
924828	Change Own Data Changes Related to Return Error Messages
903319	Composite Note: MSS ERP 2005 (Human Resources Management)
891146	ESS: Screen Control—Table T588M_ESS
879335	Additional Information about Self-Service Upgrade
878143	Use Case Entries for PersInfo Scenarios, Future Records
872892	JDI/NWDI Cookbook for ESS/XSS
870126	ITS-Based ESS Services in SAP ERP 2005
866821	Table V_T7XSSSERLNK Entry for ESS Personal Information Application
818958	ESS PersInfo: Important Configuration Tables
818957	ESS PersInfo: Guide for Configuration of Use Cases
808111	ESS/MSS: Changes in Self-Service Homepage Causes Errors
807990	ESS PersInfo: Applications Names in Lowercase Cause Error

779075	ESS LEA: Termination When Web Dynpro Application Started from UWL
761266	Self Services Patches

A.2.5   Manager Self-Services

1473671	From MSS for an Employee DPF Header
1295476	MSS Salary Development iViews Show Incorrect Salary Values
1253364	Incorrect Salary in Salary Development iView
1245140	MSS Requisition Request—Branch Help Values Incorrect
1160262	Wrong Salary Calculation When Evaluating Additional Payments
1112733	MSS Employee Profile: Integrating Other iViews
1090084	Add a Way to Include Parameters to MSS Reporting for BW
952692	Transfer of SAP MSS Functions to mySAP ERP 2005

A.2.6   Reporting

305118	Eliminating Various Query Problems in HR Which Includes the "Reporting Switches" Detailed Documentation
962241	Disable Browser Toolbar in Reporting Results iView
783608	SAP Query: Incorrect Change of InfoSet Field Texts
307413	MDT: Start BW reports from Manager's Desktop

A.2.7   Administrator Role

1374379	HR Administrator BP Versions and XSS Integration
1024326	Corrected UI for Role HR Administrator Available
972322	HR Administrator: Migration WD4A

A.2.8   Cross-Application Time Sheet (CATS)

1492583	ESS: Show Communication Key in Address Screens 13
1292967	ESS LEA: Dump on Clicking Show Team Calendar
1268877	CATS WD: "Record Working Time" Link Is Not Displayed
1258454	CATS WD: Integration with cPro without ALE Scenario
1246102	CATS WD: User Exit CATS009
1241169	ESS CATS: Heading for DISPTEXT1 and DISPTEXT2
1222812	CATS_APPR_LITE: Cancel Interface Table Records after Reset
1163465	CATS WD: Unit of Measurement Displayed in the Internal Format
1154365	CATS WD: Data Entry Profile (CVR) Not Set According to Pernr
1153197	CATS: Multiple Work Items in Approver Inbox
1151994	Error in Determining Approver When He Has More than One Role
1054540	CATS: Workflow Error When Saving Records in Timesheet
1053362	CATS: Agent Determination When WF Substitution Is Active
1041546	Error Message C R291 When You Display HR Assignments
1019376	ESS CATS: Worklist Becomes Unprotected
989453	CATS-WD: Column Widths Adjusted in CATS Web Dynpro Application
982586	ESS PersInfo: Retroactive Data Maintenance
978944	CATS: Work Item Creation with Tasks
967443	Workflow Work Items Are Not Processed Correctly
953852	Best Fit Selection for Reusing Country-Specific Services
953722	CATS Approval: Special Approval in Web Dynpro
951884	CAPS: Work Item Gets Terminated after Approval
951708	CATS: Agent Determination with CATS Workflow Tasks
944776	CATS_APPR_LITE: Cancel Interface Table Records after Reset
936179	Reuse of Country-Specific Services

923186	ESS Scenarios for Finland
919690	CATS Web Dynpro: Target Hours/Day Totals Missing
913096	CATS_APPR_LITE: Mail Sent to Manager/Approver after UNDO
894058	Column Width in the CATS Web Dynpro
887925	CATS Reporting—Document Flow Analysis
875790	RCATS_DISPLAY_ACTIVITIES—Memory Overflow
871197	CATS Web Dynpro: Search Help Fields Are Not Filled
861689	CATS Approval with CAPS: Performance Problem
858985	Deleting F4 Help for Operation Number Field on CATS Screen
814830	Notes Containing Correction Reports for CA-TS-PS Issues
808293	Support Workshop: CATS
742674	Required Information for Web Dynpro Problem Reporting
737423	Multiple Work Items Created in CATS Approval Workflow
732408	CATS_DA,CATS_APPR_LITE—Menu Entries Not Working Correctly
721799	Mobile Time Sheet 1.6 for Laptop—Composite Note
700100	Activity Allocation: Valuation of Quantities
678940	Workflow: Authoriz. for Recorders as of Release 4.70
653209	FAQ: CATS/CATM—Transfer to Materials Management
613033	Constants for Attendance/Absence Valuation
602901	Support of Country-Specific Functions
570471	FAQ 2: Confirmations in the Project System
555947	PS/PM: Confirmation by CATS (Consulting Note)
428461	CAT7: Message BK 202 "Document Contains Errors"
398050	INFORMATION: CO Cross Components (CATS)
376188	Supported User Exits from CATS in CATW Service
333884	Which Default Values Are Used When?
325722	CATS: Required Entry Field Definition for CAT2

322526	Analysis for Workflow Problems
304647	Purpose of Transactions CATSXT and CATSXC
212705	Missing CO Docs in Confirmation: Correction Program
209482	Personnel Number Check in Controlling
171491	Attendances: Proposal and Limitation
166961	CATS: Error LR121 During Transfer in Target Application
158953	Settlement in Parallel Currency Not the Same as FI Debit
155282	CO Docs for Confirmations: Correction Programs
141450	CATS: Required Fields in the Time Sheet
138267	CATS: Length of Fixed Area in Table Control
126129	Adding Customer Fields to CATS ITS
96505	CATS: Error When Creating an Error Log
81892	Implementing a New Country Version

A.2.9 E-Recruitment

997181	ERP Integration SAP E-Recruiting 600 and SAP ERP

A.2.10 Processes and Forms

1531162	ESS HCM P & F Process Not Tracked
1334453	Changes to Start Processes Application—ADOBE form Resizing
1273246	User Parameter to Disable Automatic Adobe Resizing
1266588	Automatic Height Adjustment Does Not Work
987455	New Functions in the HCM Process Search
1134887	Dynamic LTR/RTL Presentation Not Supported in Adobe Forms
1104060	Adobe LiveCycle Designer—ZCI Template Update
1101340	ISR/Adobe/ZCI: Errors in Display of Forms

1099468	Dump in Customizing Check Report: Readonly InfoType Field
1072476	ISR—Error in the Perspective for Checking the Form
1065209	SAP Enhancement Package 2 for SAP ERP 6.0
1062931	Corrections in Backend Classes of HCM Processes and Forms
1048386	SAP MSS/ESS: HCM Processes & Forms—Web Dynpro ABAP
1043755	Configuration of Start Application for Manager and Employ
1024326	Corrected UI for Role HR Administrator Available
981090	Country Availability of HR Processes and Forms
977116	Installing ECC-VPCKHR 601 on SAP ECC 600
973170	New Library for "SAP Interactive Forms by Adobe"
972322	HR Administrator: Migration WD4A
956074	Using the Update Function for Forms
955795	New Creation of Web Dynpro ZCI Forms in Form Builder
953982	Adjustments to Adobe Forms for ZCI
952693	MSS: Interactive Forms and HCM Processes and Forms
947675	ISR/Adobe: Layout Category ZCI (Composite SAP Note)
947633	Current ISR Control Libraries
944221	Troubleshooting If Problems Occur in Forms Processing
846610	How to Activate ADS Trace
834573	SAP Interactive Forms by Adobe: Acrobat/Reader Version
741381	ISR: Documentation for ISR Control Library
736902	Adobe Credentials
727168	Adobe Document Services: Patches
682619	Adobe Document Services: Configuration Guide (SAP NW '04)

A.2.11 User Management and Authorization

1241162	RHCDOC_DISPLAY in Background: Dump RAISE_EXCEPTION
1228518	RPUAUD00: Enhancement of the Documentation (Field "Action")
1226183	HR Admin: No Authorization When InfoType 0001 Is Created
1154828	Cross-Site Scripting (XSS) Attack Using Control Sequences
1154323	Authorization Trace of Applications from the Portal
1136041	Compensation Planning: Incorrect Authorization Messages
1126052	Additional Check Triggers Error Message PG038
1116744	Additional Check for Retroactive Change of Entry Date
1115700	CO-OM Tools: SE16N: Authorization Logic
1109298	SNUM: You Are Not Authorized to Use This Function
1067396	RHCDOC_DISPLAY: Runtime Error "DATA_LENGTH_TOO_LARGE"
1052242	BI Analysis Authorization: Generation
1037230	Authorization Check Not as Documented
1033149	General Improvements: Transactions SU53 and SU56
1012708	PA40: Message "Person Is Already Being Processed by User"
959358	IGS HTTP Administration Is Not Possible
944221	Troubleshooting If Problems Occur in Forms Processing
935354	Authorization Error in Transaction PA20 or PA30
902000	Analyzing HR Authorizations
853878	HTTP WhiteList Check (Security)
836478	HR Authorizations: Displaying the Data in the INDX
820317	CO-OM Tools: SE16N as a Display Transaction with Views
820183	New Authorization Concept in BI
798967	MSS: Authorizations and Roles for WD Services in ERP 2004
785345	Copying Authorization Default Values for Services
723236	Deletion of Personnel Numbers

704604	Business graphics, GeoMaps Are Not Displayed in WD Java
628962	How to Switch on the SAP JCo Trace
612585	New: Authorization Default Values for Ext. Services
597117	CO-OM Tools: SE16N as Pure Display Transaction II
570161	BAdI: Time Logic in PA Authorization Check
537138	Deactivating RPUDEL20 etc. in the Production System
514841	Troubleshooting When a Problem Occurs with the IGS
503274	CO-OM Tools: SE16N as Pure Display Transaction
496993	Authorization Objects of Shift Planning
452904	Loss of Authorization After Profile Generation
385635	Authorization Check with Employee Subgroup Change
216036	ESS and Authorizations
155650	Authorization Problems
148495	Setting Main Authorization Switches
139418	Logging User Actions
138706	Authorization Problems, Analysis Preparations
138526	Authorization Check in Reports Incorrect
130035	Authorization Check with P_PERNR Incorrect
124949	Logical Database SAPDBPNP Does Not Check P_PERNR
113290	PFCG: Merge Process When Maintaining Authorization Data
93254	RFC Short Dump RFC_NO_AUTHORITY
87861	Log Function for InfoTypes of Personnel Planning
66056	Authorization Trace with Transaction ST01
44206	Creation of InfoType log When Changing Date
30724	Data Protection and Security in SAP Systems
26909	SE16—Security
13202	Security Aspects in ABAP Programming

A.3   Transactions Cheat Sheet

The following list provides a transaction cheat sheet that you can use to quickly review useful transactions.

HRUSER	Set Up and Maintain ESS Users: Check user mapping between SAP UserID and personnel number (through InfoType 0105—Communication, subtype 0001)
KS03	Display Cost Center
OOAC	Enable AUTSW Switches in Table T77S0
OOSP	Display Personnel Development Profiles
PA30	Maintain HR Master Data
PE03	HR Features (Decision Trees) Like PINCH
PFCG	Profile Configurator (as of release 4.6)
PPOM_OLD	Maintain Org. Structure (old interface)
PPOME	Maintain Org. Structure (new interface)
PTARQ	Test Leave Request (includes a program to identify the line manager)
SE18	Business Add-Ins (BAdIs)
SE37	Function Modules
SE93	Maintain Transaction Codes
SLG1	Application Troubleshooting
SM31	Access Table
SMOD	SAP Enhancement Management
SP01	Spool Request
SU01	User Administration
SU01D	Display User Administration
SU02	Profile Creation—Manual Process (prior to release 4.6)
SU03	List of Authorization Objects
SU21	Create Specific Authorization Object

SU3	Maintain User Profile (including parameters)
SU53	Authorization Checks (displays missing authorization in the profile)
SU56	Authorization Buffer for End User
SUIM	Authorization Reporting Tree
SWU_OBUF	Refresh Org. Management Buffer

A.4   Tables Cheat Sheet

Tables are illustrated throughout each chapter and configuration steps. The following is a quick reference table cheat sheet for the tables used when deploying the self-services.

View	Name
V_T7XSSSERARGC	Assign Areas to Area Group Pages (Add and Change Entries)
V_T7XSSSERARG	Assign Areas to Area Group Pages (Find Entries)
V_T7XSSSERSARC	Assign Services to Subareas (Add and Change Entries)
V_T7XSSSERSAR	Assign Services to Subareas (Find Entries)
V_T7XSSSERARC	Assign Subareas to Areas (Add and Change Entries)
V_T7XSSSERAR	Assign Subareas to Areas (Find Entries)
V_T7XSSPERBIZFLD	Available Fields on Bizcards on PersInfo Overview Screen
V_T7XSSSERLNK	Confirmation Screen Links
V_T7XSSSERARGB	Define Area Group Pages (Add Entries)
V_T7XSSSERARGBC	Define Area Group Pages (Change Entries)
V_T7XSSSERARB	Define Area Pages (Add Entries)
V_T7XSSSERARBC	Define Area Pages (Change Entries)
V_T7XSSPERFORADD	Define Countries for Foreign Address
V_T7XSSSERSRVCG	Define Country-Specific Services (Add Entries)
V_T7XSSSERSRVCGC	Define Country-Specific Services (Change Entries)

Table A.1   Views on Tables V_T7XSS*

View	Name
V_T7XSSSERHEB	Define Headers (Add Entries)
V_T7XSSSERHEBC	Define Headers (Change Entries)
V_T7XSSSERRES	Define Resources (Add Entries)
V_T7XSSSERRESC	Define Resources (Change Entries)
V_T7XSSSERSDB	Define Servers
V_T7XSSSERSRVG	Define Service Groups (Add Entries)
V_T7XSSSERSRVGC	Define Service Groups (Change Entries)
V_T7XSSSERSRV	Define Services (Add Entries)
V_T7XSSSERSRVC	Define Services (Change Entries)
V_T7XSSSERSARB	Define Subareas (Add Entries)
V_T7XSSSERSARBC	Define Subareas (Change Entries)
V_T7XSSPERSTRUCT	ESS PersInfo, View for InfoType Structure
V_T7XSS_SER_RFW	ESS rep.framwork: Mapping of Application ID to ABAP Class
V_T7XSSCE_GRP	Group Definition Settings for ESS CE Applications
V_T7XSSREUSEUISN	Reuse of Screen Structure for New Country Version
V_T7XSSPERBIZFLC	Specify Fields for Bizcards on Overview Screen
V_T7XSSPERSUBTY	Specify Use Case and Active Subtypes
V_T7XSSPERSUBTYP	Specify Use Case and Active Subtypes
V_T7XSSCESTATFLT	Status Validity Filtering for an Assignment
V_T7XSS_GRT_IFR	View to Maintain the Dimensions of the IFrame

Table A.1 Views on Tables V_T7XSS* (Cont.)

Table	Name
T77S0	HR Switches Main Tables—Group AUTSW Regarding Authorizations
USERS_SSM	Deactivate SAP Standard Menu and Force User Menus

Table A.2 Other Tables

Table	Name
V_T591C	Enable Long Field (241) Form InfoType 0105—Communication
TRESC	Allowed Naming Space Like Z* or Y* Convention for SAP Tables
CUS_IMGACH	IMG Activities
V_T582A	InfoTypes Attributes
T526	Administrators

Table A.2 Other Tables (Cont.)

A.5 Programs Cheat Sheet

Among all the programs illustrated throughout the different chapters, here is a handy list of programs.

RPLMIT00	Provides a detailed list of employees
RPLICO10	Provides a flexible list of employee data
RPLINFC0	InfoType Overview for Employees (could be used even if made for Swiss data)
RPUAUD00	Logged Changes in InfoType Data (Personnel Administration)
RHCDOC_DISPLAY	Display Change Documents (Personnel Development)
SAPLEHUS	ESS User Utilities, Including Monitoring of User Mapping (InfoType 0105—Communication, subtype 0001)
RHRHDL00	Delete Data Records from Personnel Planning Database
RHGRENZ0	Delimiting Personnel Development Objects
RHGRENZ1	Set New End Date for Personnel Development Objects
RHGRENZ2	Delimit InfoTypes
RHGRENZ4	Set New End Date
RPUFIXDS	Repairing Data Sharing Inconsistencies (i.e., when working with ESS)

HFIUCPLO	Personnel Numbers That Have to Be Unlocked for Payroll Runs
RSTXPDFT4	Converting SAPscript (OTF) or ABAP List Spool Job to PDF
RPASR_TEST_PROCESS_ EXECUTION	Test Processes for HR Forms
FP_PDF_TEST_00	Test Program: Adobe Version Information (for Analysis Only)

A.6 Enhancement Package Checklist

Through this checklist, assess whether or not you need to install and activate enhancement packages.

We plan to use the portal administrator role.	☐ Yes	☐ No
We plan to use the HCM Processes and Forms.	☐ Yes	☐ No
We plan to use the HCM Processes and Forms for mass processing.	☐ Yes	☐ No
We plan to use the Shared Services Center functionalities.	☐ Yes	☐ No
We plan to use the Employee Interaction Center (EIC).	☐ Yes	☐ No
We plan to use the Duet functionalities.	☐ Yes	☐ No
We plan to use the latest functionalities from E-Recruitment.	☐ Yes	☐ No
We plan to use the functionalities regarding Talent Management.	☐ Yes	☐ No
We plan to use the functionalities regarding Talent Management integrated with Nakisa.	☐ Yes	☐ No
We plan to use the latest functionalities from Learning Solution.	☐ Yes	☐ No
In ESS, we have the requirement to allow personal changes in the past.	☐ Yes	☐ No
In ESS, we have the requirement to allow end users to store a foreign address.	☐ Yes	☐ No
In ESS, we have the requirement to create self-services for nonsupported countries (reuse of standard application as a start).	☐ Yes	☐ No
In ESS, we plan to use the concurrent employment feature.	☐ Yes	☐ No

In ESS, we plan to use the Web Dynpro Performance Management functionality.	☐ Yes	☐ No
In ESS, we plan to use enhanced Compensation Management functionalities.	☐ Yes	☐ No
We plan to use the HCM localization.	☐ Yes	☐ No

If you answered "Yes" to any of these quick check questions, read Chapter 1, which includes highlights on the enhancement package concept.

If none of these apply, the plain SAP ERP 6.0 release without enhancement packages is just fine for your needs.

A.7 Troubleshooting Guide

This troubleshooting guide lists the most common issues when dealing with the self-services and provides, if not the answer or solution, the different leads to investigate.

A.7.1 User "MGILLET" Does Not Exist in This Period

If the mapping of the personnel number against the SAP UserID (as illustrated in Chapter 11) is missed or has an end date in the past, the system will not be able to retrieve the information from the backend. Therefore, it will raise the error message "User >name< does not exist in this period." Verify the InfoType 0105—Communication, subtype 0001—System User Name (SY-UNAME).

A.7.2 Missing or Faulty Configuration

When the SAP NetWeaver Portal is triggering an error message such as "Entry xxx does not exist," this is usually due to missing or faulty configuration. Carefully review the following items:

▶ Is the backend configuration for self-services set up correctly? If backend configuration for self-services is fine, you may have forgotten to import this configuration into the client mapped to SAP NetWeaver Portal through Transaction SCC1, Client Copy—Special Selections.

- Is the mapping from the backend to SAP NetWeaver Portal correctly pointing to the iView or the page? Carefully check the configuration of the HPFW.

- Is the mapping from SAP NetWeaver Portal correctly pointing to the backend system? Carefully check the iView and page parameters.

- Are you maintaining master data for the right country (Molga in SAP terminology)? Is this country configured?

- Are the start and end dates in the configuration correct?

A.7.3 Portal 500 Error

This error can be triggered by SAP NetWeaver Portal for several reasons. Carefully review the configuration. According to SAP, this is a Single Sign-On (SSO) issue, so refer to SAP Note 701205 — Single Sign-On Using SAP Logon Tickets. The error message reads as follows:

The initial exception that caused the request to fail, was:

com.sap.tc.webdynpro.services.exceptions.WDRuntimeException:

ComponentUsage(FPMConfigurationUsage): Active component must exist when getting interface controller. (Hint: Have you forgotten to create it with createComponent()? Should the lifecycle control of the component usage be "createOnDemand"?)

This error occurs, if there's a Java Connector (JCo) connection that does not work.

Go to WD CONTENT ADMINISTRATOR • MAINTAIN JCO DESTINATIONS, and click the TEST link for the connections.

As soon as you can see the following error message, you should correct it:

WD Runtime Exception:

It is likely caused by: com.sap.tc.webdynpro.services.exceptions. WDRuntimeException:

Failed to resolve JCO destination name 'SAP_R3_SelfServiceGenerics' in the SLD. No such JCO destination is defined in the SLD.

Check the System Certificate Expiration Attributes

Also ask the Basis team to check the certificate expiration attributes.

You might also consider SAP Note 1045019 — Web Diagtool for Collecting Traces to build a trace and investigate further.

Further Troubleshooting Guides

Also consider this WIKI: Welcome to the SAP Technology Troubleshooting Guide: *http://wiki.sdn.sap.com/wiki/display/TechTSG/%28JSTTSG%29Main+Page.*

More documentation on the logon ticket is available at *http://help.sap.com/saphelp_ nw70ehp1/helpdata/en/f8/18da3a82f9cc38e10000000a114084/frameset.htm.*

A.7.4   Portal 503 Error

This error is triggered by the SAP NetWeaver Portal due to the fact that the SAP NetWeaver AS engine is starting. Check with the Basis team.

You will get the following error message:

> *If this state does not change within a few minutes, please contact your system administrator. Check the recommendations in SAP Notes: 943498, 764417.*

> *Message: Dispatcher running but no server connected!*
>   *Details: No details available*
>   *503 Service Unavailable*
>   *SAP J2EE Engine/7.01*
>   *Application stopped.*
>   *Details: You have requested an application that is currently stopped.*

A.7.5   Mapping SAP NetWeaver Portal to Multiple R/3 Backends

When configuring the System Landscape Directory (SLD), you normally make the SAP NetWeaver Portal point to one SAP ERP system and one HR component. This is done, as illustrated in Figure A.1, by configuring the SAP_R3_HumanResources systems.

Often, you only have one SAP NetWeaver Portal for the backend development system and the backend test system, so you need to map the SAP NetWeaver Portal to multiple backend systems.

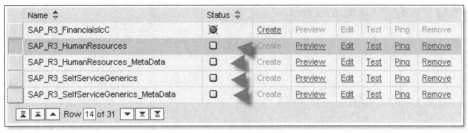

Figure A.1 Configuring SAP_R3_HumanResources Systems in SLD

To map a test portal to two different SAP systems (test and validation), we successfully tested the following solution:

1. On the SLD of the test portal, create a copy of the standard JCo destination: SAP_R3_HumanResources.

2. Rename this JCo destination as SAP_R3_HumanResourcesHRT. (HRT stands for the other target system; caution, it must be a maximum of three characters, which are normally the SAP backend ID.)

3. Edit the properties of that JCo destination so that it points to HRT (test system) and not to HRV (validation tests) anymore.

4. Do exactly the same for SAP_R3_HumanResources_MetaData → SAP_R3_Human Resources_MetaDataHRT.

5. Create a copy of the iView you want to use on the HRT system (e.g., the address iView).

6. Edit the property APPLICATION PARAMETERS, and enter the following parameter: "sap.wdarfc.useSys=SAP_R3_HumanResources:HRT&sap.wdarfc.useSys=SAP_R3_HumanResources_MetaData:HRT."

7. Include this new iView in a new page, include that page in a new workset, and include that workset in a new role. Assign this role to the users or the group of users that need to use the HRT system for ESS instead of the HRV system, as illustrated in Chapter 2.

A.7.6 Analyzing the Application Log

When receiving an SAP NetWeaver Portal error message, chances are a log is created and stored in the backend system. Run Transaction SLG1—Application Log: Display Logs.

A.7.7 ABAP Runtime Error

Another useful transaction when troubleshooting the SAP NetWeaver Portal is to look into Transaction ST22—ABAP Dump Analysis.

It highlights short dumps such as runtime errors DYNPRO_NOT_FOUND or RFC_NO_AUTHORITY.

The DYNPRO_NOT_FOUND error indicates missing or faulty configuration that you need to review, whereas the RFC_NO_AUTHORITY error means that the end user is most likely missing authorizations.

A.7.8 Authorization Issues

If you face authorization issues, as illustrated in Chapter 11, rather than using Transaction SU53—Evaluate Authorization Check, which is too "light" in terms of content, use the authorization trace via Transaction ST01—System Trace. Alternatively, ask your programmer to set a breakpoint (a STOP) in the program when calling the `Authority Check` statement.

A.7.9 Master Data Inconsistencies

As you have seen in Chapter 7, the program RPUFIXDS—Repairing Data Sharing Inconsistencies is provided to solve master data inconsistencies. This inconsistency shows up when working with self-services with the error message "! Data Record XXX (...) has grouping value "" instead of XX."

A.7.10 Locked Personnel Number

An employee or manager might report that the personnel number to maintain through self-services is locked. As you have seen in Chapter 11, you can use Transaction SM12—Display and Delete Locks to monitor these lock entries (and delete if needed and duly authorized). However, because this is a system administration transaction code, you can use the standard program HFIUCPL0—Personnel Numbers That Have to Be Unlocked for Payroll Runs to identify the locked personnel numbers and the persons locking them.

A.7.11 HttpWatch (or Similar)

As illustrated in Chapter 2, it might be wise to invest in a tracing program such as the HttpWatch, to trace the SAP NetWeaver Portal activities.

A.8 Recommended SAP Standard Courses

Standard SAP courses provide state-of-the-art training material with professional, experienced trainers so you can get the information at the source. Following is a list of recommend trainings in the field of SAP HR self-services. Check out the availability online, based on your country at *www.sap.com/education,* which contains a course search engine.

- ▶ CA500 — Cross-Application Time Sheet (new release updated to SAP ERP 6.0 in November, 2008)
- ▶ EP120 — SAP NetWeaver Portal Development
- ▶ EP200 — SAP NetWeaver Portal System Administration
- ▶ EP300 — Configuration of Knowledge Management and Collaboration
- ▶ EP600 — Configuration of the Universal Worklist
- ▶ HR130 — Introduction to HCM Enterprise Portal
- ▶ HR255 — Employee Self-Services and Manager Self-Services (also known as XSS Self-Services)
- ▶ HR270 — Learning Solution
- ▶ HR290 — ESS/MSS System Configuration
- ▶ HR316 — E-Recruiting
- ▶ HR940 — HCM Authorization
- ▶ ADM940 — SAP Authorizations
- ▶ HR580 — HCM Reporting

I am training most courses (in English) at SAP education centers, so perhaps we will meet in Belgium or in the United Kingdom.

A.9   Recommended Readings

Here are some additional (recommended) readings just to extend your knowledge, keep up your learning curve, or maintain your technology watch. These different sources of information will empower you to consolidate your self-services knowledge.

A.9.1   Online Documentation

Michael Bonrat, a great SAP HR trainer at SAP pointed out during ramp-up classes that most of us don't bother to read the documentation. Michael strongly suggests we read the documentation before posting any request for help or raising SAP messages.

Prior to any other move in regards to SAP knowledge and content, review the SAP standard documentation, either directly from your SAP system or freely online at the following addresses:

▶ **Employee Self-Services**
  http://help.sap.com/saphelp_erp60_sp/helpdata/en/f6/263359f8c14ef98384ae7a2b ecd156/frameset.htm

▶ **Manager Self-Services**
  http://help.sap.com/saphelp_erp60_sp/helpdata/en/76/77594d165144a1a9bff9aae1 e26b26/frameset.htm

▶ **Create Dynamic XSS Home Pages with Static Services Using a Simple Proxy Class**
  https://www.sdn.sap.com/irj/scn/weblogs?blog=/pub/wlg/5457

▶ **ESS Personal Information UI Enhancement without Modification**
  https://www.sdn.sap.com/irj/scn/wiki?path=/display/profile/ESS%252bPersonal%252 bInformation%252bUI%252benhancement%252bwithout%252bmodification

▶ **Customizing STACK TRACE for XSS Components**
  https://www.sdn.sap.com/irj/sdn/weblogs?blog=/pub/wlg/10796

▶ **How to Add a Custom Web Dynpro iView to the MSS Employee Profile (ECC 6.0)**
  https://www.sdn.sap.com/irj/scn/wiki?path=/display/profile/How-to+add+a+custom+ Web+Dynpro+iView+to+the+MSS+Employee+Profile+%28ECC+6.0%29

- **Hacking the New Portal iView Personalization Feature**
  https://www.sdn.sap.com/irj/scn/weblogs?blog=/pub/wlg/7152
- **Customize Icons for the Homepage Framework**
  https://www.sdn.sap.com/irj/scn/weblogs?blog=/pub/wlg/5978
- **Customize the Homepage Framework with Custom HTML Content**
  https://www.sdn.sap.com/irj/scn/weblogs?blog=/pub/wlg/6015

A.9.2   HR Expert Online

If you keep in touch with the SAP HR functionalities, why not subscribe to the HR Expert, either online or on paper? It will empower you with detailed reviews of functionalities, additional information applicable directly on your job, and business cases.

The HR Expert can be accessed at *www.hrexpertonline.com/*.

You might also want to take a look at my articles at *http://hrexpertonline.com/profile.cfm?id=17*.

A.9.3   Books

Along with the book you have in your hands, we recommend the following books from SAP PRESS that serve as extensions of this configuration book:

- Nicolescu, Klappert, Krcmar: *SAP NetWeaver Portal* (2008)
- Masters, Jeremy; Kotsakis, Christos: *Implementing Employee and Manager Self-Services in SAP ERP HCM* (2009)
- Figaj, Haßmann, Junold: *HR Reporting with SAP* (2008)
- Gatling, Ginger, et al.: *Practical Workflow for SAP* (2nd ed., 2009)
- Gillet, Martin: *Integrating CATS* (2nd ed., 2009)
- Gallardo, Manuel: *Configuring and Using CATS* (2008)
- Padmanabhan, Prashant, et al: *SAP Enterprise Learning* (2009)
- Masters, Jeremy; Kotsakis, Christos: *Enterprise Compensation Management with SAP ERP HCM* (2009)
- Masters, Kotsakis, Krishnamoorthy: *E-Recruiting with SAP ERP HCM* (2010)
- Esch, Martin; Junold, Anja: *Authorizations in SAP ERP HCM* (2008)

A.10 Social Media

Keeping ahead of the learning curve does matter, including knowing about new functionalities, troubleshooting advice, and new workarounds. Social media is a great channel to interact with peers and colleagues in your field of expertise.

A.10.1 Twitter

Twitter is a handy channel for communication and keeping informed through your time line. Follow the right people and get valuable information. Get ahead and get notified when a new blog post is released.

Here are some great individuals and groups that you should consider following. Simply add the twitter alias after this address: *http://twitter.com/XXXXX* where *XXXXX* stands for the name of the individual or groups.

Individuals

▶ **@dawncrew**
Vice President, Solution Management focused on HCM portfolio

▶ **@cmporeilly**
Director, SAP HCM Marketing for North America

▶ **@karenheatwole**
SAP HCM

▶ **@sprabu**
Entrepreneur, product designer, collaboration enthusiast, and product manager for people management software (*http://distributeddevelopment.blogspot.com/*)

▶ **@thomas_jung**
SAP NetWeaver Solution Manager specializing in ABAP development tools and UI strategy

▶ **@sap_jarret**
SAP HCM consultant, SME US Payroll, EIC, ECM, HR Expert author, SDN moderator and blogger, entrepreneur, husband, father

▶ **@hreiter**
SAP Project Manager, SAP NetWeaver techno guy, SAP HCM SME—did I miss anything?

▸ **@SteveBogner**
Works with HR and IT leaders to achieve exceptional business value through transformation of people, HRIS technology, and processes

▸ **@lukemarson**
Leading Specialist in SAP Visualization Solutions by Nakisa and Talent Management Solution Architect

▸ **@mgillet**
Freelance SAP HCM consultant, trainer, and SAP Mentor, father of two little angels, dreamer, passionate over ERP processes, globetrotter, and student pilot (on the fly)

Groups

▸ **@SCNblogs**
Connect, Collaborate and Contribute. These tweets are from SAP Community Network (SCN) blog posts (*www.sdn.sap.com/irj/scn/weblogs*).

▸ **@sapcommnet**
SAP Community Network (SCN) provides orchestrated connections to our community of SAP customers, partners, employees, and experts (*www.sdn.sap.com/irj/scn*).

▸ **@sapmentors**
SAP Mentors are SAP experts, community leaders, and influencers. These users only follow these SAP Mentors and post items relevant to the SAP Mentor initiative (*www.sdn.sap.com/irj/sdn/sapmentors*).

A list of all tweeting SAP Mentors can be found at *http://twitter.com/#!/SAPMentors/sapmentors*.

▸ **@HR_Expert**
HR Expert offers case studies, best practices, and troubleshooting advice to help you improve personnel admin, ESS/MSS, payroll, and more.

▸ **@MssEssSeminar**
The SAP Insider seminar is for teams that manage, deploy, support, and are evaluating SAP solutions for ESS and MSS.

▸ **@ToolboxforHR**
Get insights from the Toolbox for HR community, where HR professionals collaborate to solve problems and make better workplace decisions (*http://hr.toolbox.com*).

A.10.2 LinkedIn

Feel free to hook up with your SAP ESS/MSS Consultants Group peers on LinkedIn at *www.linkedin.com/groups?home=&gid=2152523*.

A.11 SAP Communities

We are all part of a an "extended family" of SAP users and contributors. We gather through the following SAP Communities and sharing platforms, so be sure to chime in, learn, discover, share, and exchange knowledge with your peers.

A.11.1 SAP Insider Network

Insider Learning Network is a global interactive website dedicated to helping SAP professionals get trusted answers to their most specific SAP questions, advance their skills, and connect with their peers with a free membership. Bringing together industry experts, SAP customers, and SAP partners, Insider Learning Network offers a single place to share with and learn from other SAP professionals, research projects and products, and find detailed technical information and advice.

Learn more at:

- *http://sapinsider.wispubs.com/*
- *www.insiderlearningnetwork.com/*

A.11.2 SAP Developer Network

SAP Community Network, which includes SAP Developer Network (SDN), Business Process Expert (BPX) Community, University Alliance Community (UAC), and Business Objects Community (BOC), has a thriving, diverse, and growing membership. By joining SDN, BPX, UAC, or BOC, you'll have access to more than one million topic threads that will provide information and training resources to help you achieve your goals and give you access to the power of true co-innovation.

The SAP Developer Network (SDN) offers deep technical content and expertise for SAP developers, analysts, consultants, and administrators on SAP NetWeaver. SDN members enjoy a robust collection of technical content, including expert blogs, technical articles, white papers, how-to guides, moderated forums, software downloads, an extensive eLearning catalog, and an open communication wiki, on a range of SAP topics.

Learn more at *www.sdn.sap.com*

HR Wiki

Follow up on questions, issues, and new information; and share experiences with peers in the wiki area for SAP HR.

http://wiki.sdn.sap.com/wiki/display/ERPHCM/ERP+Human+Capital+Management

SAP Mentors

SAP Mentors are the top community influencers of the SAP ecosystem. Most of the nearly 100 mentors work for customers or partners of SAP. All of them are hands-on experts of an SAP product or service, as well as excellent champions of community-driven projects. The following describes a SAP Mentor:

▶ Hands-on expert in an SAP product or service

▶ Collaborative attitude

▶ Good communicator

▶ Preferably working at a partner or customer of SAP

▶ Interested in improving products and services of SAP as well as the relationship of SAP with its customers, partners, and prospects

▶ Proactive engagement

Learn more about the SAP Mentors at *http://sapmentors.sap.com*.

My Blog Entries

Follow me and chime in on my blogs and wiki posts on the SAP Developer Network at *www.sdn.sap.com/irj/scn/weblogs?blog=/pub/u/252112232*.

A.11.3   Ittoolbox

This is another great place for sharing knowledge and joining online communities.

Ittoolbox Groups

Choose the SAP groups to follow according your area(s) of expertise at *http://sap.ittoolbox.com/groups*.

SAP HR Group

Follow the SAP HR group at *http://sap.ittoolbox.com/groups/technical-functional/sap-hr/*.

My Blog Entries

Follow me and chime in on my blogs Ittoolbox at *http://it.toolbox.com/people/magil/*.

A.12 Recommended Events

Taking part in the major SAP events not only gives you a great place to meet and enhance your network but also provides consolidated training and access to experts.

HR Conferences

HR conferences are organized in Europe and in the United States. For more information on conferences, see *www.wispubs.com/sap/conferences.html*.

SAPPHIRENOW

SAPPHIRE includes unparalleled global insights from customers, partners, SAP experts and executives, SAP Mentors, and networking opportunities. Get more information at *www.sapphirenow.com/*.

SAP TechEd

Each year, more than 15,000 people attend the premium technical education conference from SAP. The SAP TechEd conference empowers and connects you and your team with the essential training and community support needed to gain instant value from your IT investment. Develop practical skills through hands-on workshops and demo-enhanced lectures focused on the SAP NetWeaver technology platform and SAP BusinessObjects solutions. Learn from and network with SAP experts, customers, and community members. Find out more at *www.sapteched.com/*.

A.13 Bibliography

The following references were used in the writing of this book:

- Business Package documentation (BP ESS 1 ESS for mySAP ERP 2005), release 672—SAP Online Help, November 11, 2005

- Business Package documentation (BP MSS 1 MSS for mySAP ERP 2005), release 1.0—SAP Online Help, February 2006

- *Development Guide for Personnel Change Requests: Developing Your Own Personnel Change Requests*, mySAP ERP 2004, SAP 2002

- *Internal Service Request (ISR) Cookbook*, by Stephan Rehmann and Simon Hoeg, July 2004

- *Configuration Guide for the Reporting Workset*, release 60.1, March 2005

- *What's New in HR Reporting in R3 Enterprise*, by Michael Bonrat, SAP 2002

- *Everything You Ever Wanted to Know About HCM Reporting*, by Martin Gillet, ERP-Tips, October/November 2009

- Web Dynpro Java Foundation (SDN Contribution): *What's New in SAP NetWeaver 2004s*, by Bertram Ganz, July 2006

- *Authorization in mySAP HR*, release 4.6C, SAP Online Help, 2002

- *Authorizations in Performance Management*, SAP 2005

- *SAP Enterprise Portal Security Guide, SAP Enterprise Portal 6.0*, SAP Online Help 2004, document version 3.3

- *Enterprise Single Sign-On*, white paper by Evidian and Laurent de Jerphanion, May 2008

- *How to Configure Universal Worklist*, Version 1.00, SAP 2004

- Additional material for *Practical Workflow for SAP*, online free download from *www.workflowbook.com*

- *What IT Professionals Need to Know About Enhancement Packages*, version 1.11, by Christian Oehler, SAP 2008

- Enhancement Package 1 through 4: Master Guides, SAP standard documentation

- *HR Processes and Forms*, Media Library, SAP

- *Trends in Human Capital Management — The Emerging Talent Management Imperative*, a Knowledge Infusion white paper, July 2006

- HR250 Employee Self-Services course, SAP 2005/Q3 Material number 50078508, collection 53

- HR260 Manager Self-Services course, SAP 2006/Q2Material number 50074209, collection 53

- HR255 HCM Self-Services course, SAP 2008 Material Number 50087201, version 73

- HR255 Human Resources Self-Services, personal appendices

B   The Author

Martin Gillet (*martin.gillet@cogilius.com*) is an SAP-certified HR consultant (SAP ERP 6.0, SAP R/3 Enterprise, and SAP 4.0B) who works freelance on international projects. He graduated with honors in Human Resources Management from Belgian Haute Ecole Namuroise Catholique (HENam). Martin was also proudly appointed SAP Mentor in 2009. He is the author of *Integrating CATS* (SAP PRESS, 2nd ed. 2009), is a part of the HR Expert advisor team, and writes many articles. He also lectures at international conferences, such as SAP events and HR conferences.

Martin has worked with SAP R/3 since 1997 in the chemical, catering, pharmaceuticals, telecommunications, food, banking, and oil industries. He has focused on SAP HR since 1998 and has other SAP expertise, including XSS, LSO, E-Recruiting, CATS, reporting, authorizations, and SAP NetWeaver Portal. Martin is also keen to share his knowledge across channels such as SAP Communities and Social Media. He is also a dedicated trainer for SAP education, mainly across Europe.

Martin is also the proud father of two little angels, a dreamer, a passionate fellow about ERP Processes, and a globetrotter and student pilot (on the fly).

For more information, please go to *http://about.me/martingillet.*

Index

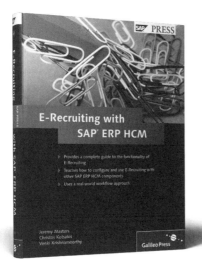

Provides a complete guide to the
functionality of E-Recruiting

Teaches how to configure and use
E-Recruiting with other HCM
components

Uses a real-world workflow approach

Jeremy Masters, Christos Kotsakis, Venkatesh Krishnamoorthy

E-Recruiting with SAP ERP HCM

This book provides a practical guide to configuring and using SAP
E-Recruitment effectively in the real-world. It is written to teach
SAP ERP HCM users and implementation teams what the E-Recruiting
tool is, so that you can use it effectively in your recruitment process and
integrate it easily with other HCM components. Beginning with an
overview, the book progresses through the configuration process from
a workflow perspective, as used in a real recruiting project. You'll also
learn how to integration E-Recruiting with other components.

358 pp., 2010, 69,95 Euro / US$ 69.95
ISBN 978-1-59229-243-1

>> www.sap-press.com

Provides all functional details on the successor of CUA

Describes integration with SAP NetWeaver and SOA landscapes

Includes two detailed real-life scenarios

Loren Heilig, Peter Gergen

Understanding SAP NetWeaver Identity Management

Whether you're thinking about an identity management solution for your company, are currently implementing one, or are already working with SAP NetWeaver Identity Management, this book covers all important aspects for the selection, implementation, and operation of the solution. Take advantage of proven concepts and tips from the authors, and learn SAP NetWeaver IdM from A to Z.

300 pp., 2010, 69,95 Euro / US$ 69.95
ISBN 978-1-59229-338-4

>> www.sap-press.com

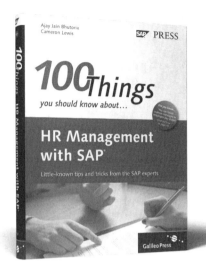

Little-known tips and tricks from the
SAP experts

Ajay Jain Bhutoria, Cameron Lewis

100 Things You Should Know About HR Management with SAP

Have you ever spent days trying to figure out how to generate a personnel report in SAP ERP HCM only to find out you just needed to click a few buttons. If so, you'll be delighted with this book — it unlocks the secrets of SAP ERP HCM. It provides users and super-user with 100 tips and workarounds you can use to increase productivity, save time, and improve the overall ease-of-use of SAP ERP HCM. The tips have been carefully selected to provide a collection of the best, most useful, and rarest information.

298 pp., 2011, 49,95 Euro / US$ 49.95
ISBN 978-1-59229-361-2

>> www.sap-press.com

Interested in reading more?

Please visit our Web site for all
new book releases from SAP PRESS.

www.sap-press.com